D1244194

On the Hunt

On the Hunt

The History of Deer Hunting in Wisconsin

Robert C. Willging

Wisconsin Historical Society Press

Published by the Wisconsin Historical Society Press
Publishers since 1855

© 2008 by State Historical Society of Wisconsin

For permission to reuse material from *On the Hunt*, ISBN 978-0-87020-405-0, please access www.copyright.com or contact the Copyright Clearance Center, Inc. (CCC), 222 Rosewood Drive, Danvers, MA 01923, 978-750-8400.
CCC is a not-for-profit organization that provides licenses and registration for a variety of users.

wisconsin**history**.org

Photographs identified with PH, WHi, or WHS are from the Society's collections; address inquiries about such photos to the Visual Materials Archivist at Wisconsin Historical Society, 816 State Street, Madison, WI 53706.

Printed in the United States of America

Designed by 2econd Shift Production Services

12 11 10 09 08   1 2 3 4 5

Library of Congress Cataloging-in-Publication Data

Willging, Robert C.
  On the hunt : the history of deer hunting in Wisconsin / Robert C. Willging.
      p. cm.
  Includes bibliographical references.
   ISBN 978-0-87020-405-0 (hardcover : alk. paper) 1. Deer hunting—Wisconsin—History. I. Title.

SK301.W493 2008

799.2'76509775—dc22

2008033216

Cover:
A satisfying day in Wisconsin's North Woods, ca. 1900
Courtesy of the Marathon County Historical Society

♾ The paper used in this publication meets the minimum requirements of the American National Standard for Information Sciences—Permanence of Paper for Printed Library Materials, ANSI Z39.48–1992.

For Deirdre, Ryan, and Molly

Contents

Preface

A man may not care for golf and still be human, but the man who does not like to see, hunt, photograph or otherwise outwit birds and animals is hardly normal. He is supercivilized, and I for one do not know how to deal with him. Babes do not tremble when they are shown a golf ball, but I should not like to own the boy whose hair does not lift his hat when he sees his first deer.
—Aldo Leopold, "A Sand County Almanac"[1]

I remember the first white-tailed buck I ever saw—the first deer I ever saw up close. All I have to do is close my eyes to relive the moment. The image of that first deer comes back with special intensity in autumn, when the air is crisp and the leaves are turning. I was twelve years old at the time.

I was in the car with my parents, my older sister to my right in the backseat. It was autumn in northern Illinois, and we were driving along a gravel road in what was to be a recreational development where people from Chicago would build vacation homes for their weekend escapes from the big city. My family lived in a Chicago suburb, and my parents had purchased one of these lots. We were looking for it for the first time, studying the little survey posts that had been driven into the ground all along the road, looking for the post that had our lot number on it.

The buck exploded out of the woods to my left, just yards in front of the car. I could see every detail of its body. He seemed huge, with a thick neck and a twelve-point rack of polished antlers. He moved from the woods onto the road in a gigantic leap, smack in front of the car. Dad hit the brakes; Mom shrieked. The buck paid no mind to us but with another leap he was past, then on the right of the car, then into the woods, white tail swaying back and forth. He disappeared almost as quickly as he had appeared.

Today, early into a new century, we have white-tailed deer populations at record high levels across most of the species' range. The sight of a white-tailed deer is commonplace for many kids, whether they live in town or country. But this was

1973, and I was a kid born in Chicago and raised in one of the city's northwestern suburbs, the last child of seven in a family that did not hunt, did not camp, did not raft rivers or climb mountains. What my family did do for outdoor recreation was have backyard barbecues in the summer, and toboggan down the village sledding hill in the winter along with thousands of other suburbanites. My friends, as far as I knew, also did not have parents or siblings who hunted or shot guns or paddled canoes, or did anything in the real outdoors. My friends and I played sports, rode bikes around the neighborhood, hiked down the railroad tracks looking for anything that might have fallen off a passing freight train. We never talked about hunting or about deer.

It was a weird set of circumstances that allowed that massive northern Illinois, corn-fed white-tailed buck to cross my path. It all began with that lot.

It had been my dad's idea to buy the lot. A developer with plans to dam Hells Branch Creek (a tributary to the Apple River, in Jo Daviess County, Illinois) to create a lake and instant lakefront property, had bought up farm fields and woodland. Nearly 3,000 acres of northern Illinois oak woodland and fallow farm fields had been carved up, marked with stakes, and sold. Somehow Dad had seen an advertisement for the development and sent in a request for more information. One night a salesman spread a large and tempting blue-and-green map across our dining room table. The blue was the future manmade lake, the green the lots for sale. There would be a marina, and a clubhouse, and an endless list of activities for kids. The offer was irresistible to my dad. He picked a lot in a projected bay of the projected lake and wrote out a check for the deposit.

Dreams of a summer home raced through our heads. Dome houses were a big thing then, and Dad soon had plans and brochures arriving in the mail with glossy photos of dome homes, the "perfect" vacation structure.

My parents were transplanted Iowans from the Mississippi River town of Dubuque. After serving as a personnel manager in the U.S. Army during World War II in not-so-exotic home-front locations such as Coffeeville, Kansas, Dad found work in Chicago. My parents, along with my oldest sister, a true baby boomer born the year the war ended, moved from Dubuque to a Chicago suburb to join thousands of other vets who were creating rings of suburbs around the Windy City. Their debt to country paid in full, they pursued the American dream of home ownership. My dad's starry-eyed purchase of the Apple River lot was an extension of his pursuit of that dream—a vacation home, the epitome of success.

Perhaps for financial reasons or simply waning enthusiasm, my father's vacation home was never built. Years later, while I was in college, he sold the lot for a loss in a poor economy.

The lot may not have helped fulfill my dad's dream, but it helped start my own. During the brief encounter with the buck I had witnessed a sort of raw wildness that I never knew existed. It did something to me. After that day I had a need to develop my own connection to the wildness I had seen in the deer. But what could a suburban Chicago kid do?

What I did was ask my parents to subscribe to outdoor magazines for me, hunting and fishing magazines: *Outdoor Life, Sports Afield, Field & Stream.* I wonder now if my parents thought that a strange request, since no one we knew hunted or even did much fishing, but they never said a negative word. I had never known anyone who had even fired a gun, until my brother married a farm girl from Princeton, Illinois, and his new father-in-law initiated him into rural Illinois culture by taking him on pheasant hunts with a group of cousins and uncles.

The outdoor magazines showed me things no one in my world could. I read about fishing for giant bass in Florida, bear hunting in Michigan, and quail hunting in Georgia. I read tales of great adventure, of killer mountain lions and grizzly bear attacks. And I read about deer hunting—a new world of rifles and cartridge loads. I read about the animal itself, how well deer can scent a hunter and how important it is to always move from downwind, about how bucks develop antlers each year, and how during the breeding season they tear up patches of earth with their hooves and rub their antlers on trees until the bark comes off. I added new words to my vocabulary, like rut and scrape and rack, although I had little opportunity to use them.

Through the sporting magazines and infrequent trips to Apple Canyon, where I searched for deer tracks in the mud and hoped for another glimpse of the giant buck, I developed my love of the out-of-doors and the adventure and excitement of interacting with wild animals

My developing passion for wildlife eventually shaped my career choice. Working with my high school guidance counselor during my senior year, I searched for a path that would support these interests. Using a new computerized survey form on which I answered dozens of questions about my interests, the career choice that came back from the "career computer" was "silvaculturist." Neither my guidance counselor nor I had any idea what a silvaculturist was. We looked it up. A silvaculturist was basically a tree manager, a forester, or, as we envisioned it, a forest ranger.

I wasn't quite sure that was what I wanted to do for the rest of my life, but it was an outdoor occupation. It was the only outdoor or natural resources–related occupation that I knew existed, and since I wanted to work outdoors, I set my sights on becoming a forester.

"Probably not much money in being a forest ranger," my counselor had said, but added, "You should do what makes you happy." He had long hair and a beard and this was the 1970s. Money wasn't important; happiness was.

The computerized "find a career" system provided me with a list of universities that offered degrees in forestry. List in my hand, my father and I attended a college fair held at the nearby Arlington Park racetrack. Representatives from colleges across the Midwest, and even as far away as California, were there, hawking the benefits of their respective academic centers. The hall was filled with wide-eyed high school seniors, all carrying plastic bags stuffed full of brochures and blank applications.

We tracked down several universities on my list, adding their brochures and booklets to my bag. The last college we searched out was University of Wisconsin–Stevens Point, a state school in a small central Wisconsin town on the banks of the Wisconsin River. As I discussed my interests with the smiling UWSP rep, it quickly became apparent that I had found The One.

I could hear the pride in the rep's voice as she described the College of Natural Resources, which she called the CNR. "There really is such a thing as a College of Natural Resources?" I asked.

"One of the largest in the nation," she answered proudly. "We offer degrees in soil science, forestry, fisheries, wildlife management . . ."

I stopped her. "*Wildlife management?* There really is a degree in wildlife management?" I knew at exactly that moment that I didn't want to be a silvaculturist, or even a forest ranger. I wanted to be a wildlife manager. It was truly a watershed moment.

That winter I sent out only one college application. In the fall of 1979, my formal education in wildlife management began.

My first official wildlife class was an introductory course in wildlife, a straightforward class focusing on the very basics of wildlife biology. I was elated to actually be taking a course with exam questions like: What is the average clutch size of a bobwhite quail? What is the scientific name for ruffed grouse? The curriculum also included a healthy dose of white-tailed deer. I learned what deer ate, when they had their young, how they survived harsh northern Wisconsin winters, and a thousand other things.

My education on the *hunting* of white-tailed deer, on the other hand, came outside the classroom. I was in Wisconsin now, and I lived in a dormitory wing with about twenty other students, the majority Wisconsin natives. The Wisconsin guys on the wing were from all corners of the state—my first roommate came from Burlington, others from small towns like Glidden, Antigo, and Two Rivers. I met people who not only deer hunted but who seemingly had been hunting their entire lives. And they were incredibly, insanely passionate about it.

Shortly after school began most of us freshmen were still in shock from being on our own for the first time, still trying to learn our way around campus. But by October, a few guys on the wing began getting up hours before sunrise, long before the first class of the day, to bow hunt. They would travel to nearby public land, such as the Dewey Marsh or George W. Mead Wildlife Areas, hunt until an hour after sunrise, and return to school. Sometimes they would hunt at sunset as well.

One day that autumn the word spread through the wing that one of the more persistent bowhunters had shot a big deer, a buck. We all went down to the street to see the deer in the back of his pickup truck. I had never seen a deer killed by a hunter before. This was my first real exposure to the Wisconsin tradition of deer hunting, a glimpse into the culture of the deer hunt: people gathered around the successful hunter who beamed with pride, still dressed in camouflaged clothes, and showing off the arrow that had served its purpose well. The night air was crisp, summer just past, and our breath hung in the air. It was something I had never experienced before but that I knew was very important.

Three semesters later I was out of the dorms, living in a typical college house (aka, a dump) with five friends. One was an ardent outdoorsman who had grown up on a commercial rainbow trout farm in Langlade County. Jeff would go home nearly every weekend during school, and on Sunday evenings he always came back with enough food to last the week: frozen venison, fresh rainbow trout, a sack of Langlade County potatoes, home-canned fruits and vegetables, and occasionally rabbits or squirrel.

The smell of wild food always seemed to be in our house. Fairly often Jeff would cook up a huge panful of potatoes (a Langlade County specialty thanks to Antigo silt loam) and venison, to be shared by whichever roommates were around at the time. My first taste of venison was another step in my early education as a deer hunter, connecting the dots from the buck in the wild to the buck in the back of the pickup truck and now to the venison on my plate.

One thing the College of Natural Resources faculty emphasized, almost daily it seemed, was the fact that, at the time, employment in natural resources occupations was difficult to obtain and the pay was generally low. Their clearly stated objective was to make us consider whether a career in natural resources management was something we really wanted. Competition for the few good jobs out there was intense.

This was the early 1980s, and the U.S. economy was in dire straits. Some CNR majors did decide to pursue careers with higher potentials of actually landing a job, and maybe even making some money at it. My roommate Jeff, who was a fisheries major with hopes of going home to manage the family trout farm, heeded the warnings and changed his major to business. Another friend switched from wildlife management to paper science, a field with some ties to natural resources (trees turn into pulp, which turns into paper products) but with the promise of steady work and a decent salary.

Soon after graduation I learned that my teachers were speaking the truth. There was intense competition for even seasonal work. After two years of scouring the job market to come up with short-term technician jobs that gave me only a few months of work at a time (and crisscrossing the country to do it) I decided to return to school to pursue a master's degree—something that had pretty much become a necessity for gainful employment in the wildlife management field.

My search led me to New Mexico State University in the southern part of the state at Las Cruces, where I would research an endangered subspecies of wild turkey, the Gould's turkey. At the time, Gould's turkeys could be found in only two areas of the United States: the Peloncillo Mountains in extreme southwestern New Mexico and at Fort Huachuca, an army base in Arizona where they had been reintroduced using stock birds from Mexico. My study site was the remote Peloncillo Mountains, a semidesert wilderness populated by a few ranchers and abundant wildlife, most of which was new to me. Mountain lions prowled the rocky highlands, and javelina roamed the mostly dry creek beds. I saw other animals that I had only read about: coatimundis, coyotes, swift fox, and burrowing owls.

And even there, in a place so very different from Illinois or Wisconsin, there were white-tailed deer. These were a southwestern subspecies of whitetail known as coues, or Arizona white-tailed deer. They are small, petite in comparison to the heavy-bodied northern deer. While the dominant deer in the area are the mule deer, frequently seen on the open grassland, the coues utilize the more vegetated habitats and the "edge" habitat between them: the grassy oak savannas and the more thickly vegetated stream and creek bed areas that support forests of pine trees and junipers.

Coues deer became the subject of my first real deer hunt. After the summer of my first field season in the Peloncillos, I had gotten to know the mountains and the Coronado National Forest that occupied much of the range exceedingly well. Back at Las Cruces, I talked to two friends about the many coues deer I'd seen during the summer. One friend, Pat, was a Wisconsinite, a fellow UWSP graduate, and an ardent deer hunter. Soon he and I and another grad student, Jim, were planning a weekend hunting trip. I borrowed a rifle from a professor who was serious about guns and had a firearms store on the side. He gave me a box of reloaded ammunition.

A local rancher who had befriended me during the summer allowed us to access the public land through his private property (referred to as "deeded land" in the West). We pitched a tent in one of the canyons and sighted in our rifles the day before the deer season opened.

That night, we sat around a crackling fire in Whitmire Canyon, smoke rising slowly in windless air. The temperature had cooled and the night was dark and clear, a stream of stars overhead. Coyotes barked from somewhere on the ridge above us. It was here, talking and laughing and trying to avoid the campfire's smoke, that I began in a small way to feel the excitement of the "night before deer season."

The hunt itself—only a weekend long—was uneventful. The deer that seemed so easy to happen upon during the summer completely eluded me. I wasn't sure what to do, or how to go about hunting a coues deer. I ended up walking up and down the open savanna of the foothills, occasionally walking a stretch of dry canyon bottom just hoping to scare up a deer, to catch even a glimpse. I never saw one.

I learned perhaps the first two important truths about deer hunting: (1) come deer season, the deer you've seen all over the place a month before will have disappeared, and (2) deer hunting isn't easy.

This New Mexico deer hunt, though exciting, was lacking something. It was missing Wisconsin: the tradition, the brisk autumn air, the fire-colored leaves of maples, aspen, and oak. Deer hunting in the Southwest may be someone's tradition, but even though I was a deer-hunting neophyte, I knew it wasn't mine.

It would be in the Lone Star State that I would kill my first deer. Upon graduation from grad school, I was hired as a wildlife biologist by the U.S. Department of Agriculture—a permanent, full-time job. My duty location was Fort Worth, in northeastern Texas. I packed my little pickup truck full of all my earthly belongings and headed east.

Texas had long and liberal hunting seasons, and plenty of whitetails. My new supervisor was a dedicated shooter and passionate hunter, and it wasn't long before I found myself regularly accompanying him to the shooting range.

Although Texas had an enormous white-tailed deer population, the big state had a dearth of public land hunting opportunities. As a result, Texas had fully developed the institution of the hunting lease. So, actually, there were *unlimited* hunting opportunities, depending on your willingness to pay for them. Options included paying for hunting by the day—typical on bigger ranches managed for big bucks—or buying into a hunting lease on a particular property—typical with the smaller ranches or farms—for a longer period.

For many years my boss and his best friend had held a hunting lease on a small ranch not far from Fort Worth. The ranch consisted of a few cattle pastures, some rocky, juniper-covered ridges, and a pond or two that held some fish. For a hundred dollars, I became a member of their hunting club for the season. With the permission of the landowner who controlled the antlerless permits, we could take a buck or a doe.

The hunting club's camp was an abandoned, dilapidated farmhouse that appeared ready to collapse. The ground floor was packed full of old junk, so our camp was on the second floor, which was reached by way of a ladder, the steps having long ago disappeared. We hauled our gear upstairs and unrolled our sleeping bags. The night before the opener was windy, and I endured a sleepless night worried that the house would simply give up and blow over.

Well before sunrise I was dropped off by pickup truck next to my stand. It was a sturdy, square permanent structure raised on four legs, furnished with a stool. The stand, at the edge of a creek bed, overlooked the creek on one side and an open pasture on the other.

Everything seemed to be in my favor. I was in a stand that had been there for a hundred years for all I knew. There was some certainty that deer would appear somewhere within my field of view. I had been shooting my .22-250 at the range for months and was very confident with my ability to accurately hit a target from a long way away.

Sitting in the stand in the predawn Texas darkness, I thought about all this. And I began to get nervous. Right then I learned a third fact about hunting. The idea of having a rifle in hand, the morning of opening day, and the idea that there would be deer around, creates a nervous sort of excitement that causes your heart to beat fast, your breath to be short, and your hands to shake.

As the sky began to lighten just a bit, I was startled by the sound of something running fast along the dry creek bottom. I knew it was a deer, but being inexperienced in the ways of hunting I didn't know what to do. Should I stand up and look? Was the deer still there? Was it a buck? My heart was pounding.

By the time I answered even the first question, the deer was long gone. Whatever it was it had run full bore down the creek bed and disappeared. I calmed down a bit. A few minutes later I noticed three deer crossing the field about 150 yards away. The distance helped keep me calm. I immediately put the scope on the deer, which were walking slowly, stopping to feed from time to time. They were all does, probably an adult and two yearlings. I focused on the largest deer, and my heart began to race again. I took one deep breath and held it. My rifle cracked. Scope down now, I watched three deer run across the field. Suddenly one disappeared as the other two continued on into the woodland near the creek.

Did I get it? Now my heart was threatening to pound out of my chest; my hands were still shaking. I flipped on the rifle safety and climbed down from the stand. It seemed to take forever to get over the barbed-wire fence and walk the distance to where I thought I shot the deer.

I was breathing heavily, and my legs were weak from the sudden walk after having been prone for so long in the stand. It took only a minute or two of searching. I could see the trail the three deer had left through the grass. About forty yards down the trail was a doe. My shot had been true—a lung shot that allowed her to run for just a few seconds before dropping.

I knelt down in the grass and ran my hand across her neck. A beautiful Texas doe, light in color and with a thin coat compared to northern deer. Fifteen years after the Apple Canyon buck bolted across my consciousness, I had become a successful deer hunter.

My education on deer and deer hunting was progressing.

While living in Texas with my wife, Deirdre, whom I'd met back at UWSP, I killed one more deer. I shot it from a comfortable ground blind on a little hobby ranch an hour west of Fort Worth. The ranch was owned by our landlords, who lived next door to the house we were renting. Though I wasn't allowed to shoot any bucks on the property (the acreage was too limited to allow for a large buck harvest), I was allowed to hunt the property by myself and to stay at a little cottage there.

The ranch was a beautiful place—open fallow fields, rugged oak ridges, a stream, and several ponds. It was good habitat for deer, as well as turkeys and mourning doves. The hunt itself was not noteworthy, just a bare-bones deer harvest. Deer were baited and fed with automatic corn feeders, common among landowners in Texas. I sat in the blind about fifty yards from a feeder. Nearing evening, the timer on the feeder kicked in. Corn was sprayed in a circle around the feeder. Within minutes several deer appeared from the woods, heading toward the feeder. I picked a larger doe still some distance away and dropped her.

I hung her in the barn for the night and brought her to the meat processor's the next day. My third hunt, and completely different from the others. I was happy to get the deer, as she provided good meat for many meals, but the hunt experience itself left something to be desired.

In 1990 I returned to Wisconsin, taking a job with the USDA in Rhinelander, the Oneida County seat. I was ecstatic to be back in the state. Deirdre and I moved in July; immediately, I was looking at the calendar and counting the days until the rifle season. After three years in Texas, even the summer weather in northern Wisconsin felt cool, a refreshing change from the oppressive southern heat. It wasn't long before the nights held a chill, the summer quickly fading into autumn.

I now had a little more deer hunting experience than when I had left Wisconsin. I had three bona fide deer hunts under my belt, with two deer killed, and had become fairly proficient in shooting. I had come back to Wisconsin ready to hunt deer, by bow as well as by rifle. Just before leaving Texas I purchased a compound bow and practiced shooting at a target in an alleyway behind the house. After settling into a rental house in Rhinelander in September, I began regularly target shooting with the bow. Not long after, I began to bow hunt in earnest.

Hunting was not just an occasional pastime but a developing passion. I studied the sporting goods catalogs and outfitted myself for Wisconsin deer hunting. First a tree stand, then camouflaged clothing, flannel shirts, long underwear, gloves, and heavy socks—things I hadn't needed for a long time. I eagerly tore into each package that arrived in the mail.

With my best friend from college, Steve, also in Wisconsin, I bow hunted most weekends, focusing on an area of the Nicolet National Forest when we had the time to travel there, or a chunk of paper company land near the small settlement of Sugar Camp when time was limited.

Our planning and discussions and target practice took place at his family's seventy-year-old log cabin at Sugar Camp on Sugar Camp Lake, located between Rhinelander and Eagle River. The cabin was steeped in Wisconsin North Woods tradition. Built of logs and lumber from long-ago Wisconsin River Valley lumber companies and set in a grove of tall hemlock, it was the perfect jumping-off place for our bow hunts. It was there, prior to heading out to the woods, that we covered ourselves with baking soda (to absorb human scent), put on our camouflaged clothes, and spent half an hour putting black, brown, and green makeup on our faces. It became a ritual.

For those who do not bow hunt—even among deer hunters—it may be difficult to understand the intensity bowhunters can develop. It is not a hunting activity that can be approached half-heartedly. A bowhunter, unless he or she relies on baiting deer, must know deer intimately in order to succeed. I learned this through a lot of frustrating trial and error.

With my bow, I was confident shooting up to twenty-five yards, thirty yards maximum. At this distance I could put six arrows in a pretty tight group. This meant I had to select a place for my tree stand—the wind's direction being of utmost importance—where I felt there was a chance of having a deer, ideally a buck, pass within my range, and remain completely unalarmed as I drew my bow and released the arrow. As I learned, this was much easier imagined than done. The deer would have to come from a direction where it could not pick up my scent, and I had to be concealed enough to be able to soundlessly draw the string on my bow, steady the arrow and myself for a shot, and fire. It was essential that the arrow flew straight and hard and hit the deer in a vital area, as arrows carry none of the supersonic force of a rifle bullet. To have this all come together takes practice, experience, and a keen knowledge of white-tailed deer behavior, as well as a healthy dose of good luck.

Although I practiced my bowshooting, I was woefully deficient in the other two factors: experience and knowledge of deer. The good luck, I discovered, was never consistent.

My first season of bowhunting taught me more about white-tailed deer than all of my previous hunting experience (which, admittedly, wasn't a lot) and my college education combined. Out of necessity, I attempted to think like a deer, to see the forest through the eyes of a deer. I learned that even the smallest things matter. The choice of a tree in which to place a stand can make the difference between a deer passing within twenty yards (which might allow a shot) or forty yards (which would not).

I learned the importance of scent and wind direction. Many times I gave in to the temptation of setting up a stand in a location that looked so perfect, but where I knew the wind direction was against me. Many times I heard the crunch of deer behind me, or the warning snort of a deer, unseen, that had identified my scent.

Mostly I learned that the whitetail is one incredible animal.

One late afternoon, hunting north of Sugar Camp, it all came together. My stand was in a good tree, and I felt invisible in my camouflage. An adult doe came trotting down the trail I was positioned over, completely unaware of my presence.

Everything worked. I quietly drew the string and steadied the arrow just as she came within range.

My arrow hit hard and she ran off into a pine plantation. I could hear the aluminum of the arrow slap against the trees. I stood on my stand, heart pounding, and looked into the woods. It had all happened so quickly—I began to doubt myself. Did the arrow hit where I had aimed? Was the deer even affected by the shot? What should I do now?

I waited a few minutes so as not to push the deer if the shot hadn't been immediately fatal, then climbed down from the stand and began the search. My worries were unnecessary. Just fifty yards into the trees, I could see the form of a deer lying between rows of pine. The shot had been perfect; adrenaline alone allowed the deer to get as far as she did.

This experience of bowhunting, of killing a large animal with a bow and arrow at an intimately close range, was profound. I admired the deer and the surroundings—the pine needles she lay on, the pattern of the red pine bark, the yellow aspen bordering the pines, the darkening sky. It all made sense.

Throughout that autumn, Steve and I were also planning the establishment of a gun deer hunting camp. We didn't have access to any shack or cabin for our camp, so we came up with an alternative: a wall tent. The location would be in the Chequamegon National Forest near Clam Lake, where we had spent a considerable amount of time while at UWSP. The Chequamegon seemed to us like the most wild and remote place in Wisconsin.

The camp was our first real stab at becoming a part of the Wisconsin deer hunting tradition. The traditional rifle season and the archery season were two different animals. Bowhunting was a sport relatively new in popularity and also more of a solo activity. Not confined to just nine days, the bowhunting season stretched from September through December. Bowhunters, a smaller subset of the deer hunting community, seemed willing to invest many hours in shooting practice, scouting, and stand time.

While we had both embraced bowhunting in a big way, it was the gun season that really excited us. The rifle season was Wisconsin deer hunting in all its glory. A hundred years of the tradition of the deer camp, the annual gathering of hunters, young and old. It was as much a celebration as a recreational activity, and we knew we wanted to be a part of it.

Steve and I were probably the most unlikely duo to be passionate about the establishment of a North Woods deer camp: I was from the suburbs of Chicago and he grew up in suburban Boston. Somehow we had both developed a respect for tradition—and for the old ways rather than the new.

I bought the wall tent after searching through dozens of brochures from manufacturers I had found in an elk hunting magazine. Steve bought a sheet metal wood stove to go in it. We learned as we went. Our first camp was located at a U.S. Forest

Service campground just outside of Clam Lake. A little unsure of ourselves, we didn't want to be too detached from civilization. We christened our camp Deadfall, not as a reference to any presumed hunting prowess but because the big aspen log we used for our tent's ridge pole almost clubbed us both as we struggled to erect the heavy canvas tent.

(Above) The spike buck taken at Deadfall Camp near Clam Lake in 1996. This was the first time we broke camp prior to the last day of deer season and also the last with the wall tent. But this season stands out as one of the best.
COURTESY OF STEVE LANE

(Below) Hunting partner Steve Lane in the kitchen at Deadfall Camp. We moved to a sixteen-foot-by-sixteen-foot log cabin in Bayfield County in 2001. With bunks, a propane cook stove, and a full-size woodstove for overnight heat, it was glorious comfort compared to our wall tent days.
COLLECTION OF ROBERT C. WILLGING

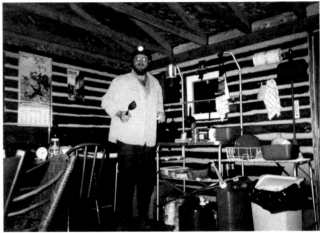

For nine days, the only thing that mattered was deer hunting. It was all we talked about at night, all we did during the day. It was our complete focus and complete freedom. We could leave the tent, rifles in hand and plans finalized, and roam the woods for the entire day, sitting in our tree stands or blinds or just carefully following a fresh set of tracks. Together again at night, we always had excited tales to tell.

As we added years to the Deadfall hunting journal, the deer hunt tradition overtook us. We developed rituals, even wrote out some bylaws, keeping in mind that a "two-man deer camp could be a fragile thing." We began to look forward to deer camp and opening day the same way a child anticipates Christmas. We spent weeks planning and discussing and speculating—and, yes, dreaming of that perfect hunt, complete with a meat pole that had at least two deer hanging from it.

Today, Deadfall is still going strong, although we replaced the original tent with a small log cabin built on some hunting land we purchased a few years back. The

cabin, however, continues the tradition. It is primitive, with no utilities. It serves only one purpose: deer camp.

✦　✦　✦　✦　✦

October 1997, in the middle of a beautiful northern Wisconsin autumn, I was diagnosed with a form of chronic leukemia. I was thirty-six. Overnight I came face to face with my own mortality. The fall activities I had grown to love—deer hunting, grouse hunting, canoeing, splitting wood for the winter—were replaced with research on treatment options, appointments with doctors, and filling out insurance paperwork. My future had suddenly become very uncertain, very complicated.

The approach of the November gun deer season seemed to be one thing in my life that wasn't complex or confusing, and I was determined to hunt. A friend offered an easily accessible ground blind on his property along the Wisconsin River south of Rhinelander. I was continually tired and had little appetite due to chemotherapy. Just getting out of the house was an accomplishment. Yet I took him up on his offer. I felt that if I could plod through the snow looking for tracks or sit out in the woods, in the cold, if only for a short while, maybe I could focus my attention on what was happening around me rather than inside of me.

I would have no traditional deer camp in the wilds of the Chequamegon National Forest as I'd had since 1990. What a difference a year can make!

I thought back to the previous season, one that now seemed nearly perfect: the traditional wall tent camp, the dry cold and perfect snow, the buck dropped with a single shot from my .30-30. Now, sitting in my friend's blind on the edge of a pine plantation overlooking the river, the cold got through to me fast, and I was just too nervous to sit for very long.

Later that week, a doe and two fawns came up the ridge and slowly walked past me, feeding along the way. I felt the familiar quickening of my heart as I watched them searching for the right plants to nip. For the first time in many weeks I was able to focus completely on something unrelated to my plight. I wished the deer would stay forever; I wished I could stay in the blind and watch them forever. I wished everything else in the world would go away and leave me alone.

But the three deer finally ambled out of sight, my back became tired, and the sun dipped below the pines. Cold seeped into my clothing and I began to shiver. Time moved on and I had to leave.

That hunt wasn't one for the hunting log or the record books, but it was probably the most important of my life. Basically I had come to believe that if I could hunt, I was alive.

After a year of chemotherapy I received the bad news: it hadn't changed a thing. My last and only hope was a bone marrow transplant. Down about fifty pounds from my normal weight and having felt like I had the flu every day for a year, I physically could not hunt during the 1998 rifle season.

Once I decided to have the transplant, there was no turning back. It was a black-and-white scenario: the procedure would either work and give me a chance to recover, or it would fail and I would die, simple as that.

I was one of the lucky ones. I started on a slow, rocky but steady road to recovery. It would take well over a year posttransplant before I felt truly healthy again.

Recuperating at home, I found myself with a lot of time on my hands and a need to keep indoors as much as possible. A nearly lifelong interest in journalism and outdoor writing had always taken a backseat to my career as a wildlife biologist. Through the years I had written when time allowed, consistently selling articles to a variety of wildlife and outdoor magazines. My homebound situation was the perfect opportunity to start writing in earnest again.

Around this time I discovered *Wisconsin Outdoor News*, a relatively new biweekly hunting and fishing newspaper. Editor Dean Bortz published some of my articles. As we talked about ideas for future stories, I told Dean I wanted to write about what hunting was like back in "the good old days." He liked the concept and suggested I expand it to include the history of deer hunting in the 1900s.

In my research, I came across an enormous wealth of resources, from old Wisconsin Department of Conservation papers, letters, and brochures to hunting and fishing magazines, local and state newspapers, as well as information and personal stories from hunters and deer managers. I produced a ten-article series covering Wisconsin deer hunting history from 1900 through 1999 that ran prior to the gun season of 2001.

Those articles were the genesis of this book. With the luxury of a book-length project, I've gone back further in time to cover Wisconsin's original deer hunters—the Paleo-Indians and the many Native American cultures that followed, as well as the settlers and pioneers who hunted deer for survival. I've also taken the story of deer hunting into the twenty-first century, with all of its controversies and complexities, such as CWD, baiting issues, and ever-burgeoning deer and human populations.

To be sure, this book is not meant to be a history of white-tailed deer management in Wisconsin, although deer management and deer hunting are intimately intertwined. Nor is it a concise accounting of the development of hunting regulations or hunting equipment or numbers of deer killed. It is simply meant to be a helpful and enjoyable exploration of where the Wisconsin deer hunt came from, what it has become, and what it might look like down the road.

With nearly twenty-five years of deer hunting experience behind me, I am still fascinated by whitetails. I've learned that the white-tailed deer is a remarkable animal, something much more than just the target of a hunter's rifle. Deer hunting is something greater as well. It has myriad components: the smell of the woods in autumn, the blaze orange or camo clothing, the meticulous cleaning of a fine rifle, wood smoke, blood trails in the snow, rifles lined up in gun racks.

It is a cliché to some now to say that deer hunting is primeval, somehow a very part of our being, something contained in our DNA. Modern thinkers scoff at this idea and toss it aside as just some excuse hunters use to justify their need to hunt. However, it is not conjecture that no other man-animal relationship in the world is as old and as important as the human-deer relationship. Deer have been escaping and frustrating man—vanishing into the forest with uncanny ability—for just as long. Deer and human interactions through thousands of years created the structure and parameters of today's hunt.

Simply put, the deer hunt is an irremovable component of our very being. Some of us just don't know it yet.

Acknowledgments

I'd foremost like to thank Dean Bortz, editor of *Wisconsin Outdoor News (WON)*, who originally supported the idea of tracing the history of Wisconsin deer hunting in ten articles. These *WON* articles covering deer hunting in the 1900s served as the launching point for this book.

Special thanks also go to Keith McCaffery, retired Wisconsin Department of Natural Resources (DNR) northern forest research biologist, Rhinelander, whose knowledge and memory of white-tailed deer management is beyond compare. His willingness to share that knowledge with me was an enormous factor in ensuring the accuracy of several chapters in this book. I'd also like to thank Bruce Kohn, also a retired DNR northern forest research biologist, Rhinelander, for providing information and access to publications for the original *WON* articles, and Keith Warnke, DNR big-game ecologist, Madison, for his assistance.

Thanks go to Peter David, wildlife biologist with the Great Lakes Indian Fish and Wildlife Commission (GLIFWC), Odanah, who took the time to conduct a thorough review of the draft manuscript and provide numerous insightful comments. Steve Lane, Wimbledon, North Dakota, and Hiles, Wisconsin, my primary deer hunting partner and founding member of Deadfall Camp, also deserves thanks for a careful review of the manuscript (and for providing comments to keep me honest).

Thanks also to everyone who openly shared their personal stories and/or photos of their own special deer hunting experiences or helped in other ways with the development of this book: Joyce Bong Erickson, Poplar; Mike Edwards, Superior; Marge Engel, Winchester; Lewie Falk, Poynette; Peggy Farrell, Stevens Point; Buck Follis, Brule; Connie Ghiloni, Winchester; Jonathon Gilbert, Odanah; Mike Herbst, Hartford; Todd Herbst, West Bend; Jeff Koser, Rhinelander; Jan Loven, Fort Worth, Texas; Bill Nohl, Ashland; Connie Rollman, Rhinelander; Jim Rollman, Rhinelander; Trygve Solberg, Rhinelander; Brian Tessmann, Waukesha; Dr. Christine Thomas, Stevens Point; Dorothy Uthe, Mercer; Mike Vlahakis, Rhinelander; Werner "Zim" Zimmer, Rhinelander; Ed Zydzik, Phillips; as well as the unnamed old-timers and other hunters encountered in the deer woods.

This book would have been impossible to complete without the assistance and support of the following:

Kate Thompson and Laura Kearney, Wisconsin Historical Society Press, Madison.

The dedicated staff of the Rhinelander District Library who processed numerous interlibrary loan requests for me and kept the microfilm reader running—and, perhaps more important, remained committed to keeping the library, originally built through a Carnegie grant received in 1903, a free and open functioning facility in spite of threats to funding and the privacy of its patrons.

This book also is a result of my passion for wildlife and the outdoors, an interest that was fostered by numerous educators throughout the years including Jim Bertoglio, Prospect High School, Mount Prospect, Illinois; wildlife management professors at the UW–Stevens Point College of Natural Resources, Drs. Lyle Nauman, Jim Hardin, and Neil Payne, now retired; and the late Dr. R. K. Anderson, and Dr. Sanford Schemnitz, professor emeritus, New Mexico State University, Las Cruces, New Mexico.

Lastly, I am indebted to Sean Naze, Dr. Dhimant Patel, Dr. Bill Drobyski, and Jim Myers for helping to get me here.

The Animal

The white-tail is the American deer of the past and the American deer of the future.
—Ernest Thompson Seton[1]

The white-tailed buck steps tentatively out of the spruce forest. He is intensely alert, eyes sharp to any movement, nostrils constantly testing the breeze, ears twitching, listening for anything out of the ordinary. There is nothing to cause alarm, no scent of a predator, the only sound the gentle rustling of the leaves of a few distant aspen trees. Satisfied, he takes two small bounds. Completely out of the dark woods, he seeks the succulent browse that can only be found at the forest edge. He puts his head down just long enough to grab a mouthful of vegetation, then it is up again, senses monitoring every aspect of his environment.

It is late summer in the region of the western Great Lakes. The six-year-old buck is in his prime: heavily bodied, strong, and healthy. A thin red summer coat is transforming into the sleek gray of winter. Growing from pedicles on his skull is a magnificent set of antlers, still covered with velvet; thin skin and blood-filled capillaries allowed the antlers to grow and develop. Shortly, the blood flow to the velvet will stop, and the dried tissue will be rubbed off by the buck, leaving antlers of polished bone. Thrown into the heat of the rutting season, the buck—in mad pursuit of females to breed—with few thoughts of food, will lose considerable weight.

But for now the living is easy. As the sun begins to touch the treetops toward the west, the buck continues to feed for several minutes until a sound from the forest causes him to snap his head up, all senses on alert. He looks downwind, the direction from which the sound came. He does not move, not even to chew the fresh greens in his mouth. He waits; he assesses. There's nothing to send him running, but he is more cautious as he resumes his feeding.

Again there is the noise, and the head is back up. This time the buck stamps his front feet and takes a step toward the sound, feeling that something is not quite right. He is on a higher plane of alertness, every nerve on edge. His instinct is to leave the area, to circle downwind, to try to identify the source of the new sound. Then there is an explosion of sound and movement.

A saber-toothed cat had been patiently hunting the deer. Well before the buck appeared, the cat had taken up an ambush position downwind of a trail that lately had been frequented by deer intent on browsing the forest edge in the afternoons. The large cat had hit it big when the buck appeared. Although a smaller deer would be easier to take down and kill, the sabertooth—at five and a half feet long, 700 pounds, and in possession of canine teeth more than six inches long—was not intimidated by a healthy buck deer.

Sensing the buck's nervousness and intent to move, the cat, which had been slowly closing the distance to the buck, started with a tremendous rush toward the deer, great bounds covering ten feet in an instant.

Without thought, reacting only with instinct and adrenaline, the buck whirls and propels himself away from the cat with the power of his back legs. The buck is back in the thick spruce, bounding with great leaps of his own farther and farther from the cat. The sabertooth pursues but only for a moment, its energy spent on the charge. The effort was a futile waste of energy for the great cat. It moves on in search of easier prey, perhaps a giant ground sloth or a young wooly mammoth.

The buck also stops. He turns, listens, watches, waits. There is nothing. He knows the cat has given up the chase. The buck has made another successful escape in a life that is all about escape, all about survival.

This may have been a typical scenario for a white-tailed deer 12,000 years ago in the land that someday would be called Wisconsin. By this time the glaciers from the most recent ice age had left Wisconsin and receded well up into Canada, leaving behind a landscape of lakes, marshes, bogs, and parklike forests of spruce and aspen[2]—a landscape we might recognize as northern Wisconsin and Minnesota today.

This was late in the Pleistocene epoch, a geological time period that began roughly 1.65 million years ago to 2.48 million years ago, and ended in the relatively recent time of about 10,000 years ago.[3] The Pleistocene is commonly known as the Ice Age, when the earth saw incredible changes in climate resulting in several periods where glaciers covered and uncovered much of Canada and the northern United States.

The whitetail was there through it all. It is thought that the whitetail's ancestors (the deer that would develop into what we know today as the white-tailed deer) traveled from Eurasia into North America by crossing over the Bering Straight land bridge, which connected the Chukchi Peninsula of Siberia with the Seward Peninsula of Alaska, sometime in the Pliocene epoch, which lasted from 5.3 million to 1.8 million years ago.[4] These deer may have been small in stature and possessed small, simple forked antlers.[5] Once in North America, one lineage of these deer, keeping to the cool northern temperate mixed forests, developed greater body size and large, many-tined antlers.[6] This evolutionary line produced moose, caribou, and, more than three million years ago, the most ancient of all deer species in North America: the white-tailed deer.[7] Whitetails, more tolerant of heat than their relatives, spread across the continent and even found their way to South America.

The white-tailed deer shared an Ice Age landscape with a bewildering variety of mammals, most of them now extinct; many, though, were "king-sized" versions of similar animals we still have today. There was a bison with horns that spanned seven feet and a beaver the size of a black bear. For many thousands of years whitetails shared the forest and swamps, the prairies and woodlands with a great number of hoofed animals, such as wooly mammoths, mastodons, horses, tapirs, peccaries, camels, pronghorn antelope, and bison.[8]

The Pleistocene landscape was also populated by myriad predators, all perfectly capable of hunting, killing, and eating hoofed prey, including white-tailed deer. Familiar predators—the gray wolf, mountain lion, wolverine, and bear—exist in North America today.[9] Deer also were relentlessly hunted by nightmarish Ice Age predators such as dire wolves—larger versions of today's gray wolf but with more powerful jaws and teeth—and the giant short-faced bear, which was bigger than a grizzly, with males that may have weighed more than 2,000 pounds. And there were the cats: the familiar saber-toothed cats as well as American cheetahs and a formidable species of Ice Age lion, long-legged and tipping the scales at nearly 800 pounds, dwarfing the African lions of today.[10]

On the road to evolutionary success, the whitetail had to overcome some major obstacles. In order to survive it had to compete intensely for food and living space with the many species of Pleistocene herbivores, some numbering in the hundreds of thousands, and at the same time develop ways to evade the multitude of predators that were constantly on the prowl for deer meat.

Whitetails were to accomplish all this and more. By the end of the Ice Age, most of the large mammals that had existed alongside the whitetail had become extinct. Some were unable to cope with ever-changing climate and habitat conditions. Others were unable to cope with a recently arrived and highly intelligent predator: humans.[11]

In contrast, the whitetail not only survived but flourished, having developed into one of the most widespread and adaptable wildlife species on the continent. "The whitetail was very good at avoiding extinction," wrote noted deer biologist Valerius Geist.[12] While many mammals became highly specialized during the Pleistocene and therefore more vulnerable to extinction when conditions changed, whitetails took a different tack. Deer became adaptable and opportunistic. Their generalized food habits allowed them to exploit and occupy a wide variety of habitats. Whitetails could seek out and select the high-quality vegetation they required, but could also survive for long periods, such as during bleak northern winters, on extremely poor foods. This adaptability and ability to shift food sources as climate and vegetation changed made them a highly successful creature, able to survive just as well in the palmetto swamps of the south, the plains and woodlots of the southwest, or the swamps, bogs, and mixed forest of the north.

Thousands of years of relentless pressure from predators forged the whitetail into a species with a remarkable ability for sheer survival. Geist wrote: "To evade predators, white-tailed deer had to be able to avoid ambush, day or night, be concealed from the sharp eyes and talons from the air, outrun sprinters such as the American cheetah or the giant bulldog bear, discourage long distance runners such as the dire wolf, decoy away fawn killers, and fight off those that could be defeated with its limited weapons."[13]

To survive tooth and claw, talon and fang, deer developed what has been called a security or survival "toolbox"—an impressive array of strengths, behaviors, and instincts that allowed them to escape predators more often than succumb to them.

A doe explodes through a Vilas County clear cut. Speed is key to the whitetail's survival.

PHOTO BY MATT ERLANDSON, WWW.TRAMPERSTRAIL.COM

Foremost in the toolbox is speed. When danger looms, a whitetail can explode with a burst of speed and disappear so quickly that a predator has a difficult time with pursuit. To accomplish this, deer sacrificed energy efficiency for velocity, forsaking a more energy-efficient but slower transverse gallop for a fast but energy-intensive rotary gallop.[14] At full gallop a whitetail may exceed thirty miles per hour and can clear obstacles as high as eight feet.[15] The goal of an escaping deer is to bolt away so quickly that all contact between predator and prey—sound, sight, and scent—is broken, leaving a predator wondering what happened.[16]

To be able to run headlong into the thickest cover at top speed, the whitetail must know its home range intimately. It must know every tree, rock, stream crossing, and rocky ledge. Deer are very loyal to their home area, for this is where they are most secure.[17] Geist succinctly summed up the importance of this knowledge: "The deer knows where it is going, whereas the pursuing predator does not."[18]

Whitetails developed into professional escape artists, and the escape does not consist of only a quick burst of speed. A deer will change direction in an instant, pause to assess a predator's progress, back-track, or circle to get downwind, all of which add to the predator's—or hunter's—frustration.

To react to danger, a deer must be able to detect and analyze potential threats. It must know when to flee and evade a predator, and when not to react so that precious energy isn't wasted on constant false alarms.

The whitetail is extremely good at detecting motion, but less skilled at discerning an object—even a predator—that is standing completely still. In the predator-rich environment of the Ice Age, however, detecting motion was perhaps the most important specialization for vision. As is common with species that are generally pursued in the game of predator-prey, a deer's eyes are located on the sides, rather than the front of the skull. This allows deer to perceive movement nearly from all sides. With eyes angled slightly forward, whitetails have some binocular vision (that is, they can see three-dimensionally), but they can also see along their flanks to detect objects behind them.[19] Overall, a white-tailed deer has a 310-degree arc of sight, making it a very difficult animal to sneak up on.[20]

To further confound an ambush by a hungry predator, whitetails posses both a tremendous ability to detect scent and an extremely keen sense of hearing, the deer's large ears turning to capture every sound. Deer expert Leonard Lee Rue felt that hearing more than any other sensory perception triggers cautious or evasive behavior.[21]

On the alert: Predators are often thwarted by the whitetail's acute hearing ability.
WISCONSIN DEPARTMENT OF NATURAL RESOURCES

Scent is important to whitetails for many reasons. Much of the communication between deer is scent related. The rutting buck can detect the smell of a doe in estrus, and individual deer can identify others from the scent they leave. The whitetail's highly developed sense of smell is an important asset when danger looms. The faintest whiff of a predator can send a deer packing.

With a full complement of defense mechanisms, a healthy adult deer—unimpeded by deep snow or some other obstacle—is not easy prey. However, a newly born fawn with wobbly legs and weighing less than ten pounds can do little by itself to avoid a predator. As a consequence, predators may concentrate their hunting efforts on the more vulnerable fawns in the spring.[22] But the same predatory pressures that provided adult deer with a survival toolbox also threw in a few tools to aid in the survival of fawns to reproductive age.

A newborn fawn, lying helplessly on the forest floor, is built not for escape but for concealment. For at least its first week, the main survival strategy for a fawn is to keep out of sight. The doe will let her fawn nurse and then leave to feed for herself, returning infrequently. After nursing, the fawn will generally choose its own place to bed down, some distance away from where the doe stood. While she is gone, the fawn remains motionless—its characteristic spotted coat breaking up the outline of its body and serving as an effective camouflage.

A fawn's coat serves as camouflage while it beds down.
Photo by Jack R. Bartholmai

This stage of a fawn's life does not last very long, as fawns double their birth weight in about two weeks. After about a week, the fawn already is displaying an ability to run; a two-week-old fawn is very fleet of foot and generally will attempt to flee from danger rather than stay put.

While the physical characteristics of young deer develop quickly, the experience needed to survive the daily rigors of the wild takes longer to accumulate. To this end, the fawn will stay with its mother throughout the autumn and winter, until new fawns come in the spring. The doe will chase away last year's fawns as she concentrates on the new crop during the summer.[23] By autumn, the doe and the new fawns will regroup with the yearlings. The combination of a protective mother, fast growth rate, and an early ability to stay concealed, add up to relatively high survival rates for newborn whitetails.

By the end of the Ice Age, the white-tailed deer had evolved into one formidable survivor—an animal that was also the embodiment of grace and beauty in form and motion.

This was the animal people found as they entered the scene around the Great Lakes on the heels of the receding glaciers, arriving in the midst of, and, according to some theories, assisting with, the great extinctions of the late Paleozoic about 13,000 years ago. As the saber-toothed cats, dire wolves, and American lions dwindled and disappeared, humans took over as the top-level predator of whitetails. When what may have been their primary prey—mammoths and mastodons—also

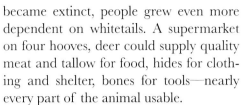

A doe and its offspring
PHOTO BY MATT ERLANDSON, WWW.TRAMPERSTRAIL.COM

became extinct, people grew even more dependent on whitetails. A supermarket on four hooves, deer could supply quality meat and tallow for food, hides for clothing and shelter, bones for tools—nearly every part of the animal usable.

Of this relationship, cultural anthropologist Richard Nelson wrote: "[P]eople and deer have lived together on this continent for a very long time, and not as distant strangers, but in the constant, intense relationship of predator and prey."[24]

The very sight of a mature buck quickens the pulse of any deer hunter in autumn.
WISCONSIN DEPARTMENT OF NATURAL RESOURCES

The First Hunters

The basis of the Indian existence was the food quest, and the basis of the food quest was the hunt. The hunting instinct had been implanted in him unnumbered ages before, while he was still a nomad on the steppes of Siberia. It was this instinct that had brought him to the Americas, where in spite of continual climate changes he had always possessed a huge territory teeming with apparently inexhaustible supplies of game.
—Jon Manchip White, *Everyday Life of the North American Indian*[1]

It was the end of winter when the old mastodon finally died. Suffering for many months, the great animal—too tired, too weak to press on through the deep and heavy snow—laid its six tons of bulk down.

It died alone. Infirm and unable to keep pace with a small group of others, it had been left behind. The others had wandered farther north the previous summer, moving deeper into the boreal forest—closer to the edge where the spruce and fir met arctic tundra, closer to where the enormous continental glacier still towered a mile high.

A vegetarian of massive proportions, the mastodon could not supply itself with the hundreds of pounds of food—spruce needles, moss, twigs of pine and cedar—it needed daily to sustain life.

The beast breathed its last in a small opening amid a forest of balsam fir, aspen, and spruce. For a month or so the mastodon's carcass lay in the deep snow. But as the warmth of spring grew and the snow melted, animals now had access to an enormous quantity of meat. The feeding began.

First the beasts of prey, the Ice Age predators that were not too proud to scavenge a free meal, scented the decaying carcass. Dire wolves and short-faced bears feasted, clawing, ripping, and tearing away the softening flesh. Birds circled down to peck at the exposed meat, carrying chunks away. Then the smaller animals crept in, the gray wolves and fox, the fishers and weasels.

By midsummer, the feeding had waned as the carcass was decomposing in the warmer air. Myriad insects buzzed around or crawled on the remains. By the end of the short Wisconsin summer there were only bones.

Amid the huge bones of this mastodon, grass and forbs grew green and lush, fertilized by the return of the mastodon's nutrients to the earth. It was nutritious browse that the white-tailed doe and her two fawns sought. Winter was approaching, and these last days of feeding on summer's vegetation were important. The health and weight of the deer at winter's onset would determine their survival during the bleak months.

The doe worked her way across the grassy field, feeding occasionally as she moved, until reaching the area of the mastodon bones, where she began to feed in earnest. The fawns, nearly four months old, followed a little behind, more independent than even a week before.

Intent on feeding, the fawns had not noticed the first stone-tipped dart that flew between them, toward the broadside of the doe. Another dart flew past. By this time the doe had made a high jump in the air, attempting to run to the security of the forest. The run did not last long, as both darts had hit their mark, one piercing her lungs and another breaking her right hip. As she crashed to the ground, the naïve fawns were not alarmed, only curious and alert. Suddenly, apparitions appeared from the forest edge, animals on two legs running into the field; more darts were in the air, one piercing one of the fawns. Alarmed now, the other fawn sped into the thick cover and was gone.

The doe is dead, only yards from where she had been feeding. The fawn, disabled by the stone-tipped dart, lies kicking in the grass. A hunter kills the deer with a thrust of a lance.

There are four hunters, short in stature but extremely muscular. All are dressed in animal hides, including hides bound around their feet. They organize quickly to carry the deer from the field. Their camp is only a few minutes' walk away on a highland ridge overlooking a small river. Several women and small children express satisfaction upon the sight of the animals. The women begin to skin the deer carcasses using sharp stone cutting tools specialized for the purpose. The hides are fleshed, the meat carefully cut from bones using other stone tools; tendons are severed and bones set aside as material for future tools, the hides for future clothing and blankets.

A large portion of the fresh meat is seared over an open fire. What's not quickly consumed is sliced and laid across wooden racks near the fire to dry. As darkness overtakes the camp, beds of deer and elk hide inside shelters built of sticks and birchbark beckon the women and children. The four hunters crouch around the fire. Overhead is a nighttime sky ablaze with stars.

Members of this camp were representatives of Wisconsin's first people, referred to as Paleo-Indians by archaeologists. These people were perhaps direct descendants of the first human beings to enter North America by way of the Bering Sea land bridge about 14,000 to 13,000 years ago.[2] Traveling southward from Alaska inside an ice-free corridor with the Pacific Ocean on one side and the towering edge of the Continental Glacier on the other,[3] they dispersed across the continent in a remarkably short amount of time, working their way south and east in perhaps only a thousand years.[4]

It is thought that Paleo-Indians arrived in what would become Wisconsin about 11,500 years ago, first inhabiting the southwestern coulee region, an area not touched by the most recent period of glaciation.[5] As the climate warmed and the ice sheet receded northward, exposing more and more of the landscape, Paleo-Indians expanded their range in the region.

These people were nomadic, traveling in highly mobile family bands that may have consisted of several pairs of adults and several children, perhaps numbering fifteen to twenty-five.[6] As subsistence hunters, they were on the move most of the time, going from one temporary camp to another, following the seasonal movements of big-game animals.[7]

By the time Paleo-Indians found the region of the western Great Lakes, it is likely that mastodons—probably much more common in the region than mammoths—still existed.[8] Dozens of mastodon sites have been discovered in Illinois and the Lower Peninsula of Michigan.[9] Although only one mastodon kill site has been documented in Wisconsin, the Boaz site in Richland County, it is likely that mastodons were wide ranging in the state after the glaciers receded.

The end of the Ice Age and the relatively swift retreat of the glaciers was a time of great climate change. In Wisconsin, the boreal forest—the habitat of thick spruce and fir—receded to the north along with the glaciers. Southern Wisconsin transitioned to oak forests and open grasslands, while the northern part of the state grew drier and transitioned into forests of hardwoods and pine.[10]

With mastodons dwindling in numbers and becoming nonexistent in much of the region—climate change, perhaps coupled with intense hunting pressure, pushed the mastodon out of the region and to eventual extinction 10,000 to 8,000 years ago[11]—Paleo-Indians by necessity would become dependent on other sources of food and animal products. Elk, bear, moose, woodland caribou, and white-tailed deer all could be found in the region.[12] Paleo-Indians had to adapt and change hunting methods and strategies to efficiently take these "smaller" game animals. The whitetail perhaps presented the greatest challenge, for it already possessed the survival capabilities gained through millions of years of escaping and eluding predators on the North American landscape.

It was white-tailed deer that were on the minds of the four Ice Age hunters as they sat around their campfire, discussing the deer they had seen during the day, the two they were able to kill and take back to camp, planning the next day's hunt. The predawn morning would find them staking out a trail through the woods leading to an open sandy spot on the river. It was a place where they had learned that a large deer often sought water just at daylight. If they were lucky, they would be able to ambush the deer and, as had happened near the mastodon skeleton, take it down with powerfully launched stone-tipped darts.

Like whitetail hunters on the eve of a hunting season today, the men carefully inspected their equipment. The oldest of the hunters held a piece of wood about two feet long. The piece had been carefully worked so that it was narrow and somewhat flattened at one end. At this flattened end there was a spur, a small knob. The other end was wrapped with strips of deer hide, a handle for gripping. He passed it to another hunter who admired it, turned it in his hands, ran a hand across the smooth board. He gripped the handle with his right hand and raised the piece of wood slightly above his shoulder. It felt right, just right, and the hunter returned the instrument to the older man, nodding in appreciation.

The men also examined several handcrafted spears—longer than an arrow at about five feet, and each tipped with a large, sharp-edged stone point. The opposite end was designed to fit perfectly onto the knob at the flattened end of the wooden piece.

This "spear thrower" was the weapon the hunter had used to kill the doe earlier in the day, the weapon that allowed the hunter to fire the spear, or dart, with deadly accuracy and high speed from a considerable distance, perhaps thirty to forty yards. The ancient weapon is known today as the atlatl (pronounced *AT-lat-tel*), named after the Aztec words for water and thrower.[13] The atlatl represented an advance in hunting technology that revolutionized Paleo-Indian hunting.[14]

The atlatl was deceptively simple, a piece of wood or bone, carved somewhat to enable the hunter to fit the dart onto a spur, or pin. To fire the dart, the hunter held the "loaded" atlatl above and behind his shoulder and then slung it forward, propelling the dart at distances greater than could be obtained simply by throwing it. For example, if the hunter could throw a spear fifty feet with his arm, the atlatl would allow him to launch it 300 feet.[15] The hunters had discovered a key to weapons technology: a way to harness the power of potential energy in a tool that could be both accurate and portable.

The word atlatl generally refers to just the wooden or bone launcher. However, the launcher was really only one part of a three-component system that represented the very height of Paleo-Indian technology. The other components included the wooden shaft of the spear and the stone point, the early "broadhead" associated with Paleo-Indian culture, which these hunters created and left scattered across the continent.

The heavy stone point resists the acceleration of the spear, causing the back of the spear to travel faster than the front. The spear shaft has been described as a

The Paleo-Indians' weapon of choice was the atlatl, which increased both the speed and power of the spears they threw, enabling them to take down mastodons as well as whitetails.

COURTESY OF CAHOKIA MOUNDS STATE HISTORIC SITE, PAINTING BY LLOYD K. TOWNSEND

long, loose spring that, when accelerated by the atlatl, compresses and stores energy. That energy is then used to push the shaft away from the atlatl, enabling the dart to launch smoothly and effectively.[16]

The importance of the stone spear or dart point for hunting cannot be understated. There were two types of stone points associated with Paleo-Indians: the Folsom and the Clovis, named for the locations where they were first discovered (Folsom and Clovis, New Mexico). A finely finished Clovis spearpoint was a beautiful thing. Typically about four to five inches long and perfectly symmetrical, its razor-sharp edges were the result of careful pressure flaking.[17] In creating a new point, the hunter would carefully hammer away the outer stone to make a "blank." Some blanks were used as knives or scrapers; others were chipped and shaped into points and then attached to a foreshaft, replacing a broken point.

Materials used for points were usually very high quality. There were certain quarry sites favored by the Paleo-Indian, including quarries at the lower Rock River in Illinois, the Thunder Bay area of Ontario, and the Silver Mound site in Jackson County, Wisconsin.[18]

One can imagine the Paleo-Indian hunter of 10,000 years ago. The elder passing a prized atlatl down to his son, an atlatl that had provided well for the band, that had helped feed them through long periods. And perhaps the son felt a certain sense of pride when he took his first deer using the atlatl given to him by his father, who had passed down his understanding of the weapon along with his knowledge of the whitetail and the tactics of the hunt. This complex interaction between human hunters—the weapon used, the prey sought, the necessity of passing hunting knowledge to the next generation—was the very emergence of a culture of hunting tradition that exists to this day.

As the sky began to brighten in the east, the hunters were again in pursuit of meat. Downwind of the small sandbar in the creek they crouched, motionless and obscured by underbrush, and waited. The sound of crunching leaves betrayed the

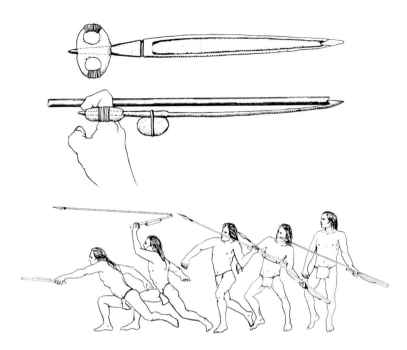

A depiction of how the atlatl was held (top) and thrown (bottom).
Courtesy of Royal BC Museum

deer's approach. As it tentatively stepped out of the forest cover toward the watering place, the hunters saw a large buck with a heavy set of antlers still fuzzy with velvet. After a few moments of analyzing the slight northwest breeze for any hint of danger and listening intently for the same, the buck stepped to the water and began to drink.

A second later came the sounds of sticks breaking and shuffling in the brush. In his excitement, the youngest of the hunters had stumbled. The other hunters immediately thrust their arms, firing darts from the atlatls at the already alarmed animal.

The buck, with the advantage of a second's warning, was in motion before the atlatls were fired. Every nerve of the deer's body knew there was danger in the brush, a predator no different from the saber-toothed cats or short-faced bears or any of the other Ice Age predators that had relentlessly stalked, harried, and attempted to ambush the deer's ancestors for millions of years. The deer had been hard wired for escape. With great splashing leaps, the animal was across the creek, then up the bank into thick underbrush, and then utterly and completely gone. Not one of the darts had hit their mark.

The hunters would regroup, make another plan, make another hunt. The hunt was critical to their survival.

As the Ice Age glaciers receded, Paleo-Indians adapted to their environment's changing conditions, their specialized hunting practices giving way to a more generalized hunting-gathering life.[19]

The Paleo-Indian most likely transitioned into new groups of Native Americans.[20] These new cultures—collectively known as Archaic culture, a period that began about 10,000 years ago and lasted up until about 3,000 years ago[21]—adapted to meet the challenges and opportunities of a post–Ice Age world.

Although they began looking to more diverse food sources, the Archaic people still relied heavily on hunting. Many of the technological changes they made centered on the need to take wild game. The atlatl became their principal weapon, as the hand-thrown spear was of little use for the smaller game available in postglacial Wisconsin. The large fluted Clovis and Folsom spear points of the Paleo-Indian were

Certain sites were preferred for the quality of the material available for spearpoints, such as that used in these Clovis points.
WHS MUSEUM 1984.6.8, 1984.6.7, 1984.23, 1968.234.124; PHOTO BY JOEL HEIMAN

replaced by a wide variety of somewhat smaller dart points. The smaller points, which allowed the darts to fly faster and farther, could more efficiently take down game such as the white-tailed deer.[22]

Another advance in the development of the spear point occurred between 6,000 and 4,000 years ago when the Archaic period Indians of the Western Lake Superior region discovered exposed veins of nearly pure copper. Great Lakes Archaic Indians were the first to experiment with metal fabrication technologies in North America, learning various techniques to cold and hot hammer copper into useful tools, from metal spear points to knives, harpoons, and fish hooks.[23] The copper spear points—essentially metal broadheads—would be used for white-tailed deer hunting.

As the centuries passed, Archaic Indians became less nomadic, instead forming larger, more stationary settlements—likely spending winters in rock shelters and summers in semipermanent camps along productive rivers and streams.[24] Rather than being dependent on just large game, they increasingly began to utilize the abundance of resources postglacial Wisconsin afforded: fish, clams, wild rice, and waterfowl from the lakes and rivers, acorns from the oak trees, nuts, berries, and other fruit from the forest, and small game such as squirrels, snowshoe hares, and ruffed grouse.

In the centuries that followed the Archaic period, the Native American hunter-gatherer society continued to diversify. Advancements in methods to process, preserve, and store food—baskets, pottery, and cooking utensils—allowed for more time to be devoted to tradition and ritual. The hunt for game, though not the life-encompassing task that it had been for the Paleo-Indian, remained a central focus of Native American society. Even though women, as the primary gatherers of other foods, were actually bringing in more food than the hunter, it was the male hunter who received the greatest respect and admiration.[25]

Deer hunting for these early Native American hunters was not sport or casual pursuit; it was a deadly serious activity. This was increasingly apparent as larger bands or tribes formed. It has been estimated that members of a band of about one hundred people would require a minimum of four pounds of meat per person each day to ward off starvation. To provide this amount of meat, the hunters of the band would have to kill an average of at least four deer a day.[26] Realizing that a successful hunt was never a sure thing, and that the survival of the band may depend on the hunter's success, a deep reverence for the animal hunted became an integral component of Native American world view. This often included the idea that the successful hunt required the cooperation of the animal hunted—a willingness on its part to give itself to the hunter.

According to the Mississippi Valley Archaeology Center, deer became the most important animal hunted in the Wisconsin region, a title it has kept to this day.[27] The whitetail was a very practical animal, well worth the difficulty and time investment required to obtain it. The deer was the perfect size for a single hunter to kill, butcher, and take back to camp, and it provided all for the Indian hunter. It was a source of meat, fat, and hides for clothing, bedding, and shelter; the bones and antlers could be fashioned into implements from knives to fish hooks.[28] As one of the most important wildlife species hunted, the whitetail took on an increasingly important cultural significance. But while hunting tradition and culture evolved through the centuries, hunting weapons technology made slower progress.

The less nomadic Archaic period Indians diversified their diet while still relying on deer as a food source.
WHI IMAGE ID 33814

✦ ✦ ✦ ✦ ✦

Since the last days of the Ice Age, the atlatl and its relatively heavy, stone-tipped dart was the hunter's chief weapon, supplemented by lances, spears, and stone knives. Through the centuries, atlatl technology was improved upon somewhat, making the atlatl more versatile and efficient. Archaic peoples used broadheads on their spears that were smaller than Clovis and Folsom points and could more easily penetrate the hide of the animals hunted. Another atlatl advancement was the development of weights, or bannerstones. The bannerstone would slide underneath the throwing board, likely adding more power to the system. As the dart itself resisted the weight of the heavy point and stored energy like a spring, the bannerstone may have served to supplement the weight of the stone point.[29] Some bannerstones may have been designed to silence the ziplike sound of the atlatl's swing or, as may have been the case with some intricately carved weights, to provide some level of spiritual power or good luck.[30]

The Native American deer hunter had perfected the atlatl, and certainly a point was reached where improvements, if any, would be insignificant. For thousands of years the atlatl had served the prehistoric hunter of the upper Great Lakes well. It had evolved into a versatile weapon that could take a goose in the marsh, a fish in the creek, and, above all, a whitetail in the forest. But it certainly had its limitations. It was inaccurate beyond thirty or forty yards, the long darts were cumbersome to transport, and it required a relatively wide, clear area to shoot. Although the system took advantage of some stored potential energy, the velocity of the dart was very much limited by the strength of the throwing arm of the hunter. Could there be a better tool for the hunter's arsenal, something more deadly than the spear, the stone knife, and the atlatl?

The great innovation was the bow and arrow, which found its way from the Old World to the region of the upper Great Lakes perhaps 1,500 years ago.[31] As the atlatl had been a revolutionary advancement over the simple hand-hurled spear, the bow and arrow was many more times an advancement over the atlatl.[32]

The bow and arrow differed from all previous weapons technology in that it could take the low-grade power of a hunter's arm, store and multiply it as potential energy in the bow itself, and allow a rapid release of the energy to send an arrow with great velocity and accuracy to distances not possible with the atlatl.[33] The bow and arrow rapidly replaced the atlatl as a deer hunting weapon, although in some parts of North and South America the atlatl continued to be used for hundreds of years after the bow arrived on the scene.

Despite the successes hunters had with the atlatl, the bow and arrow possessed great advantages over the older system. The obvious advantages suggest why it was developed.[34] To start, arrows were shorter and lighter than atlatl spears, and were tipped with much smaller stone points, making them easier to transport. The arrowheads were triangular points, stemmed or notched for attachment to the arrow. These small points required fewer raw materials and much less time to make compared to spear points. The entire system gave the hunter greatly increased mobility. With his bow in one hand and an animal skin quiver holding a dozen potentially deadly arrows, the hunter could range across the landscape for miles.

The bow and arrow opened up a new world of opportunity, giving the Indian more freedom while hunting. In pursuit of whitetails, the Indian developed new techniques for still hunting—for quietly, slowly stalking deer in the very places they fed, or bedded down, or yarded during the deep snow times. The bow and arrow was sleeker, less cumbersome than the atlatl and its long spear, and didn't require much space to shoot—just a clear lane wide enough to let the arrow zip through without obstruction. The bow and arrow was really the first stealth weapon.

The Indian deer hunter, constantly under the intense pressure to mount one successful hunt after another, always having to match his intellect, skill, and weaponry against an animal that had been designed by nature over the course of millions of years to thwart the hunt at every opportunity, took to the bow and arrow immediately and made it very nearly a part of his being. Nowhere in North America was this more apparent than in the Native American deer hunters of the region of the upper Great Lakes.

The Subsistence Hunters

I see in this fine village filled with young men, who are, I am sure, as courageous as they are well built; and who will, without doubt, not fear their enemies if they carry French weapons. It is for these young men that I leave my gun, which they must regard as the pledge of my esteem for their valor; they must use it if they are attacked. It will also be more satisfactory in hunting cattle and other animals than are all the arrows that you use.
—Nicolas Perrot, French trader and explorer[1]

For nearly two days the Indians had been watching and waiting. Waiting since a Huron Indian scout had materialized in the humid air of July 1634 on the shores of Green Bay and told the Ho-Chunk people encamped nearby news that would eventually change their world forever. The Huron explained that he was with a flotilla of birchbark canoes, an expedition from far to the east that was two days' travel away. The expedition consisted of seven Hurons and a Frenchman called Nicolet.

Samuel de Champlain, governor of New France, had sent Sieur Jean Nicolet on a journey from Quebec across the upper Great Lakes and down into Lake Michigan with the hope of negotiating a peace between the Ho-Chunk and the Odawa and Huron. Odawa and Huron were acting as middlemen for trade in the Green Bay area, which prevented the French from exploring and trading in the unexplored region west of Lake Michigan.[2]

The Ho-Chunk knew of the French, as European colonial interests had already had a profound impact on tribes from Michigan to the Eastern seaboard. But the Europeans were relatively late in reaching the Wisconsin region, and the Ho-Chunk had not yet seen a white man.[3] The Ho-Chunk dispatched several braves to accompany the Huron scout back to the expedition, to assist them. By the time Nicolet's canoe slid ashore (believed to be in present-day Door County) thousands of Indians were there to greet him.[4]

A French Jesuit priest and friend of Nicolet's, Father Barthelemy Vimont, later reported the event: "He wore a grand robe of China damask, all strewn with flowers and birds of many colors. No sooner did they perceive him than the women and children fled, at the sight of a man who carried thunder in both hands—for thus they called the two pistols that he held."

According to Father Vimont, each of the chiefs present ordered a feast to be prepared, and at one of these banquets "they served at least sixscore beaver."[5] It is likely that the feast included an abundance of fresh venison as well.

The Indian societies that the first European explorers encountered in what was to become Wisconsin had many aspects in common. By the 1600s Wisconsin Indians utilized the wealth of resources provided by the land. They gathered wild rice, nuts, and roots and made sugar from maple sap. They hunted and fished. They practiced agriculture to some degree, particularly the growing of the "three sisters"—corn, beans, and squash—as well as tobacco. They lived in semipermanent villages, in lodges made of bark, saplings, and rushes. Spring to fall they traveled mainly on foot or in birchbark canoes; in the winter, travel was via snowshoes. The lives of Wisconsin's Indians were, however, to be forever altered by a series of events that occurred to the east, several years after Nicolet's journey.

The Iroquois Confederacy battled the Huron. The defeat and subsequent scattering of the Huron finally opened up Wisconsin to the French.[6] By the late 1650s, considerable numbers of French traders and explorers, as well as refugee tribes escaping the violence in the east, were moving into the Wisconsin region.[7]

One of the tribes that migrated to Wisconsin during this time was the Ojibwe, who settled along the south shore of Lake Superior. When we think of the archetype of the Indian hunter—bow and arrow in hand, silently stalking the northern wilderness of pine and birch in pursuit of game such as the white-tailed deer—it is the image of the Ojibwe that most often comes to mind.

The environment in which the Ojibwe lived dictated their way of life. The northern environment of Canada, northern Wisconsin, and Minnesota was harsh. The land was rugged and rocky, the soil thin, and the winters were extreme with brutal temperatures and heavy snowfalls. The world they occupied was not unlike that which covered all of Wisconsin just a few thousand years before—a land of lakes and rivers, swamps, bogs, and forests of towering pine. The Ojibwe survived on the nuts, berries, and wild rice they could gather, the fish they could catch, the animals they could trap, the wild game they could kill.

The Ojibwe also understood that deer were the great provider. The whitetail provided not just food but also materials for clothing, tools, and building. Deer did not migrate out of the area each year, as did the migratory waterfowl. They did not den up and sleep the winter away under a blanket of snow like the bear. Smaller than elk or moose, a deer could be hunted and killed by one man; it could be easily transported, easily processed, and it provided a wealth of materials, from venison steaks to feed the band to bone antlers for tools and tanned hides for clothing.

Because the Ojibwe lived in the far north, with more limited resources than in other regions, a large territory of land was required to provide for their needs. By necessity, the Ojibwe were nomadic, having to move frequently as the seasons and food supply dictated.

Robert Bieder, professor of American history at Indiana University, wrote in *Native American Communities in Wisconsin*, "Despite summer fishing and hunting, there was seldom enough food to last through the year, and so the autumn, winter, and spring were given over to hunting large game. A severe winter that depleted the animal populations or reduced its nutrient value sometimes resulted in starvation of whole family units."[8] As much food as possible was processed and stored for the coming winter, but the Ojibwe knew that would not be enough. Once ricing season waned, thoughts turned to autumn big-game hunting and the progression toward the winter camp.

The breakup of the tribe and the movement of small bands to winter camps were accomplished in unhurried stages during autumn and early winter. Transporting supplies could require several trips to a temporary camp, and often several temporary camps—from which the bands might spend several days hunting—were established until the final winter camp was reached.[9] During these autumn hunts, small groups of hunters traveled together, each group heading to a different area.[10] According to Carol Mason in *Introduction to Wisconsin Indians*, hunting success was more often related to how well the groups could disperse across the hunting range than the success of individual hunters.[11]

In December, or the "Little Spirits Moon," the Ojibwe would finally make their winter camp—an area specifically sought, for they had hunted it for a number of years and knew the territory well.[12] The leader would assign hunting territories to the able-bodied men. While the women of the camp spent most of the daylight hours scavenging for firewood, the men hunted.[13] When storms and cold prevented the hunters from pursuing deer and other game, they would stay in camp, mending their weapons and snowshoes. In winter camp, the hunters didn't travel far so they could return each night.[14]

The first documented mention of Ojibwe winter pursuit of deer in Wisconsin appears to have been by the French explorer Radisson, who was in northwestern Wisconsin the winter of 1661–62. He wrote: "The weather continued so three dayes that we needed no racketts [snowshoes] more, for the snow hardened much. The small staggs are [as] if they were stakes in it after they would make 7 or 8 capers. It's an easy matter for us to take them and cutt their throats with our knives."[15]

By February, sometimes called the "Hunger Moon," food supplies would have been dwindling. The hunting was getting harder by the week. With fewer signs of big game, the hunters traveled farther afield on their snowshoes, searching for the tell-tale tracks of a whitetail or perhaps a deer yard that might hold several deer.

As trees cracked and popped on those coldest of winter nights, the hunters, secure inside their shelters, "worked on animal traps and tools, made drums and rattles, flaked arrowheads for hunting, and shaped new bows."[16] They told hunting stories of the past and planned strategies for the next day's hunt, as had countless generations of hunters before them. Perhaps, most importantly, the hunters paid quiet homage to the spirit world.

"The Chippewa [Ojibwe] world was filled with a host of spirits which controlled the weather, affected the health of the hunter, and above all, allowed the hunter to kill game," wrote Dr. Edmund Danziger, professor of history at Bowling Green State University in Ohio, in *The Chippewas of Lake Superior*.[17] Ojibwe hunters performed various practices connected with hunting. When game was scarce and hunting success elusive, Ojibwe medicine men would create potions to attract game. These preparations were used by unsuccessful hunters who believed themselves bewitched.[18] According to Sister M. Carolissa Levi in *Chippewa Indians of Yesterday and Today*, game that was killed while the hunter was using "medicine" was subject to many taboos. For example, a woman was not allowed to eat the head, liver, and kidneys of this game. Also, the meat was not to be given away, as this would destroy the efficacy of the charm.[19]

There were other, more subtle rituals as well. A hunter never sharpened his knife just before hunting, as the Ojibwe felt this would show overconfidence and doom the hunt. If a hunter left for the field and found that he had forgotten something necessary for hunting, he returned and called off the hunt: turning back signified failure, which meant the hunt for that day was also doomed to failure.[20] The presence of a hooting owl held a dark significance for the hunters; encountering an owl while hunting was considered a bad omen.[21]

Prior to the hunt, great thought was also given to what the hunters were about to do. Sister M. Inez Hilger recorded interviews from Ojibwe people in Wisconsin and Minnesota in the 1930s, such as this story about a boy's first hunt: "The first time that I went hunting my father called me: 'Witigoc, you are ready to go hunting (I was told this a few days before we left home). Don't say anything disrespectful about the deer. Don't boast, saying, I am going to kill a deer, or I am going to shoot two deer. Don't talk that way. God made the deer so he can hear you say that. Simply be quiet and don't talk; and then you will get deer.'"[22]

Good-luck charms were also an important component for a successful hunt. According to Sister Hilger, "The charm most effective in hunting on the LCO [Lac Courte Oreilles] reservation was the foetal inclusion found between the skin and the visceral lining of an animal—those for rabbit and deer predominating."[23]

Prayer to a Deer Slain by a Hunter

I had need.
I have dispossessed you of beauty, grace, and life.
I have sundered your spirit from its worldly frame.
No more will you run in freedom
Because of my need.
I had need.
You have in life served your kind in goodness.
By your life, I will serve my brothers.
Without you I hunger and grow weak.
Without you I am helpless, nothing.
I had need.
Give me your flesh for strength.
Give me you casement for protection.
Give me your bones for my labors,
and I shall not want.

—Ojibwe prayer[1]

NOTE
1. Basil Johnston, *Ojibway Heritage* (Lincoln and London:
   University of Nebraska Press, 1990), 57–58.

The enormous importance of white-tailed deer to the winter survival of Ojibwe bands in the Wisconsin region eventually led to conflict between the Ojibwe and the Dakota Sioux, one of the tribes present in Wisconsin prior to the arrival of the French. The Sioux had occupied northwestern Wisconsin, and, like the Ojibwe, also depended heavily on a winter deer supply.

As the Ojibwe became established in northern Wisconsin, they were eventually drawn farther to the west and south from the shores of Lake Superior, continually looking for productive territory to support their hunting during the long winters. The transition zone between the north country and the mixed forest of central Wisconsin supported more deer, which attracted the Ojibwe hunting parties. The Sioux also relied on this area for winter deer meat.

This no-man's-land of deer habitat was known as the "debatable zone" and neither the Ojibwe nor Sioux could hunt the area freely as both groups were formidable warriors as well as hunters. Any hunter seeking deer in the debatable zone had to be keenly aware of the possibility of deadly enemies in the woods. Mason believed that since no one group could freely hunt the debatable zone, overhunting of the deer population was avoided.[24]

The Ojibwe proved the greater warriors: by the mid-1700s, they had forced the Sioux out of a region as far south as the mouth of the Chippewa River. Ojibwe success in battle eventually pushed the Sioux completely out of Wisconsin and west of the Mississippi.[25]

Wisconsin tribes that occupied areas south of the northern forest did not rely on big-game hunting to the extent of the Ojibwe and the Sioux. Climates in central and southern Wisconsin were more favorable for agriculture, and many tribes in this region were able to cultivate, harvest, and store large amounts of agricultural products.

While the Ho-Chunk of the Lake Winnebago area relied on a wide variety of wild and cultivated food supplies, the white-tailed deer was still extremely important to them. The Ho-Chunk home range—described as "rolling open prairies crossed by rivers and dotted with lakes and stands of hardwood timber"[26]—was good deer country. Seventy percent of all animal remains found in an excavated refuse pit from the Crabapple Point Ho-Chunk village site on Lake Koshkonong were from white-tailed deer.[27]

Unlike the Ojibwe, the Ho-Chunk did not migrate to winter hunting camps. Their villages, with solid lodges, were fairly permanent.[28] As winter approached, the Ho-Chunk left in large hunting parties to search for deer and bear. "Deer were often driven past concealed hunters or were caught in traps," wrote Bieder.[29]

Cold temperatures and snow in December, which the Ho-Chunk referred to as the "When Deer Shed Their Horns Moon," were signals for hunting parties to return to their villages. Inside their warm bark lodges, "tales of summer hunts and war adventures were told over the fires."[30]

The Native Americans who inhabited Wisconsin from the time of first contact with the French to the region's era of European settlement used a variety of methods to hunt and take whitetail, which were adapted to meet the specific environment of the tribe: the terrain, the climate, the quality of the habitat. After contact with European culture, deer hunting methods became a mix of the ancient and the new.

A. W. Schorger, a wildlife professor at the University of Wisconsin in the 1950s and 1960s who documented the early history of many wildlife species in Wisconsin, wrote:

Prior to the introduction of firearms, the Indians had four methods of hunting deer. These are described by George Copway, an educated Ojibway [*sic*], who spent considerable time in Wisconsin:

1. Snaring. The deer was snared by placing a rope noose made of wild hemp along the runways. When caught the deer choked to death.
2. Stake Trap. Sharp stakes were driven into the ground beside a log over which a deer was expected to jump. When successful the stake pierced the deer's vitals.
3. Water Drive. Deer were run into the water by the dogs and then could be easily taken; or they were exhausted by a chase in deep snow.
4. They were killed with bow and arrow at salt-licks or at the borders of lakes and streams where they were accustomed to feed. An Indian could shoot a deer at a distance of 50 paces. Flambeaus made of birch bark or other combustible materials were used for night hunting. In this way a very close approach to the animal could be made. Candles were subsequently used in place of torches.[31]

The torch hunt described by Copway was a common hunting method of the Ojibwe and was widely documented. J. G. Kohl, a German scientist and historian, traveled North America in the 1850s and spent a considerable amount of time with the Ojibwe. He recorded one of the earlier accounts of the method:

There is one peculiarity among these Indians, however, that they also entrap deer by fire, and shoot them from their canoe at night. This curious mode of hunting, which I heard of both among the Ojibbeways [*sic*] and the Sioux, is only customary in the mosquito country, for I never heard of it elsewhere, and besides, mosquitos are an important factor in rendering it possible. The deer and stags are driven into the lakes and rivers by these little tormenting insects. They will stand at night for hours in the shallow water refreshing themselves, or will walk some distance up the stream. The Indian hunters drift down the stream towards them; and, in his canoe, an Indian will make less noise than in his soft moccasins on the snow. In the bows burns a light, or torch, which they make very neatly of birch-bark. The strips employed for such torches are bound together with a quantity of rings. The flame burns down from one ring to the next, and bursts them one after the other, while the lower ones still keep the torch together. These torches are fixed in a cresset provided with a board behind, like a dark lantern. The light throws its beam forward, while the hunter cowers in the shadow of the board. The gently approaching boat does not, strange to say, startle the animals in the least: they stand, on the contrary, quite quiet, and stare at it. When the hunter has so managed that the animals cannot scent him, he can come close up to them and kill them at ease, as the light shines on them. The animals are so little startled by the light, that they will, on the contrary, rush towards it; and cases have been known in which they wounded the hunter with their antlers. There is no sort of hunting in which a man can approach game with equal security, and nearly all the Indians of North America seem to be acquainted with this novel mode of hunting.[32]

Setting fire to the prairies of southern Wisconsin was one method used by Native Americans to take deer.
COURTESY OF THE INDIANA STATE HISTORICAL SOCIETY

Native Americans living in more open country, such as the prairie and oak savanna country of central and southern Wisconsin, employed a more dramatic use of fire to hunt deer. "An old and often described method of deer hunting in southern Wisconsin was to fire the prairies and oak openings," noted Schorger. "Reliance was generally placed on driving the deer into lakes or stream valleys where the hunters were stationed."

The method was still being used in the early nineteenth century when an early resident of Beloit, P. P. Crane, described the procedure in that area: "Also in the fall of 1837, when the prairie grass had become old and dry, smokes were seen rising on the prairies, some days in one direction, others in a different direction. It was ascertained that these fires were started by Indians for hunting purposes. Whenever they wanted to take a deer, a rifle party would go forward, leaving others behind . . . and as the flames approached, the deer would bound along to get away from the fire, and then rush toward the riflemen and be shot down."[33]

A tactic that seems to have been used by both the northern Ojibwe and southern tribes was a "fence drive." By today's standards this method seems impossibly labor intensive. However, the rewards of being able to take several deer during a fence drive more than compensated for the labor involved. This method as used by Wisconsin Menominee was described in *The Story of American Hunting and Firearms*:

The Menominee prepared for the hunt by felling many trees to form a V, which ran for several miles through the woods. The trees were dropped so that their trunks remained attached to the stumps but lay close to the ground, all extending in the same direction. When the drive began, a band of hunters concealed themselves at the apex of the V. Other hunters—and sometimes their women and children—gathered at the wide end of the V, and walking slowly and noisily forward, moved towards the bottleneck. The deer fled before them, but the drive had to be well paced. If the hunters moved too fast, the deer became panicky and leaped over the fallen logs and out of the V. But where the hunters proceeded cautiously, the deer followed the line of least resistance inside the barricade and finally found themselves trapped.[34]

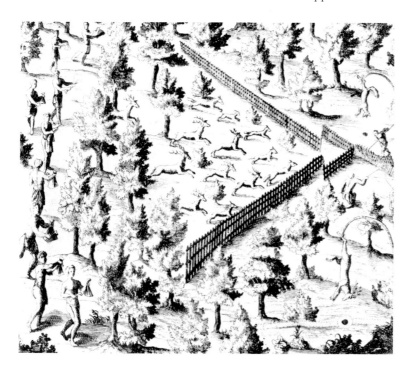

Illustration of the effectiveness of fence drives, another deer hunting method used by Native Americans, from a book by French explorer Samuel de Champlain.
WHi Image ID 58811

According to McCabe and McCabe in *White-Tailed Deer Ecology and Management*, as late as the 1880s, Indians in northern Wisconsin drove deer along fences twelve and fifteen miles in length built of felled trees. The fences were constructed in such a way that the animals could not break out of the narrowing funnels. Fence Lake in Vilas and Marquette counties may have been named for this hunting technique.[35]

In 1944 Victor Barnow in *Wisconsin Chippewa Myths and Tales* recorded the experience Tom Badger, an elderly Ojibwe, had with this type of hunting:

We used to travel a lot because my father had to keep on the move, looking for game.

We picked berries every day. . . . Then we stopped picking berries and made a deer fence. I helped by clearing the leaves away, so that my father wouldn't make a noise on the leaves when he walked along. We made the fence by felling trees, lining them in a row. After the fence was laid, we cleared a patchway for my father. We made the fence about five miles long. The deer couldn't get across it. My father walked along the other side of the fence, along the cleared pathway.

The fence at Clear Lake went for five miles down to the lake. My mother was waiting on the other side of the lake, and my father stayed on his side of the fence. When the deer came to the fence, they would follow it down to the lake and then start to swim across. I sat with my brother and sisters next to my mother. We'd warn her when we saw deer coming. Then she'd get in her canoe and paddle up to the deer and spear it with an iron tipped spear. . . . We didn't go with her in the canoe because it might tip over. After she speared the deer, she'd drag it to shore and skin it.[36]

The use of water was a component of other variations of the drive. "It was common to organize a deer drive that pushed whitetails to a promontory extending into a river or lake, and when the game plunged into the water it was pursued by waiting canoemen," according to Charles F. Waterman in *Hunting in America*. "A deer swims swiftly, and drawing abreast of it with a single canoe is not simple, for the animal will alter its course so quickly that only an adroit paddleman can follow."[37]

Another hunting method was to drive deer into lakes and rivers, as seen in this 1836 painting of Sioux pursuing a whitetail from their canoes.
SMITHSONIAN AMERICAN ART MUSEUM, GIFT OF MRS. JOSEPH HARRISON JR.

Schorger wrote of deer hunting on Lake Winnebago, as recounted by J. G. Thompson, who arrived in Neenah in 1846: "When a deer was driven into the lake by wolves, the Indians would pursue in a canoe. A loop, bent on the end of a hickory pole, was slipped over the deer's head and the canoe drawn sufficiently close that the animal could be dispatched with a tomahawk."[38]

The time-honored method of still hunting, or stalking a deer, was likely used by all the tribes in Wisconsin. In fact, *Waupaca* is a Ho-Chunk word for "stalking place"—where one went to hunt deer.[39] Stalking is most associated, however, with the northern tribes, where the terrain and the social structure were not favorable to large communal hunts. "Particularly in the north, where deep snows and cold temperatures were obstacles to drive hunts," wrote McCabe and McCabe, "snaring and stalking, and using snowshoes to 'run down' deer were favored techniques. Under these conditions, even with whitetails congregated in deer yards, hunting was energy expensive work."[40]

A 1929 government bulletin described the technique used by the Ojibwe to still hunt deer: "According to the Chippewa [Ojibwe] . . . it is the habit of a deer to jump, then trot, and then walk in a circle when it is trying to evade a hunter, but a deer never crosses its own path when it has completed the circle. Knowing this, a Chippewa hunter circles outside the circle traveled by the deer, then closes in, and frequently finds the deer tired out and lying down near the place where it began the circle."[41]

"Before they possessed horses, speed of foot must have been even more highly prized," wrote Kohl. "As they were compelled to hunt all their game on foot, what is called 'running down the game' was quite ordinary. . . . They frequently do so, for instance, with the elk, especially in winter, when the animal has difficulty in getting over the snow, and breaks through, while the Indian easily glides over it with his snow-shoes."[42]

According to McCabe and McCabe, John Muir related that in the mid-1880s in central Wisconsin, Indians literally ran deer down. "In winter, after the first snow, we frequently saw 3–4 Indians hunting deer in company, running like hounds on the fresh, exciting tracks. The escape of the deer from these noiseless, tireless hunters was said to be well-nigh impossible; they were followed to the death."[43]

Like hunters of today, the Indians of the past had accessories to assist the hunt. Every Indian camp kept a supply of dogs, the only domesticated animal the Indians of Wisconsin possessed, many of which were used to help them with the hunt.[44] They also used a variety of calls and lures to attract deer. Potawatomi hunters were known to "rattle up" deer by clashing two antlers together to simulate the noise of sparring bucks, a sound that attracted rutting bucks. Ojibwe would cut down cedar trees in the winter and come back at night to shoot the deer that were feeding on the cedar slashings.[45]

Early Wisconsin Indians used many tactics and techniques to hunt white-tailed deer. Some of these methods are known and used by modern hunters. However, the factors that kept the Indian hunter out on the trail of the whitetail were much different from what motivates today's deer hunter.

"Adventure and excitement were much less motivating factors in Indian hunts than was the pragmatic need for food," wrote McCabe and McCabe.[46] Hunting was a career; it was work, plain and simple. In fact, in many Indian dialects the words for "hunt" and "hunting" are synonymous with "work" and "working."[47]

Prior to the arrival of Europeans, Wisconsin's Native Americans generally did not expend effort to hunt beyond what was practical, as there really was no reason for them to kill more deer than were needed for immediate use or could be processed into jerky or pemmican (a combination of meat, fat, and dried berries) and stored. According to McCabe and McCabe, stockpiling hides for the sake of material possession was rare.[48] But after European culture and weapons began infiltrating these Indian cultures, deer hunting was no longer tied just to the need to survive harsh northern winters. For some, an interest in trading hides to European fur traders increasingly became part of the equation.[49] And while guns may have made the Native American hunter more efficient, Mason notes that "hunting also became more wasteful as once useful things were no longer kept."[50]

The well-balanced relationship between Indian hunters and the white-tailed deer they had once depended on for survival had been permanently disrupted by

The European influence on the Native American hunter is embodied in the new weapons that became available.
WHi Image ID 2103

the encroachment of European and American values and culture. As Indian society was relegated to smaller and smaller chunks of territory in the early 1800s, a new hunter came onto the Wisconsin landscape.

The Market Hunters

Civilized man, with the arteries of commerce and the development of more luxuriant taste, could easily dispose of his surplus for cash with which to buy the luxuries he craved, and his weapons made it easy for him to obtain a much greater supply of game and furs than he himself could use. Hence the slaughter began.
—Junius Henderson and Elberta Louise Craig, "Economic Mammalogy"[1]

The fur trade turned the whitetail—the animal that had provided for the Indians through countless winters, the animal that Ojibwe hunters were careful never to offend for fear of reprisal and a failed hunt—into just another commodity, with the Indians helping to supply the white merchant's trade.[2] The slaughter of deer that took place in the wilderness of Wisconsin was fueled by the European public's demand for products made from deerskin. In between the Indian hunter and the European consumer was a four-thousand-mile-long network of traders, shippers, craftsmen, and merchants. Deer hides from whitetails killed in the virgin forests, the oak savannas, and the unbroken prairies of Wisconsin ended up as gloves and shoes in storefronts in London and Paris.

As French dominance of the western Great Lakes region gave way to the British in the 1700s, the trade in deer hides intensified, with England becoming the almost exclusive destination of American deer hides. After the Revolutionary War, however, foreign markets became largely inaccessible and, by 1800, deerskin had lost prominence in the hide trade.[3] While deer were still being sporadically killed for the market, the market was just not there. Deer populations had declined to the extent that commercial hunting was no longer profitable, although the U.S. government still bought most of the available hides for domestic use.[4]

Whereas the Indians' traditional subsistence hunting of whitetails had little impact on deer numbers, the relentless pursuit of whitetails for the hide trade took its toll on deer populations. It has been estimated that as a result of Indian-

European deerskin trade activities, deer populations nationwide were reduced by as much as half of what they had been before European contact.[5]

The Indians also suffered as a result of their intense exploitation of deer and other wildlife for the market, with their complex deer hunting culture but a shadow of what it had been prior to European contact.[6] John James Audubon described the effects: "For as the Deer, the Caribou, and all other game is killed for the dollar which its skin brings in, the Indian must search in vain over the deserted country for that on which he is accustomed to feed, till, worn out by sorrow, despair, and want, he either goes far from his early haunts to others, which in time will be similarly invaded, or he lies on the rocky seashore and dies."[7]

With the Northwest Territory under firm American control and open for settlement, thousands of farmers, miners, and loggers began to migrate to the region. In the early 1800s, the Indians of the Northwest Territory, of which the Wisconsin region was a part, still roamed freely across the land; in the eyes of white settlers, though, they were a hindrance to growth and development. Under the stern relocation policies of President Andrew Jackson, including the Indian Removal Act of 1830, Wisconsin Indians were facing forced exile out of the territory to places west of the Mississippi, or onto northern Wisconsin reservations. In a last, futile effort to reclaim their Illinois homeland, a band of about 1,200 Sauk (now called Sac), Fox, and Kickapoo, led by Black Hawk (Mucatamish-Kakaekg), attempted to retake their village, defying orders from the U.S. government to leave. From June through August 1832, Black Hawk's band was pursued by U.S. Army troops. In August, Black Hawk surrendered and many of the remaining Sac and Fox in Wisconsin were massacred.[8] The Black Hawk War effectively put an end to violent conflict between white settlers and Wisconsin Indians.

In *A Century of Wisconsin Deer*, Otis Bersing wrote:

> The Blackhawk War of 1832 marked a turning point in land-use which concerned deer in several ways. One of the most important results of the war was the removal of large numbers of Indians to reservations west of the Mississippi River and in northern Wisconsin. Their absence gave deer an opportunity to increase for awhile in southern Wisconsin. At this time the civilian population of the state was less than 5,000. Regular settlement of the southern part of the state began after the Blackhawk War—prairies were fenced and plowed.[9]

While the removal of Indians from southern Wisconsin effectively eliminated subsistence or commercial hunting by Indians, it also gave a green light to once wary settlers to put vast areas of virgin prairie to the plow. The farms that began

Alterations to the southern Wisconsin landscape by pioneer farm families created a mixed "edge" habitat favored by deer.
WHi Image ID 26720

to dot the southern Wisconsin landscape created a patchwork of pasture, cropland, and woods.[10]

Many of these changes benefited the whitetail. As a creature of "edge" habitat, the opening up of forests, as well as the fragmenting of great expanses of prairie by settlers for agricultural production, provided whitetails with improved habitat. The rolling landscape of southern Wisconsin, looking much different from only fifty years before, again began to support sizable deer populations in the early decades of the nineteenth century. Deer had a reprieve of sorts, and populations began to recover from the devastation of the hide trade era.

In *Wildlife in Early Wisconsin*, A. W. Schorger wrote:

In spite of Indians and mining developments, deer were abundant in southwestern Wisconsin in the 1830s. Hoffman found large herds on the prairies in February 1834. Smith wrote of the summer of 1837: "The deer are often seen sporting over the prairie, and in the groves and oak openings; they frequently aroused out of the high grass, and as the rifle of the hunter has not yet sufficiently alarmed them in their secret lairs, they are in a measure less wild than in parts more densely settled: I have often seen them in my rambles, quietly gazing at the traveller, until he passed by."[11]

Unfortunately this positive rebound of the whitetail population in Wisconsin did not last for more than a few decades. The 1800s were a time of incredible change in the region. By the time Wisconsin became a state in 1848, hundreds of settlements and villages, as well as cities such as Milwaukee and Madison, had been established across the state. A territorial population of just thirty-one thousand in 1840 had exploded to more than ten times that number just ten years later. The entire upper Midwest region was booming, with the city of Chicago having completed the construction of its first railroad and the important Illinois and

Michigan Canal that linked Chicago with the Illinois River and thus the Gulf of Mexico.

The initial resurgence of more intense deer hunting pressure came from these early pioneers. Many of the earliest of pioneer farmers were giving up on worn-out farms of New England, lured west by the promise of the fertile prairies of southern Wisconsin. The rebound of southern Wisconsin deer numbers in the early 1800s was timed nicely for their arrival.

While these pioneers may have come with some livestock in tow, they were far from self-sufficient. With little capital until the farms became established and productive, the settlers relied on what nature could provide, and, as with all of the cultures that preceded them, the pioneer farmer found that the white-tailed deer was the great provider: deer hunting put meat on the table and buckskin clothing on their children.

The pioneer hunter took deer and other wildlife without any regulations to impede his kill. He also was not much concerned with any notions about overhunting, as E. B. Swanson noted in his review of the use and conservation of Minnesota game from 1850 to 1900: "The profligate attitude of white settlers . . . was based upon the assumption that game must all disappear eventually, hence no thought of the future need spoil their pleasure of the day."[12]

Although the pioneer farmer supplemented his larder by taking deer at any time in any season, deer populations may have held their own if simple subsistence hunting was the rule. However, two major themes came together during this early period of Wisconsin history that changed the face of deer hunting in Wisconsin: settlement and commerce. As pioneer farmers put the virgin Wisconsin prairies under the plow, trade networks and commerce grew as fast as the settlers' wheat. Wagon roads began to link small communities with larger towns, and those with the growing cities.

In a sort of parallel to the Indians' transition from relying on deer solely for subsistence toward more of an emphasis on commercial use in the 1600s, Wisconsin settlers in the 1800s would experience a similar transformation. However, the commercial, or "market," hunting of the 1800s was destined to dwarf the early Indian commercial trade in both intensity of the kill and value of the products sold.[13]

Nineteenth-century market hunting began on a small scale and was primarily a hide trade. As early as 1810, whitetail hides were purchased by hide buyers in St. Louis, Prairie du Chien, Milwaukee, and Chicago.[14] Rather than being sent overseas, hides were shipped to eastern U.S. manufacturing centers, such as Philadelphia, to be tanned and sold for use in leather products.[15] The processing of deer hides for leather developed into a significant part of the U.S. economy in the early nineteenth century: by 1815, hide tanning was estimated to be a $12 million to $20 million industry.[16] Deer hides provided a much-needed source of domestic leather

An H. H. Bennett photo of a Ho-Chunk woman tanning a buckskin.
WHi Image ID 7358

Lac du Flambeau Indians tanning deer hides.
WHi Image ID 43220

prior to the large-scale cattle industry that developed later in the century after the West had been explored and settled.

"Deerskins were used for leatherstockings, hats, caps, gloves, breeches, aprons, waistcoats, doublets, entire suits, coats, belts, shoe uppers, and boot linings," McCabe and McCabe wrote. "Deerskin also was used in window panes in lieu of glass, as rugs, wall covers, snowshoe netting, upholstery fabric, bellows, harnessing, saddles, handbags, book binding, and for most leather products requiring a soft durable hide."[17]

As the Indians had relied on whitetail bone and antler as material for a myriad of tools, the early-nineteenth-century American also found many uses for various deer parts. Items such as knife handles, umbrella stands, coat racks, buttons, and even forks were made from deer antlers; deer hair often became the stuffing of a pillow or chair.[18]

However, by mid-century the commerce in whitetail products began to take on an added dimension. Advances in railroad transportation allowed venison—once a by-product of the hide trade and only used or sold locally (if at all)—to be shipped to markets far from the original hunt location. It was commerce in venison that really fueled the incredible era of whitetail exploitation seen after 1850. As railroads began to connect the far-flung Wisconsin settlements with larger urban markets, whitetail market hunting expanded with each new rail line. According to Schorger:

The local consumption of deer was comparatively small until the construction of railroads provided easy transportation to the large cities. . . . Scarcely a newspaper failed to comment on the scarcity or abundance of deer and the price of venison. In December, 1850, a load of 22 deer was brought to Milwaukee and the lot purchased by the Plankinton Hotel. A quarter of a century later, the following comment was made in Milwaukee: "Venison is so plenty in this market that the pedestrians wish there was some public park for deer instead of having them occupy the sidewalks."[19]

Whitetails hunted for the market in the late 1800s easily found their way to upscale restaurants from St. Paul to Boston. In 1876, venison was a breakfast item at the Palmer House in Chicago.

COURTESY OF CHICAGO HISTORY MUSEUM

PALMER HOUSE.

BREAKFAST.

Friday *January 7th 1876*

Stewed Oysters.   Fried Oysters.

Black Tea.   Coffee.   English Breakfast Tea.   Chocolate.   Green Tea.

BROILED.

Beef Steak.	Mutton Chops.	Pickled Tripe.	Ham.
Calf's Liver.	Breakfast Bacon.	Beefsteak, with Onions.	Veal Cutlets
Pigs' Feet.	Pork Chops.	English Mutton Chops.	Spare-ribs of Pork.
	Tenderloin of Pork.	Venison Steak.	

FRIED.

Corned Beef, Hashed.   Apples, with Salt Pork.   Calf's Liver, with Salt Pork.   Mush.
Mutton Chops, Breaded.   Pigs' Feet.   Veal Cutlets, Breaded.   Grits.
Sausage Balls.   Sausage.

FISH.

Broiled Whitefish.   Codfish Balls.   Fried Lake Trout.
Codfish in Cream.   Smoked Haddock.   Broiled Salt Mackerel.

STEWED.

Kidneys   Chicken.   Tripe.
Smoked Beef, in Cream.

COLD.

Roast Beef.   Ham.   Smoked Beef Tongue.
Mutton.   Spiced Salmon.   Pickled Lamb Tongues.

EGGS.

Fried.   Poached.   Scrambled.   Boiled.
OMELETS—Plain, with Rum, Parsley, Ham and Cheese.

POTATOES.

Baked.   Fried.   Stewed.   Minced.   Lyonaise.

BREAD, &c.

French Rolls.   Corn Bread.   Muffins.   Plain Bread.
Corn Cakes.   Dry Toast.   Butter Toast.   Milk Toast.
Cracked Wheat.   Graham Rolls.   Boston Brown Bread.   Oatmeal Porridge.
Graham Bread.   Maple and Loaf Sugar Syrup.   Wheat Cakes.
Buckwheat Cakes.

Breakfast Wines.

	PTS.	QTS.		PTS.	QTS.
Sauterne	$ 75	$1.00	Medoc, (Claret)	$ 75	$1 00
Haut Sauterne	1 25	2 00	St. Julien, "	1 25	2 00
Chablis, (White)	2 00	3 50			

HOURS FOR MEALS:

Breakfast from 6:30 to 11:00 o'clock.	SUNDAY—Breakfast at 8 o'clock.	
Dinner " 1:00 to 3:00, and 5:00 to 6:30.	" Dinner from 1:30 to 3:30, and 5:00 to 6:30.	
Tea " 6:00 to 8:00.	" Tea " 6:00 to 8:00.	
Supper " 8:00 to 11:30.	" Supper " 8:00 to 11:30.	

FOR CHILDREN AND NURSES.

BREAKFAST, 6:30 o'clock.   DINNER, 1 o'clock.   SUPPER, 6 o'clock.

THIS HOUSE IS ENTIRELY FIRE-PROOF.

✦ ✦ ✦ ✦ ✦

Even before the Civil War, the combination of subsistence hunting by settlers and hunting by a growing rank of market hunters had caused a significant reduction in deer numbers in the oak forests and prairies in the extreme southern part of the state.[20] By the start of the war, subsistence and market hunting had expanded into some central and northern counties.

The close of the war in 1865 sent thousands of young and weary veterans back to the farms and villages of Wisconsin with little more than the clothes on their backs and perhaps a rifle in their hand. Also a new tide of settlers poured into the state, intent on homesteading a productive piece of land.[21] Men looking for a way to make a living in postwar America, or at least a little extra cash, turned to the whitetail and the rising demand for venison.

Shortly after the Civil War, an advance in railway transportation greatly promoted the shipment of venison: in 1867, refrigerated rail cars began to be used on trains running between Chicago and New York City.[22] The new cars could keep meat, including venison, fresh for up to ten days in warm weather, enabling venison to be shipped from Wisconsin and Minnesota to the New York and Boston markets.

The venison would likely end up in a butcher shop or as a main item on the menus of the finer hotels and restaurants. Market hunting was definitely not limited to deer, though: the menus would also offer wild trout, quail, and an assortment of waterfowl. A Philadelphia man commented on the wild game available in St. Paul in 1870: "You can eat grouse three times a day if you please, and the finest flavored of trout and venison are a drug on the market."[23]

The seemingly insatiable demand for wild game in the marketplace led market hunters to take advantage of deer populations that had increased in the north earlier in the century. Market hunters relentlessly pursued deer during the second half of the century, and enormous quantities of venison and hides found their way to market annually. The principal venison markets from 1870 to 1900 were Chicago, St. Paul, Boston, Omaha, New York, and Philadelphia.[24] Bersing wrote: "In 1885 . . . it was estimated that 10,000 deer were shipped out of the state. A large number were shipped to Chicago and labeled as 'mutton.' A newspaper tells of the oldest and most experienced hunter in the vicinity of Eau Claire killing 3 tons of venison in 1886."[25]

The figures were staggering, as noted by Schorger:

It was stated in January, 1866, that 3,000 deer had been brought into Eau Claire over a period of three months. Many of these were hauled to Sparta to be shipped by rail to Milwaukee. The deer season of 1879 at the village of Colby was considered only fair, but there were shipped from that station fifty whole deer weighing 6,334 pounds, and 1,860 pounds of saddles, making a total of 8,194 pounds. There were shipped from Peshtigo during the season of 1882, 1,047 saddles of venison. The total weight of saddles, hams, and carcasses shipped was 67,726 pounds. The aggregate annual shipments from the various railway stations must have been enormous.[26]

✦　✦　✦　✦　✦

Killing deer as an avocation rather than just to put meat on the table to feed a family meant that a market hunter had to maximize his take and reduce his costs to make a profit. Through much of the market hunting period in Wisconsin, prices paid for venison stayed steady at about six or eight cents per pound. "The fairly stable prices over time . . . indicate a continual supply of venison," wrote McCabe and McCabe, " . . . but it is incorrect to assume that under such pressure deer populations were maintained at levels of sustained yield."[27]

The ideas of fair chase and sportsmanship were not held by the market hunter of the 1800s. Time and ammunition were valuable commodities and the more of each expended per animal killed translated directly into fewer profits for the hunter. As the waterfowl market hunters of the time devised punt guns and sink boats to slaughter birds on a massive scale, the market hunter after whitetails used every conceivable method to take deer. There were no regulations, or if there were, they were not followed nor enforced. The market hunter took many of the old Indian hunting methods and combined them with modern technology and a dose of ruthlessness.

To Stem the Slaughter

WITH PIONEER SETTLERS AND AGGRESSIVE MARKET HUNTERS using just about any method that might result in the take of a deer, the odds for long-term survival of a white-tailed deer in southern Wisconsin in the years preceding the Civil War were not good.

"Wanton deer killing by means of fires, hounding, hunting for the market, and other unsportsmanlike methods, along with the influx of settlers, accounted for the decline of deer, or the wiping out of the herd, in many southern counties before the Civil War," wrote Otis Bersing in *A Century of Wisconsin Deer*.[1]

As Wisconsin's population and economy continued to grow and transportation networks expanded across the state, even more pressure was put on a declining deer herd by market hunters fueling a huge demand from urban centers such as those in Milwaukee and Chicago.[2] As deer began to disappear from southern Wisconsin counties, the hunters turned their sights to central Wisconsin and eventually to regions farther north.[3]

The excessive and uncontrolled slaughter of deer had already begun to cause some public concern by the mid-1800s, resulting in

To Stem the Slaughter (continued)

the first legal restrictions placed on the hunting of deer. "Hardly had Wisconsin been granted statehood in 1848, and the first legislature and governor elected, than the first deer control law was passed," wrote Bersing. "It provided for the protection of deer by closing the season for five months only, from February 1 to July 1, in 1851."[4]

This legislation resulted in what is regarded as Wisconsin's first official deer season, since before 1851 deer could be legally hunted at any time. However, the measure was largely symbolic as it was not enforced in any significant way until 1887. It also still allowed the taking of any type or amount of deer.[5]

While the 1851 law was certainly a step in the right direction, it would take many years and numerous attempts at legislating deer hunting before real results were achieved. Rather than being based on any sort of conservation goal or real understanding of the biological needs of the species, the early regulations typically were political in nature, simply reactions to localized depletion of deer numbers.[6]

Early regulations were often unclear and confusing to the hunter. A statewide regulation could conflict with numerous local provisions that took precedence, resulting in a situation where a method of hunting acceptable in one part of the state might be illegal in another.[7] Since uncontrolled market hunting was the most obvious threat to deer numbers in the state, early regulations frequently attempted to put a lid on the excesses of commercial exploitation of the

herd. Many attempts were made to curtail market hunting by restricting both the transportation and sale of deer. Bersing described the ever-changing laws regarding the shipment of deer:

> Shipment of deer or venison out of state was prohibited state-wide in 1878 and 1879, but was permitted again from 1880 to 1882. During this time, however, in 1879, a local law prohibited the shipment of deer out of Door County unless the deer were taken within six miles of the southern county line. From 1883–1894, out-of-state shipment was prohibited anywhere. In 1895, shipment was permitted with a limit of two per trip when accompanied by the owner. After 1897, licensed nonresidents could take their legal deer out of state.[8]

Regulations regarding the possession and sale of venison also could be confusing. From 1860 to 1876 the sale of venison was prohibited during the closed season.[9] Beginning in 1877 venison sales were permitted during the open season and up to fifteen days after its close.[10] This time frame was reduced to eight days after the end of the season in 1889; it changed to three days in 1896 and to five days in 1897.[11]

Aside from restrictions on the shipment and sale of deer, specific methods—many of them reliable weapons in the market hunter's bag of tricks—began to be targeted as well. The dangerous and indiscriminate set gun, which

To Stem the Slaughter (continued)

sometimes took human lives as well as deer and whatever other wildlife might have the misfortune to come across it, was first outlawed in 1869.[12] Shining of deer was outlawed in 1883; the use of salt licks in 1905.[13] The killing of deer in water or on top of ice was banned in 1897.[14]

Employing dogs for deer hunting became increasingly unacceptable to the public in the mid-1800s, but, like the other regulations, it proved to be a moving target for many years. Bersing described these attempts: "In 1871, the legislature passed the first local law for Door County only, prohibiting the use of dogs while deer hunting. A similar law later prevented the use of dogs in Kewaunee County. From 1876 to 1886, a general law prohibited the use of dogs, state-wide, but a law, local in nature, enacted in 1877 and in force until 1888, permitted the use of dogs for hunting deer only in Ashland, Bay-field and Douglas Counties."[15]

The use of dogs was again prohibited state-wide from 1889 to 1900, but for the 1901–02 season, the law allowed the use of dogs in six-teen southern counties, which was expanded to include twenty-eight southern counties for the 1903–04 season.[16] Finally, in 1905, the use of dogs was banned statewide.[17]

✦ ✦ ✦ ✦ ✦

The confusing structure of deer hunting regulations that were being developed in Wisconsin in the mid-1800s might have been a nightmare for a hunter intent on following the letter of the law.

However, in reality, the laws weren't much of an issue for most hunters as they weren't followed anyway.

According to Stanley Young in his piece about deer and American pioneers, it wasn't until the 1890s that deer protection took on a more serious nature. "Restrictive game laws were regarded as a minor nuisance in the 1880's and a real menace in the 1890's," he wrote.[18]

Despite myriad regulations on the books, it wasn't until the establishment of the game war-den system in 1887—thirty-six years after the first deer season had been set—that there were any significant attempts at enforcing the laws.[19] The governor was authorized to appoint four wardens but only appointed two, which were perceived as political appointments.[20] In 1891 enforcement capabilities expanded with the formation of the Office of the State Game and Fish Warden. The State Warden was given the authority to appoint one or more deputies per county.[21] Acknowledging the challenges, Burton Dahlberg and Ralph Guettinger wrote, "Imag-ine the gigantic and seemingly impossible task confronting the early game warden faced with a century-old habit and man's philosophy that wild things were his for the taking."[22]

With game wardens now in the field to enforce laws, more consistent statewide regu-lations were enacted. In 1897 a bag limit was established for the first time, setting the number of deer that could be taken during the season at two of either sex or any size.[23] That year, deer hunting licenses were required for the first time,

To Stem the Slaughter (continued)

at a cost of one dollar for residents and thirty dollars for nonresidents (the nonresident fee was reduced to twenty-five dollars in 1899).[24]

As the end of the 1800s approached, a new perspective on wildlife—a conservation ethic—was developing, born in part from the realization that natural resources, including the deer herd, were not limitless and must be managed more wisely if they were to be there for future generations to enjoy. This shift in perspective coincided with a move away from hunting primarily for subsistence or the market toward sport or recreational hunting.

The death knell for the market hunter came in the form of national legislation, the Lacey Act of 1900, which prohibited the interstate shipment of wild game taken in violation of state law. The Lacey Act, as well as simple deer scarcity, effectively put an end to market hunting in Wisconsin after the turn of the twentieth century.[25]

Wanton disregard for the new game laws certainly continued into the early 1900s, but increasingly restrictive deer hunting laws—which included shortened seasons and closing seasons altogether in counties with few deer—became the trend as the Wisconsin public struggled to conserve and wisely use the white-tailed deer that was so much a part of its heritage.

NOTES
1. Otis S. Bersing, *A Century of Wisconsin Deer* (Madison: Wisconsin Conservation Department, Game Management Division, 1956), 7.
2. Ibid., 10.
3. Ibid.
4. Ibid., 9.
5. Richard E. McCabe and Thomas R. McCabe, "Of Slings and Arrows: An Historical Perspective," in *White-Tailed Deer Ecology and Management*, ed. Lowell K. Halls (Harrisburg, PA: Stackpole Books, 1984), 71.
6. Bersing, *A Century of Wisconsin Deer*, 11.
7. Ibid.
8. Ibid.
9. Ibid., 24.
10. Ibid., 27.
11. Ibid., 32–36.
12. Ibid., 25.
13. Ibid., 30, 41.
14. Ibid., 36.
15. Ibid., 11.
16. Ibid.
17. Ibid.
18. Stanley P. Young, "The Deer, the Indians, and the American Pioneers," in *The Deer of North America* ed. Walter P. Taylor (Harrisburg, PA: The Stackpole Company, 1956), 25.
19. Burton L. Dahlberg and Ralph C. Guettinger, *The White-Tailed Deer in Wisconsin*. Technical Bulletin No. 14 (Madison: Wisconsin Conservation Department, Game Management Division, 1956), 33.
20. Bersing, *A Century of Wisconsin Deer*, 13.
21. Dahlberg and Guettinger, *The White-Tailed Deer in Wisconsin*, 33.
22. Ibid.
23. Bersing, *A Century of Wisconsin Deer*, 14.
24. Ibid.
25. McCabe and McCabe, "Of Slings and Arrows," 70.

The market hunter killed deer lured to baits, salt licks, and live deer decoys, shooting them from blinds, trees, or elevated platforms. They mounted drives or used dogs to loosen deer from the thickets. To maximize kill and reduce manpower, a variety of indiscriminate but deadly tools were used, including snares, deadfalls, poison, pitfall traps, and the infamous set gun: a miniature gun attached to a tree or pole along a deer trail that fired a bullet at whatever snagged the trigger wire.[28]

Fire hunting or "jacklighting" with torches in canoes, as the Ojibwe did for many years at Lac du Flambeau and other northern places, was a favorite method of the market hunter. The method was deadly, as deer along the banks of streams and lakes stood watching while the quiet canoe slipped closer. The market hunter, however, replaced the bow and arrow of the Ojibwe with the shotgun or repeating rifle.

An old tool of the fur trade, leghold traps also were used by market hunters to take deer. Oliver Newhouse, the developer of high-quality manufactured leghold traps explained their use in a trappers' guide published in 1869:

> For taking Deer a trap must be a strong one, and the jaws should be spiked, and so shaped and adjusted that when sprung they will open about half an inch to prevent breaking the bone. The trap should be placed in the path of the deer where it crosses a stream and enters a lake; and it should be set underwater and concealed by some covering. If it is as heavy as it ought to be (say three or four pounds' weight), it should not be fastened at all or even clogged; as the animal is very active and violent when taken, and will be sure to break loose . . . if his motions are much impeded. If the trap is left loose, the Deer, when caught, will make a few desperate lunges and then lie down; and will seldom be found more than ten or fifteen rods from where he was taken.[29]

With no enforced limits on season or types of methods used, deer were hunted 365 days a year for the most part, even in the depths of severe winters when deer were concentrated and vulnerable in yarding areas. Schorger wrote of the winter deer slaughter: "There are many references to the effect of the winter of 1856–57 on Wisconsin deer. Joseph V. Jones came to Durand in Pepin County in 1856. That winter the snow was six feet deep on the level so that deer were unable to travel. Many were killed with clubs and hundreds starved. The situation was equally bad in Grant County where the deep, crusted snow permitted a great slaughter. The deer were killed by simply knocking them on their heads."[30]

An 1857 newspaper account from Prairie du Chien detailed the winter deer killing in that area:

> A friend of ours killed a drove of seven last week in one day. He followed a path made through the hard crust, until they could scarcely walk and with a Sharpes

rifle shot them down one after the other. We thought last summer, when noticing some Frenchmen bringing home each morning from 5 to 8 deer, obtained by Fire Hunting on the Wisconsin and Paint Creek, that they would soon kill off all the Deer; but we are now convinced that deer hunting in December exceeds Fire Hunting five hundred percent, for the very reason that the animals are now rendered helpless by the deep snows, and are murdered by every farmer's boy in the country. Some three sleigh loads of venison passed our office every day last week and as many more this week.[31]

Similar weather conditions prevailed the winter of 1868–69. A crust formed on the snow in Door County in February and deer were slaughtered in wholesale fashion. Ambrose Hummel of Green Bay, for one, killed eighty-eight deer that season along the Menominee River.[32]

The winter of 1887–88 was another tough one for deer, and a productive one for market hunters in northeastern Wisconsin. The *Madison State Journal* reported in 1888 that "[t]wo hunters at Bryant, Langlade County, caught a herd of 17 deer in the deep snow and killed all of them."[33]

While Wisconsin deer populations had withstood thousands of years of pursuit by humankind, they could not endure the endless pursuit by the modern market hunter. The abundant deer numbers that greeted the first white settlers in southern Wisconsin began to succumb to the onslaught. Decades of market hunting were taking its toll.

The reduction, and in some areas the total elimination, of deer from the Wisconsin landscape followed the direction of settlement, occurring earliest in the most southern and southeastern counties, then moving northward and westward.

According to Schorger, deer had become scarce in Rock County by the 1850s and had disappeared altogether around Janesville by 1856.[34] Just to the north in Dane County, Schorger documented that "the last deer was killed on the site of Madison in 1847. It was an old buck that had a trail over University Hill. Few deer were killed in the county between 1850 and 1900."[35] In December 1884, not a single deer was known to have been killed in the county during the season. Two deer, seen near Arlington in Columbia County on August 28, 1881, were considered a rare sight.[36]

Deer had been abundant in the Milwaukee area when the city was established in the 1840s and continued to be common until 1852.[37] Deer were considered scarce in Waukesha County by 1857.[38] Dodge and Jefferson were two counties where overhunting reduced or eliminated the deer population fairly early. Deer were very scarce in Jefferson County by 1855, and in 1857 it was reported that deer were so rare around Watertown that it was not worthwhile hunting them.[39]

Market hunters in Richland County quickly reduced the deer herd in the 1850s. In 1856 a Richland County newspaper noted: "Richland County, we will venture to say, has furnished more venison for the eastern markets this winter, than has any other county in the State"[40]

After the Civil War, the list of counties where whitetails had been aggressively pursued by market hunters kept growing and began to include some central Wisconsin counties. Deer were reported scarce in Fond du Lac County by 1865 and confined largely to the eastern edge of the county. "Hunters complained of scarcity of deer in 1872," wrote Schorger. "From this date forward only an occasional deer was killed."[41]

By 1882, Sauk County had only a remnant deer population, probably surviving in thick cover along the Wisconsin River.[42] Eau Claire County was not productive for market hunters by 1886 due to low deer numbers.[43] Portage County deer populations had greatly declined by 1888.[44]

Schorger felt that a low point in the state's deer population was reached about 1890, caused almost entirely from overshooting.[45] Bersing, however, believed, the Wisconsin deer population probably reached the lowest point in the early 1900s, before World War I.[46]

The disappearance of the whitetail from southern Wisconsin did not curtail the excesses of market hunting. As numbers declined in the south, hunters moved to central Wisconsin, and then farther north as numbers became depleted in the central counties. At the time some speculated that deer had simply "migrated" north. The average citizen was not knowledgeable enough about deer and deer biology to realize that the deer had not migrated; they were systematically being eliminated by overhunting and the advance of settlement.[47]

In the latter half of the 1800s, when the future for deer in Wisconsin looked extremely bleak, deer numbers actually began to rise in northern Wisconsin. Northern Wisconsin had always held deer, but deer numbers were fewer because of the relatively unproductive deer habitat of the dense northern forests. The great northern forest—a mixture of white and red pine and hardwoods such as maple, hemlock, and basswood—covered so much of the land that deer had a difficult time finding food in many places.[48]

While enormous quantities of potential lumber stood silent and unexploited in the north, early Wisconsin settlers relied on wood products imported from the East. The first sawmill in Wisconsin may have been built as early as 1809, but little northern lumbering occurred until the cessions of Indian lands in 1837 and

1842.[49] At that time the north was still a vast wilderness accessible primarily by water routes. By the 1850s, however, logging interests were working their way north and, by 1869, lumber production had reached more than one billion board feet. Wisconsin quickly ascended to fourth place among the country's timber-producing states.[50]

White pine logging was the first great assault on the northern forest. The huge pines provided a lot of return for the effort, and they were plentiful and convenient to the streams and rivers required to transport them to sawmills. The white pines were felled and shipped to market at breathtaking rates from approximately 1850 through the 1890s. The Chippewa River Valley, one of the great white pine watersheds, boomed after the Civil War. It had produced forty million feet of lumber in 1858, but by 1884 the annual harvest was more than four hundred million feet. Lumber from Chippewa Valley white pine made its way to twenty-three states and territories to the West in 1891 and 1892.[51]

As railroads networked through the North Woods, loggers were less dependent on waterways and could get deeper into the woods. Railroads also allowed for the transportation of hardwoods, which could not effectively be floated. North Woods logging transitioned into a hardwood logging phase from about 1890 through the early 1900s.[52]

The rapid pace of deforestation in the north in the late 1800s was astonishing. At that time few involved in the logging industry held any thoughts of sustainable timber production, and few lost any sleep over the exploitation of the incredible forest resource. The pines and other trees were there to be taken and used to feed the demands of an ever-expanding America, including the need "to clear the land and provide roads and other infrastructure that would lead to a permanent agricultural economy."[53] In 1897 a USDA forestry agent warned that of 130 billion board feet of pine that had once been present in Wisconsin, only seventeen billion board feet remained.[54] It took only about four decades for the timber barons and the loggers to clear most of the white pine from the entire northern portion of the state.

Lumberjacks dwarfed by a Wisconsin white pine felled by ax and crosscut saw. The pine logging industry of the mid- to late 1800s fed the growing nation's demand for lumber, transforming the primeval forest of northern Wisconsin.
WHi Image ID 6771

The first passenger train arrives in Merrill, Lincoln County, on the Chicago, Milwaukee & St. Paul railroad, in 1885. Trains were symbolic of the increasing access to the North Woods—and the intense deforestation that followed. A booming deer population thrived on the new growth in the former forests.
WHi Image ID 24899

The wholesale and rapid conversion of the mature northern forest into a vast area of "cutover"—a mess of stumps and slash prone to wildfire—had a great impact on whitetail numbers. As each new tract of big woods was logged and the trees carted off to the mills, new, young growth—shrubs, forbs, and young, succulent tree growth—replaced the big trees. Ironically the devastation of the pineries greatly improved deer habitat. According to the Wisconsin Woodland Owners Association in *One Hundred Years of Wisconsin Forestry, 1904–2004*, "Opening the forest to sunlight by axe and fire fostered a growth of plants, which formed superb food and cover for deer."[55]

Schorger documented the rise of deer numbers in the northern counties:

Ashland County: Apparently they did not become common in the Ashland region until the late 1870s. In the fall of 1880, deer were reported plentiful and in excellent condition. Deer were reported as numerous in 1885 and 1886 around Glidden.[56]

Bayfield County: In the late fall of 1883, David Downer, while hunting at Cable, killed nineteen deer, the two largest weighing 225 and 240 pounds respectively.[57]

Douglas County: Deer [were] rare until about 1875, after which date the increase was quite rapid. In December, 1876, one hunter killed twelve deer in a short time; and eleven years later the slaughter was "immense." It was estimated that 1,000 deer would be shipped from the county during the hunting season of 1897.[58]

Iron County: This county was late in acquiring an abundance of deer. In 1874 Joe Current and his uncle killed about twenty deer at Moose Lake in a period of two weeks. Deer were unusually plentiful in 1890. It was stated in 1892 that deer were unknown at Hurley seven years previously (1885).[59]

Sawyer County: Deer were plentiful in 1884 and a considerable number were killed. Many deer were killed in the fall of 1892.[60]

Vilas County: In the early days deer were not common. Deer were plentiful in 1895.[61]

This upswing in the deer population did not go unnoticed as market hunting increased in the north, aided by the access the railroads afforded. Another result of the boom in the logging industry was settlement of the north, which provided a ready market for venison.

A Chippewa Falls–area logging crew poses in front of their camp on a winter's day in 1875. Market hunters provided much of the venison served at northern Wisconsin lumber camps.
WHi IMAGE ID 4177

Deer habitat in northern Wisconsin was first altered by loggers, then settlers. This advertising card issued by the Land Department of the Wisconsin Central Railroad promoted Wisconsin land sales to European immigrants.
WHi IMAGE ID 24505

Logging towns popped up all across the north as people came to work in the woods or to provide services to the loggers and the logging camps. According to Bersing, "The population of the north jumped from about 35,000 inhabitants in 1870 to over 100,000 in 1880."[62]

The lumber camps themselves had a great demand for venison. Schorger wrote:

The traffic in venison became enormous in the latter part of the nineteenth century. The lumber camps bought deer directly from professional hunters, or hired men to shoot for the camp mess. For example, the winter of 1868–69, James Terry engaged to hunt for John Sterling who had two camps on the North Fork of the Eau Claire River. He received his board and $4.00 per deer. Up to the first of January of this winter, he killed 38 deer and two bears; and up to the first of January the following winter, 47 deer. These were moderate bags.[63]

On the heels of the loggers came the settlers. Believing the great promotions by the railroad companies and the state about opportunities for farming in the cutover, pioneers headed north for their piece of paradise.

These early settlers, like those of southern Wisconsin a generation before, quickly came to rely on deer to support themselves and their families. "The resourceful immigrants soon came to terms with the forest . . . and found it to be a good provider," wrote Frederick Hale in *The Swedes in Wisconsin*. "The forest and lakes also furnished most of the meals before agriculture got well underway, and many of them afterwards too. Swedes found familiar and palatable

Vast tracts of desolate stump land, simply known as cutover, were left in the aftermath of pine logging.
WHi Image ID 3990

freshwater fish of many species. The men hunted grouse, prairie chickens, geese, ducks, and deer much of the year."[64]

Farming the cutover was not an easy task. Huge stumps, rugged terrain, rocky soil, and cold winters—some of the same impediments that had prevented the early Indians from pursuing agriculture to any great degree—faced the cutover settler. In this harsh environment, the hunting of game, particularly deer, pulled the settler through, as documented by Robert Gough in *Farming the Cutover*: "Albert Stouffer, who moved in 1886 as a ten-year old to the town of Bashaw in Washburn County remembered that 'fish and game were plentiful. . . . Deer fed on our rutabaga patches and it was only necessary to go up river a few bends to get all the mallards we wanted.' "[65]

There were settlers in the north who became more hunter than farmer, as the northern environment favored the hunter. "Some cutover settlers never cleared

Northern Wisconsin deer camps of the late 1800s often included dogs. This 1885 photo of a typical camp shows a bag of massive mature bucks as well as younger bucks, does, and fawns.
WHi Image ID 1930

much land because limited agricultural activities satisfied the desire for security, independence, and a close relationship with the natural environment that had attracted them to the cutover in the first place," wrote Gough.[66] A Rusk County school teacher later recalled that, early in the twentieth century, "[h]unting and fishing were the general hobbies; sometimes I used to think they were the vocation and farming was the hobby."[67]

As the 1800s closed, deer remained common and even plentiful in many northern counties, despite the pressures of market hunting and a continuing subsistence hunting culture. Deer numbers in the cutover probably peaked and began to decline around the turn of the century. By 1910, deer numbers in southern Wisconsin had already bottomed out while a combination of intense hunting and uncontrolled wildfires in the north finally negated the growth seen in the late 1800s.[68]

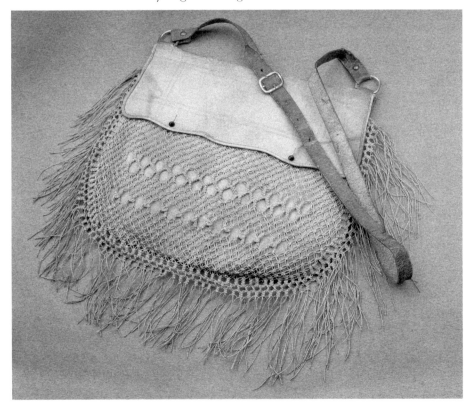

Hunting equipment in the 1880s included knotted-twine bags, the design of which came from English and German settlers. While such bags were available commercially, instructions on making one's own were found in such publications as an 1884 issue of *Harper's Bazar*. This bag was discovered in the summer home of the Sawyers—Oshkosh lumber barons—whose members, male and female, were avid sportsmen.

COUNTIES FREQUENTED BY DEER IN 1897

Source: Map is based on "Laws of Wisconsin 1897", Chapter 221, Section 9, which designates counties frequented by deer.

This map from Otis S. Bersing's, *A Century of Wisconsin Deer*, published in 1956, depicts approximate whitetail range in 1897. By this time deer were rare in southern Wisconsin.

A Century of Wisconsin Deer

✦ ✦ ✦ ✦ ✦

By the end of the 1800s, the overall outlook for whitetails in Wisconsin was gloomy. Most of southern and central Wisconsin no longer held significant numbers of deer. Although logging opened up the big woods and promoted a northern deer population increase, deer in the north were at risk of suffering the same fate as the southern herd. However, at this same time American society was overhauling its attitude toward natural resources and, in particular, toward wild animals.

In less than a century, the American wilderness experienced by Lewis and Clark had largely been tamed and settled. By the late 1800s there was a growing awareness that the country's natural resources that at one time seemed endlessly abundant did indeed have limits. Passenger pigeons, which in the 1840s darkened the sky over southern Wisconsin, were nearly extinct, and the white-tailed deer, which had sustained humans for so many years, were so severely overhunted that their future survival was uncertain. A new idea of wise use and conservation of natural resources was taking hold, promoted by prominent Americans such as Theodore Roosevelt and John Muir.

These ideas came too late to save the doomed passenger pigeon, but they helped the whitetail. There was at the turn of the century a growing segment of the population who actually did care about deer and deer populations, and ultimately the future of deer in the state. These thinkers felt that, unlike the elk, caribou, and bison, it was not inevitable that deer would disappear from the Wisconsin landscape as settlement and civilization encroached on their habitat. Real, enforceable legislation to curtail and eventually eliminate market hunting and regulate the subsistence and sport harvest of deer began to be passed. However, the road to recovering and maintaining healthy deer populations in the state would not be an easy one.

The idea of hunting for sport rather than the market developed hand in hand with the idea that hunting needed regulations if deer populations were to remain stable enough to prevent the species from vanishing in the state. The whitetail transitioned from decades of being simply a commodity to the subject of an enjoyable and challenging week or two in the woods. This idea was huge.

Carl and Roy Linnell of Black River Falls pose with a trophy whitetail buck mount, ca. 1895. The era of the sport hunter had begun.
WHi Image ID 29160

The Rise of
the Sportsman

The real hunter doesn't slam car doors and clank off into the woods. He pays attention to breezes, he notices rubbings, he sees a variety of distances from food to resting areas and watering spots. He puts all this information together and uses it at the right time of day, quietly and with that special alertness, that sixth sense, and he sees deer. If he chooses to shoot or not, if he wants a trophy or roast venison, that is his final option, but he has derived his basic satisfaction from solving the problem.
—Gene Hill, *A Listening Walk*[1]

Americans were optimistic as the first decade of the new century began in 1900. The country was poised for great things. Railroads were spreading across the United States, cities were being electrified, and industry was expanding. America was growing at a fast pace, eager to take its place among world leaders.

William McKinley was reelected president in November 1900 on a Republican ticket with Theodore Roosevelt as his running mate. Fate carried by an assassin's bullet made Roosevelt president in 1901; he dominated American politics for the remainder of the decade. An intense and spirited sportsman and adventurer, he was destined to be at the forefront of the era of American conservation that was on the rise.

Conservation of natural resources was not on the minds of most Wisconsin deer hunters in the early "ought" years. The state's population was just more than two million people in 1900, most of whom lived in farming or rural areas.[2] While deer populations had reached historic lows in states to the east, and hunters there faced increasingly restrictive or closed seasons, Wisconsinites had some reason to be optimistic about hunting prospects: deer numbers were actually increasing in some areas. The trick was to go to where the deer were.

Market hunting, increased human settlement with a heavy reliance on deer for subsistence, and habitat changes had decimated deer populations in most eastern and midwestern states by this time. Southern Wisconsin was typical of the situation. By the turn of the century, deer were so rare in southern counties that the mere observation of a single deer was fodder for excited talk and speculation at the

Clarence Hood hunting near Spring Green, early 1900s. By this time, deer were rare in southern Wisconsin.

barbershops and taverns. Deer mainly existed in areas of heavy cover, such as along creeks and rivers.

This wasn't the case in northern Wisconsin, however. During the first years of the 1900s, most northern counties reported deer to be plentiful and hunting to be good. A Rhinelander newspaper, *The New North*, reported deer during the season of 1901 to be numerous and stated that "already a large number have been brought to this city."[3] It was ironic that the whitetail had been literally shot out of southern counties, where the farm, field, and forest habitats were more favorable to deer, while herd populations seemed to be increasing in the northern forest, which had typically been poor habitat because of its heavy forests and hard winters.

The favorable blip in deer populations in the north was mostly due to changing habitat conditions in the wake of large-scale North Woods logging. The era of the great pineries was coming to a close,

A unique photo of two hunters, including Fred E. Blake of Fond du Lac (right), poling a deer on a raft across a northern Wisconsin river in the early 1900s. Many modern-day hunters use boats or canoes to access remote areas for a try at a trophy deer—the legendary "swamp buck."

but logging was still big business in northern Wisconsin. In its aftermath, deer benefited from the brush and second-growth forests replacing the big trees.

Hunting and Fishing with the Indians

ON MAY 29, 1848, WISCONSIN BECAME THE THIRTIETH state accepted into the Union. The population required for statehood had been met by 1840 as European immigrants flooded into the region in search of freedom and good farmland. As settlers spread across southern and central Wisconsin establishing pioneer farms and raising first-generation Americans, the economy of the state flourished. By the 1870s, after the Civil War, pioneers flowed toward northern Wisconsin, where white-pine logging further fueled the economy.

By the early to mid-1900s, these original Wisconsin pioneers began passing away in large numbers, and their knowledge of what life was like when Wisconsin was young was frequently lost. Fortunately, a few of these pioneers recorded their experiences for posterity. William George Nohl, known as W. G., was one of them.

Nohl was born in 1861 on the Sheboygan County homestead established by his father, an immigrant from the Alsace-Lorraine region, in 1846. Nohl's father had bought six lots in Milwaukee from Solomon Juneau, but he moved to the unsettled woods of Sheboygan County—purchased for $1.25 an acre—after hearing the area had better land with fewer rocks. The immigrants found wild country where the howling of wolves kept them awake at night. Native Americans welcomed the settlers with a pow-wow and showed them how to grow fine corn by placing a chunk of fish into each seed hole.

After receiving a frontier education at the schoolhouse built on his family's farm, W. G. worked as a clerk for a dry goods and grocery store in Sheboygan and at a sawmill in Manitowoc County before heading to the wilderness of the North Woods in 1877. He took a job as a clerk in a general merchandise store in Butternut, Price County.

Nohl was able to experience firsthand the traditional hunting and fishing existence of the Ojibwe living in the area. His words are an intimate record of a brief period in North Woods history, when early settlers and Native Americans interacted against a backdrop of primeval forest. At the time, large-scale white-pine logging was just beginning in the region.

"After following the clerking in the store for a time, and in the fall of the year I was approached by a man, Jim Cody, whether I would go with him and hunt with the Indians. My answer was yes," Nohl recollected more than sixty years later.[1]

Nohl and Cody planned to spend the forty-five-day hunting season with the Indians hunting deer, partridge, and other game in preparation for winter. When they arrived at the hunting grounds about ten miles northeast of Butternut, they found a traditional Ojibwe camp: "We arrived at the hunting grounds near the North Fork of the

Hunting and Fishing with the Indians (continued)

Flambeau River. Their wigwam was put up with long poles covered with tanned deer and bear hides, large enough to seat 50–60 persons," wrote Nohl. "After supper A-na-kwad (Chief Cloud) came and visited us. I had to smoke the pipe in peace in order to be with them on their hunting and fishing grounds and to be their friend."

After the ceremony the chief stated that Nohl was "made a pale face Ojibwa Indian." The Indians then called him "Chippewa Bill."

"After I was instructed and painted with 'vin rouge' and an Indian suit handed to me I hit the hay. We rose early morn and in due time prepared for the hunt after the fleet footed deer. I loaded my .44 Winchester rim fire (there were no center fire cartridges in them days) and started out early with the Indians and my pal Jim Cody."

Nohl, Cody, and the Indians spent the next few weeks hunting timbered country covered with virgin pine and hemlock. "A person or a hunter could see a deer from a distance of a mile as there was no underbrush, except alders along the creeks and rivers," Nohl noted.

There was only one lumbering operation in the area at the time, the camp of George Calligan, and the hunters knew the logging slash attracted deer. Early one morning, when they went into the area where the logging was taking place, they encountered this scene:

[A]s deer browse on the hardwood tips of trees green cut down in order to remove the pine logs from its place to the skid way; we discovered numerous tracks of deer; Cody informed me to take a station on a deer trail whence the deer come and go to the feeding place, and Jim Cody took another stand and several Indians were driving with their Anamosh dogs. As I stood quite a while near a large pine stump I noticed a movement coming towards me. . . . I noticed a nice big buck came towards me from the west on account the wind was with him he could not catch the scent of me. I thought to myself, brace up young man, get the first shot; took good aim and let go the .44 between the antlers, the buck made a high jump and landed close to me, coming towards me, was ready for fight, but fired another shot and killed him.

Wolves were often observed by Nohl and Cody, as were other predators, such as lynx discovered at camp: "All at once by the fire two lynx up on a tree made a terrible noise, we got busy with our .44's and the light from the fire could see their eyes plain and we let go . . . and down came the lynx, we placed them on a place to find later for the bounty."

Some of the deer shot by the hunting party provided food for the camp; some was sold to a butcher in Fifield who supplied meat to the lumber camp.

Nohl and Cody finished their time with the Indians by hunting partridge and fishing through the ice for musky. They then returned to Butternut.

Hunting and Fishing with the Indians (continued)

Eventually Nohl opened his own Indian trading store. Due to his respect for the Ojibwe culture and his willingness to learn the local language, he conducted a brisk business. In 1895 he relocated to Ashland County, where he was extremely active in the conservation of fish and wildlife through the years. In the 1930s he established a summer resort at Mission Springs just west of Ashland on Chequamegon Bay. Nohl's Mission Springs Resort is still in operation today, owned by W. G. Nohl's grandson, Bill Nohl.

Bill Nohl said his grandfather was fluent in the Ojibwe language. "He shot a .33 Winchester," remembered Nohl. "He hunted deer until he could no longer stand."[2]

A true Wisconsin pioneer, W. G. Nohl passed away in 1951 at the age of ninety.

NOTES
1. William G. Nohl, "Reminiscences, undated," Wisconsin Historical Society Archives. RLIN Number WIHVOO-A1554. Call Number SC 1919.
2. Bill Nohl, personal communication, June 2008.

Because of the scarcity of deer elsewhere, northern Wisconsin began to see a new phenomenon: an increase in hunters from somewhere besides northern Wisconsin—primarily from southern counties but also from outside the state—who traveled north for the opportunity to hunt deer. "The annual slaughter of deer began Monday morning and for several days prior to that time, hunters came pouring into the city from every direction," reported *The New North* in 1901.[4] In 1905 the newspaper noted that "hunters from the south are arriving on every train."[5]

These hunters represented a new and growing segment of the American hunting population: the sportsman. Rather than hunting out of the necessity to feed a family or, as in the case of the market hunter, for profit, the sportsman placed primary value on the experience of the hunt. This new breed of hunter was willing to travel, sometimes great distances, simply for a fulfilling recreational hunting experience.

Getting to the northern counties to pursue the sport of deer hunting was not particularly difficult, and it was getting easier. Although automobiles were scarce (only about 8,000 existed in the entire United States in 1900) and roads on which to drive them few, railroads were booming. These "roads" provided hunters access to the very heart of the northern deer country. The state and the railroad corporations, anxious to sell land and increase settlement in the north, promoted the idea of using the rails to reach deer. The 1904 "Official Railroad Map of Wisconsin" included text that stated, "The northern portion of Wisconsin may be justly called a sportsman's paradise, both for fishing and hunting. Deer hunting along the lines of the Wisconsin Central is exceptionally good during the open season."[6]

The major railroads, as well as smaller, local lines, such as the Dunbar and Wausaukee in Marinette County, Hazelhurst and Southeastern in Oneida County,

Members of the Echo Lake Hunting Club, 1920, at their deer camp
located near Pembine in Marinette County.
WHi Image ID 24434

and Chippewa River and Northern in Gates (later renamed Rusk) County, passed through small settlements and logging camps with now-forgotten names like Bagdad, Sillhawn, and Veazy. It was a good situation for hunters, who typically set up camps in proximity to railroad access or used abandoned logging camps, of which there were many. Locals with horses and wagons were eager to provide transportation for hunters and gear.

The season framework itself was a pretty simple affair. In the "ought" years, the deer season ran for twenty days each year and, except for 1900, when the season started November 1, the seasons began November 11. Since 1897, hunters could take two deer of either sex. This continued until 1909 when a one deer, either sex bag became law. A deer license cost a Wisconsin resident just one dollar; a nonresident paid thirty dollars. Licenses were generally bought from the county clerk at the local courthouse, and the county was allowed to keep 10 percent of the revenue from each license sold.

Photographs of early hunting days in northern Wisconsin, created by Hugo O. Schneiders, a dentist, conservationist, and sportsman from Wausau.
WHi Image ID 58608, 58609

A meat pole of a deer camp from the early 1900s bends under the strain of seven deer. The Winchester and Marlin repeating rifles brought to deer camp by the five hunters served them well.

There was a requirement to tag deer with a paper tag prior to transport or shipping. After receiving numerous inquiries regarding the proper shipment of deer, *The New North* printed the law: "No deer or part of a carcass can be shipped, but must be accompanied by the hunter, with coupon section 'B' of his license attached to it. If a non-resident, sections B and C are to be attached to the carcass or part of the deer."[7] This rule was not strictly followed; when it was, many a hunter returned from the woods to find his tag was no longer attached to his deer.

Hunters had complained about the paper tags for years. A hunter from Milwaukee, Judge Neele B. Neelen, had taken two deer in Vilas County in 1901. *The New North* printed some of his comments regarding the season:

There is one amendment to the present game law that ought to be adopted. It relates to the tags which, according to law, must be attached to the deer before they can be shipped. The paper tag, now used, is not sufficient, because it is lost too easily. It is simply a frail piece of paper and easily blown away.

Successful deer hunters at a northern Wisconsin tent camp near Donald in Rusk County, 1904.
WHi Image ID 28309

The deer are sometimes carted twenty or thirty miles before they get to a railway station where they may be shipped. I know a prominent business man in this city who was obliged to give away a deer he had shot because the tag was lost between the camp and the railway station. I always wrapped my tag up in a piece of cloth and tied it tightly to the deer's horn, so that it could not get lost. I should suggest that a tin tag might be used and attached around the deer's neck with wire.[8]

Metal locking tags replaced paper tags in 1920.
WHS Museum 1967.186.1, 1967.151, 1969.464.21;
Photo by Joel Heiman

It wasn't until 1920 that the problem was solved. The new tag, which consisted of a strip of tin with a ball at one end, was sturdier than its predecessor. After the strip was slid through a deer's gambrel, one end was pushed into the ball, locking it permanently. "The new tags must be a source of interest to those hunters who received them," stated Wisconsin Conservation Commissioner W. E. Barber, "for many have written for new ones because they inadvertently locked theirs while experimenting with them."[9] The new metal tags were destined to tempt hunters to lock them prematurely for decades to come.

In the early years of the decade, deer hunting regulations were minimal and enforcement of those laws limited due to the scarcity of game wardens. When wardens were present, their performance in pursuit of violators frequently was lackluster. *The New North* sarcastically reported on the actions of the local wardens in 1902:

> At Last! At Last! Our State Game Wardens Have Captured Someone Who Has Been Violating the Law.
>
> The first crop of hunters of the season of 1902 was rounded up in Paul Browne's Municipal Court rooms last week. They are all good citizens who probably went hunting just this once during the year. They were in [the] charge of Deputy Game

Three adult bucks were among the deer taken by these hunters, possibly from the Wausau area, around the turn of the twentieth century.
COURTESY OF THE MARATHON COUNTY HISTORICAL SOCIETY

Must have been a great hunting spot: Some of the same hunters from the previous photo pose in front of another season's take of fine deer.
Courtesy of the Marathon County Historical Society

Seven hunters from the Wisconsin Rapids area show off their success from a late 1800s deer hunt. Hunters included Julius Gash, A. F. Billmeyer, Alpha Snyder, Henry Sampson Jr., George Snyder, H. A. Sampson, and Joe Snyder. With the exception of a shotgun, each hunter possesses a lever-action rifle.
Courtesy of McMillan Memorial Library, Wisconsin Rapids

Seventeen deer, including several nice bucks, hang according to size from the meat pole of Johns Gudegast's deer camp near Rhinelander in Oneida County. Gudegast was an early settler who later became successful in the land and timber business.
COURTESY OF MIKE VLAHAKIS

Wardens E. A. VanAerman and Martin Berg, who caught them in the act of hunting deer with dogs. They were promptly convicted, in fact plead guilty, and were fined $25.00 and costs which they paid. This is the first arrest that has been made in this county during the deer hunting season for any violation of the game laws and at least 260 deer have been killed in this county the present season. It is a fine illustration of the ridiculous inefficiency of our present system of protecting game, and brings to view the tireless, tenacious, sleuth-like following which game wardens have given the hunters in this vicinity! There have been at least twenty parties of hunters in Oneida county out for deer with dogs during the season, and a good many were out before the season opened. Not an arrest has been made. Not a complaint, nor a whimper has been heard from any of the game wardens. Deer have been slaughtered plentifully and unlawfully throughout the northern woods this year. The law regarding the time, dogs and headlights has been disobeyed with an openness and wantonness that has never been equalled. Madison official dispatches as to the game wardens effectiveness are simply laughable. Talk indulged by game wardens and the showings made by the papers which seek to praise the system and defend its efficiency are ridiculous in the face of the facts. People up here know what these facts are, if they are posted. We believe that fewer deer would be illegally hunted and killed, if the duty of enforcing laws regarding game was in the hands of the daily constituted officers of towns and counties and the game wardens' positions were all abolished. Let a heavier penalty be inflicted in case of conviction of violation of these laws and let the officers of a town and county attend to their enforcement. The game warden business is a farce so far as this section of the state is concerned. It is no joke with the taxpayers however, but the ineffectiveness of the system has been so well disproven that some sort of change should be made.[10]

Whether the criticism of the local wardens was wholly warranted or the result of local politics, it was true that the early wardens were not always successful in their attempts to enforce game laws. They were few and far between in a part of the state still vast and remote. The accusations against a "system" that let game-law violators off with a slap on the wrist—if even that—symbolized the growing feelings of many residents of small North Woods towns that the state was not doing enough to pass and enforce regulations to control deer hunting.

The running of deer with dogs was still a common practice in some areas in the early 1900s, though not allowed by law or acceptable by general public opinion. Accepted methods to bag a deer varied by locale, but in many locations it was still anything goes. Most often, deer were taken by recreational hunters sitting on stumps near runways or paths of travel, by still-hunting (the practice of slowly stalking a deer), or during deer drives.

Hunting over a salt lick from a high point or scaffold was common in areas with lower deer populations. The use of salt licks was banned in 1909, but it would be many years before the practice disappeared. Set guns, the old market hunter's tool, were banned in 1869 but continued to be used into the early 1900s. A deer hunter was killed by a set gun during the 1905 season.

Taylor County deer hunters at camp in 1907 with their dogs and an assortment of game including some great bucks and a bear. At the center of the photo is John Brandt, the great-grandfather of Mike and Todd Herbst who supplied the photo—both avid hunters today.
Courtesy of Mike and Todd Herbst

The Deer Rifles We Once Used

IMAGINE WHAT MIGHT HAVE BEEN THE TYPICAL Wisconsin deer camp of 1908. It would have been located in one of the northern counties, in the cutover region that had begun to support large numbers of deer. In fact, an abandoned logging camp bunkhouse, one of many dotting the landscape, may have served as the deer camp headquarters.

Perhaps half a dozen hunters, friends, and relatives from one of the growing towns of southern Wisconsin would have traveled to the north via rail, in a Chicago & Northwestern or Chicago, Milwaukee & St. Paul coach car. They may have asked the conductor to let them off at a spot along the tracks, or they might have traveled to a depot where they could hire a local to take them to camp by horse-drawn wagon. If they were successful in taking deer, their quarry would travel home in much the same way—with the exception of riding in the baggage car.

The six men may have included a Civil War veteran or two, likely a grandfather or uncle who may have been in his late teens or early twenties when he enlisted with one of the many Wisconsin regiments headed east from Madi-

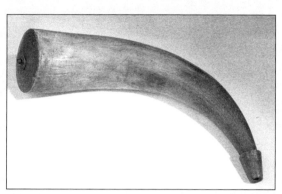

Hunters used cow or ox horns, which were lightweight and spark-proof, to hold their gunpowder. This powder horn dates to the 1830s.

son or Milwaukee, but now in his mid- to late sixties or early seventies. Middle-aged men in their forties or early fifties—children born during or shortly after the war years who were now shopkeepers or salesmen back in town—and their boys, small-town kids who welcomed in the turn of the century and were raised on stories about Custer's last stand, the romance of the Wild West, and Grandpa's Civil War experiences made up the rest of this camp.

The arms and ammunition the group may have brought in their pursuit of white-tailed deer were likely a diverse and unique mix of old and new firearms, for the deer hunter of the early 1900s was able to reap the benefits of the advances in rifle technology that had occurred since the Civil War. The advantages and disadvantages of the individual rifles were sure to have been fodder for lively nighttime discussions.

Prior to the Civil War, just about any firearm capable of killing a deer was used by those early American hunters who killed deer for trade or market, or the pioneer settler who killed deer to put food on the table. Daniel Boone's famous Kentucky rifle—a one-shot, long-range muzzle-

The Deer Rifles We Once Used (continued)

loader born of the needs of the early American woodsman—might well deserve the title of the first deer rifle.[1] Except in the hands of very skilled shooters, these early weapons were not particularly reliable or accurate. The advent of

A woman poses with a trophy buck and a lever-action Winchester in a photographer's studio around the turn of the century. In the early days of regulated deer hunting, female hunters, often referred to as modern day Dianas in reference to the Roman goddess of the hunt, were uncommon but not rare.
COURTESY OF MIKE VLAHAKIS

the Civil War, however, changed the firearms situation forever.

The reality of the Civil War was that battles were won and battles were lost and as thousands of soldiers on both sides shed their blood and gave their lives, the war ground on in a bloody stalemate. Both sides, but particularly the industrial North, actively sought advances in technology in an effort to produce the edge that would win the war. Rifle technology in particular made great strides during this period.

"The Civil War was the climactic event toward which all arms developments of the period had been leading. It provided the crucible in which all ideas would be tested, all theories refined. . . . With 4,137,304 men in uniform at one time or another, huge quantities of arms were needed," wrote Larry Koller in *The Fireside Book of Guns*.[2]

In *Winchester: The Gun That Won the West*, Harold Williamson wrote: "The demand for firearms coupled with a rapid development in technology at the time resulted in a greater variety of guns during the Civil War than in any other major conflict in history."[3] According to Koller, before the war's end the Union had officially recognized about eighty different models of rifles.[4]

The most significant advances in rifle technology during this period included the introduction of practical breech loaders—rifles loaded from the breech end of the barrel, rather than the muzzle end (muzzleloader)—that utilized a self-contained rimfire metallic cartridge (allowing for fast and reliable reloading). These advances

The Deer Rifles We Once Used (continued)

helped push the rifle far beyond anything Daniel Boone may have ever envisioned.

Incorporating these new technologies was the Spencer lever-action repeating rifle. Patented by Christopher Spencer in 1860, it fired a .52-caliber rimfire cartridge and allowed a soldier to shoot seven times before reloading.[5] While most soldiers during the war were resigned to use more abundant but less effective .58-caliber Springfield Model 1861 muzzleloaders, a sizable number of Spencer rifles were purchased by the military and were the most widely used Civil War repeating rifle.[6] Another capable repeater used by troops was the famous rifle designed by Benjamin Tyler Henry and produced for military use in 1863.[7] The Henry rifle, chambered for a .44 rimfire cartridge, was not popular with the military and few saw service in the regular army during the Civil War in comparison to the Spencers.[8]

Civil War–era advances in weaponry proved a great benefit to an ever-increasing number of game hunters, both market hunters and recreational sportsmen. After the war, the quest for better game hunting rifles became a major factor in continued rifle development. Though the Henry rifle was never officially adopted by the military, it was well received by the game hunter. Easier to handle and shooting a more powerful cartridge than the Spencer, the Henry became a favorite of the sport hunter.[9]

With an eye still on the military market, rifle manufacturers also began to consider the game hunter. In 1866 Oliver F. Winchester's New Haven

Arms Company began producing the first rifles to bear the Winchester name—the Model 1866— shortly after the war.[10] A repeater chambered for .44 rimfire, the Model 66 was produced in a military version as well as two sporting styles.[11] Basically an improved version of the Henry, this rifle proved popular with hunters: about 157,000 were produced from 1866 through 1891.[12]

Winchester found success with the 1866, but big-game hunters were looking for something with more firepower. The answer came in the form of the Model 1873, perhaps the best known of all Winchester repeaters.[13]

The 1873 was primarily chambered for a black-powder .44-40 cartridge utilizing the relatively new centerfire technology.[14] Although the centerfire cartridge—a major advance that allowed for thicker cartridge cases that could take heavier loads as opposed to the rimfire cartridge—had been developed during the Civil War period, it really came into its own after the war. Koller wrote that the Model 1873 was an improvement over the Model 1866 in many ways, including the more powerful cartridge, which held forty grains of black powder as compared to twenty-eight in the Model 1866.[15]

As popular as the 1866 was, the 1873 was embraced by game hunters, and its popularity far surpassed the 1866: while the model was in full production between 1873 and 1919, more than 700,000 were made.[16] Originally chambered

The Deer Rifles We Once Used (continued)

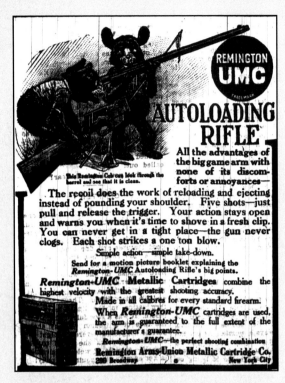

The autoloading rifle developed in the early 1900s, such as the Remington Model 18, represented an advance beyond lever-action technology.
THE NEW NORTH, OCTOBER 24, 1912

for .44-40, other calibers followed, including the .38-40 in 1879 and the .32-20 in 1882.[17] Koller called the Model 1873 "the first American repeating rifle that can be legitimately classified as a deer hunting weapon."[18]

The year 1873 was important for another rifle development as well. The U.S. Army, which had only grudgingly accepted some repeating rifles, such as the Spencer rifle, during the Civil War, remained biased against repeaters and adopted

a Springfield Model 1873 single-shot carbine as its official rifle.[19] This new Springfield was chambered for the .45-70 centerfire, which, according to Williamson, was destined to become the standard against which all others were measured.[20] With seventy grains of black powder, the .45-70 could be accurate at great distances, such as those encountered by soldiers, or big-game hunters in the Western Plains.

Rifle manufacturers were quick to adopt the new, more powerful cartridge for the sportsman. Both Remington and Sharps began making single-shot sporting rifles chambered for a .45-70 cartridge that could send a 405-grain bullet to its target at distances of 600 yards or more.[21]

To meet the demand for more powerful loads, John Browning developed a new lever-action repeater for Winchester that could handle the bigger loads such as the .45-70.[22] The Model 1886 was one of the many Winchester lever actions made famous by Theodore Roosevelt.

Extolling the virtues of the Model 1886, Koller wrote: "In the .45-70 the hunter had almost instant command of 8 reserve cartridges. No other rifle of the black powder era surpassed the dependable Winchester in firepower and the ability to knock down the biggest game within the limit of its range."[23] A testament to its popularity, the Model 1886 was manufactured until 1935.[24] According to *Outdoor Life*, the Model 1886 is "considered by some to be Winchester's greatest lever actions" and is ranked by the magazine as one of the top twenty-five deer rifles of all time.[25]

The Deer Rifles We Once Used (continued)

By the late 1880s the black-powder era was coming to a close as developments in smokeless powder provided a superior alternative. Smokeless powder allowed for a much higher velocity through more controlled and consistent burning of the powder.[26] According to Koller, "For sporting arms the invention of smokeless powder opened the doors to a golden era of gun technology."[27]

Perhaps one of the most enduring advances in terms of deer hunting rifles that came from the availability of smokeless powder was legendary gun designer John Browning's design for Winchester: the Model 1894, the first Winchester designed specifically for smokeless powder.[28] Browning chambered the Model 94 for the .30-30, the first smokeless powder hunting cartridge. Almost immediately, the Model 94 shooting a .30-30 cartridge became *the* standard rifle for deer hunting.[29]

Another popular line of quality repeating rifles for deer hunting was the long line of Marlin lever actions, differing notably from Winchesters by having a side ejection system. "The 1893 Marlin was actually the first truly modern lever action for the medium power deer cartridges, .32-40 and .38-55. In those times a .32-40 was a satisfactory load for whitetails, easy and economical to shoot," wrote Henry M. Stebbins in *Rifles: A Modern Encyclopedia*.[30]

As far as many Wisconsin white-tailed deer hunters of the turn of the century were concerned, deer rifle development could have stopped with the Winchester Model 94 or Marlin Model 93 chambered for .30-30. However, while significant changes in lever-action repeaters were not in the future, many great strides in hunting rifle development were yet to come. "The time from 1900 to 1920 plus saw the fervid development of the autoloader, the beginning of bolt-action popularity, and some modernization of existing lever actions, which hold their own in spite of innovations," Stebbins wrote. "Probably in most hunting camp sessions the automatics got the most discussion, pros and con."[31]

Our deer camp hunters of 1908 were at an interesting place in Wisconsin deer hunting history. The older hunters may have favored the arms they were familiar with from their younger days—Civil War–era weapons, rimfire single-shot rifles, or early repeaters chambered for relatively low-powered black-powder loads—outdated by turn-of-the-century standards but still serviceable in the hands of an experienced Wisconsin deer hunter.

Almost certainly some of the hunters, perhaps the middle-aged ones who grew up in the midst of the lever-action advancements, would have packed various examples of this golden age of the lever action: the famous line of Winchesters, the 1866, 1873, and 1886, shooting black-powder loads, and of course, the Model 94, with the smokeless .30-30 cartridge.

The equally formidable Marlin lever actions, cherished for the beauty of the stock, such as

The Deer Rifles We Once Used (continued)

the Marlin 1893, were touted as "the best rifle for big game" in the 1908 Sears, Roebuck & Co. catalog (where it sold for about sixteen dollars) and available chambered for the popular .30-30 as well as .32-40 and .38-55.[32]

Perhaps it was the younger hunters who were most excited about the latest advances—advances that left behind the deer rifles of the 1800s, heralding the new century—such as the new Winchester Model 1907 "self-loader" (the name Winchester gave to what we know today as semiautomatics) chambered for a .351 cartridge.[33]

Advances would come at a rapid pace in the early twentieth century, including the acceptance and eventual enormous popularity of the bolt-action rifle after World War I. An equally popular cartridge developed by the U.S. Army in 1906 for its Springfield bolt-action military rifle, the .30-06, was destined to earn its own well-deserved place in deer hunting history.

But for the northern Wisconsin deer camp of 1908, the gun rack most likely held a diverse collection of arms that spoke to America's rough and colorful past: rifles with origins in the bloody Civil War, "sporterized" military rifles, those rifles used on the Western Plains as the "West was won," those toted by T. R. on horseback as he tended his Dakota cattle, and those designed specifically to hunt wild game. Small bore, big bore, rimfire, centerfire, both odd and familiar calibers, black-powder and smokeless cartridges, with maybe a sprinkling of the very new and modern—whatever variety of hunting arm

the deer camp of 1908 may have possessed, their purpose during the hunting season would be singular: the taking of white-tailed deer.

NOTES

1. Larry Koller, *The Fireside Book of Guns* (New York: Simon and Schuster, 1959), 169.
2. Ibid., 75.
3. Harold F. Williamson, *Winchester: The Gun That Won the West* (South Brunswick and New York: A. S. Barnes and Company, 1952), 32–33.
4. Koller, *The Fireside Book of Guns*, 75.
5. Ibid., 78.
6. Ibid., 80.
7. Williamson, *Winchester*, 33.
8. Joseph W. Sheilds Jr., *From Flintlock to M1* (New York: Coward-McCann, 1954), 119.
9. Koller, *The Fireside Book of Guns*, 79.
10. Williamson, *Winchester*, 49.
11. Ibid.
12. Dean K. Boorman, *The History of Winchester Firearms* (New York: The Lyons Press, 2001), 34.
13. Ibid., 36.
14. Ibid.
15. Koller, *The Fireside Book of Guns*, 169–170.
16. Boorman, *The History of Winchester Firearms*, 43.
17. Ibid.
18. Koller, *The Fireside Book of Guns*, 169.
19. Sheilds, *From Flintlock to M1*, 112.
20. Williamson, *Winchester*, 51.
21. Boorman, *The History of Winchester Firearms*, 46.
22. Ibid., 60.
23. Koller, *The Fireside Book of Guns*, 182.
24. Boorman, *The History of Winchester Firearms*, 60.
25. "25 Greatest Deer Rifles Ever," *Outdoor Life*, www.outdoorlife.com/article_gallery/25-Greatest-Deer-Rifles-Ever.
26. Sheilds, *From Flintlock to M1*, 141.
27. Koller, *The Fireside Book of Guns*, 168.
28. Boorman, *The History of Winchester Firearms*, 61.
29. Koller, *The Fireside Book of Guns*, 171.
30. Henry M. Stebbins, *Rifles: A Modern Encyclopedia* (Harrisburg, PA: The Stackpole Company, 1958), 10.
31. Ibid., 20.
32. Sears, Roebuck & Co., Chicago, Illinois, Catalog No. 117, 1908, 728.
33. Boorman, *The History of Winchester Firearms*, 69.

The firearms being used in the North Woods were a unique mix of old and new technology. Great strides in rifle development had been made since the Civil War, spurred on by demands from both the military for accurate, dependable weapons for use on the western frontier and the growing ranks of sportsmen looking for the perfect game rifle. A Wisconsin deer camp might have in its armory a wide variety of firearms chambered for an equally wide variety of cartridges. Civil War–era weapons, or "sporterized" versions of them, were readily available and popular with hunters after the war.

Whatever the method or firearm used, it became clear by the deer seasons of 1905 and 1906 that more and more hunters were killing more and more deer in northern Wisconsin. A newspaper report from Woodruff warned, "The slaughter of deer is likely to be greater this year than it has been for some time. If this continues for a few years more, those swift footed animals of our American forests will soon be as rare a sight as the buffalo."[11]

In the early 1900s it was difficult to know just how many deer were being killed during each deer season. Most estimates of the kill were based on the numbers of deer shipped south on the railroads. In 1907 the state's chief warden reported that about 5,600 deer had been transported by the railroads. But he estimated the kill at 10,000, allowing for deer taken straight home or those consumed at camp.[12]

The railroads provided hunters of the late 1800s and early 1900s access to the northern deer woods and the means for successful hunters to transport their deer home. These hunters stand with rifles and deer on the railroad platform at Harshaw in Oneida County. WHi Image ID 28310

Another gauge of hunting pressure was the number of licenses sold. A 1908 newspaper report gave a conservative estimate of 75,000 hunters in northern Wisconsin—an unprecedented number for the time.[13] After the 1908 season, the state's chief warden, again using the number of deer transported (6,268) as a base, estimated the deer take at 11,000—a 1,000-deer increase from the previous year.[14] In response, *The New North* noted, "At this rate it can be plainly seen that unless steps are adopted for more rigid game laws that in time there will be few deer left to kill."[15]

Residents of the small logging towns like Rhinelander, Mercer, and Hayward were witness to the thousands of sport hunters pouring into the north, as well as to the thousands of deer heading south by rail. "Up to the present time few deer have been brought to the city although the express car of every train thru here for the last few days has been loaded with carcasses," reported one North Woods newspaper.[16] However, as had already occurred in eastern states, by the end of the decade, Wisconsin deer hunt-

Larger-than-life deer awaiting transport.
WHi Image ID 28307

ing philosophy was gradually shifting from an "anything goes" attitude to a "save the deer" attitude. Sportsmen realized that changes must be made if the sport of deer hunting was to survive.

Sportsmen's clubs were formed across the state, with very similar agendas. In January 1909, forty sportsmen, including the local game warden, assembled at Rhinelander City Hall to establish the Rhinelander Hunting and Fishing Club. The club immediately addressed deer season regulations, drafting a resolution to forward to the state legislature urging adoption of a law to license all nonresident hunters and to limit hunters "to only one deer per license issued each season." They also recommended a closed season for all game during the first ten days of November, possibly with the intent to reduce illegal preseason hunting.[17]

A deer hunting party poses with deer and supplies by a train on the Chicago, St. Paul, Minneapolis & Omaha railroad in 1912. Hunters were frequently dropped off along the tracks to set up a tent camp or to occupy an old logging camp for the deer season. When the hunt was complete a train would be flagged down for the trip home.
WHi Image ID 28305

Perhaps the most significant recommendation from this hunting club was one echoed by others across the north: the idea that the one-deer bag limit should be for bucks only. "W. B. LaSelle, one of the most enthusiastic nimrods in the county, has made it a rule for several seasons to kill only bucks," reported a Rhinelander newspaper. "Mr. LaSelle opines that if sportsmen adhered strictly to this rule it would tend to prevent the extermination of deer."[18]

The reduced bag limit from two to one deer did occur for the 1909 season, but it was still an either sex rule. However, the growing fear that deer would become a memory akin to buffalo was very real at the time. In the next decade, Wisconsin deer hunters would begin to see a steady movement toward "buck only" laws, closed seasons, and deer refuges. The deer protection movement was beginning.

Successful hunters, each with a fine northern Wisconsin buck—and a couple of does—prepare to head south from the depot at Ladysmith in Rusk County.
Courtesy of Mike Vlahakis

In 1910, as the first decade of the new century closed and the next one began, the country hadn't been involved in a major armed conflict since the Civil War. The United States was awash in prosperity and purpose. The horse-and-buggy days were slowly becoming history as the public demanded new roads on which to drive their increasingly affordable automobiles. Wisconsin's population had grown to well beyond two million people.

In the early 1900s, sport hunters had many options for spending their disposable income.
Appleton Post-Crescent, November 19, 1926

Prosperity meant extra money in the pockets of many Wisconsin sportsmen. Those dollars often were spent on modern rifles and shotguns, cartridges, and outdoor clothing designed just for the new breed of outdoor "sport." Around 1910 a Wisconsin deer hunter could buy almost all of his gear and clothing through the enormously popular Sears, Roebuck & Company catalog. A new lever-action Winchester 1894 .30-30 cost just $15.53. A sporterized version of the Swiss Army Vetterli, featuring a Mauser-type bolt action, could be purchased for $7.00. The latest in rifle technology, the "self-loading" Winchester Model 1907, was $18.90.[19]

Black-powder cartridges were available in a wide variety. A fifty-round box of black powder .44-40 or .38-40 cartridges sold for about seventy cents. The old Spencer black powder cartridges, the rimfire .56-50 and .56-52 were still available and cost about $1.00 for a box of fifty. Center-fire cartridges with smokeless powder were a little more expensive. A box of twenty .30-30 cartridges, either with a soft point or "Metal Patched" bullet, sold for sixty-four cents. A tan duck canvas rifle case, or "cover," could be purchased for sixty-seven cents, a heavy leather case for $1.64. A wool Mackinaw hunting coat, or "frock," cost $2.17.[20]

Prosperity also allowed for the annual deer hunt trek to northern Wisconsin, which was fast becoming a cherished tradition. Thousands of sport hunters boarded the railcars of the Chicago & Northwestern, Wisconsin Central, and the "Soo" each November to be transported from southern and central Wisconsin villages and cities to the wild and remote reaches of the North Woods. The *Wausau Daily Record-Herald* reported on November 10, 1910, that "the rush for the deer fields has been on for several days and still continues. Every north bound passenger train on the St. Paul road has been packed with sportsmen bound for the northern woods."[21]

A northern Wisconsin hunt was an enduring tradition for this group of hunters from the Wausau area, ca. 1900: Walter Ohrmundt, Carl Fitzke, August Ohrmundt, Frank Helke, Robert Nickel, Otto Zahn, Frank Zastrow, and Charles Lenz.
PHOTO COURTESY OF THE MARATHON COUNTY HISTORICAL SOCIETY

The early 1900s were romantic times and young men—fueled by the polar exploits of Roald Amundson and the African adventures of Theodore Roosevelt—dreamed of outdoor adventure. The deer hunt fulfilled, at least in part, these dreams. A man could take gear and his trusty .30-30 rifle, board a train for the "big woods," and for a week or two be free of the staid conventions of the early twentieth century. The groundwork for the Wisconsin hunting tradition was set as the annual deer camp became more than a quest for game—it became a rite.

Throughout the 1910s, deer hunting in the state still translated into a strictly northern Wisconsin hunt. Deer were scarce, still declining in much of central and southern Wisconsin. Early in the decade, deer were becoming rare enough in Marathon County that successful hunts were described in detail by the newspapers. The 1910 hunt of Paul Pophal of Wausau was front-page news. Pophal, who was lucky enough to shoot a nice 196-pound buck near Kelly, was quoted as saying, "There are more deer in Marathon County this year than ever before because of the thick growth of underbrush that has sprung up. There are deer within three miles of the city and it is not necessary to go out of the county to hunt."[22]

Pophal's hunt was not the experience most central Wisconsin hunters were finding in the woods in 1910. In general, their experiences were more similar to that of Carl Krieger, who brought four other hunters seventeen miles east of Wausau for "a six mile tramp," during which the men didn't see sign of a single deer.[23] Toward the decade's end, Marathon joined the growing number of counties completely closed to deer hunting.

Deer hunting had been banned in forty southern and central Wisconsin counties by 1910. In counties that had deer seasons, the hunt of 1909 had initiated a one deer, either sex bag after more than a decade of two deer, either sex limits.[24] Not until 1943 would Wisconsin hunters again be able to take more than one deer per hunter in a single year.

The Deerfoot Lodge

ON NOVEMBER 12, 1929, A VERY SPECIAL PARTY WAS held at the Wausau Club in honor of B. F. Wilson's seventieth birthday. In attendance were nearly all the living members of Deerfoot Lodge, and many of their friends. Several of the guests wore their age-worn hunting togs, and hours were spent in joyful remembrance of the heydays of a classic early Wisconsin deer hunting lodge.

The Deerfoot Lodge officially came into existence in 1910, when a group of Wausau-area businessmen decided to purchase thirty-seven acres of land and an old saloon on the south shore of Laura Lake in Vilas County for the purpose of establishing a deer hunting lodge. The initial lodge membership read like a veritable "Who's Who" of Wausau society and industry leaders at the time. Most of the men had ties to Wisconsin River lumbering, paper, and power-development industries and included such notables as Cyrus Carpenter "C. C." Yawkey, David Clark "D. C." Everest, Neal Brown, Mark Clayton Ewing, and Charles Gilbert.

M. B. Rosenberry's detailed account of Deerfoot Lodge has preserved the memory of a grand old traditional deer camp that existed in northern Wisconsin during the early days. WHS LIBRARY PAMPHLET 99-5202

With their backgrounds in the business world, the men naturally decided they needed to incorporate. On March 8, 1910, they filed articles of incorporation with the Wisconsin Secretary of State, perhaps making Deerfoot Lodge the first Wisconsin corporation ever established for the purpose of deer hunting. At this time, the annual meeting was set as the day after opening day of deer season, which at the time was November 10.

Founding fathers of the lodge rarely missed an open season throughout its twenty-five-year history. Judge M. B. Rosenberry, the official lodge secretary, kept impeccable records of lodge hunts, which survive today as a manuscript compiled by Rosenberry in 1940. "A History of Deerfoot Lodge: Memories of Happy Hunting" offers a remarkable glimpse into Wisconsin's deer hunting past.[1]

According to Rosenberry, Deerfoot Lodge's origins actually dated back to 1906, when logging company owner B. F. Wilson invited Wausau resident Neal Brown to go deer hunting with him in the vicinity of Star Lake in Vilas

The Deerfoot Lodge (continued)

PHOTO MEMORIES OF DEERFOOT LODGE

A TRAINFUL FOR DEERFOOT LODGE
Back row - Left to right: D. C. Everest, Judge Ewing,
J. M. Duer, E. A. Gooding (in doorway), Emil Brastz,
J. W. Laut, H. A. Patterson. Front row on platform:
B. F. Wilson, C. C. Yawkey, Neal Brown (Hand on
wheel), P. M. Wilson, W. H. Bissel (leaning on rail).
C. S. Gilbert, (extreme right). Sitting on platform--
M. C. Ewing. OnGround--G. K. Gooding, G.D.Jones.

THE SLEEPING SHANTY

COOK SHANTY AND DINING ROOM

Deerfoot Lodge

More images capturing Deerfoot.
WHS LIBRARY PAMPHLET 99-5202

County. Around 1900 Wilson's company was under contract with the Milwaukee-based Land, Log and Timber Company to log 800 million board feet of pine timber in the Star Lake area. The logging company had previously purchased a homestead on the north shore of Laura Lake, near Star Lake; this site would serve as the hunting party's base camp. Brown organized a group of seven hunters, most of whom would become future Deerfoot Lodge members.

The group continued to hunt the area through the 1909 season. During that hunt, Wilson proposed that the party look into purchasing a property for sale on the south side of Laura Lake to establish a permanent camp. "The matter was discussed and before we left camp it was finally agreed that if the property could be procured at a reasonable price it should be purchased," wrote Rosenberry.

The property the group ultimately purchased consisted of a saloon, the saloon keeper's house, and some outbuildings, one of which was a simple square "shanty" known as the Snake House into which "lumberjacks were thrown when they became so intoxicated they could not navigate, hence its name."

The Deerfoot men converted the saloon into their dining hall and renovated the residence to accommodate "sixteen men, two in a bed." The Snake House also was renovated, becoming sleeping quarters for guides and overflow guests.

The Deerfoot Lodge members were fortunate to acquire the services of Charlie Anderson, a local resident and woodsman who had been associated with the original party since their first hunt in 1906. He became the property's permanent caretaker after the lodge's incorporation in 1910.

"It was Charlie who made Deerfoot Lodge possible, for as Caretaker and Quasi-host, any member of the Lodge could go there at any time of the year and find warm shelter, food and a hearty welcome," wrote Rosenberry.

✦ ✦ ✦ ✦ ✦

When the lodge was established in 1910, deer hunting in the north was still a primitive affair.

The Deerfoot Lodge (continued)

The buildings of Deerfoot Lodge on the shores of Lake Laura in Vilas County.
WHS LIBRARY PAMPHLET 99-5202

Lodge members climbed aboard the train in Wausau and disembarked at Star Lake. From there it was by horseback to the lodge. Although Deerfoot Lodge was situated amid hundreds of acres of cutover, it was an unpopulated chunk of the state. "The whole territory for many miles to the north and east of Star Lake was at that time unoccupied," wrote Rosenberry. "We very seldom saw the tracks of other hunters." The members knew just how big the country was, and they had detailed rules to follow if lost, as well as certain landmarks that delineated the boundaries of their hunting grounds. "There was always the danger on a dark stormy day of a hunter becoming bewildered," noted Rosenberry.

Hunting success at the lodge peaked in 1912, when a record was set with thirty-one deer—nineteen bucks and twelve does—taken. Using 1912 as an example of a typical season, Rosenberry described the members' hunting strategies: "We employed two methods of hunting, first the drive method, and second tracking and still hunting. It may be said that our still hunting was oftentimes not very still but nevertheless we succeeded in bagging a good deal of game."

Interestingly, the hunter's primary mode of transportation in the field was by Indian pony. At the time of the establishment of Deerfoot Lodge, at least two bands of Ojibwe existed in the area. The Partridge Lake Band, led by Mary Escanaba, had several ponies broken to the saddle. "Each year we rented these ponies from Mary Escanaba for fifty cents a day," noted Rosenberry. "The ponies were a great help in bringing back the deer."

With twenty-four hunters in camp for the 1912 season, opening day would have been a flurry of activity. A regular logging camp–style breakfast of coffee, toast, hot cakes, sausages, potatoes, bread, camp doughnuts, and more was available. "There was no formality about breakfast," wrote Rosenberry. "Some were on

The Deerfoot Lodge (continued)

time, some were late, some were very late, but those who were late had no ground for complaint."

The Indian ponies were saddled, gear was readied, and the serious hunters were usually at their posts by sunrise. Some of the more woods-experienced members of the lodge served as guides, placing hunters at their posts and then pushing the deer toward the shooters. "These drives generally yielded from two to three, sometimes four or five deer," noted Rosenberry.

The men of Deerfoot Lodge developed a culture of tradition for the camp, both in the field and inside the lodge. Stories were told and

AT DEERFOOT LODGE, AUG. 29, 1925. Left to Right: C. S. Gilbert, M. B. Rosenberry, J. W. Laut, C. C. Yawkey, B. F. Wilson, E. A. Gooding, Walter Alexander, A. L. Kreutzer, G. P. Ewing, W. H. Bissell.

Members of Deerfoot Lodge, 1925, many of whom were prominent Wausau businessmen.
WHS Library Pamphlet 99-5202

retold, poems written, and songs sung so that the lodge developed its own oral history, like an ancient tribe. A Big Game Medal was acquired and awarded annually to the lodge member who brought back the largest deer.

As the 1920s came to a close, Deerfoot Lodge began to fade as well. After the record thirty-one deer taken in 1912, hunter success slowly declined, reaching new lows in the 1920s. Only two deer were taken in 1921, and six were killed during the lodge's last official season in 1928. The founding fathers of Deerfoot Lodge, old men by this time, realized that the world had changed around them. Original members including Neal Brown and M. C. Ewing had passed on. Younger hunters were leaving Deerfoot to join other, perhaps more exciting, camps. In 1930 original member B. F. Wilson lamented the changes in a letter to members: "I agree with you that Deerfoot is a thing of the past so far as hunting is concerned. There is plenty of game but the country is too open and accessible to automobile hunters and they certainly are a wild lot."

Deerfoot's end was assured after Charlie Anderson took ill and died in Rhinelander in 1931 at the age of eighty. The decision to sell Deerfoot Lodge was hard but inevitable. The original members had paid $1,200 for the property in 1910 and were asking $1,500 for it in 1935. Even though they knew it was worth more due to many improvements to the old buildings, they accepted an offer of $1,300

The Deerfoot Lodge (continued)

```
        APPENDIX F

   H U N T I N G   S O N G S
             O F
   D E E R   F O O T   L O D G E

             By

        JAMES M. DUER

          PARODIED

FOR THE FAMOUS "BEAR DINNER"

TUNE--Working on the Railroad.

             I

Each fall we go to hunt the deer,
A band of ardent nimrods,
At Deer Foot Lodge we take our cheer,
For standing on the run-way.

CHORUS.

I've been standing on the run-way,
All the live long day;
I've been standing on the run-way,
For a deer to come my way;
Can't you hear the captain's orders,
Rise up so early in the morn,
Can't you hear the captain shouting,
Charlie, blow your horn.

             II

Our ardent hope and fondest dream,
Is bringing down the winner,
As forth we steal at dawn's first gleam,
To stand upon the run-way.

CHORUS.

             III

When evening shadows gently climb,
We turn our faces homeward,
And dream of better luck next time,
From standing on the run-way.
CHORUS.
```

```
             IV.

Around the fire light's ruddy glow
We gather close each evening,
And swap our yarns of weal or woe,
From standing on the run-way.
CHORUS.

   ANTICIPATING THE 1914 HUNT

   TUNE--"On Wisconsin."

             I.

On to Deer Foot, on to Deer Foot,
With its plenty and good cheer,
On to Deer Foot, on to Deer Foot,
To hunt the wily deer,
On to Deer Foot, on to Deer Foot
To drive dull care away,
And make us all feel so happy, young and gay.

             II.

On to Deer Foot, on to Deer Foot,
With its laughter and its fun,
On to Deer Foot, on to Deer Foot
To get them on the run,
On to Deer Foot, on to Deer Foot,
But may we all take care,
Never shoot till we're sure a deer is there.

             III.

On to Deer Foot, on to Deer Foot,
To drive and track and stand,
On to Deer Foot, on to Deer Foot,
To work to beat the band,
On to Deer Foot, on to Deer Foot,
Oh! may we have good luck,
And several of us get a fine big buck.

   DEDICATED TO THE 1914 HUNT

   TUNE--"John Brown's Body."

We love to see the bounding
Of the rapid running deer
O'er the knobs and pot holes
Where we hunt him ev'ry year;
```

Deerfoot Lodge members were serious hunters but still made time for fun—
including rollicking renditions of songs created for deer camp.
WHS Library Pamphlet 99-5202

The Deerfoot Lodge (continued)

from Edward C. Koepke of Chicago, concluding the sale on October 14, 1935. Upon liquidation of the lodge and receiving his share of the proceeds, member M. P. McCullough wrote in a letter to his fellow lodge members: "There will probably never be another Deerfoot Lodge, or anything like it, for our crowd, and it does hurt to have it pass out of our lives. Deerfoot Lodge really made a record and brought every one of us closer together."

For twenty-five years, these captains of industry who had largely been born and raised in the decades right after the Civil War drew on their own experiences, their own perceptions and desires, to create, as others were also doing at the time, the foundation and the pattern for the North Woods deer camp that persist to this day. Perhaps influenced by the legendary King Arthur and his knights, tales of rough-and-tumble California frontier life, and Jack London's stories of far north adventure, the men of Deerfoot fused together the sense of camaraderie and the importance of tradition with the excitement of hunting a quarry as fine as the whitetail. In doing so, they created the very soul of the Wisconsin deer camp.

As John Madson wrote: "For as long as men have hunted they have banded into special hunting packs with their own taboos, traditions, and rituals. And sometimes the companionship and the rituals become more important than the hunt itself, and sometimes the greatest pleasure is in anticipation and recollection, with the hunt only serving to bond the two."[2]

NOTES

1. M. B. Rosenberry, "A History of Deerfoot Lodge: Memories of Happy Hunting," August 1941, Wisconsin Historical Society Pamphlet Collection. Call Number: 99-5202.
2. John Madson, "Why Men Hunt," in *A Hunter's Heart: Honest Essays on Blood Sport*, ed. David Peterson (New York: Henry Holt and Co., 1996), 131.

Deer hunting regulations were becoming increasingly stringent—a contrast to the weak and confusing deer hunting regulations of the late 1800s. Most Wisconsin newspapers provided a summary of regulations just prior to the season as a caution for the hunters ready to venture back up north to deer camp. A 1912 account from Rhinelander exhibits how many regulations targeted the wild and indiscriminate methods of the market and subsistence hunters:

The laws restrict the hunting of deer to the last 20 days of November and geographically to certain counties in the north. It is also unlawful to use dogs in hunting, to hunt at night, or to kill deer in the water and on the ice. Pits, pitfalls, traps, and snares of all kinds are prohibited. A ban is placed on the use of artificial lights also, and the placing of salt in any place for the purpose of enticing deer. Hunting from elevated platforms or scaffolding is prohibited. Moose are prohibited at all times and at all places. It is also unlawful for a hunter, whether a resident or non-resident of the state, to kill more than one deer in one season or to have in his possession the skin of any deer when it is in the red coat or any fawn when it is in the spotted coat.[25]

Despite the tightening of deer hunting regulations and some increased zeal on the part of wardens in pursuing offenders, the old methods persisted in many locales.

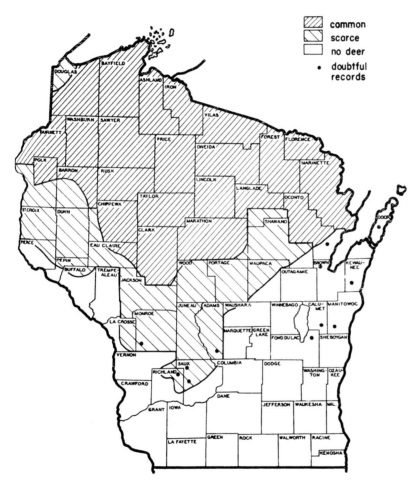

APPROXIMATE RANGE OF WHITE-TAILED DEER-1912

- ⧄ common
- ⧅ scarce
- ☐ no deer
- • doubtful records

Source: "Mammals of Illinois and Wisconsin" by C. B. Cory.

This map shows that by 1912, deer were becoming less numerous in southern and central Wisconsin.
A Century of Wisconsin Deer

Perils of the Early Days of Wisconsin Deer Hunting

TODAY WISCONSIN DEER HUNTING IS CONSIDERED AN extremely safe activity. Despite the fact that for a few days each November hundreds of thousands of hunters—most armed with high-powered rifles—take to the field intent on shooting at a whitetail, hunting accidents are relatively rare and fatalities caused by firearms are even rarer. This wasn't the case in the early days of Wisconsin deer hunting.

The newspapers of the early 1900s were laden with reports of death and destruction. In the days before the development of strong federal and state regulations designed to protect the public's health and well-being, and with relatively primitive medical practices and facilities, death by accident was a common occurrence and came in a multitude of ways. Farmers routinely were killed by machinery or livestock, train

An educational photo from 1926 illustrates what not to do when walking in the woods while hunting. High rates of injury and death in the early years of Wisconsin deer hunting were the black cloud over the sport. Eventually, more stringent regulations as well as hunter education programs greatly improved safety.
WHi IMAGE ID 9445

Perils of the Early Days of Wisconsin Deer Hunting (continued)

accidents killed both passengers and railroad workers, fatal logging accidents were notoriously common in the North Woods, and in November of each year deer hunting accidents were added to the collection.

An account of an accident that occurred near Merrill in Lincoln County in the fall of 1900 was not unusual for the time:

> Fred Sell was found dead yesterday on the ice of the Copper river, five miles north of here, by several hunters who spent the day near the place. Attracted by prolonged howls of a dog they discovered the remains. He had evidently been crossing the river when the ice broke through and in going down the hammer of his gun caught on the edge of the ice. The bullet struck him under the chin, shattered his brain and passed out behind his ear.[1]

A less serious hunting incident was reported the same day from Merrill: "Len Hinch of Dudley, a summer resort north of here, was shot in the arm by Edward Heard, who took the man for a deer. The bullet pierced Hinch's clothes but passed out without fatally injuring him."[2]

Both accidents highlight the two most common causes of serious deer hunting accidents in the early years of sport hunting as well as in years to come: the shooting of one hunter by another who shoots without identifying the target, and the self-inflicted gunshot wound

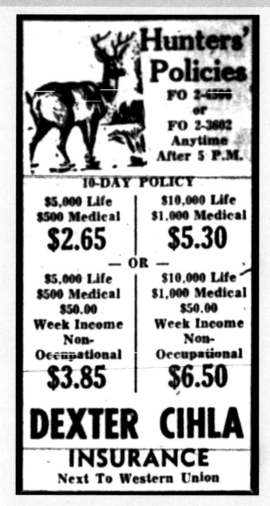

Special short-term deer hunter life and health insurance policies could be purchased prior to the season in many North Woods towns in the 1950s and '60s. Whether necessary or not, they provided some sense of security.
THE NEW NORTH, NOVEMBER 15, 1957

caused by mishandling a weapon (frequently a lever-action rifle). Of course, there were a multitude of variations of these types of accidents.

Perils of the Early Days of Wisconsin Deer Hunting (continued)

"An accident of a peculiarly-distressing nature happened near Iron Mountain, Michigan, yesterday," it was reported from Marinette in 1900. "Fyde Shaddock, a well-known resident of that place, and Peter Weber went out to shoot deer. They traveled about eight miles, when Weber got a shot at a deer. The shot took effect, but the bullet passed through the animal and entered Shaddock's side, inflicting a wound from which he cannot recover."[3]

Tragically, historical accounts of deer hunting accidents include many involving children, since in the early days of deer hunting there were no restrictions regarding a hunter's age. A November 1900 report from Sparta, Monroe County: "A 9-year old son of Thomas Jenkins was accidentally shot while hunting by his 4-year old brother. The bullet entered just below the heart. It is not known how serious the wound may prove."[4]

In what might seem ghoulish detail to a reader today, a newspaper report matter-of-factly described a gun-handling accident in the Wausau area also in the fall of 1900: "Adolph, the 15-year old son of William Kornhusk, a farmer in the town of Wausau, was accidentally shot and instantly killed last evening. He and his brother had been out hunting and on their way home stopped at a neighbor's and set the gun down near some planks. In picking it up the hammer hit the plank, discharging the gun. The charge . . . entered the lad's head near the right eye, blowing off the top of his skull."[5]

Until deer populations began to recover in central and southern Wisconsin in the 1950s and 1960s, hunter pressure and, consequently, hunting accidents were concentrated in the big deer woods of the north. A northern newspaper reported on the end of the 1912 season with a noticeable sigh of relief:

> The deer hunting season of 1912 in this state is now a thing of the past. Hunters are out of the woods and one can now feel almost safe to walk through the brush without fear that he may become a subject for the undertaker. The list of fatalities in the northern woods this fall was heavy. Most of the deaths were due to carelessness of hunters mistaking human beings for deer. Lack of caution in handling guns was also responsible for several accidents.[6]

As deer hunter numbers increased to more than 100,000, hunting accidents also increased. The 1915 deer season, when an estimated 149,000 deer tags were sold, tallied thirty-three hunters killed and thirty-six injured. The next year the state game warden had some words of advice: "Captain C. W. Rickerman, of Madison, state fish and game warden, hopes to greatly reduce the killed and wounded during the season's deer hunting in Wisconsin by urging all hunters to wear red caps. These articles of apparel will serve as a sort of headlight. Captain Rickerman also urges hunters to curb their enthusiasm to the extent of refraining from shooting at every moving object."[7]

Perils of the Early Days of Wisconsin Deer Hunting (continued)

At this same time, safety issues became a part of the heated controversy over the one-buck law. Proponents of the law cited increased safety as a positive aspect of it. "One good thing about the one-buck law is its tendency in decreasing the number of hunting accidents in the northern Wisconsin woods," an old Rhinelander area hunter was quoted by the press as saying in 1916. "The majority of hunters look carefully at what they intend to shoot before pulling the trigger, and while they may not hesitate to kill a doe, are not apt to shoot a man. Hunters are learning not to shoot at everything that moves."[8]

While hunters were awakening to the need to be safer in the woods—and many were voluntarily wearing red and practicing safe gun handling—accidents continued to follow the same old pattern. In 1921, for instance, the *Wausau Daily Herald* reported on two hunting-season deaths: "Two Wisconsin hunters have been killed during the opening six days of hunting season.

Temporary hunter insurance offered by the Flieth Insurance Agency of Wausau in 1968 included coverage in the event of heart attack.
Wausau Daily Record-Herald, November 14, 1968

Christian Hansen, twenty year old Baronette youth, was killed by Frank Brown, veteran huntsman, who mistook him for a deer. Curt Benlow, forty-seven, Clinton, was killed when a rifle fell from the hangar and was discharged, the bullet piercing his heart."[9]

It wasn't until 1945 that the wearing of red became mandatory. The regulation read that at least 50 percent of a hunter's upper-body clothing must be red, "including caps and sleeves of garments."[10] The red law came in a year of a short five-day deer season that many felt would add to hunting hazards. The press reported: "Because of the shorter than normal season, the hazards probably will be greater than usual, officials declared. . . . [A] larger concentration of men in the woods is expected."[11] Also in 1945, several of Wisconsin's more populated counties were designated as "shotgun only" for the first time.[12]

The red law and increasing emphasis on safety seemed to be improving the accident statistics. A report from the 1949 season, also a short, five-day season, summed up the most recent numbers: "Wisconsin's five day season

Perils of the Early Days of Wisconsin Deer Hunting (continued)

Hunter safety students who receive a minimum of ten hours of instruction receive these patches upon graduation.
WISCONSIN DEPARTMENT OF NATURAL RESOURCES, BUREAU OF HUNTER SAFETY

for shooting deer which ended Wednesday was one of the safest on record despite what may have been a record kill. The latest count showed seven dead from gunshot wounds while hunting compared with 12 deaths—10 by gunshot—last year when bucks only could be shot. In 1947, six out of 221,672 died of gunshot wounds and in 1946, the all-time high of 21 dead and 41 wounded was recorded with 200,190 hunters in the field."[13]

In 1951 orange became another color that met the visibility requirement. "Under a new law,

50 percent of a deer hunter's jacket, excluding the sleeves, and 50 percent of the visible part of the cap must be red or orange," reported the *Rhinelander Daily News*.[14]

Four years later a heavy deer season loss of life was reported: "Wisconsin's nine day 1955 deer hunting season closed at dusk Sunday leaving at least 20 hunters dead—one of the heaviest tolls of modern times."[15] However, out of the twenty dead, twelve had died of heart attacks. Regardless of that fact, the eight persons killed by firearms represented the highest gun accident death toll since 1942.[16]

It was in the 1950s that an increasing number of hunter-safety and firearms handling courses were offered to the public by volunteer instructors, often certified by the National Rifle Association. The first official state-sponsored hunter education class was held in Dunn County near Boyceville on August 24, 1967. The program, simply named "Hunter Safety," was voluntary.[17]

In 1967, yellow was allowed as another color option for hunters' clothing.

With the opportunity for hunters to take part in a growing number of hunter-safety training opportunities and the continued use of safety colors for clothing, the deer woods seemed to be getting much safer by the 1970s. The press reported, "Only two deer hunters were shot to death during the 1972 season, the lowest toll since the state began keeping records in 1940. Another 38 were injured during the season."[18]

Although eleven hunters died from gunshot wounds during the 1978 deer season, statisti-

Perils of the Early Days of Wisconsin Deer Hunting (continued)

cally it was one of the safest deer seasons in many years, with a low percentage of hunting accidents and fatalities per 100,000 hunters. "One of the most alarming statistics that came out of the 1978 report was that of the 119 shooting accidents that did occur, 97 or 81.5 percent of them occurred within the same hunting party. That included 10 of the 14 fatal shootings statewide," reported the *Rhinelander Daily News*.[19]

While deer hunting safety had come an incredibly long way since the early days, accidents still occurred, a frustrating issue for deer managers and hunter-safety advocates alike as they knew that most, if not all, hunting accidents were preventable. In 1980 another step was taken in the attempt to make hunters more visible to each other: hunter orange, more commonly known as blaze orange, became the required safety clothing color. In 1979 a newspaper reported on the coming requirement: "This hunting season will be the last for the traditional hunting red. Beginning with the 1980 season hunters will be required to wear the blaze orange. The law states that during the 1980 gun deer season, 50 percent of the outer garment worn by hunters above the waist must be blaze orange including the hat."[20]

Blaze orange had its critics at first, mostly those unhappy with having to give up the old red wool Mackinaw for hunting. However, blaze orange was quickly elevated to the status of a Wisconsin icon, right next to brats, beer, whitetails, Lombardi, and Lambeau. In fact, the favorite cold-weather gear at late-season Packers games is often the heavyweight blaze-orange clothing worn during deer season—making for a mix of green, gold, and blaze orange in the stands.

With progressive regulations designed to increase deer hunting safety, such as the adoption of blaze orange, in full force in the 1980s, it seemed that, ultimately, safety still came down to the personal responsibility of each individual hunter. "It can be said over and over, but as long as there are still hunting accidents, hunters must plan mentally and physically for their hunt and then hunt their plan," said Mel Lange, Wisconsin Department of Natural Resources law enforcement safety specialist for the North Central District, in a November 1982 *Rhinelander Daily News* article. "Every year throughout Wisconsin hunters are being shot by their hunting partners and, in most cases, investigation has found that failure to adequately plan their hunt, or not following the plan, has resulted in death or injury. Almost 75 percent of all hunting accidents involve members of the same hunting party who do not mean to hurt anyone else, but without maintaining mental control over their hunting situation get involved in an accident."[21]

The last big step toward removing the careless hunter from the safety equation occurred in 1985 when it became mandatory for all hunters born on or after January 1, 1973, to successfully complete a "Hunter Education and Firearms Safety" course in order to purchase a hunting license. The course offered today covers much more than simple gun safety rules. Participants

Perils of the Early Days of Wisconsin Deer Hunting (continued)

certainly learn about firearms—how they work and how to handle them—but they are also instructed in wildlife species identification, habitat, and management, responsibility and ethics, conservation, handling outdoor emergencies, and law enforcement and one's role in hunting's future. The minimum number of hours for a hunter safety course is ten; the average length is eighteen hours, which includes a combination of indoor classroom and outdoor gun-handling and shooting activities.[22]

According to the DNR, hunting accidents have steadily declined since formal hunting education courses began; by 1996, there were 90 percent fewer accidents than in 1967.[23] Considering the huge number of hunters who participate in the annual rite that is the Wisconsin deer season, it is clear that the efforts of many committed individuals have transformed a once very dangerous endeavor into one that with training and a good dose of common sense can be an extremely safe and enjoyable activity for hunters of all ages.

NOTES

1. "Hunter Kills Himself," *Rhinelander Herald*, November 1900.
2. Ibid.
3. "Shot Goes Through Deer, Wounding Man," *Rhinelander Herald*, November 1900.
4. "Mistaken for a Deer," *Rhinelander Herald*, November 1900.
5. "Boy's Head Blown Off," *Rhinelander Herald*, October 1900.
6. "Deer Season Ends: Many Fatalities Occur in This Part of Wisconsin," *The New North*, December 5, 1912.
7. "Asks Deer Hunters to Wear Red Caps," *The New North*, November 5, 1916.
8. "Claims Buck Laws Check Accidents," *The New North*, November 30, 1916.
9. "Hunting Season Takes Its Toll," *Wausau Daily Herald*, November 18, 1921.
10. "Hazards Greater Due to Shorter Hunting Season, Officials Believe," *Rhinelander Daily News*, November 21, 1945.
11. Ibid.
12. "A Chronology of Wisconsin Deer Hunting: From Closed Seasons to Antlerless Permits," Wisconsin Department of Natural Resources, news release, November 14, 2003.
13. "One of the 'Safest' Seasons Brought Record Deer Kill," *Rhinelander Daily News*, November 25, 1949.
14. "Going Deer Hunting? Better Study These Rules for 1951," *Rhinelander Daily News*, November 9, 1951.
15. "Deer Hunting Season Ends with 20 Dead," *Rhinelander Daily News*, November 28, 1955.
16. Ibid.
17. "History of Wisconsin's Hunter and Bowhunter Education Programs," Wisconsin Department of Natural Resources, provided by Tim Lawhern, DNR hunter safety administrator.
18. "Hunting 'Army' Arriving," *Rhinelander Daily News*, November 16, 1973.
19. "Last Season's Deer Hunt Was Safe One for State," *Rhinelander Daily News*, November 18, 1979.
20. Ibid.
21. "If You're Not Sure, Then Don't Shoot," *Rhinelander Daily News*, November 21, 1982.
22. "Hunter Education," Wisconsin Department of Natural Resources, www.dnr.state.wi.us/org/es/enforcement/safety/hunted.htm.
23. "History of Wisconsin's Hunter and Bowhunter Education Programs," Wisconsin Department of Natural Resources, provided by Tim Lawhern, DNR hunter safety administrator.

WOUNDED DEER KILLS A MAN

Struggle in Wisconsin Lake Ends in Death of Sportsman.

Antigo (Wis.) Dispatch to St. Paul Dispatch.

That a fight with a wounded deer ended in the death of David Gibson was revealed when the body of the hunter was found late today in Sawyer Lake, near here. Gibson was out hunting Monday and wounded a large deer, which plunged into the lake. Gibson followed the wounded animal and was killed in the struggle.

WASHINGTON POST, NOVEMBER 29, 1914

In 1912 Stanley Curry, the principal of the Three Lakes School in Oneida County, was killed while hunting when buckshot fired into his legs after he accidentally triggered a set gun placed for deer. *The New North* reported the incident: "The gun responsible for the accident was no doubt heavily loaded as the charge shattered both of the unfortunate man's legs. The gun which caused Mr. Curry's death had evidently been placed in the woods for the purpose of killing deer. It was a trap arrangement, the trigger connected by a wire to a concealed spring. The parties who set the gun are not known although the people of Three Lakes are said to have their suspicions as to who the guilty ones are."[26]

✦ ✦ ✦ ✦ ✦

Northern Wisconsin deer numbers seemed too plentiful in some areas and declining in others. In 1912 deer were thought to be in abundance in many areas due to "excessive rain and lack of fire."[27] A Rhinelander paper reported, "In some localities in northern Wisconsin the animals [deer] have been reported scarce, but this does not seem to be the case in Oneida County."[28] There were, however, increasing signs that deer numbers were actually declining, even in the big northern woods. Earlier in the decade it was reported from Oneida County: "From all over this county and other parts of northern Wisconsin comes the report that deer are not as numerous as in former years, as the timber is rapidly being cut, or destroyed by fires, the animals seek other haunts, roaming to the wilder and more remote regions. The guns of the pot hunters are also doing much towards diminishing the deer."[29]

During the deer season of 1912, Governor Francis E. McGovern and his entourage abandoned their hunting grounds in Langlade County to try greener pastures in Ashland County. "They were on their way to Glidden, where they will continue the hunt after having found deer in the vicinity of Elcho scarce," reported *The New North*.[30] It was also reported in 1912 that in northern Michigan, just across the border, deer numbers were "rapidly growing fewer in numbers."[31]

Nevertheless, a preseason prediction for the 1913 season was optimistic: "November 11th is the magic date, and the nineteen days following that will be just as important. The word has come down from the north that the woods are full of deer this year, and many a rifle that was put away last fall 'forever' has been brought out and made ready for the annual trip north."[32]

Despite such optimism, the 1913 hunting season didn't produce as expected. "That fewer deer were killed in northern Wisconsin during the hunting season of 1913 than last year is the opinion of deputy game wardens and others who are in a position to know," wrote *The New North*. "The lack of snow was a large factor in decreasing the annual slaughter of deer, tracking being impossible."[33]

While weather and absence of the all-important tracking snow certainly had some bearing on the reduced deer kill, hunters were beginning to realize that there really were fewer deer in the woods. "There also appeared to be a scarcity of the animals not noticeable in previous years," noted *The New North*. "Hundreds of old-time hunters who journeyed into the Wisconsin woods in quest of venison returned without their quarry, due it is said, to the scarcity of game and unfavorable weather conditions."[34]

Those that had a statewide perspective saw a bigger picture—and it was not good. The problem was that with the only healthy deer numbers occurring in the northern third of the state, the burgeoning numbers of sport hunters had concentrated there. Harvest records, although based on rough estimates, were broken repeatedly in the first two decades of the new century, the majority of the take coming from northern counties such as Ashland, Bayfield, Douglas, Sawyer, Iron, and Oneida. While deer populations in the North Woods seemed healthy, they weren't limitless.

In 1911 state game warden John A. Scholts estimated a total statewide population of only around 20,000 animals, which was perhaps a conservative number. According to a newspaper account, Scholts also stated prior to that year's deer season that 80,000 licenses had been sold.[35] Whenever increasing sport hunting pressure was added to the challenges of harsh northern winters, abundant predators, and postlogging wildfires, the northern population was bound to decline.

The northern herd had grown somewhat in the late 1800s and early 1900s, due primarily to the improved habitat for deer in the cutover land. But by 1910 a combination of intense hunting pressure and uncontrolled wildfires had resulted in a significant population decline.[36] The hunting public was beginning to take notice, a consequence of which was additional hunting regulations in the early 1900s, including the one-deer bag limit rule enacted in 1909.[37] In 1915 mounting concern about the dwindling deer population meant another regulatory step: Wisconsin's first buck-only season.

The one-buck law was a firestorm of controversy from the start, and sportsmen came down on both sides of the issue. In 1916 F. B. Moody of the State Conservation Commission anticipated a hard fight over the one-buck law in the Legislature's 1917 session. He stated that "opinion regarding the buck law is divided through the state, some believing it to be a good thing both for the preservation of deer and the prevention of accidents, while others declare that it should be wiped off the statutes."[38]

Those opposed to the one-buck law felt it was the cause of many does being shot and left to rot in the woods—the same argument that detractors of the one-deer bag limit had used a few years earlier.

A Spooner newspaper condemned the law during the first one-buck law season of 1915: "Nearly every returning hunter tells of finding many does and fawns dead in the woods. The so-called 'buck law' is being widely condemned. One old-time hunter remarked that it would take at least five years of a closed season to replenish the deer that will be left dead in the woods this season."[39]

The comments of Dr. H. L. Garner of Rhinelander, published in *The New North* during the second one-buck season in 1916, shared this opinion. Garner declared the one-buck law "to be one of the greatest farces ever placed upon the statutes of Wisconsin." He felt that "over one half the deer shot during the season are does. Many hunters when they sight a deer in the distance are unable to ascertain its sex and shoot in the hope that the animal is a buck. When they find that they have killed a doe they leave the carcass in the woods, fearing contact with the wardens."[40]

The one-buck law may have been the first great deer management controversy Wisconsin had experienced. As with any great controversy regarding deer, there was another side with its staunch advocates. Many in favor of the one-buck season promoted the idea that it prevented many hunting accidents since it forced hunters to be more aware of what they were shooting.

"One good thing about the one-buck law is its tendency in decreasing the number of hunting accidents in the northern Wisconsin woods," an "old hunter" told *The New North* in 1916. "The majority of hunters look carefully at what they intend to shoot before pulling the trigger."[41]

The very root of the one-buck law, however, was the growing belief that any hunting of does was detrimental to the deer population. For its supporters, the one-buck law was critical: it would save deer from outright extinction in the state.

Conservation Commission member Moody was correct: there was a legislative fight over the one-buck law; it was repealed in time for the 1917 deer season, but not without compromise. While the bag limit returned to one deer, either sex, the traditional twenty-day season was reduced to ten days, beginning on November 21 rather than November 11.

With the one-buck law repealed, alarmed Conservation Commission officials sympathetic to the one-buck law urged hunters to voluntarily refrain from shooting does. The *Wausau Daily Record Herald* reported, "Notwithstanding the law permits the killing of does, the conservation commissioners ask the sportsmen to spare them, for it is upon them that we must depend to produce the deer supply for the coming years. If the sportsmen kill the deer indiscriminately, it will be a matter of but a few years until the sport of deer hunting is a thing of the past."[42]

The Conservation Commission's official statement read in part: "Three years open season under our present law will wind up deer hunting in Wisconsin during the lives of our present sportsman. So we ask you, men, in your own interest, if for no other reason, that you spare the does."[43]

The Conservation Commission also called on hunters to be extremely cautious in the woods, since they felt the return to an either-sex season would raise the risks of fatalities as hunters felt free to shoot at anything. "We have issued up to the present time 56,000 deer tags which, after making liberal deductions, indicate that there will be over 50,000 hunters in deer territory this season," stated the commission. "This is a much larger army than is mobilized in any of Uncle Sam's camps in the United States, and we caution hunters to look twice before they shoot, or the casualty list will exceed those from France."[44]

Although the one-buck law had been repealed and either-sex hunts were held in the decade's last three years, the writing was on the wall: 1910 to 1920 was to go down in history as a decade of transition and change, a hybrid between the liberal, anything goes attitude of the "ought" years and the ever-growing idea that something drastic must be done to save Wisconsin's deer and preserve the hunt. Central to the controversy was the belief that restricting or banning the taking of antlerless deer was the key to long-term deer survival.

In 1919 W. E. Barber, head of the Wisconsin Conservation Commission and a strong proponent of the one-buck law, addressed the members of the Portage County Fish and Game Association in Stevens Point:

> This year and next there is an open season for deer in Wisconsin, but for the 10 years following there will be a closed season just as sure as the sun shines. It seems impossible to get proper legislation to protect the deer. This year 75,000 licenses were issued to deer hunters in Wisconsin who will soon be going into the north woods. What would happen if one-fourth of that number shot one deer? There would not be a dozen deer left.
>
> When you have a buck law you will have deer as long as the state stands. This has been proven in 10 states and in Wisconsin too, before the buck law was

repealed. Now there is an open season on bucks, fawns and does in the state. Eighteen thousand deer were killed last year in the state, mostly does. A year from now the conservation commission may hold hearings throughout the state and closed counties. Petitions will be circulated calling hearings and closing up counties. If this is not done the deer will be wiped out.[45]

The passage of time would bring some credence to Barber's statements. In the next decade, Wisconsin hunters would see the return of the buck law as well as statewide closed seasons.

In a fitting symbol of the change that was upon the sport of deer hunting in the "Roaring Twenties" *The New North* reported in 1924 on what may have been one of the first documented deer-vehicle collisions in the state: "An automobile driven by Wesley Turbin of White Lake collided with a large buck deer on Highway 64 near Merrill. The damage to the car consisted of two bent fenders, a bent axle, and a broken lamp. Mr. Turbin considers himself fortunate that he emerged from the wreck unhurt."[46]

The auto itself was changing the very nature of the deer hunt as state and county highways constructed at a rapid pace were connecting small northern Wisconsin communities with those of central and southern Wisconsin. The days of nearly complete reliance on the railroads for both the transportation of hunters to deer territory and the shipment of deer back home were coming to a close. In 1920 a Rhinelander newspaper reported, "It is estimated that at least five thousand hunters are in the woods of Oneida County. Every train into the city has carried extra coaches to accommodate the 'red caps' and hundreds have made the trip to this locality by automobile. Nimrods from every section of the state and many from neighboring states are here for their annual hunt."[47]

Early in the decade newspapers reported that fewer deer were being shipped home on the railroads as a result of better roads. In 1922 it was reported that "cars were responsible for the transportation of bucks from the north woods and it is therefore out of the question to secure any kind of an idea of the number of deer taken out of the woods."[48] In previous years the number of deer shipped south on the rails formed the basis for the statewide deer kill estimate. In 1921 numbers began to be based on a deer kill census postcard that hunters were asked to mail in.

While automobile travel was regarded as a positive development, the new decade brought one not so welcome change: the return of the infamous one-buck law and the raging controversy that accompanied it. The one-buck bag limit, first enacted in 1915, had been repealed by the legislature in 1917. After holding hearings in the twenty-seven counties open to deer hunting, the Wisconsin Conservation Commission brought the one-buck law back in 1920. As one-buck law proponent

Conservation Commissioner W. E. Barber stated prior to the start of the 1920 season, "The commission is going to use every effort possible to demonstrate the one-buck law as a conservative measure for does and fawns."[49]

At the crux of the debate was the dilemma sportsmen faced about how to ensure the sport's future while at the same time protecting and rebuilding the dwindling deer herd. As with many Wisconsin issues, the debate often had a north versus south flavor. Many northern Wisconsin sportsmen favored the one-buck law and sincerely wanted it to work in order to prevent a statewide closed season for deer. Many southern Wisconsin sportsmen were calling for complete protection of the herd.

In December 1920 Fred Williams, a Three Lakes representative at the Wisconsin Fish and Game Protective Association annual meeting in Madison, stated:

> While northern Wisconsin sportsmen favor the buck law, they do not wish to see a closed season for a couple of years, such as most of the downstate hunters are working for. They advance the theory, and it is practical, that if the season is closed for a number of years, then the downstate man will ask for an open season on deer of any sex and size. Too many men are of the opinion that this fall showed them that buck deer were exterminated. Such is far from the fact. Any wise hunter of deer will tell you why the bucks were not to be found when the season opened last November. There are plenty, if the laws are builded [*sic*] as they should be for the protection of the deer and not for the blood thirstiness of hunters who are after meat, rather than after clean sport.[50]

From Logging Camp to Hunting Camp

ALTHOUGH HE MAY NOT HAVE REALIZED IT AT THE TIME, Walter Knight, the son of a homestead farmer residing in the town of Georgetown in Price County, was fortunate to experience firsthand the last days of Wisconsin big-timber logging. In 1976 Knight's childhood remembrances of working at the Finnish logging camp his father helped build five miles from the family farm in the early 1920s were typed up for posterity. Inadvertently, Knight also recorded in detail the transition of a white pine logging camp into an early Wisconsin white-tailed-deer hunting camp.

"The camp was a two-room log building consisting of cook shack and bunk house. The log walls were chinked in with mud and hammered-in strips of wood," wrote Knight. "It took several loads of lumber to make the roof and floor, but that too was from local timber."[1]

His description of the camp continues: "The bunks in the bunk house were double-decker, two men to a bunk, with a bench running along side the bottom bunks where the men could sit in the evening. A stove made from an oil barrel furnished heat for the room. Wood three feet long and properly stoked would keep the fire all night."

From Logging Camp to Hunting Camp (continued)

The camp was built for the purpose of logging what was probably one of the last commercially significant stands of the big woods—the old growth forest of hemlock and pine—in the region. "The piece of timber logged was about three miles long and averaged half a mile wide," Knight remembered. Forty lumberjacks of Finnish ancestry occupied the camp, which operated for only three years.

Initially the camp operated as turn-of-the-century logging camps had for decades. The massive old-growth trees were felled in the winter by hand and hauled out of the woods on sleighs pulled by draft horses. "They used a rutter to cut ruts for the runners and iced the road with a tank hauled by a team of horses," wrote Knight. In the last year of the camp's existence (although the year isn't specified, it's likely 1926 or 1927), the horses were replaced with a Caterpillar tractor.

The camp closed its doors after the tract of big timber had been cut. By the 1920s the era of Wisconsin white pine logging marked by literally billions of board feet of logs heading down river to the mills had essentially been over for several years in most of the state. In its wake were millions of acres of "cutover"—land denuded of forest and covered with slash left behind by the logging. Spotted across the cutover were numerous abandoned logging towns and hundreds of abandoned logging camps like the one known by Knight.

The cutover habitat was more favorable to the whitetail than the primal forest of old, and deer populations shot up after the turn of the century. Abandoned logging camps made convenient and cozy deer camps for the hunters streaming north on the railroads each year.

What had become known as the Old Finn Camp became the hunting camp of Walter Knight's family and friends. "After the . . . timber was cut, the camp was used for a hunting camp for the next four or five years," wrote Knight. "The hunting crew, usually relatives from Eau Claire, Menomonie, Mauston and Durand were Ed Cronk, Ernest Cronk, John and Clarence Vasey, Mike and Stanley Sands, Preacher Thompson, Herman Watland, Gene Sanders, my father and I. Occasionally there were others."

Knight described the operation of the logging camp turned deer camp:

My father was captain of the crew and organized all the drives. The hunting country was a network of blazed-out trails with deer stands at various places. Drives were made with standers and drivers alternating. The hunting season lasted ten days and ended up with nearly everyone getting his buck. Some of the older hunters would say at the end of the season that they thought this would be their last trip, but they invariably came back again and again.

In the evening, hunting stories started—usually pretty well colored. Every time a man would miss a deer, he had to put a dime in the "kitty" and the

From Logging Camp to Hunting Camp (continued)

money made from this source went for camp improvement. The poorest shot donated the most towards camp comfort. After the kitty was handed around for donations, the trading started. Each man had something to trade and the game, of course, was to best the other guy. Once one of the hunters came prepared with some very good counterfeit money. He loaded the camp with it.

My father would get up long before daylight and make sourdough pancakes and would be ready for the hunt at the break of day. This hunt was the high point of the year for the hunters.

The camp that was built from the logs and lumber of virgin forest eventually suffered the fate common to many other abandoned logging camps. A raging cutover wildfire, fed by the ample amounts of dried slash left from the old logging days, burned through the camp, sending back to the earth anything made of wood. "The only evidence of the exact spot would be the old mammoth cook stove and maybe the oil barrel heating stove," Knight wrote. "The country has changed so much in the last fifty years that I'm sure I couldn't find it myself."

NOTE
1. Walter Knight, "The Old Finn Camp," a typed reminiscence, 1976. Wisconsin Historical Society Archives Manuscript Collection, Northern Great Lakes Center Area Research Center, Ashland, WI (RLIN Number WIHV85-A1142).

The opposite faction of sportsmen, opposed to the one-buck law, claimed "that the bucks are not so numerous and a few years of the buck law will see them depleted."[51] Most who fought the law felt a buck-only season led to the needless destruction of does and fawns. Fred P. Schlin, a strong opponent stated, "When some city man comes to hunt for a week he doesn't want a doe, simply for the reason that there will be no way for him to take her out of the woods and home. So for the first couple days he will be careful, but when there seems to be nothing but does, he gets angry and starts plugging deer which he is not sure of. That is why in northern Wisconsin it is not unusual for a hunter to find three or four does every season that haven't been drawn. One doesn't find any bucks."[52]

Regardless of a deer hunter's stand on the issue, it was becoming apparent in the early 1920s that the one-buck law was not doing enough to stabilize the deer herd. Hunter numbers had surged in 1918 after the close of World War I, and even though northern newspapers consistently reported deer to be plentiful—perhaps to ensure the annual arrival of the "army of redhats" that were becoming important to local economies—actual deer kills were declining. After the one-buck season of 1920, the seasonal kill was estimated at about 20,000 deer. After four more consecutive buck-only seasons, the take for 1924 was estimated to be 7,000 deer.[53]

Often the northern newspapers or local wardens attributed lower buck kills to poor weather or inopportune timing of the breeding season. Fred P. Schlin had no use for these excuses and wrote about these northern contradictions in *Outdoor Life*:

TWO MENASHA MEN BRING DEER BACK FROM NORTH

Menasha—Albert Maas returned from Three Lakes Monday with a 205-pound deer which he captured Sunday. Hary Goretzki returned from the vicinity of Superior with one weighing 100 pounds. Many automobiles passed through Menasha Monday and Tuesday with deer strapped to the running boards.

Appleton Post-Crescent, November 18, 1924

"Every year when the figures [deer kill] are published in the newspapers they are accompanied by statements from game wardens in the northern part of the state showing why so few were taken out when so many hunters were out. These excuses are varied, but a stock one is that the game kept to the impenetrable swamps during the open season and thus escaped."[54]

Schlin believed, like many others, that the one-buck law was not doing anything to protect the Wisconsin deer herd. "I don't know what law will save the deer but that [one-buck law] certainly will not."[55]

What was urgently needed to protect the dwindling supply of deer, thought many sportsmen and conservationists, was complete protection: a statewide closed season.

The New North quoted part of an article by Schlin that appeared in the December 1924 issue of *Outdoor Life*: "I notice that Minnesota has a new law whereby the deer season is open every other year and Wisconsin has not so much game as Minnesota. I think it is high time for the same law to be put into effect in Wisconsin, and possibly it would be a good idea to put a two- or three-year closed season on to start. Too much protection is bad, but a very few more years under the present system will see Wisconsin with no deer left to protect."[56]

In January 1925 the newly formed Minocqua Chapter of the Izaak Walton League promoted the idea of closing the deer season for a period of three years.[57] The push for a statewide closed season finally culminated in 1925 with the implementation of alternate closed seasons, as Minnesota had already been doing. Exactly ten years after the first-ever Wisconsin "one-buck law," the state had its first statewide closed season for deer hunting.

In early fall 1926 a northern newspaper summarized the attitudes toward the first closed deer season in the history of Wisconsin deer hunting: "Many deer have

Digest and Summary

OF THE

WISCONSIN GAME LAWS

In force and effect until changed by the
Legislature of 1927

ELMER S. HALL
Commissioner of Conservation

Madison, Wisconsin

COURTESY OF WISCONSIN DEPARTMENT OF NATURAL
RESOURCES, BUREAU OF WILDLIFE MANAGEMENT

been seen in the woods and on the highways of this section during the present summer. While many assert that the closed season of last year did little to increase the number of deer, others state the closed season has given the deer a respite from hunters and allowed them to multiply rapidly."[58]

In the alternate years when the season was open, the season dates changed from the familiar November 11 opening day to a late-season opening on December 1, but still running the usual ten days. In 1926, *The New North* reported, "Hunters in many parts of upper Wisconsin express dissatisfaction over the lateness of the deer season. . . . It is their contention that a large number of does will be killed, it being claimed that time of year the meat of the bucks will not be palatable. In several counties hunters will make a strong protest to the next legislature that the deer season be switched back to November."[59]

A deer season that didn't start in November was a strong sign that the times certainly were changing. The second half of the 1920s had only two open seasons—bucks only, with a one deer limit—a far cry from the liberal, long seasons of a generation before. One thing that hadn't changed, however, was the cost of a resident hunting license: still only one dollar, although the required deer tag now cost fifty cents.

As actual hunting opportunities diminished in the 1920s, hunters turned their attention to the protection and rebuilding of the herd. The idea of deer refuges—areas where no hunting of deer would be allowed, even during open seasons—was gaining in popularity. In 1926 the National Playground Association, a group composed of Milwaukee and Chicago sportsmen, purchased thousands of acres of land near Boulder Junction in Vilas County and applied to the state for a permit to establish a game refuge on 1,500 acres. The area would remain a refuge, with no hunting or even loaded firearms allowed on the property, for five years.[60] Areas officially recognized as refuges were protected by law, with fines for violations.

As opposition to the one-buck law tempered, Wisconsin deer hunters embraced wholeheartedly the idea that probably the most important component of a plan to save Wisconsin's deer was the absolute and complete protection of does. The

Beginning in 1928, deer hunters were required to wear an official license button while hunting. This requirement continued for two more consecutive open seasons during the alternate closed-open season framework that existed from 1925 to 1935.

COURTESY OF MIKE VLAHAKIS, PHOTO BY JEFF KOSER

A deer hunter wearing a hunting license button poses with a nice buck.

COURTESY OF MIKE VLAHAKIS

stringent protection of the deer "factories" was backed by Wisconsin sportsmen so strongly that the idea became enshrined in the very ethics of deer hunting. John Madson wrote about this era of deer hunting history in 1961: "Does and fawns became virtually sacred, and were gently set in the same category as home, mother and flag."[61]

The early ideas for protecting and growing the deer herd became institutionalized in Wisconsin game regulations as well as in the minds of most Wisconsin deer hunters in the 1920s. The measures were good ones, necessary in the context of the times, in that long transition from the days of the market hunter, who cared very little about the animals he was slaughtering for profit, to the enlightened world of the conservationist sportsman, who realized he must protect deer if there was to be a future for the sport of deer hunting. The next decades would bring with them new and complex problems caused by a dynamic, rebounding deer herd, and a host of new concerns and controversies for Wisconsin deer hunters to sort out.

DEER POPULATION - 1929

Source: Game survey undertaken by conservation wardens and
selected sportsmen in 65 counties.

Estimated deer numbers by county based on a survey taken by conservation
wardens in 1929. Deer remained rare or in very low numbers in southern and
central Wisconsin.

A CENTURY OF WISCONSIN DEER

The Deer Wars

Some people ask why men go hunting. They must be the same kind of people who seldom get far from highways. What do they know of the tryst a hunting man keeps with the wind and the trees and the sky? Hunting? The means are greater than the end, and every deer hunter knows it.
—Gordon MacQuarrie, "Just Look at This Country"[1]

In mid-November 1930, most of the 700 residents of Drummond in Bayfield County turned out to watch the Rust-Owen Lumber Company, which had been in existence since 1882, saw its final pine log. In nearly fifty years, it had cut an estimated two billion board feet of lumber, much of it old-growth white pine.[2]

The closing of the Rust-Owen mill was symbolic of the final, quiet end to the glorious days of Wisconsin white pine logging. Though nearly all the big pines were felled years before, Rust-Owen had reserved a tract of virgin white pine, which became the very last logs sawed at the mill.

A symbol of the end of an era, the closing of one of the last big sawmills in northern Wisconsin also was a sign of the times. "The lumbering industry in Northern Wisconsin is no longer viewed with pride as the state's largest and most prosperous industry," reported a newspaper covering the Rust-Owen story. "In fact the lumber business in this part of the state is rapidly decreasing until it may scarcely any longer be classed as 'big business.'"[3]

Closing the mill drove 200 men into the ranks of the unemployed and left the other Drummond residents wondering what the future held. The folks of Drummond were not alone in their fears. In 1930 the United States was sinking deeper into the depths of the worst economic collapse the industrial world had ever known: the Great Depression.

Hard times didn't dampen the Wisconsin deer hunter's enthusiasm for the annual hunt. Following the alternate-year closed season of 1929, hunters headed

The Dane County clerk, Selma Fjelstad, issues a hunting license in 1934. For many years the only place to purchase a deer hunting license was at the county clerk's office. Wisconsin Conservation Department personnel were not allowed to issue big game licenses until 1951.
WHI IMAGE ID 49113

to the northern Wisconsin deer range for the 1930 open season in droves. "Whether times are prosperous or otherwise," reported a northern newspaper, "the sale of hunting licenses does not appear to be falling off very materially."[4]

Perhaps because of an increased demand for inexpensive meat or a need to escape the realities of the economic crisis, deer hunter numbers steadily increased throughout the 1930s. Nearly 80,000 hunters purchased the required deer tag in 1930 and 1932; by 1938, tag sales topped 100,000 for the first time.[5]

The actual numbers of deer taken by hunters also were increasing. The 1930 open season, with its estimated deer take of 23,000, was considered by many hunters to be "the most successful Wisconsin has had for many years."[6] Rhinelander's *The New North* reported, "Many old-time hunters say there are more deer in hunting sections of the state today than there have been for many seasons past."[7]

The "old-timers" were right. Deer numbers were finally on the upswing. Leading up to the next open season in 1932, hunting prospect reports continued to be upbeat: "Reports coming to the conservation department indicate a plentiful supply of deer this year. Continued success of the one buck law, reduced number of wolves and other predators, and favorable breeding seasons the past two years account for the increases."[8] During the one-buck open season of 1932 more than 36,000 deer were taken—about the same number as the estimated kill for the seasons of 1924, 1926, and 1928 combined.[9]

The Fox Kill-Every-Deer Bill of 1931

DURING THE SPRING AND SUMMER OF 1931, NEWSPAPERS across Wisconsin had many big stories to cover: Eliot Ness had finally collared Al Capone, the Chicago gangster with ties to Wisconsin's North Woods, on charges of income-tax evasion and conspiracy to violate prohibition; President Hoover was attempting to deal with the nation's worsening economic crisis; and the tallest building in the world, the Empire State, opened in New York.

In northern Wisconsin, however, one of the biggest headline grabbers and front-page stories that spring was a piece of state legislation that had become known as the "Fox kill-every-deer bill."

On April 7, the *Rhinelander Daily News* summarized the main provisions of the bill: "Under the Fox kill-every-deer bill, three counties that have been closed for over 10 years would be thrown open again; hunters would be allowed to shoot at any deer over a year old, regardless of whether it was a buck or a doe; the season would be held in mid-November when deer are mating and hasn't [*sic*] taken refuge in the deep woods for the winter; and an open season on all deer would be declared every year."[1]

North Woods conservationists, sportsmen, resort owners, and the general public were not happy with the bill. "[C]onservationists in this part of the state are inclined to believe the state legislature has gone completely insane," reported the paper. "With an annual open season before cold weather sets in, the deer slaughter probably would be complete the first year in counties like Oneida, which not only must

furnish hunting for their own sportsmen, but for downstate and Illinois shooters who pour into the Land o' Lakes counties."[2]

The Oneida County Conservation Club called an emergency meeting after learning of the bill. "'They want to kill off all our deer next year and we must stop it!' warns the notice of Thursday night's meeting as sent out by Eugene Kabel, secretary of the Conservation club," the *Rhinelander Daily News* reported.[3]

A local North Woods legislator, S. J. Gwidt, vowed to fight the bill every step of the way, taking his case right to Governor Phil La Follette if necessary.[4] "He [Gwidt] charges that northern Wisconsin assemblymen deserted the conservation movement and listened to selfish arguments from southern Wisconsin hunters who want one big year of killing all the deer, and don't care if deer are exterminated," reported the *Rhinelander Daily News*.[5]

The "Fox" in the Fox kill-every-deer bill was Jerome Fox, a Calumet County Democrat from Chilton who served in the Assembly in the early 1930s. (He later ran for governor in 1938 as a "New Deal" Democrat, but lost in the primaries.)

To fully understand northern rancor over the Fox bill, it must be put into historical perspective and placed in the context of the state of deer management in Wisconsin in the early 1930s. With the exception of buck-only seasons in 1915 and 1916, until 1920, all that Wisconsin hunters had known were "any deer" seasons in which bucks, does, or fawns were fair game. Until 1916, hunters also had known deer

The Fox Kill-Every-Deer Bill of 1931 (continued)

seasons that ran for twenty days.[6] The early 1900s saw a steady increase in the number of hunters who by necessity headed north each November to where deer were still relatively numerous—unlike the situation in central and

The state Legislature, supported by the Conservation Commission (a precursor to the Natural Resources Board), responded to public demand to protect does and fawns and, beginning in 1920, again instituted the one-buck law. Going a step further in 1925, the Legislature passed a

RHINELANDER DAILY NEWS, APRIL 24, 1931

southern regions. By 1918 there were an estimated 53,000 sport deer hunters, and there was a growing perception from those in the "deer counties" of the north that "any deer" seasons were going to lead to the extermination of deer from the state. Many felt that the only way to save deer from this fate was the strict adherence to buck-only seasons.

law allowing for alternate closed deer seasons, with the first statewide closed season occurring in 1927.[7]

In accordance with the alternate year open-season plan, 1931 was slated as a closed season. The northern Wisconsin public, with a vested interest in healthy deer numbers for the sake of tourist as well as hunter dollars, was solidly behind the one-buck law and the alternate closed seasons. The Fox bill, with its provisions for open

The Fox Kill-Every-Deer Bill of 1931 (continued)

seasons every year, allowing again the taking of does along with bucks, and an earlier than normal opening date, enraged many in the north.

When the Assembly passed the bill on April 24, the news seized the headline of the *Rhinelander Daily News*. The accompanying Associated Press report gave the details: "The assembly today passed the Fox bill repealing the one-buck law and cutting the deer hunting season to five days, beginning the third Saturday in November in even-numbered years. The vote was 54 to 27."[8]

County governments in the north were quick to react to the bill's passage. The *Rhinelander Daily News* reported on action taken by the Vilas County board on April 25: "At a one day meeting, the board adopted a resolution petitioning the legislature and conservation commission to close the season in Vilas County, because of the expected general slaughter made possible under the Fox kill-every-deer bill passed by the state assembly yesterday."[9]

Steady opposition in the north to the Fox bill eventually resulted in a greatly altered bill coming out of the Senate. In June the *Rhinelander Daily News* reported: "Members of the Oneida Conservation club expressed themselves as well pleased with the action yesterday of the state senate in altering the Fox 'kill-every-deer' bill to such an extent that it has lost almost all of its objectionable features."[10]

In the end, the alternate closed season policy as well as the one-buck law remained a part of Wisconsin deer hunting regulations for

1931. Despite deer numbers in the north growing during the 1930s to the point where serious range damage was leading to winter starvation in the deer yards, state hunters would not see another antlerless deer season until the highly controversial "split" season (a four-day, buck-only season followed after a three-day rest by a four-day antlerless season) of 1943.

The 1930s were a time of great change in deer management in Wisconsin. Prior to 1933 the state Legislature alone generally set game regulations through legislation. A myriad of diverse and sometimes conflicting bills came and went through the Assembly and the Senate. After 1933, the Conservation Committee, with guidance from the Conservation Congress, began to set deer season regulations, which resulted in the more consistent application of regulations statewide.

NOTES

1. "Conservation Club to Meet, Discuss Fight," *Rhinelander Daily News*, April 7, 1931.
2. "Assembly Backs Kill-Every-Deer Plan for North," *Rhinelander Daily News*, April 3, 1931.
3. "Conservation Club to Meet, Discuss Fight," *Rhinelander Daily News*, April 7, 1931.
4. Ibid.
5. Ibid.
6. Otis S. Bersing, *A Century of Wisconsin Deer* (Madison: Wisconsin Conservation Department, Game Management Division, 1956), 23–50.
7. Ibid., 16–17.
8. "Measure Asks for Repeal of One-Buck Law," *Rhinelander Daily News*, April 24, 1931.
9. "Would Check Vilas County Deer Hunting," *Rhinelander Daily News*, April 25, 1931.
10. "Fox Deer Bill Liked Locally," *Rhinelander Daily News*, June 6, 1931.

DEER SEASON OPENS SATURDAY

BE SURE IT'S A YEAR-OLD BUCK

Nimrods, many of them getting up before breakfast November 24, will be out after the season limit of one buck not less than one year-old (spike horn). The above cartoon, found in the stored cut files of The New North will give the average person who does not care to hunt, a mild idea of what deer hunting in the woods and around the farms represents during the open season. Hunters are prohibited from hunting deer between one hour after sunset and one hour before sunrise of the following morning.

Deer are plentiful this year and many bucks have been seen in the woods recently. Some of the old timers say that deer are more plentiful than they have ever been in the County. The number will be considerably reduced after the seven-day season ends. Thousands of hunters will be in the woods but many will experience the "buck fever" feeling.

Venison steaks and roasts will be served in many Oneida county homes for the next two weeks and it is also supposed venison roasts will take the place of turkey on some Thankgiving tables this year. It is hoped that all families needing the meat for food, will be fortunate enough to get a spike horn or larger buck this season.

A newspaper cartoon from 1934 satirizes the annual invasion of hunters to the North Woods.
THE NEW NORTH, NOVEMBER 22, 1934

Aside from increases in the deer kill, there were other, sometimes subtle indications of an expanding deer herd. Incidents of deer quietly starving to death in the winter yards of isolated areas of northern Wisconsin were reported as early as 1930.[10] Dead deer were found each spring with increasing regularity.[11]

The move toward strong protection of the herd, which began in earnest during the 1920s, fully developed in the 1930s. The buck-only, or "one-buck," hunting season, a reality since 1920, had become much less controversial as deer protection attitudes took hold. *The New North* reported, "The presence of more deer in the woods this year than two years ago caused many hunters to comment and there is a growing sentiment in favor of the one-buck law, which is primarily responsible for the increase in deer."[12]

The alternate-year closed seasons were also perceived as a key to increasing deer numbers: "[I]t is plain to see that the making of the deer season only in alternate years is necessary for the preservation of the sport in Northern Wisconsin," a newspaper commented in 1930.[13]

Another necessary component of the strategy to grow Wisconsin's deer herd, many felt, were the deer refuges. Deer refuge areas, where deer were afforded complete protection, gained in popularity in the 1930s. Conservation Department director H. W. MacKenzie proudly reported in a review of 1936 accomplishments that "a total of 400,000 acres of permanent and 400,000 acres of temporary refuges were set up prior to the opening of deer season."[14]

The Deer Revolt of 1930

A JUDGE, A COUNTY SHERIFF, A DISTRICT ATTORNEY, a game warden, and several illegally killed white-tailed deer. These were the main players in a northern Wisconsin deer season drama in 1930.

What began as an Oneida County judge's simple recommendation that any confiscated deer or deer found dead in the woods during the upcoming hunting season be turned over to charitable organizations to help feed needy families developed into a widely reported standoff between the state and the county.

The story, known as Oneida County's deer "revolt," began innocently enough about one week before the opening of the 1930 season, set to begin December 1. As winter's grip approached, small towns across the north already were slipping into the grips of the Great Depression. America's industrial collapse had sent many in Oneida County, as elsewhere, to the breadlines. The outlook for the winter was bleak.

Enter County Judge H. F. Steele.

Since the 1930 hunt was to be a buck-only season, there were bound to be many does and fawns shot and left in the woods. Judge Steele saw an opportunity to help feed the poor. In a letter to the Wisconsin Conservation Commission, the judge wrote:

Many families in this county are suffering from the general depression and are seriously in need of public aid and especially of provisions with which to maintain themselves and their families. . . . As the open season for the hunting of deer

approaches, it seems quite obvious that many animals will be confiscated because they are unlawfully taken. It has occurred to the writer that it would be very helpful if instead of selling these animals . . . it might be possible for your commission to authorize its wardens to turn over at least a portion of confiscated animals to some of our charitable organizations who are in good faith endeavoring to alleviate conditions among the poor.[1]

The Conservation Commission was apparently in no mood to entertain ideas—even charitable ones—that tampered with the state's jurisdiction over wild game. Earl. L. Kennedy, Oneida County's recently elected district attorney, was informed over the telephone by Paul D. Kelleter, the state conservation director, that the commission would not approve Steele's proposal. In accordance with state law, any deer killed illegally and confiscated by a warden, or found in the woods and recovered, was property of the state. The sale of this venison by the wardens to the highest bidder, typically hotels and resorts, was the accepted practice.[2]

The whole thing might have ended there. Judge Steele was not inclined to pursue the matter. However, District Attorney Kennedy had other ideas.

Kennedy thought it was well within the rights of the county to appropriate this venison and see that it made its way to the needy. Only a few days before Steele's request, the county had

The Deer Revolt of 1930 (continued)

formed a relief committee to address the ever-growing needs of the unemployed. Kennedy was a member of that committee.

The *Rhinelander Daily News* reported on November 26 that "he [Kennedy] believes that state law gives county officials, through the office of the court, the right to seize and dispose of venison and make such disposition of any proceeds as the judge may order."[3]

Despite the refusal of the Conservation Commission to sanction the county's plan, Kennedy pushed on. On November 28, the *Rhinelander Daily News* published a letter from Kennedy that was counter to the Conservation Commission's decision: "Owing to the fact that a large number of does and fawns are left in the woods each hunting season, and for some reason or other the people do not report the same to the officers, the undersigned, by authority of Section 29.05 of the Wisconsin statutes, requests that all persons knowing of a doe or fawn being killed or left in the woods bring it or report the same to Hans Rodd, sheriff of Oneida County."[4]

The district attorney was in effect attempting to usurp the authority of the state by instructing hunters to transport illegally killed deer directly to the county courthouse. The press recognized the precedent-setting nature of the move. "This is the first time, so far as known here, that county officials have decided to act independently of the conservation commission in a matter of this kind," wrote the *Rhinelander Daily News*.[5]

Emotions were already at fever pitch regarding the 1930 season. With nearly two-thirds of the state closed to hunting, downstate deer hunters flocked to the open counties of the north, provoking the ire of locals. Many in the north considered deer numbers to be low and questioned the wisdom of having a deer season at all, and editorials lambasted the state's deer management policies. The scene was set for the north to fight back, if only just a little.

While the commission had not given Judge Steele the courtesy of a formal reply, the matter was finally formally addressed on November 29 at a meeting in Milwaukee. "Members of the Wisconsin Conservation Commission meeting here today took notice of a situation that has arisen in Oneida County with the announcement that the commission itself will take charge of all confiscated property, including deer, in accordance with the provisions of the hunting laws," reported the Associated Press.[6]

The commission's answer to Oneida County was clear: "The commission will disperse of all confiscated property as the statutes provide with the view of preventing further willful violations of the hunting laws."[7]

Unwavering and confident that state law granted the county the authority to carry out his plan, D.A. Kennedy left Rhinelander for, the Associated Press reported, "a hidden hunting cabin four miles from anywhere in the town of Minoqua, where it will be impossible to reach him." There was a deer season to attend to. Kennedy indicated that he would "come out of the woods one day next week to see how things are developing."[8]

The Deer Revolt of 1930 (continued)

Rhinelander Daily News, November 28, 1930

When questioned about what course of action he would take if any deer were brought in to him, Sheriff Rodd said he would "hang them up and then let the authorities argue about it."[9]

It was widely believed that the local warden, A. J. Robinson, would demand any deer obtained by the county. But two days into the season the standoff had yet to be tested. "Neither Warden Robinson nor Sheriff Rodd had any does reported to them so far, so the 'Oneida county revolt' has developed no warfare so far," reported the *Rhinelander Daily News* on December 2.[10]

As the days passed without any deer finding their way to Sheriff Rodd, speculation mounted that the woods-wise needy of Oneida County didn't really need anyone's help in obtaining venison. "Meanwhile Oneida county's revolt moves peacefully along without any does being brought in, and a well-founded rumor is being circulated that many of Oneida county's poor people are placing their trust in the old adage that 'the lord helps those that help themselves,'" the *Rhinelander Daily News* reported.[11]

Finally, the county obtained two does—one brought in by a hunter, the other found by Undersheriff John Farman and Deputy Sheriff Harvey Rodd after a hunter reported its location. As expected, Warden Robinson requested that the deer be turned over to him. Farman refused, as both Sheriff Rodd and D.A. Kennedy were still out hunting. It was becoming clear that the matter would have to be resolved when all the players had returned from their hunting camps.

The revolt was receiving increasing publicity across the state, and other northern Wisconsin

The Deer Revolt of 1930 (continued)

counties were awaiting the outcome. "The Oneida county deer situation has drawn the attention of other counties in the north, where officers would like to use confiscated venison to aid the poor if the attempt should prove successful," the *Rhinelander Daily News* reported.[12]

The *Vilas County News Review* commented: "There is no doubt but what the right in the affair is on the side of Oneida county and if they are successful in putting across this method of game disposal it will be followed by all the counties that have open seasons on deer."[13]

When Sheriff Rodd returned from the field he immediately "joined the ranks of Oneida county's 'revolting' officials when he refused a demand of Warden A. J. Robinson that does now held by the county be turned over to him."[14]

Several more does eventually were brought to the courthouse. By season's end, Sheriff Rodd held five illegally killed deer. Ironically, the fate of those five deer rested with the man who had started the revolt: Judge Steele.

During the course of issuing "John Doe" warrants for the arrests of those responsible for the illegal kills, D.A. Kennedy also made a motion that the deer be disposed of through local charitable organizations.[15] On December 12, the judge dutifully ruled that the court could not legally give the does to the poor. However, in an interesting twist, he ordered Sheriff Rodd, as an agent of the state by right of his position, to sell the venison to the highest bidder. The proceeds would go to the Conservation Commission.[16]

The last chapter of the deer revolt occurred when Sheriff Rodd sold all five does at a public sale on December 13. William S. Raven, a local builder, purchased the five deer for five dollars.[17]

"Immediately after his purchase . . . he announced his intention of turning all five does over to the Citizen's relief committee . . . with the expectation that the committee would distribute the venison among the needy," reported the *Rhinelander Daily News*.[18]

The revolt was officially over, with both sides claiming victory.

———

NOTES

1. "Give Seized Game to Poor, Request," *Rhinelander Daily News*, November 26, 1930.
2. Ibid.
3. Ibid.
4. "'Bring Does to Sheriff'—Kennedy," *Rhinelander Daily News*, November 28, 1930.
5. Ibid.
6. Associated Press, "Express Doubts Over Deer Move," *Rhinelander Daily News*, November 29, 1930.
7. Ibid.
8. Ibid.
9. Ibid.
10. "Deer Slaughter Light First Days," *Rhinelander Daily News*, December 2, 1930.
11. "1930 Hunters End Third Day Seeking Deer," *Rhinelander Daily News*, December 3, 1930.
12. Ibid.
13. Ibid.
14. "Rodd Refuses State Demand for Dead Does," *Rhinelander Daily News*, December 8, 1930.
15. "Gano Is Freed," *Rhinelander Daily News*, December 11, 1930.
16. "Warden to Get Confiscated Deer?" *Rhinelander Daily News*, December 12, 1930.
17. "Raven Buys Five Does for Needy," *Rhinelander Daily News*, December 13, 1930.
18. Ibid.

The original intent of the game refuge system was to "promote a successful wildlife program and to conserve and perpetuate an adequate supply of game and game birds, thereby insuring to the citizens of this state better opportunities for hunting and recreation."[15] However, by the mid-1930s, as winter starvation in deer yards—particularly in refuges—increased to alarming levels in areas where populations had become much larger than the habitat could support, game managers realized that deer could not be stockpiled.

The idea that there could be a surplus population of deer (as well as other game animals) that if not taken by the hunter's gun would surely be taken by nature's less efficient methods of starvation and disease was a bold new concept. It signaled the birth of modern wildlife management.[16]

Along with scientific game management, other progressive ideas developed during the hard times of the 1930s would benefit Wisconsin deer hunters for generations to come. Thousands of acres of fire-scarred, tax-delinquent cutover lands left behind by the previous generation's timber barons were incorporated into federal, state, and county public forests. "County forest crop lands now total 1,739,140 acres, an increase of 116,000 acres over last year. These county forests constitute the largest and most rapidly growing class of public forests in Wisconsin," reported Conservation Department director MacKenzie in 1938.[17] The federal government was actively buying tax-delinquent cutover lands during this period. In 1933 the Nicolet and Chequamegon national forests were officially established by presidential proclamation.[18]

Beginning in 1933, the young men of Franklin Delano Roosevelt's Civilian Conservation Corps reforested these areas by planting trees by the millions each year across northern Wisconsin. In 1938 alone, more than 25 million trees raised in state nurseries were planted on public forestland, including 11 million planted on county forestland.[19] New forest crop laws promoting the sound management of privately owned forestland also allowed for hunter access to these lands.

Another first that occurred in the 1930s was the establishment of an archery season. In 1930, "bow and arrow" hunting was allowed in Wisconsin for the first time since the development of regulated sport hunting—but only during the regular gun season in those counties open to deer hunting.

Only one deer was taken with a bow in 1930, a spike buck killed in Vilas County by Roy Case of Racine, an early proponent of the archery season.[20] Case became the first licensed archer to legally take a white-tailed deer with bow and arrow in North America. Often referred to as the "father of Wisconsin bow hunting," Case is credited with coining the term *bowhunter*.[21]

The first separate "archery only" season was established in 1934 and limited to Columbia and Sauk counties, where deer were making enough of a comeback

Cutover public forestland being replanted. New growth proved an enticing meal for whitetails and deer population in the north grew in the early 1930s.
WHI IMAGE ID 58597

to cause damage problems for farmers but weren't yet numerous enough to allow gun hunting.

"In Columbia and Sauk counties of south central Wisconsin, deer hunting with bow and arrow only will be permitted in the first experiment of the state in archery. The counties embrace the well-forested Quarzite hills of the Baraboo range, long known to be the home of hundreds of deer protected from riflemen by law," reported the *Rhinelander Daily News*.[22]

The archery season took a step forward in 1936 when an early seven-day antlerless season, from October 25 to 31, was held. Archers taking their single allotted buck during this season would not be allowed to gun hunt during the rifle season, and bowhunting would no longer be allowed in conjunction with the regular season.[23]

"Archery enthusiasts are preparing for the advent of Wisconsin's first special archers' season on deer by tuning up their bowstrings, improving their technique and aim by frequent practice sessions, and visiting their favorite bowyers and fletchers for new equipment or repairs," reported *The Wisconsin Sportsman* in 1936.[24]

Only about one hundred hunters took part in the new early archery season, and only one deer was killed: Chester Sroka, the Portage County fire chief, took a nice mature buck. "With proof that their weapon is powerful enough for deer, archers are already looking forward to another season," reported *The Wisconsin Sportsman*. "Many of them are planning to persuade the conservation department to permit a yearly open season in these counties for archers and to extend the season for a longer period with no bans on the sex of the deer to be killed."[25]

A delegation of archery enthusiasts, including Roy Case, Aldo Leopold, and Chester Sroka, met with the Conservation Department officials in January 1937 to promote their ideas of a more liberal archery season. The archers were successful in gaining support for a twenty-day bow season that fall. Officials also felt that the season's range could expand to include several counties in addition to Sauk and Columbia. *The Wisconsin Sportsman* reported that Conservation Department Director MacKenzie "indicated that he was in favor of it [archery], feeling that it was a sportsmanlike way to hunt, and should be encouraged."[26]

The January conference paid dividends for archers. The bow season of 1937 started in early October and ran for twenty days. Additional counties included Manitowoc and Dane. However, the new Wisconsin bow season was still in its infancy. "Wisconsin's bow and arrow season for deer in Columbia, Manitowoc, and Sauk Counties and part of Dane County has come to a close without the loss of a single animal," *The New North* reported. "Using bows that will send an arrow through the body of a deer or pierce a heavy plank, the archers combed the deer inhabited areas of the four counties and report having had numerous shots. In all cases reported to the conservation department the deer were missed."[27] Hunter participation totaled 134.

Roy Case, shown here in 1930 in Vilas County with the first deer killed in Wisconsin with a bow as part of a regulated hunting season, was a tireless promoter of bowhunting in the state.
COURTESY OF THE WISCONSIN BOWHUNTING HERITAGE FOUNDATION

The Master Bowman from Winchester

Art LaHa was nationally known as an expert bowhunter. Hunters came from across the country to attend one of his annual Vilas County bowhunting camps.
COURTESY OF CONNIE GHILONI

I MET ART LAHA, AS THOUSANDS OF PEOPLE INTERESTED in Wisconsin bowhunting have, by finding him at the Bear, the supper club/hunting camp he built and presided over in Winchester, a very small community in northern Vilas County. A friend and I had traveled from Rhinelander to Winchester to check out the Bear and hopefully run into LaHa, whom we had heard so much about after becoming interested in bowhunting just a few years before. Art LaHa was a Wisconsin bowhunting legend, known for his expertise with a recurve, incredible tracking and trailing skills, and great involvement in promoting the sport in the state.

We arrived before the dinnertime crowd. LaHa told us stories as he gave a tour: the bunk rooms that served as quarters for bow camp or for those hunting deer just over the border in Michigan; mounts of some of the game animals he'd taken with his bow, the centerpiece being a full-body mount of a polar bear; and a lounge room where we were shown LaHa's movie of his hunting experiences in Alaska, with commentary by him. We then made our way to the bar for a beer. LaHa came from behind with a large ziplock bag full of smelt. Someone had given him more than he could use.

We exited out into the chill night air, my head full of bowhunting images, a bag of smelt in my hand. It was a unique experience, and we didn't immediately recognize its importance until later. Sadly it had occurred when LaHa was in failing health and would soon be gone. It was only after his death in 1994 that I learned more about the man and understood why he was thought of so highly—so well respected not just by bowhunters but by all who knew him.

The Master Bowman from Winchester (continued)

✦ ✦ ✦ ✦ ✦

LaHa was born in Winchester in 1920. The town basically existed because of a sawmill, which is where LaHa's father, and nearly every adult male in town, worked. The LaHa family was also very good at utilizing the resources the North Woods provided: wild game and fish, berries and nuts.[1]

In 1934, the year Wisconsin had its first official "bow and arrow" season for deer (held in only two southern Wisconsin counties) a teenager named Art LaHa was fast gaining the expertise with a bow that would lead to a life committed to practicing, improving, and promoting the sport of bowhunting.

It was the influence of a French Canadian grandmother, Agnes Languey—a tall, rugged woman who loved the outdoors and could hunt and track wild game as well as anyone—that first got young LaHa interested in hunting game with a bow.

Marge Engel, resident of Winchester, fellow bowhunter, and life-long friend of LaHa and his wife, Ruth, said that LaHa's grandmother was the one who taught him how to shoot a bow.[2] It was the Depression era and people had to put food on their tables, which frequently meant out-of-season hunting. She taught him to hunt with a bow because it was quiet and didn't alert the wardens.[3] She also taught LaHa to walk backward across a road so that the wardens wouldn't know where he was.[4] According to LaHa's second daughter, Connie Ghiloni, "Dad used to tell the family that he had fed seven families during the Depression," referring to using his prowess with the bow to put food on the table of hard-pressed neighbors.[5]

LaHa was a ready pupil and took naturally to the woods, soaking in everything his grandmother could teach him. It was through Agnes that LaHa obtained his first bow: a hand-crafted longbow, given to him by lumberjack friends of hers. Since commercially made arrows were not available in the North Woods, LaHa set out to make his own, using birch dowels for shafts,

Art and Ruth LaHa. Ruth became an accomplished archer and bowhunter in her own right after marrying Art in 1940.
COURTESY OF CONNIE GHILONI

The Master Bowman from Winchester (continued)

barred owl feathers for fletching, and metal cut from an old car clutch plate for arrowheads.[6]

From the time LaHa acquired that first bow, bowhunting became a passion. But skill with a bow didn't pay the bills. After attending high school in Eagle River, LaHa married Ruth Benson, his high school sweetheart, in 1940 and went to work as a meat cutter for the A&P grocery store in Eagle River.[7] LaHa would travel to help open new stores, and wherever he went he got people interested in bowhunting. "They called Dad a bowhunter, but he was really a teacher," said Ghiloni.[8] In 1949 LaHa moved back to Winchester to open a small store and run his own meat-cutting business.

In the early 1940s, bowhunting was in need of some good public relations. During the first five open bow seasons in the 1930s, a total of nine deer had been killed.[9] Though hunter numbers had grown from forty in 1934 to 1,200 just five years later, the sport was still foreign to most Wisconsin deer hunters, many of whom believed that the bow and arrow was not capable of effectively killing big game.

The 1940 bowhunting season, which ran for thirty-one days (October 1–31), was no longer confined to southern Wisconsin: it was allowed in thirty-eight counties—including many north-central counties, such as Vilas and Oneida—for the first time.[10] Not everyone welcomed this expansion of the bowhunting season. "In the north, bowhunters were thought of as 'scum of the earth,'" recalled Dorothy Uthe, a Mercer-area historian and friend of LaHa. "The editor of the

Vilas County News did everything in her power to discredit bowhunters, calling them 'bloody drunks.'"[11]

Marge Engel also remembers the anti-bowhunting sentiment that existed in the north during this period: "Boulder Junction hated bowhunting; the whole community was against it, calling bowhunters derogatory names and claiming they just wounded deer."[12]

These attitudes did eventually change, said Engel, especially when people realized that some of the bowhunters were the same people who came back north in the summer and spent money then, too.[13]

LaHa worked with other bowhunting proponents in the 1940s, including Roy Case of Racine and Larry Whiffen of Milwaukee, to organize the Wisconsin Bowhunters Association with the purpose of establishing an organization that could educate the public and lobby in support of archery hunting.

Also helping to change attitudes toward bowhunting was LaHa's strict adherence to an ethical code, including the idea that a bowhunter must know how to trail game and do everything possible to locate wounded animals.

In 1949 LaHa was able to expand his involvement with bowhunting by operating bowhunting camps each fall. LaHa would rent local Winchester-area resorts during the bow season to serve as a base for his guiding business. Marge Engel, who worked for LaHa at his store, was drafted to be the cook at these annual camps. Engel also became a formidable bow-

The Master Bowman from Winchester (continued)

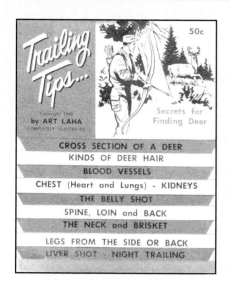

Art LaHa's "Trailing Tips" booklet
COURTESY OF CONNIE GHILONI,
PHOTOS BY JEFF KOSER

hunter herself, often hunting with LaHa's wife, and was known as the "Little Beagle" for her expert trailing skills.[14]

The bow camps proved to be extremely popular. As LaHa's reputation as a master bowman grew, people from across the country would sign on for LaHa's instruction. "The men always had a good time at camp," Ghiloni said. "They loved to listen to Dad and he just loved to tell stories."[15]

Engel remembers that at first it was just the men who came up to bow camp. But they had so much fun they brought their wives along next time as a vacation for them. "At first they didn't hunt, but Art would put them on drives," said Engel. "Soon they started taking up bowhunting themselves. Art introduced a lot of women to the sport."[16]

LaHa's camps also had a big influence on the number of deer taken by archers in Vilas County. Kevin Wallenfang wrote in *Wisconsin Natural Resources*: "Laha [sic] would often have as many as 100 bowhunters in his camp each week, and in some years accounted for more than half of the total archery deer kill for the county. In 1949, some 266 of the statewide archery harvest of 551 deer were taken in Vilas County."[17]

Those who came to hunt with LaHa were held to his strict ethical standards.

"Dad was strict about finding deer," said Ghiloni. "He didn't want to make bowhunters

The Master Bowman from Winchester (continued)

look bad. If someone couldn't find a deer Dad would have them out all night looking, with lanterns and eating sandwiches in the woods, until they found the deer. He would let the warden know that they would be out there so he wouldn't wonder what was going on."[18]

To aid bowhunters in trailing deer, LaHa produced a pocket-size booklet, "Trailing Tips," in 1960. "Trailing Tips" sold for fifty cents and contained an enormous amount of detailed information, straight from LaHa's own experience. The booklet provided a mini whitetail anatomy lesson, with a color diagram of the cross section of a deer showing the position of major organs, and another section describing the major blood vessels of a deer, also with a diagram. Other sections covered the different types of deer hair and where they are located. The booklet also contained descriptions of what to look for when trailing deer according to whether the arrow hit the chest, kidneys, spine, legs, or belly.

The last page of "Trailing Tips" contained ten reminders from LaHa that reflected the level of capability he desired all bowhunters to possess, as seen in tip number three—"Find arrow and correctly interpret looks of blood, hair, food particles, slime, tallow"—and tip number four—"Be perfect in identifying deer hair, then you will use correct trailing tactics."[19] Nearly every bowhunter had a copy of LaHa's booklet in his or her back pocket.

LaHa's and others' efforts to promote bowhunting in Wisconsin really began to pay off in the 1970s. The archery harvest stayed under 10,000 annually until 1974 (forty years after the first official season), when it broke the 10,000 mark for the first time with a take of 12,514.[20] Just six years later, however, the archer take surpassed 20,000, with a 1980 harvest of 20,954.[21] Bowhunting was finally becoming an accepted component of the deer hunting scene in the state. In 2007, archers killed a record 116,010 deer.[22]

LaHa passed away in 1994. In 1996, he was posthumously inducted into the Bowhunter's Hall of Fame.

NOTES

1. Dorothy Uthe, *Art LaHa: A Northwoods Legend* (Decorah, IA: Anundsen Publishing, 1993), 13.
2. Marge Engel, interview with the author, June 27, 2008.
3. Ibid.
4. Uthe, *Art LaHa: A Northwoods Legend*, 21.
5. Connie Ghiloni, interview with the author, June 27, 2008.
6. Dorothy Uthe, interview with the author, September 2000.
7. Uthe, *Art LaHa: A Northwoods Legend*, 42.
8. Connie Ghiloni, interview with the author, June 27, 2008.
9. Otis S. Bersing, *A Century of Wisconsin Deer* (Madison: Wisconsin Conservation Department, Game Management Division, 1956), 133.
10. Ibid.
11. Dorothy Uthe, interview with the author, September 2000.
12. Marge Engel, interview with the author, June 27, 2008.
13. Ibid.
14. Uthe, *Art LaHa: A Northwoods Legend*, 59.
15. Connie Ghiloni, interview with the author, June 27, 2008.
16. Marge Engel, interview with the author, June 27, 2008.
17. Kevin Wallenfang, "Hunters Take a Bow," *Wisconsin Natural Resources*, October 1996, 20.
18. Connie Ghiloni, interview with the author, June 27, 2008.
19. Art LaHa, "Trailing Tips: Secrets for Finding Deer" (Clarendon Hills, IL: Distributed by American Archery Co., 1960).
20. Wisconsin Game and Fur Harvest Summary, 1930–1982, Wisconsin Department of Natural Resources, 1983.
21. Ibid.
22. "2007 Wisconsin Big Game Summary," Wisconsin Department of Natural Resources, April 2008, 6.

An archer with a young buck to bring home on the hood of his Chrysler automobile in 1940.
WHi Image ID 28312

Interest in the bow season slowly but steadily grew, as did the length of the hunt and the amount of territory open to bowmen. The 1939 season ran for thirty days and included several northern Wisconsin counties, including parts of Ashland, Burnett, Douglas, Iron, and Marinette.[28] The 600 hunters who participated in that season's hunt were mavericks, still learning the ancient art of hunting with a bow and arrow. A record kill of six bucks—the first killed by archers since Sroka's buck in 1936—was made. After the 1939 season, a newspaper reported, "Archers believe that in the future there will be thousands of people hunting with bow and arrow. A bag of six deer with bow and arrow this year is expected to greatly stimulate interest in the primitive weapon. Archery clubs have been formed in many communities."[29]

It was clear by the end of the 1930s that bowhunting in Wisconsin was taking hold and would become a fixture on the hunting scene for decades.

Bowhunting buddies pose with a very respectable ten-point buck taken in Marinette County by John Voell (far right) of Fond du Lac in October 1943.
WHi Image ID 28304

Bowhunting legend Fred Bear poses with a nice buck arrowed in the North Woods. Bear played a significant role in establishing a bowhunting season in Wisconsin.
WHi IMAGE ID 28308

◆ ◆ ◆ ◆ ◆

The growing willingness of hunters to spend many hours in pursuit of an animal was showing itself in another way in the 1930s. Perhaps due to more than a decade of buck-only seasons, hunters began to develop a greater appreciation for the difficulty involved in taking a trophy-sized animal. "There is no animal in these parts so cunning, wary, and alert as the white-tailed deer stag!" wrote a northern outdoor reporter in 1938. "It is the sagacity of the white-tailed buck that makes deer hunting worthwhile—open the season on does and it would be like shooting cattle in a barnyard."[30]

While large bucks with nicely developed racks had always been a cause for comment, a greater amount of press was starting to be given to trophy bucks. Accurate weight and antler measurements began to be reported in the newspapers for the first time in the 1930s. "Deer heads are being mounted in many sections of the state as a result of the recent season and one head reported to the Conservation Department has horns numbering 43 sizeable points plus additional smaller ones. If these points are all of standard size laid down in records, it is probable that Wisconsin has established a new deer head record for the country," reported a newspaper in 1937.[31]

The New North stated in 1939:

Record heads are the rule in Wisconsin. Last year the state had reports of more than 50 bucks weighing over 270 pounds, dressed. Inquiry developed that only 10 had actually weighed their deer on scales. Dick Kay of Washburn took the biggest buck in Bayfield county, a buster of 321½ pounds dressed weight. Had Kay weighed this deer before dressing, he might have been credited with a world record, now generally acknowledged to be held by a 388 pound deer taken in New York State by Henry Ordway in 1890.[32]

That same year, it was also reported that "Fay Hammersley of Madison had another giant buck, taken in Juneau County. Dressed weight was 315 pounds and the antlers of this buck were the biggest the state could find last year, a 24 inch outside spread, both beams 5½ circumference; 10 points on one side, nine on the other side."[33]

Hammersley's buck was one of numerous record-quality bucks reported as taken in the 1930s. Others included the Boone and Crockett Club–listed buck taken by Earl Holt in Bayfield County in 1934. (The club started its formal recognition of trophy animals in 1932.) *The Wisconsin Sportsman* described the rack:

The victim of Mr. Holt's marksmanship boasted a set of really remarkable antlers, which were somewhat palmated, like those of a caribou, and in number of points and breadth of beam surpassed those of any white tail deer recorded in Prentiss N. Gray's 'Records of North American Big Game.' Holt's buck has 39 points and the circumference of the main beam is 7½ inches.[34]

A fourteen-point buck taken by Carl Laughnan and a ten-point buck taken by Russell Hegg during the 1934 deer season made the trip from Douglas county hunting grounds back to Madison tied to the front fenders of an automobile. The days of transporting deer back home by rail were only memories by this time.

WHi Image ID 16168

By the 1930s, deer strapped to automobiles were a common sight on Wisconsin roads during and after deer season. Two bucks as well as a timber wolf made the trip home with these hunters.

Courtesy of Mike Vlahakis

The alternate-year closed season structure that began in 1925 continued into the 1930s. The ten-day season length that had started back in 1917 continued for the 1930 and 1932 open seasons. After three seasons with a December opening day—1926, 1928, and 1930—the season's start returned to a more traditional late-November opening in 1932; its length, however, was reduced to seven days beginning in 1934.

If the pattern of statewide closed seasons in odd-numbered years was adhered to, there would have been a closed season in 1937. But with a consistently expanding deer herd—which in some locations clearly was an overpopulated herd—game managers felt there needed to be a deer hunt in 1937. This proposal, the first serious suggestion to curb rising deer numbers, might well be termed the first shot fired in the ensuing deer wars.

Newspapers editors across the state were inundated with letters from hunters commenting on the proposal. *The Wisconsin Sportsman* summarized some of the letters. It was clear where the battle lines had been drawn: again, a raging deer management controversy was largely north versus south.

The editor of *The Wisconsin Sportsman* wrote:

> Before and after every deer season there seems always to be much heated discussion pro and con. The deer probably has more friends among the general population than any other wild animal. It seems to have the power of stirring, with its liquid brown eyes, the sympathy of John Q. Public, of creating within him righteous wrath at the very idea of anyone shooting this most attractive animal.[35]

Those who wrote in favor of having an open season in 1937 were largely from central and southern Wisconsin counties. It was easy to see the rebounding deer numbers in these counties, as farmer complaints increased and deer dead along roadsides became a common sight.

A letter to the editor of the *La Crosse Tribune and Leader Press* stated:

> To us it is surprising to see how some people jump to defend these animals year in and year out. If they would only consider some of the factors pertinent to the situation, disregarding any idealism they might have, we are sure they might see the problem in a somewhat different light. If there isn't an open season this year, it will be necessary to do considerable artificial feeding this winter. We believe that a little idealism in regard to Wisconsin deer is a swell thing, but we contend that a little practical sense must also be used.[36]

A letter to the *Milwaukee Journal* criticized the newspaper's support of a closed season: "I have had your paper in my home for ten years, always bought your Sunday paper, but I think you are going too far in printing untrue things about the deer hunting season. We have plenty of deer, so quit your knocking."[37]

After the *Capital Times* ran a picture of twenty-two deer hunters each standing proudly next to a buck with comments suggesting the photo be a case for the closed season, an irate hunter wrote: "I noticed your 'picture editorial' of 22 hunters with 22 deer, and you say it would be a good idea if the conservation commission would look at this picture before deciding to have an open season again this fall. Yes, I think it is a good idea for the conservation commission to study this picture, for when 22 hunters can bag 22 bucks in seven days, it proves there is no shortage of deer in the state."[38]

Most of the sentiment against a season for 1937 came from northern counties by those who had experienced the enormous tide of deer hunters every season and observed deer stacked in great heaps at the railway stations. In more recent years, the north had experienced an influx of summer tourists who liked nothing better than to observe the wild animals of the north—particularly the beautiful whitetail. So the animal's population had taken on a new importance to the local economies.

Joseph Mercedes, executive director of the Heart O' Lakes Association in Rhinelander, wrote to the *Milwaukee Journal*:

> One of the most destructive moves that can be made to kill off our tourism industry is to allow an open season on deer this year. I come in contact with thousands of tourists each year and I find that they are most interested in seeing our wild game, rather than fishing. I have as my guest at present Mayor Joseph Allen of Des Moines. He is here with his family for the first time. I spent the better part of two days driving through the woods to enable his family to catch a glimpse of our deer. We finally succeeded in seeing three. The visitors were thrilled beyond words.[39]

A writer to the *Ladysmith News* suggested the Conservation Department had ulterior motives for open seasons: "It hardly seems to be the sentiment of Rusk county folks that an open deer season is called for this year. One suspects that the conservation department may be actuated by the desire to have income from deer licenses and this desire finds expression in the opinions of many of its wardens that deer are plentiful."[40]

Due to the controversy, the 1937 season turned out to be a compromise season much like the season of 1917 that brought back the "any-deer" season but cut the season length in half. The 1937 season was held, but only for three days. Despite the season's abbreviated length, about 90,000 hunters bagged 15,000 bucks.[41]

As the 1930s drew to a close, nearly twenty years of buck-only hunting had changed the way sportsmen viewed deer and deer hunting. But problems were brewing that would soon pit the new ideas of scientific game management against age-old beliefs and a deeply divided public.

Complete protection of does, along with closed seasons and deer refuges, while accomplishing the intended goal of growing the deer herd, had allowed populations in many areas to grow out of control. Neighboring states of Minnesota and Michigan had already experienced population crashes, as thousands of deer died of starvation during the winter of 1937–38 due to the inability of the winter habitat to support the growing numbers.[42]

Wisconsin Conservation Department deputy director Ernie Swift was one of the first to sound the warning, although not many hunters in the state were ready to listen. In 1939, Swift wrote a paper, "The Problem of Managing Wisconsin Deer," that described the rocky road deer management was headed down and addressed the critical need to manage the deer herd based on the rather new principles of scientific deer management. He was blunt. Although he felt public involvement in the deer management process was crucial, he chastised those who made arguments based only on personal opinion.

"From three to ten days of every year or every other year, the average hunter studies the deer problem through the sights of a .30-30 while the balance of the year his research is restricted pretty much to the barber shop," Swift wrote. "If he is a business man of the north and has a cottage on a near-by lake, his research is confined to the road out to the cottage in the evening and back to work in the morning."[43]

Swift saw deer management as something like an agricultural science and used terms new to the deer hunter of the day but familiar to us today. He wrote, "The first concern of the state is to make available the surplus or harvestable crop, safeguarding a renewable seed stock. For the past several years the only logical way to save that seed stock has been to allow only the killing of forked horn (antlered) bucks, and through an adequate refuge system."[44]

Swift emphasized that the buck-only seasons, the closed seasons, and the refuge system had allowed the herd in some areas to grow past the land's capacity to support those deer numbers. Trouble was ahead.

"There seems to be ample proof that deer have been increasing over a period of 25 years and this not only comes from the findings of the department but is also borne out by hunters, loggers, and woodsmen familiar with certain territories, some of them as long as 40 years," Swift wrote. "This is evident in Vilas county, the Flambeau river country in Price and Sawyer counties, the Clam Lake region in Bayfield, Sawyer, and Ashland counties and in central Wisconsin."

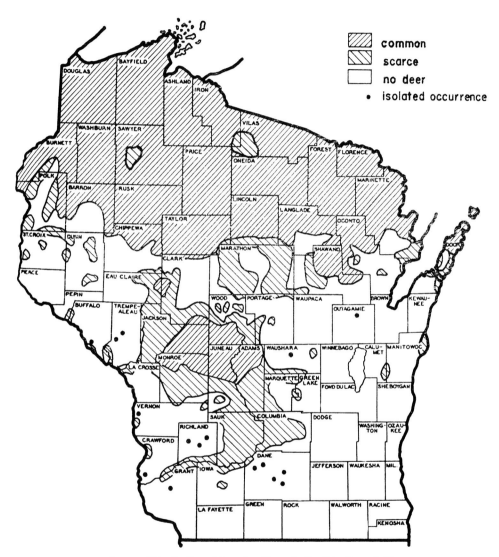

WHITE-TAILED DEER IN WISCONSIN
SUMMER RANGE
AS OF 1938

common
scarce
no deer
• isolated occurrence

Source: "The Problem of Managing Wisconsin Deer" by Ernest Swift.

As habitat improved and regulations took hold in the late 1930s, deer numbers and occupied range began to expand, reversing the trend of previous decades.

A Century of Wisconsin Deer

The whitetail's range was expanding as well. "In fact, the deer are now common in many central, southern and western counties where they had been extinct for many years," noted Swift, "and in some other counties where practically extinct, a substantial increase has been noticed."[45]

He continued: "The spread and increase of deer is further in evidence by the gradually increasing amount of damage to crops, gardens, shrubs and trees, paid from deer tag money by the state. The number of deer killed on highways by automobiles is also definitely increasing each year."[46]

After decades of a general attitude among hunters that does needed complete protection in order to save the seed stock, Swift concluded that years of buck-only seasons had skewed the sex ratio to favor does. A continued combination of the status quo—high takes of bucks and closed deer seasons—would do nothing to bring the population in a balance with the carrying capacity, that is, the number of deer the habitat could support.

Swift's ideas, while solidly anchored in facts and real observations rather than anecdotes and personal opinion, stood in direct opposition to the general hunting public's perception of how deer should be managed. Northern interests were still fighting for closed seasons to preserve the deer for the tourists. Southern interests wanted to go back to open, any-deer seasons to address burgeoning problems associated with more deer on the landscape.

Swift responded to those who felt the any-deer season was the answer, with this:

> If the sex ratio has become unbalanced by the killing of too many bucks, a general open season on all deer is not necessarily the answer. Instead of 100,000 deer hunters, we would have possibly 130,000 or 150,000 hunters. The ease with which does and fawns can be killed during a deer season is generally known throughout the state. An open season on all deer would cause a real, man-sized revolution. Everybody from smooth-faced boys and blushing brides to old men in wheel chairs would stampede the woods to witness the last stand of the deer and put their tag on a doe or fawn that father or brother Jim shot for them.[47]

Addressing those who still clamored for closed seasons, he wrote:

> The plea of some persons that we should have no open season is certainly not the answer to the question. Imperfect as the attempts of man may be to bring a balance in conservation efforts which in the past he has disregarded, at least we have come to one great milestone of where it is recognized that a balance is necessary if all types of conservation are to move forward.[48]

Swift saw common ground between the different factions and provided a succinct quote from an article by Dr. Rudolph Bennitt, a professor at the University of

Missouri: "I would like to point out once more that all of us who are interested in wildlife at all, from the dyed-in-the-wool game-hog to the most extreme protectionist, are seeking the same thing whether we realize it or not. If we want more wildlife to enjoy without killing it we can get it only by increasing the carrying capacity of the lands and waters. If we want a larger crop to harvest, year after year, our method must be the same and the objective of the non-hunter will be attained as well. We all seek a larger breeding reserve. The only difference is that some of us wish to leave the entire surplus to be killed by natural factors; others wish man to take a fair share of the surplus."[49]

Swift stated that the 1939 Wisconsin deer herd was "not in 'deplorable' condition, nor is our problem 'acute' at the present time; but when the management of an excessive doe population is necessary in any locality, it does seem evident that a general open slaughter of all deer is not the remedy. The situation should be taken care of before that is necessary."[50]

The answer to the problem, in Swift's opinion, would have to include some limited take of does since decades of complete doe protection were responsible for the imbalance observed in the Wisconsin herd. Swift knew the killing of does, something not permitted in Wisconsin since 1919, was inevitable. Any system to allow for a limited take of does would have to be highly regulated. Knowing this could be a tough sell, he asked the question, "Are hunters as yet ready to accept these additional restrictions and a limited number of licenses issued in the name of good management? Or is all this controversy after each hunting season really born of a desire to see everyone get a deer so that none of the hundred thousand would be 'skunked'?"[51]

In 1939, Swift advocated for a hunting season that would include the removal of does. Now the question was, would anyone salute?

World events would soon put Swift's question on the back burner.

In the early morning hours of December 7, 1941, Japanese submarines and aircraft carrier–based planes were attacking Pearl Harbor in Hawaii, the site of one of the principal American naval bases. By the time the surprise attack ended, approximately 3,000 Americans had been killed or injured. The United States could no longer assist the war effort from the sidelines. On December 8, Congress officially declared U.S. entry into World War II.

On the home front, talk of battlefield maneuvers in the Pacific and Europe dominated café, tavern, and barbershop discussions. When men, young and old, had thoroughly informed each other of their opinions on the war effort, discussions often turned back to another volatile subject in Wisconsin at the time—deer management.

The groundwork for what would later be referred to as the "deer wars" had been laid during the preceding two decades. A declining deer herd and diminishing hunter opportunities occurred hand in hand with a growing awareness among Americans that it was a good thing, an ethical thing, to conserve rather than squander our natural resources. But six statewide closed seasons, the first in 1925, primarily one-buck laws

The voluntary sportsmen's license became available in 1937, with a portion of the fee going toward the purchase of refuges and hunting grounds.
COURTESY OF WISCONSIN DEPARTMENT OF NATURAL RESOURCES, BUREAU OF WILDLIFE MANAGEMENT

since 1915, and huge tracts of land designated as protected game refuges (with the northern cutover region a veritable deer pasture of new growth) all contributed to a situation that was termed a deer "irruption"—a severe increase in population—by game managers.

Aldo Leopold, chair of the Department of Wildlife Management at the University of Wisconsin, described the stages of a deer irruption in a 1943 paper that became part of the Wisconsin Conservation Department's publication *Wisconsin's Deer Problem*. Leopold wrote that, in the early stages, the growing deer population begins to overbrowse its highest quality food sources, so much so that a deer line, or browse line, becomes apparent. At this stage, deer still winter well. But as deer populations continue increasing, a browse line appears on lower-quality browse, and weaker animals, including fawns, begin to die during hard winters. "At this stage conifer plantations begin to show deer-damage, and reproduction of palatable browse has ceased to survive," wrote Leopold.[52]

In later stages, if the herd is not reduced by shooting, the herd's numbers peak, the range deteriorates even further, and the end result is massive starvation over the winter in deer yards. It is only then, when the adult does begin to die, that the population begins its decline. "Downgrade by starvation always begins during a hard winter," wrote Leopold.[53]

If there is no intervention by game managers or hunters, deer numbers eventually drop below the carrying capacity of the land and level off. The implications were clear: either let Mother Nature balance deer numbers with available food supply through starvation during the brutal northern winters, or let hunters intervene and remove the number of deer necessary to allow the herd to keep in balance with the land's ability to support a given population.

Leopold believed that, in 1943, northern Wisconsin and some areas of central Wisconsin were in the early stages of deer irruption, and that immediate, significant reduction of the herd was imperative.[54] Leopold explained that years of overprotection of the deer herd, compounded by removal of wolves—a natural predator—in the north, had set the stage for deer irruption. "Buck laws are admirable for a herd that needs building up," Leopold wrote, "but hardly for a herd in need of reduction." If not regulated by hunter harvest, Leopold warned, the herd will regulate itself by massive starvation and range destruction.[55]

In 1940 a study of deer yard conditions, primarily in northern Wisconsin, had been initiated under the direction of the Wisconsin Conservation Department to add scientific credibility and some hard facts to the Wisconsin "deer problem." The study team examined more than 250 deer yards to assess and document the condition of the habitat. The results of the "deer research project," reported by project leader W. S. Feeney in 1943, were startling but confirmed what game managers had already come to understand: the northern Wisconsin winter deer range was in a deplorable condition and had a greatly diminished capacity to support deer.[56]

The study found that more than two-thirds of the deer yards assessed were heavily overbrowsed and deer numbers were exceeding carrying capacity on a sustained basis in three-quarters of the yards. Cedar, a preferred deer food source, was browsed clean in 90 percent of the study area, and balsam fir, regarded as a "starvation" food, had experienced increased browsing. A mild

The necessary paperwork for a Wisconsin resident to hunt deer in 1940–41: The license, which sold for one dollar, was issued by a county clerk. A postcard attached to the license served as a report of deer taken and needed to be returned to the Wisconsin Conservation Department by February of the next year.

COURTESY OF WISCONSIN DEPARTMENT OF NATURAL RESOURCES, BUREAU OF WILDLIFE MANAGEMENT

winter in 1941–42 prevented massive starvation that season, since deer could range out of the yards to find food. The next winter, however, was a hard one, and Feeney found dead deer littering the yards; nearly 80 percent had died from outright malnutrition and starvation. He observed:

> [O]f the dead deer found, 77 percent were fawns, of these the ratio of bucks to does was approximately equal. Occasionally the misleading statement has come out that 1200 or 1300 deer died in Wisconsin last winter. Over 1400 deer were found, but since only a very small percentage of the winter range was cruised this number could be multiplied considerably to arrive at the actual total starvation losses. Though this mortality runs into the thousands, it is difficult to estimate the total reliability. We do know, however, as far as could be determined by counting live fawns and dead fawns that all of last year's fawn crop was lost in several of the browsed out deer yards.[57]

With the hard evidence provided by the deer study, a Citizens' Deer Committee consisting of nine members and chaired by Aldo Leopold made formal recommendations to the Conservation Commission in 1943. In general, their recommendations were extensions of the ideas put forth by Ernie Swift in 1939. The committee stated:

> We see no remedy except to reduce the deer herd to what the yards can carry without losing their good natural winter food plants.
>
> We are convinced that artificial feeding without herd-reduction is no remedy, for it does not relieve the overdraft on natural food plants. States which have tried feeding report that it does not relieve overbrowsing, and may aggravate it.
>
> Artificial feeding of deer is different from artificial feeding of birds, for the latter has no effect on the future supply of natural bird foods.
>
> The present starvation of fawns is not reducing the herd. Only the removal of does can do so. It is not practical to distinguish does from other antlerless deer in setting open seasons.[58]

With a deer herd thought to number more than half a million, the committee believed that an antlerless deer season posed no threat of an overharvest of does: "We conclude that every deer hunter could take an antlerless deer for at least one season, and perhaps for several seasons, before a sufficient reduction will have been made. We conclude that no danger of an over-reduction exists, provided the antlerless deer season be restricted to overpopulated counties."[59]

The Citizens' Deer Committee took votes on eleven questions related to the deer problem. Question number six—"Should herd reduction begin in 1943?"—received a unanimous "yes" vote.[60] The bottom line, according to the committee, was: "If the herd is not shot down, it will starve down."[61]

The Conservation Commission concurred that an antlerless season was imperative, but recognized it was going to be an extremely hard sell to the hunting public as well as the deer-protectionist public. Wisconsin had not had a deer season that allowed the killing of does and fawns since 1919. Younger hunters weren't even born then, and older hunters had a tough time remembering the "any deer" seasons of the past. In the years that had passed since those liberal seasons, killing a doe had become almost taboo.

There also was a contingent that believed herd reduction would best be accomplished through a strictly antlerless season, not an "any deer" season. An antlerless-only season for 1943 had been a recommendation of the Citizens' Deer Committee.

With deeply divided factions, the end result was an awkward compromise for 1943: a buck-only season and a separate antlerless season, each four days long and separated by three days.

Prior to this unique deer season, no one knew what to expect. "It's a screwy deer season this year—perhaps the screwiest in history—with shell shortages, gas and meat rationing and a doe season thrown in to complete matters," commented one newspaper. "Nonetheless, to many sportsmen it's the most important time in the year and some of them live from year to year for the thrills and the remembrances of it."[62]

The buck-only part of the season occurred with little comment. But as the antlerless season began, emotions ran high. "Hunters in Oneida County early yesterday morning began the antlerless deer season with the slaughter rivaling that on a Russian battlefield," reported the *Rhinelander Daily News*. "As Warden Harley T. McKeague expressed it, 'the county was strewn with blood and guts from one end to the other,' adding, 'you can quote me on that.'"[63]

Despite the emotional impact of the antlerless season, hunter participation was at a record level. "Deer hunting license sales will reach a record total of at least 148,000 in Wisconsin this year," according to an estimate from Roy Straus, head of the Conservation Department's licensing division, reported by the *Rhinelander Daily News*.[64]

The 1943 split season also resulted in a record take of deer: the combined season estimate totaled more than 128,000 deer. Only 45,000 deer had been taken during the previous year's buck-only hunt. In terms of increasing harvest and reducing the deer herd, the split season was a success. But it turned into a public relations nightmare for both the Conservation Department and the Conservation Commission. The double shock of a season on does and fawns coupled with a tremendous number of animals killed was too much for most of the public to bear.

Newspaper editorials across the state, such as this one from the *Oshkosh Northwestern*, blasted the Conservation Department and the Conservation Commission:

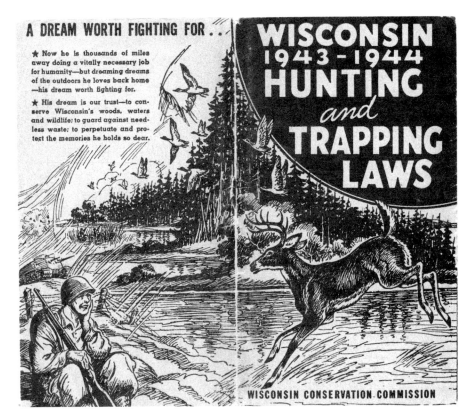

The hunting and trapping regulations pamphlet for the 1943–44 seasons employed the image of soldiers fighting in World War II to encourage those on the home front to protect Wisconsin's natural resources.
COURTESY OF WISCONSIN DEPARTMENT OF NATURAL RESOURCES, BUREAU OF WILDLIFE MANAGEMENT

Judging from the large number of deer transported through Oshkosh during and at the end of the recent double shooting season, by way of automobiles and railroad express, the slaughter in the woods of northern Wisconsin must have been tremendous. . . . *Considering* the whole affair, with a total of eight hunters killed in accidental shooting, it is probably not likely that this herd-thinning experiment will again be tried soon by the state conservation commission. After seeing the extent of the slaughter, many persons cannot help wondering if there are any more deer left in the woods.[65]

The *Capital Times* shared similar concerns:

Wisconsin's double-header deer season, permitting four days of indiscriminate killing of does and antlerless deer and four days of buck shooting, has come to an end with a wholesale slaughter of deer which tops all records. The full respon-sibility for the mass destruction of a large part of the state's deer herd this year lies squarely on the shoulders of the state conservation commission. Arguing that there was insufficient feed in the north woods for the deer, the commission for an eight day period virtually took off all bars. A hundred thousand or more bucks, does, young bucks, and fawns were destroyed as a result of commission bungling, and there is reason to believe that the quality of the deer herd has been impaired for a long time to come.[66]

In northern Wisconsin, the general sentiment was close to rage. The *Forest Republican* wrote, "[T]he north is not burned up over the shooting of big bucks but the slaughter of fawns, does and small bucks is what has thousands of northwoods folks riled up. . . . Every time we think of the big slaughter, we wonder what in the h--l is the matter with those conservation nit-wits down south. The past season was really disgusting. . . . All this makes the northwoods citizen mad enough to vote for a closed season next year and then go out and violate all fall."[67]

The *Vilas County News-Review* wasn't so diplomatic: "Horror piled upon horror during the buck-doe season. The woods actually were smeared with blood wher-ever one walked. Even men accustomed to killing a buck each season turned their eyes away in disgust. A shudder of distaste went down the spine as car after car loaded with does and Christmas trees left the country.

"Human greed, ugliest of human emotions, aroused by the promise that there were 'lots of does,' became a gigantic force that brought wreckage and possible temporary disaster to the herd."

The paper went on to say, "The days of cowardly evasion are over. Northern Wisconsin has come of age during this deer season."[68]

Central and southern Wisconsin newspapers mostly reflected a different atti-tude, one based on the impressions of hunters in those regions. The *Marshfield News Herald* wrote: "But we have no fear that so many deer were killed in the dual season that the herd is anywhere near depletion. If anything, not enough deer were taken to permit the remainder to feed on their winter ranges without over-browsing them."[69]

Those with the perception that the deer herd had been shot to pieces felt their concerns were justified when the winter following the 1943 season brought deep snows, which magnified the downward trend in the deer population.[70]

Hotly debated deer management issues didn't keep hunters out of the woods during the war years. In the early 1940s, annual hunter numbers continued their steady increase well past 100,000. The reason for the record number of licenses sold for the split season of 1943 was often attributed to "the desire to supplement limited wartime meat rations."[71]

Rationing had other impacts on hunting during this period. "Faced with limited gasoline and ammunition supplies, hunters have been doing some close figuring to be able to get out in the woods," reported the *Rhinelander Daily News.*[72]

Deer Season Manhunt

IN THE AUTUMN OF 1942, AMERICA WAS BECOMING deeply involved in World War II. Since the Japanese attack on Pearl Harbor the previous December, the United States had committed itself to the war in Europe as well as the Pacific, and young men were going overseas by the thousands.

With the rationing of gasoline and ammunition prevalent, those on the home front wondered what the 1942 Wisconsin deer season would see for hunting pressure. The one thing that was clear was that, of those who could hunt, most would be heading to northern Wisconsin, as they had for years. They would be drawn north for the camaraderie and tradition of the North Woods deer camp, and also because many counties in southern Wisconsin remained closed to all deer hunting due to low deer numbers. The 1942 season was set to open on November 21 and run nine days in the thirty-one counties that had a season, with a forked buck–only bag restriction.[1]

With hunters concentrating their efforts in the north, the Wisconsin Conservation Department needed special wardens from the south to assist the northern Wisconsin wardens with deer season law enforcement. The 1942 season also had a new law enforcement concern: it was the first year back tags were required.

Albert Reif, the thirty-three-year-old supervisor of Kettle Moraine State Forest, was one of those department employees assigned to deer season duty in the North Woods. Reif was sent to Florence County to assist game warden Floyd Sanders. Neither man could foresee the great tragedy that would occur just days before the opener.

On November 18, the Wednesday prior to opening day, Reif and Sanders were patrolling the woods along the Wisconsin-Michigan border about three miles northwest of Iron Mountain, Michigan, when a gunshot echoed through the autumn woods.[2] Someone was getting a jump on the season. They proceeded toward the area to investigate.

Approaching the area where the shot had come from, they discovered a man near a 1930 Oldsmobile on a side road about fifty yards off U.S. Highway 2. Reif began a standard interrogation of the man, who was dressed in a blue flannel shirt and whipcord breeches—typical North Woods attire. Sanders investigated the inside of

Deer Season Manhunt (continued)

the car and noted the backseat was filled with camping gear.[3]

While Sanders was searching the backseat, another shot rang out. Jumping out of the car he saw that Reif had fallen to the ground, shot in the head, and the man in the blue flannel shirt was standing there, pistol in hand.[4]

"They exchanged shots, the slayer backing into the woods and Sanders following him, dodging from tree to tree," reported the Associated Press.[5]

Sanders picked up Reif's automatic pistol and emptied both his own and Reif's gun but failed to hit the murderer. Without ammunition, Sanders briefly became the pursued. He escaped by circling through the woods. The man in the blue flannel shirt was able to double back to his car and disappear. When Sanders returned to the scene of the crime he found that the man had dragged Reif's body into the woods, and the Olds was gone.[6]

Immediately the manhunt began. "Twenty-two Michigan State police and 16 Wisconsin officers in addition to [Florence County] Sheriff Grell's deputies have been assigned to the hunt, with more officers to arrive today," the Associated Press reported on November 19.[7] State police and wardens from both states combed the woods along the border, and detectives followed up on every lead.

"Possibility that the slayer of Albert Reif, Wisconsin forest supervisor, was the same man who is wanted for questioning about the fatal shooting of a woman and her eight-months-old daughter near Oconto Falls several weeks ago was being investigated today by Florence and Oconto county authorities," the press reported on November 20.[8] The lead proved false and, after three days, the trail of the killer seemed to grow cold.

"Meanwhile, search for Reif's murderer continued unabated through the wild forest-lands of Wisconsin and northern Michigan, with law enforcement officers of both states admitting they had unearthed no definite clues to the man's whereabouts."[9]

A hopeful lead was reported on November 24 when a story from Rhinelander seemed to be a break in the case. "A possibility that a gun theft suspect who was arraigned in county court yesterday may have been implicated in the slaying of Albert Reif, was being investigated here today," reported the *Rhinelander Daily News*.[10] That lead, however, also proved false.

Search for Slayer Of Conservation Officer Widens

FLORENCE, Wis., Nov. 19 (*AP*)— A John Doe warrant charging murder was issued today for the slayer of Albert E. Reif, 33-year-old forest supervisor who was shot yesterday as he questioned a man about gunfire in the woods three miles northwest of Iron Mountain, Mich.

Dist. Atty. Allen Wittkopf directed issuance of the warrant after a coroner's jury had returned a verdict that Reif died of a gunshot wound fired by a person unknown.

County authorities said that a bullet had been removed from Reif's head and appeared to have been fired from a .38 calibre weapon.

Search for the slayer continued in northern Wisconsin and Upper Michigan, but authorities said they had uncovered no definite clues.

Michigan state police found an abandoned automobile near Norway, Mich., last night. It bore

RHINELANDER DAILY NEWS, NOVEMBER 19, 1942

Deer Season Manhunt (continued)

Days went by with no developments in the case. Anxious residents of Florence County and across the Michigan border in Dickinson and Iron counties began locking their doors at night. The hundreds of deer hunters now in the woods wondered if there was a murderer prowling nearby.

On November 28, the story ended as quickly as it had started. A Michigan fire warden near Sagola realized that a local woodsman, who had gone into town to purchase food, fit the description of the suspect.[11] The man was quickly apprehended.

Emil Schroeder, a forty-six-year-old woodsman and trapper arrested by the Michigan state police, lived alone in a remote cabin. He offered no resistance and readily confessed to authorities. According to the press, the slayer "admitted that he was pursued into the forest and that he counted the shots fired by the officer until sure the guns were empty. Then he returned to his car and drove to his isolated cabin."[12]

The man told authorities that he had feared for his life and fired in self-defense because Reif "was pulling a gun from his pocket."[13]

With a full confession in hand, and a positive identification by Warden Sanders, Sheriff Grell and Warden R. A. Nixon brought the man to Florence to be arraigned before Judge Irving W. Smith.[14] Schroeder was later held in the Marinette County jail (because of lack of jail facilities at Florence) to await trial.

On Sunday, November 29, the 1942 Wisconsin deer season came to a close, and, with

Albert Reif's killer in jail, so, too, did the story of a deer season tragedy.

Reif was buried in Milwaukee, the home of his parents. A native of Switzerland and graduate of Michigan State University, he had worked for the Conservation Department since 1932.[15] Reif's slayer was convicted of second-degree murder and served seven years at the state prison in Waupun.

NOTES

1. Otis S. Bersing, *A Century of Wisconsin Deer* (Madison: Wisconsin Conservation Department, Game Management Division, 1956), 95.
2. "Hunter Shoots State Officer," *Rhinelander Daily News*, November 18, 1942.
3. "Search for Slayer of Conservation Officer Widens," *Rhinelander Daily News*, November 19, 1942.
4. Ibid.
5. "Hunter Shoots State Officer," *Rhinelander Daily News*, November 18, 1942.
6. Ibid.
7. "Search for Slayer of Conservation Officer Widens," *Rhinelander Daily News*, November 19, 1942.
8. "Seek to Link Slayer With Death of Two Others," *Wausau Daily Herald*, November 20, 1942.
9. Ibid.
10. "Gun Theft Suspect Is Questioned on Warden's Slaying," *Rhinelander Daily News*, November 24, 1942.
11. "Trapper Admits Slaying State Forest Supervisor," *Wausau Daily Herald*, November 30, 1942.
12. Ibid.
13. Ibid.
14. Ibid.
15. "Search for Slayer of Conservation Officer Widens," *Rhinelander Daily News*, November 19, 1942.

The government didn't miss the fact that so many hunters continued to head to northern deer camps despite wartime rationing. The Office of Price Administration (OPA) notified hunters that investigators "will be on the job to ask for and check gasoline coupon books." The OPA warned hunters that "the fellow who cannot make the trip without securing extra gasoline from somewhere . . . had better forego deer hunting this year or take the chance of ending up with less gasoline than he has now or perhaps none at all."[73]

One group of hunters not worried about gasoline rationing included soldiers home on leave. Many lucky enough to receive furloughs in November headed straight to the deer woods. "Two Three Lakes servicemen got home at the right time and succeeded in bagging deer," reported the *Rhinelander Daily News* in 1943.[74]

One serviceman in the woods during the 1943 season was the famous fighter pilot Richard Ira Bong of Poplar. Bong had already downed twenty-one Japanese planes when he took to the woods while home during a furlough. He was hounded by the press. "Capt. Bong, who is home on leave from the bigger sport of bagging Japs, took to the woods early today with a party of relatives and friends in pursuit of deer," a newspaper reported.[75]

As the war came to a victorious close in 1945, servicemen by the thousands returned to Wisconsin and began new traditions of deer hunting. Deer tag sales

Purchasing war-rationed shotgun shells in Madison, 1944
WHi Image ID 40781

topped 200,000 in 1946, and continued to climb the remainder of the decade. In the 1948 buck-only season, a record 248,954 deer licenses were sold. Though the hunting pressure was great, only about 42,000 bucks were taken during the nine-day season, as compared to 53,520 in 1947 and 55,276 in 1946.[76] It seemed that when constrained by a buck-only season—which was the case for five years after the uproar over the 1943 split season, with a few exceptions in some agricultural counties—increased hunting pressure was not enough to reduce the deer herd.

Home for the Hunt

JOYCE BONG ERICKSON REMEMBERS THE GREAT EXCITEMENT that was filling the small Wisconsin farmhouse on that cold November evening in 1943. She remembers the people who were filling the farmhouse as well. Friends and neighbors were crowding into it, and so were the reporters.

The reporters were there to wait for the arrival of Captain Richard Ira Bong, the U.S. Army flying ace who had already shot down twenty-one Japanese warplanes. Joyce, in ninth grade at the time, along with the rest of the Bong family, was simply waiting for Dick.[1]

Twenty-three-year-old Dick Bong had just completed his first combat tour as a pilot of a P-38 fighter and was coming home to the family farm near Poplar, a small town in northern Douglas County, for some well-earned R&R. Captain Bong's feats in the South Pacific were already legendary. The humble, unassuming Wisconsin farm boy was famous, a national hero.

"It was an exciting time," Joyce told me in 2002 as we sat in the dining room of the farmhouse where the Bong children grew up. "Every-

one wanted to see Dick. He hadn't been home in over two years."

Dick Bong had enlisted in the Army Air Corps aviation cadet program in January 1941 at age twenty. The end of that year brought the Japanese attack at Pearl Harbor and thrust the United States into the war in the Pacific. Bong eventually found himself at the controls of a P-38 Lightning in the southwest Pacific. With a combination of skill, a cool head, and just the right amount of moxie, Bong blossomed into a top fighter pilot.

While the temperature dropped outside, the scene inside the farmhouse was one of warmth and revelry. Sister Nelda played the piano, with the crowd, including the twenty-nine members of the ROTC band, American Legion members, and some former professors of Bong's from Superior State Teachers College, joining in on song.[2]

Finally, just after 1:00 a.m., headlights flashed in the darkness. Captain Bong had arrived.

The reporters bombarded Bong with questions while the photographers set up shot after

Home for the Hunt (continued)

shot. Members of the Superior American Legion Post presented Bong, his father, and his seventeen-year-old brother, Bud, with rubber-soled hunting boots, the result of a "Boots for Bong" campaign. A box of shells for Bong's 300 Savage was presented by "Doc" Miller, a former professor, on behalf of the Superior Junior Chamber of Commerce.[3] These were welcomed gifts as both rubber and ammunition were rationed during the war.

Dick Bong poses in the barn next to opening-day bucks for photographers eager to capture the World War II flying ace's Wisconsin deer hunt on film. To satisfy the throng of reporters and allow Dick to hunt the remainder of the season in peace, the story—for the moment—was that Captain Bong shot the ten-pointer. The photo quickly hit the front pages of newspapers across the country.
Courtesy of Joyce Bong Erickson

Home for the Hunt (continued)

Like most northern Wisconsin boys of the time, Bong was an ardent hunter. He'd arrived just in time for the Wisconsin gun deer season.

After his mother moved the crowd out around 3:00 a.m., Bong was able to get some sleep. The next day would be spent preparing for the hunt. "In the afternoon, we drove to Superior to get some wool hunting pants and other hunting gear for Dick," wrote Carl "Bud" Bong, Richard's younger brother, in his book, *Dear Mom: So We Have a War*.[4]

The next morning was the opener—the first day of the first half of the unique 1943 split season. The first four days of the season were for antlered bucks only (forks or better), followed by a three-day break, and finished with a four-day antlerless season.

The blue skies of the Pacific Theater were far away for Captain Bong, as an old-fashioned Wisconsin deer hunt began. After a big farm breakfast of bacon and eggs, fried potatoes, toast, and plenty of coffee, Bong, his father, and his brother waited for the hunting party to assemble at the Bong house. Uncles and cousins and neighbors arrived in the darkness. The early-morning talk wasn't about Dick's flying or the war effort, but about what deer trails to guard and which direction the wind was coming from.[5]

On opening morning, Bong's father shot a respectable ten-point buck, and his uncle Roy Bong hit and wounded an eight-pointer. The hunting party gathered and went after the wounded deer. Bud dropped the buck with a quick shot after they jumped it in a thick spruce swamp.[6]

The reporters and photographers continued to follow Bong's every move, insisting on posed photo shoots, making it difficult for him to enjoy the hunt. The story was just too incredible for the reporters to ignore—a local farm boy turned war hero pursuing his passion for the Wisconsin deer hunt.

"It isn't too well known that Dick and our father decided to tell the reporters that Dick had shot the ten-point buck killed by our father," Joyce recalled nearly six decades later. "They did it so the reporters could get their story and leave Dick to hunt in peace."[7]

With photos of Captain Bong, his rifle, and the two opening-day whitetails flashing across the country, the satisfied reporters backed off for the remainder of the season.

The Bong hunting party mounted drives through the deep snow, managing to take seven bucks during the buck-only season and two does during the antlerless season.

Bong wasn't able to bag any deer, although he did take five shots at a standing buck on the second morning of the hunt, missing the deer completely, according to his brother Bud. For Bong to miss the mark not once but five times—he was, after all, a seasoned fighter pilot and deer hunter—something was definitely wrong. In his book, Carl confessed to being the probable cause of the problem:

Earlier in the summer, I had written a letter to Dick in an effort to persuade him to finance the purchase of a 29s Weaver Telescope Sight for the 300 Sav-

Home for the Hunt (continued)

age. Dick okayed the deal and I got the scope sight. Then I made the mistake of mounting the sight on the rifle myself. (A seventeen-year-old can do anything, you know.) I drilled out the holes all right, but somehow I botched the job of threading one of the holes and the result was that one of the set screws came loose and the sight was no longer on target.[8]

Although Bong was not able to put his trusty Savage to productive use, he was, however, able to eat all the fresh venison he could hold.

Shortly after deer season, Bong was sent to Washington, D.C., for a public relations tour that included a visit to New York City to take part in a nationwide radio broadcast. The farm boy from Poplar was wined and dined by senators and congressmen, got a tour of the city, saw a Broadway play, and rode the subway.[9]

Even amid the bright lights and glamour of the Big Apple, Wisconsin and the deer hunt weren't far from his mind.

"How is the venison holding out?" he wrote to his mother from the Ambassador Hotel in New York on December 22, 1943. "Still got plenty of steaks left, I hope. I'll sure be ready for some when I get home again."[10]

Bong returned home to spend some quieter time with his family. In early January, Captain Bong boarded a train bound for Minneapolis and eventually California to begin his second tour of duty.

Richard Ira Bong went on to shoot down a total of forty enemy planes, and damaged or pos-

sibly shot down another eighteen—the greatest fighter record in the history of American warfare.[11]

In December 1944, Bong was relieved of combat duties and reassigned to Wright Field in Dayton, Ohio, where he would begin testing the newly developed—and problem-plagued—Lockheed Shooting Star P-80 jet-powered fighter. After two months of learning about the aircraft, he was relocated to the Lockheed plant in Burbank, California, for serious flight testing. Although Bong knew that several pilots had died in P-80 test flight mishaps, he was unconcerned, showing the same intense determination at Lockheed that he had exhibited while in combat.[12]

On August 6, 1945, the same day the United States dropped an atomic bomb on Hiroshima, Captain Bong's P-80 crashed forty seconds after take-off, killing him.[13]

All those photos taken by the eager photographers during the deer hunt of 1943 now serve as part of the legacy of Dick Bong.

――――――

NOTES

1. Joyce Bong Erickson, interview with the author, 2002.
2. Carl Bong, *Dear Mom: So We Have a War* (Minneapolis, MN: Burgess Publishing, 1991), 309.
3. Ibid.
4. Ibid., 309–310.
5. Ibid., 310.
6. Ibid., 310–311.
7. Joyce Bong Erickson, interview with the author, 2002.
8. Bong, *Dear Mom: So We Have a War*, 311.
9. Ibid., 315.
10. Ibid., 327.
11. Carl Bong and Mike O'Connor, *Ace of Aces, The Dick Bong Story* (Mesa, AZ: Champlin Fighter Museum Press, 1985), 201–202.
12. Ibid., 172–173.
13. Ibid., 191.

But by 1949, with deer herd numbers estimated at over a million, the Conservation Commission could no longer ignore the need for severe herd reduction. With the antlerless-only ice broken in 1943 and now faced with the dire need to manage the ever-growing deer herd, the commission approved an antlerless-only deer season for 1949, as originally recommended by Aldo Leopold in 1943. The antlerless season permitted the shooting of does, fawns, and spike bucks—those bucks with antlers not having spikes or forks greater than two inches in length—as well as fork bucks with forks less than two inches long.[77]

"Wisconsin's bitterly contested antlerless deer season, first step in a major program to control the nation's largest deer herd, opens tomorrow," reported the *Rhinelander Daily News*.[78] However, instead of the expected negative commentary typically found in the northern Wisconsin press, the paper held its verdict on the 1949 season—a sure sign that public sentiment and understanding was changing in favor of herd management, rather than strict herd protection.

The paper did comment on those vehemently opposed to the antlerless season: "They don't like to see the little animals in the kill. They let their Bambi-inspired sentimentalism obscure their consideration of the total picture of deer herd development and health in its relation to an overall appraisal of natural resources.

"The time for making a real appraisal of the results of the 1949 deer hunting season will be in the summer of 1950. Judgments reached before then will be more speculative than reasonable."

The paper had this to add: "It is not, by old-time standards, a 'pretty' season. It is a meat hunt. There is little of the sporting element about it. It was not intended to be."[79]

The 1949 deer season was technically the first season in Wisconsin's history of regulated deer hunting during which the shooting of mature bucks was not allowed. The Conservation Department did, however, remind hunters that spike bucks were legal game.

"Mature bucks may parade their trophy antlers in safety. This year they are not legal targets, for the first time in Wisconsin's 100-year history," reported the *Rhinelander Daily News*.

As an example of how differently the press was reporting on the 1949 season as compared to the 1943 season, the article went on to say: "Biologists hope that a lot of tags will find their way to deer carcasses. The herd is estimated to number well over a million at present and biologists say it must be reduced sharply before mass starvation takes place in browsed out areas."[80]

Although many had resigned themselves to the "meat hunt" and were beginning to accept the critical need for herd reduction, last-minute attempts to stop the antlerless hunt were made by the usual northern Wisconsin factions. Area sportsmen's groups urged the Conservation Commission to abandon the hunt plans. Petitions against the antlerless hunt signed by thousands of North Woods residents in Oconto, Marinette, Florence, Forest, and Langlade counties were presented to the commission in early November, to no avail.

DeByle's Department Store in Rhinelander encouraged hunters to gear up for the 1949 season. Cartoon deer at the top of the advertisement provide a commentary on the season's antlerless-only regulation.

Rhinelander Daily News, November 7, 1949

"The conservation commission cold-shouldered appeals from some northern Wisconsin sportsmen's groups yesterday to stop the doe and fawn shooting season starting November 19th," reported the press.[81]

In 1949 the deer refuge system was still thought of as a hedge against excessive harvest. More than 800,000 acres in nineteen counties were protected as refuges. Many of these acres were in central and southern Wisconsin counties, including Iowa, Juneau, Waupaca, and Columbia. However, even with a dangerously high deer population in the North Woods, refuge acres in Oneida, Florence, Bayfield, and other northern counties remained. Attempts to close 3,500 acres in the town of Sugar Camp in Oneida County for the 1949 season were abandoned after intense protest from locals.

Once again controversy did not keep hunters—whatever attitudes they subscribed to toward the "doe" season—from pursuing their favorite activity in 1949. A new state record of nearly 300,000 hunters covered field and forest, swamp and bog to take more than 159,000 antlerless deer.[82] The state had taken a giant leap in the direction of effective deer herd management while providing increased opportunity for sportsmen. The next decade would see a continuation of efforts to balance deer numbers with the land's carrying capacity through the taking of antlerless deer, including the first any-deer season since 1919. Controversy, however, now a permanent component of deer herd management in Wisconsin, would not be far away in the new decade.

✦ ✦ ✦ ✦ ✦

"Kenneth Weeks, 17, spent a cold weekend tramping through woods in the Iron River area but he didn't get a deer," reported a statewide news wire in November 1951. "Monday he decided to look around the marshland of his father's farm at Eldorado where deer had been spotted off and on. A few minutes later he bagged an eight-point buck, practically in his backyard."[83]

Weeks's buck was one of the thirty-four deer reported killed in Fond Du Lac County during the 1951 Wisconsin hunting season. It was statewide news for the simple fact that it could be done. Fond Du Lac County had not had an open deer season since 1897. Finally fading from the Wisconsin deer hunting scene was the idea that deer could be found only in the remote reaches of northern Wisconsin. Years of increased protection of the herd, along with new philosophies of conservation and scientific game management, were beginning to pay big dividends for Wisconsin sportsmen.

Hunting opportunities in the early 1950s were greater than they had been for decades. There were fifty-five counties open to some form of firearm deer hunting—either rifle or shotgun—during the 1951 season. Not since 1906 (the season prior to the first general closing of thirty-six counties) were more counties open to deer hunting.[84] However, unlike the early 1900s, when deer were scarce or nonexistent in most central and southern Wisconsin counties, deer were becoming common across the state.

By the early 1950s, deer hunting had become one of Wisconsin's greatest institutions. Nearly 25 percent of all Wisconsin males old enough to hunt purchased a deer tag, which meant that about one out of every six males age twelve or older hunted deer. In 1950, deer tag sales topped 300,000 for the first time. The favorite rifle of the day was still the time-honored .30-30, though the bolt-action .30-06 was gaining in popularity.

Large numbers of hunters were taking record numbers of deer. Following the antlerless-only deer season of 1949, during which nearly 160,000 does, fawns, and spike bucks had been taken, were the any-deer seasons of 1950 and 1951—the first since 1919.

The any-deer seasons, which allowed licensed hunters to take one deer of any sex or age, were designed to allow an adequate harvest of antlerless deer—something deemed crucial by deer biologists—while also allowing buck hunting. In theory, this season structure would allow those against any taking of does and fawns to pursue a buck hunt, while others could help reduce the surplus of antlerless deer.

On the eve of the 1950 season, the *Rhinelander Daily News* commented on the changing times:

It hardly seems like deer hunting time. With the examples of recent years still fresh in memory, you could expect pyrotechnical prologues full of fiery speeches and calls of alarm to the populace.

But here we are, opening a record breaking season tomorrow 8 a.m. with a record number of hunters in the field and a record bag in prospect. Gone with the snows of yesteryear are the bitter yowls of partisan deer management.

Of course, if this seven-day any-deer season doesn't produce the good results in surplus reduction, meat saving and equalized distribution the manager promised, there may be new outcries even before there's new snow.

At any rate, the years of wrangling apparently have produced this one season that leaves everyone happy, or at least mollified.

The trophy hunters can look for bucks to their hearts' content, and the meat hunters can pick a tasty doe or yearling.[85]

While the any-deer seasons weren't accompanied by the usual public outcry and harsh editorials, many factions still vehemently opposed the taking of does and fawns. A newspaper reported in 1950 that "[h]unters in the Chequamegon Bay region around Ashland tell of coming across posted signs that read 'Don't shoot does and fawns. Save our deer for future hunting. To hell with those Madison Hoodlums.'"[86]

The majority of sportsmen, however, were slowly beginning to accept the need and purpose behind the liberal deer seasons. Altogether, approximately 300,000 deer had been killed during the antlerless season of 1949 and the any-deer season of 1950. With the second any-deer season scheduled for 1951 to further reduce the herd, even the northern press—long the most vocal critic of liberal deer seasons—was beginning to significantly soften.

Prior to the 1951 hunt, the *Vilas County News-Review* wrote: "We have gotten a little cagey about the deer season as the years have passed. Oh, we used to howl with the rest of them and we are afraid that we howled a little louder than any of them.

"Each year proved us wrong. One year we would say that the deer were all gone, and the very next year thousands of deer were taken out on fenders, and we couldn't help feeling a little foolish."[87]

COURTESY OF WISCONSIN DEPARTMENT OF NATURAL RESOURCES, BUREAU OF WILDLIFE MANAGEMENT

The editorial concluded: "Let us keep our heads about this and refrain from making up our own theories. We are having an any deer season this year and nothing can stop it. Let us observe, watch, and gather statistics while this season is going on."[88]

While the venom of northern editorials seemed to have subsided as the hunting public gradually accepted modern deer management ideas, people were still apprehensive. In November of 1951, the *Marinette Eagle-Star* reported: "As the third liberal deer season gets under way, there is cause for concern over the future of the Wisconsin deer herd and grumbling on the part of some hunters over restricted areas. It is probable that the harvest of deer this season will dictate the end of an any-deer season for several years to come."[89]

The 1951 season saw approximately 300,000 hunters bag nearly 130,000 deer, bringing the total take from the three liberal seasons of 1949, 1950, and 1951 to nearly 450,000—or nearly double the total taken in twenty years throughout the 1920s and 1930s. Game managers and sportsmen alike nervously looked toward a more conservative approach to future seasons.

"The state has now had three exceptionally liberal shoots on deer in succession," wrote the *Green Bay Press-Gazette* in 1951. "The necessity for caution in the future will be underlined by the fact that no one had the slightest notion of the numerical total of the deer herd before this enthusiastic shooting era began."[90] As was the case after the 1943 split season, the 1950 and 1951 hunts were followed by deep-snow winters, which again magnified the perception of herd reduction.[91]

Conservation Department director Ernie Swift was quick to caution sportsmen to prevent the pendulum of deer management from swinging too far in favor of shooting. "Too many people have the opinion that deer herd management is merely a matter of a liberal or a conservative season. Deer management is not that simple," Swift said. "An any-deer season can reduce the herd very rapidly where the country is accessible, and where a high population is advertised to the hunters."[92]

The main problem Swift saw with deer management in the early 1950s was uneven hunting pressure. Accessible areas were hunted hard, while remote areas were barely touched by hunters. Also, as the rest of the state opened up to hunting, the historic heavy pressure in northern deer counties was decreasing. The very areas that needed herd reduction the most were not being hunted enough to effect change.

Compounding the problem was a trend Swift himself had first observed in the 1940s: the advent of the transient hunter. Due to the availability of good automobiles and increased road access to northern Wisconsin hunting areas, a growing

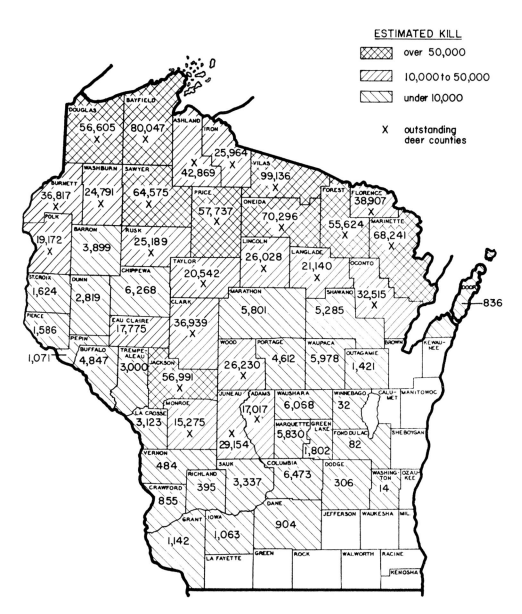

The estimated total deer harvest by county from 1932 to 1954.
A CENTURY OF WISCONSIN DEER

number of hunters were forsaking the hunting camp system of old. This new breed of hunter spent only enough time in the woods to bag his deer—usually just opening weekend—and then returned home. By necessity these hunters stayed close to the roads.

Rather than spend a week or more at the traditional deer camp, these hunters were filling up hotel rooms in northern deer towns. "Two big bucks, hanging from the marquee of the Hotel Fenlon in downtown Rhinelander, attracted considerable attention over the weekend," the *Rhinelander Daily News* reported in 1955. "The deer were bagged by downstate hunters staying at the hotel. Hundreds of persons stopped to inspect the deer Sunday and many took snapshots of the animals."[93]

When mandatory deer registration began in 1953, Wisconsin Conservation Department staff recorded information on these sheets.
WHS Series 271, Box 1

Some hunters didn't even waste time on the niceties of hotels. "An unusually large number of hunters from the southern part of Wisconsin saved expenses by sleeping in their cars Friday and Saturday nights," a northern newspaper reported. "These groups were making drives bright and early both mornings, anxious to fill their licenses and head back home for hot food, warm sheets and baths."[94]

The growing reliance on automobiles to reach hunting areas became a problem when the weather turned bad. Several deer seasons during the 1950s were accompanied by deep snows and sometimes bitterly cold temperatures. During the 1956 season, a blizzard that dumped upward of twenty inches of snow on parts of the north was followed days later by a storm that added four to eight more inches.

"For those who are going to keep the Thanksgiving fires burning, here's a comforting note from the weatherman: The way it looks right now, the deer hunters may be out of the woods by Christmas. The second severe snowstorm of the season—deer and autumn seasons, both—lashed across the northwoods," reported the *Rhinelander Daily News.* "Conservation wardens in the central north said that not only were many town roads and fire lanes choked with snow, but were blocked further by the stalled cars of hunters who tried—too late—to make it out of the woods Tuesday night."[95]

Lewie Falk, who began hunting in the Boulder Junction area in the late 1940s, remembers well a season of tremendous snows. "We got bogged down in the snow on our way to hunt, and while we were digging out the car another eight inches fell on top of it," Falk recalled. "We couldn't see the road in front of us."[96]

Falk also noted that plain old cold feet kept a lot of hunters from venturing too far from the warmth of camp or cabin. "We just didn't have the footwear like we do today," he said. "Most hunters wore uninsulated, high-topped boots with rubber overboots. We really couldn't stay out in the woods very long when it was cold."[97]

Getting enough hunters into remote, less accessible backwoods areas in order to reduce the surplus deer populations was a problem the Conservation Department grappled with throughout the 1950s. Following the liberal seasons and big kills of the early 1950s, the state held five consecutive buck-only seasons beginning in 1952. As expected, the buck-only seasons resulted in greatly reduced kill.

By the middle of the decade, after years of lowered annual harvests (fewer than 40,000 deer were taken in each season from 1952 to 1956), the problem of overpopulation was again critical. Instead

These "Report of Game Killed" postcards from the 1953 deer season served as a means for the Wisconsin Conservation Department to gather data on the deer harvest.
WHS Series 271, Box 1

Hunting was cause for many a celebration, as seen in this North Woods newspaper. *RHINELANDER DAILY NEWS*, NOVEMBER 13, 1959

of going back to the any-deer season to accomplish antlerless deer reduction, the state took another big step toward balanced deer herd management in 1957 with the development of the "party permit."

The party permit system in effect allowed for a regulated antlerless season tucked inside a regular buck season. The permit, which was issued to a party of at least four hunters, allowed the group to take one extra "camp deer" of any sex or age. Party permits allowed for a more even taking of antlerless deer, thereby softening the criticisms of taking does and fawns. Despite a fierce autumn storm that dumped as much as fifteen inches of snow north of a line from Green Bay to La Crosse, three days into the nine-day hunt, initial results of the first party permit season were encouraging.

"The State Conservation Department said today preliminary reports indicated this year's deer kill may run close to double that of last year," reported the *Rhinelander Daily News*. "Ruth L. Hine, department biologist, said the heavy kill so far is due to the camp meat licenses."[98]

The popularity of party permits increased in 1958, as hunters became accustomed to the new system. Also, sporting goods stores were able to issue party permits, whereas the previous year permits could be obtained only through a state conservation department station. The 1958 season saw another record broken for the number of hunters in the field. "With all the enthusiasm and abandon of Frenchmen storming the Bastille, an estimated 300,000 hunters will invade Wisconsin's forests, bush, bog swamps and meadows for the state's 1958 gun deer season which opens Saturday morning," reported the press.[99]

With good deer hunting opportunities across nearly the entire state, the North Woods had now become an area with relatively light hunting pressure, a great difference from a generation before. To encourage the take of more deer in this area, the 1958 season allowed for an extra week of hunting in the north following the statewide nine-day season. Pressure in the north was less than anticipated for the initial season.

"With the rest of the state open during the first nine days of the season, hunting pressure in the far northern counties was extremely light with an average of less than four hunters per square mile. This average meant hunting grouped here and there with many miles devoid of hunters," wrote the *Rhinelander Daily News*.[100]

To make the extended season structure more effective in reducing northern herd numbers the following year, the special northern hunt came before the regular nine-day season. In 1959, a resident deer hunting license cost just four dollars, ten dollars for a nonresident. A party permit was five dollars.

With hundreds of thousands of hunters pursuing abundant deer in all but four Wisconsin counties in the autumn of 1959, the "deer wars" were a thing of the past.[101]

The Herd Grows and Records Are Broken

And in living my good and reasonable life, I suspect I should sometimes kill some beautiful animal and eat it, to remind myself what I am: a fragile animal, on a fierce fragile magnificent planet, who eats and thinks and feels and will someday die: an animal, made of meat.
—Stephen Bodio, *On the Edge of the Wild*[1]

As deer hunters prepared for the opening of the rifle season in November 1969, many of them packing boxes of grub and gear for the annual trip to a northern deer camp, three men were preparing to complete their own journey. Just days before the season's start, the astronauts of *Apollo 12*, Conrad, Gordon, and Bean, had flown to the moon and made the second landing on the lunar surface. As deer season got under way on November 22, the three men were already hurtling back toward Earth. The star-filled early morning skies gazed upon by deer hunters had new meaning in the autumn of 1969.

The course for the decade was set back in 1960 with the election of young John Kennedy to the presidency. Kennedy was determined from the start to lead the country in bold, new directions. But the new president also held some age-old ideas. As president-elect in November 1960, he visited his running mate Lyndon Johnson at Johnson's Texas ranch.

"President-elect John F. Kennedy got two deer when he went hunting Thursday. . . . Johnson also got two deer," a news wire reported.[2]

In the autumn of 1960, about 335,000 Wisconsin hunters prepared to enjoy deer season as well, although there was much debate as to what the first season of the decade would bring. The largest take of deer since the advent of mandatory deer registrations had occurred in 1959, when more than 105,000 deer were killed. The high kill, as usual, prompted public outcries about the slaughter of the deer herd. Much of the controversy centered on the party permit, in place for the fourth consecutive year in 1960.

After the Nicolet National Forest publicized statewide a plan to offer free maps to hunters, the editor of the *Forest County Republican*, Jack Kronschnabl, vented his frustration. Kronschnabl wrote: "Three consecutive party permit seasons have reduced the Forest county deer population so low that deer as a major tourist attraction has ended here. It was almost impossible to show tourists even one deer during the past summer. Last year's wild deer season caused a heavy slaughter of deer in the Forest county areas."[3]

Echoing the sentiment held by many in northern Wisconsin, Kronschnabl felt that by allowing the take of does by way of the party permit the future of the northern herd was in jeopardy. "And there will be even less deer here during the next three or four years as a result of decreased reproduction of deer because of the four party permit deer hunting seasons," he wrote.[4]

The party permit, which allowed four members of a hunting party to take one additional "camp" deer of either sex, was first used in 1957 as a new approach by the Wisconsin Conservation Department to maintain a stable deer herd. Until the advent of the party permit, mechanisms to address deer overpopulation had usually been "any-deer" seasons, which allowed for drastic, across-the-board reductions, or "antlerless-only" seasons, which targeted does and fawns but angered most sportsmen.

"In terms of effecting a deer harvest the party permit plan is a modest compromise between strict protection and a liberal kill," wrote Dick Hemp in the *Wausau Record-Herald* in 1960.[5]

The prospect of a fourth party permit season in 1960 had pushed the Oneida County Board in early November to adopt a resolution against the continuation of the party permit system.[6] However, the Conservation Department stood fast against party permit opposition. In a report, the department emphasized that after three years of party permit hunting the deer herd remained healthy and was still expanding.[7] The department explained:

> Deer managers are particularly sold on the party permit in Wisconsin because it does not chop down the numbers of does, something that often happens with an either-sex season. This allows a sustained take from year to year, and predictions are that properly used the party permit could assure Wisconsin sportsmen of from 75,000 to 100,000 deer every year for many seasons to come.
>
> Game managers also point out that the party permit can provide a limited method of attracting hunters to inaccessible areas, can sharply reduce illegal kill and crippling loss, control deer numbers in specific spots better than an either-sex regulation, provide a limited harvest of does in areas close to centers of population and stimulate hunter interest in the deer management program

because of the high percentage of hunters who are members of a successful party.[8]

Some regulatory changes related to the party permit were made prior to the 1960 season. One new rule required at least two members of the "party" be present when a party permit deer was registered in order to "slam the door on the selfish individual who tries to circumvent the law by purchasing licenses for friends or relatives or borrowing them from disinterested hunters so that he may take both a party deer and a buck for himself."[9]

A regulation unrelated to the party permit required for the first time that hunters transporting deer to registration stations leave a part of the deer open to public view.[10] This regulation was enacted in an attempt to reduce the number of deer transported illegally from camp or hunting area to home without being registered. It also called for the snapped tag to be located where it couldn't be manipulated by the hunter during transport, thus preventing a quick snap of the tag if stopped by a warden.[11]

While emotions regarding the deer season had been relatively light toward the end of the 1950s, by 1960, the stage was set for a new eruption—one again based on north-south differences of opinion.

"Many area sportsmen contend the local deer herd has been drastically depleted by three consecutive party permit seasons. They say this northeastern part of the state has been 'overshot' and point to the absence of deer signs along fire lanes and sand roads and within the woods," reported the *Rhinelander Daily News*.[12] The party permit was, however, extremely popular among hunters in much of the rest of the state.

Controversies related to the party permit were not quieted by the results of the 1960 deer season. The deer harvest was slightly more than 60,000—including 25,000 taken with party tags—a great reduction from the 1959 season. Even though the Conservation Department predicted a reduced harvest due to regulation changes, the numbers were even lower than expected, which seemed to validate the arguments against the party permit. Unseasonably warm weather during much of the nine-day season was certainly partly to blame as well.

A northern newspaper wrote: "The opening brought weather that was more like that at the start of the fishing season. The weather was mild with waters high in the streams, rivers and swamps. The woods and fields were noisy—and there was no snow for tracking."[13]

Aside from very warm temperatures and lack of snow, other possible reasons for the light harvest were reported. "And probably most important of all, the deer have had excellent grazing because of the wet fall and aren't particularly hungry," wrote the *Rhinelander Daily News*. "They don't have to come out of their lowland

1961-1962 WISCONSIN
Big Game
HUNTING REGULATIONS

**IN A
BUCK SEASON —**

- Most of the deer you see are illegal
- Don't shoot them — it's wasteful
- Law compliance plus suitable regulations can mean better hunting for you

This is not a complete set of hunting laws, but contains the information you are most apt to need in hunting big game (deer and bear). Separate pamphlets are being issued to cover waterfowl seasons and small game seasons. They are available at license depots and department stations if you wish to hunt game other than that listed herein.

The open seasons are shown on maps. Bag limits are state-wide, except as specified.

If you have any questions, contact any conservation warden, ranger station, or conservation department field man or station.

Publication No. 714–61
WISCONSIN CONSERVATION DEPARTMENT
Madison 1, Wisconsin

COURTESY OF WISCONSIN DEPARTMENT OF NATURAL RESOURCES, BUREAU OF WILDLIFE MANAGEMENT

swamp areas for food. And most hunters don't relish pushing deep into the swamps to drive them out."[14]

Whatever the reasons for the reduced harvest of 1960, public opinion helped eliminate the party permit: the Legislature enacted a two-year moratorium.

Whether kills are very high or very low, lamented the Conservation Department, there will be those who say the deer are nearly all gone. In 1961 the Conservation Department distributed an educational publication, "Venison Stew . . . With Ingredients for Good Deer Management," designed to address the misconceptions regarding deer management and the idea that whatever season had just passed was responsible for the near eradication of the herd: "This old refrain has been fearlessly chanted in the face of the facts for the past 23 years. This season was no exception. Adding the figures, however, shows that between 1937 and 1960 Wisconsin hunters bagged 1,465,872 deer, not counting the numberless thousands that starved, died of wounds, or were otherwise wasted.

"As a matter of fact, the much maligned 1960 hunt which produced 61,000 was the 8th best in Wisconsin's entire deer hunting history."[15]

The department attempted to break down the sentiment against shooting antlerless deer—the hard-to-shake idea that does must be protected in order for the herd to survive that was an outgrowth of the 1920s and 1930s "save the deer" movements. (The Disney movie *Bambi*, released in 1942 and rereleased about every ten years until the video age, promoted the idea that the caring doe and helpless fawn shouldn't ever be the target of the hunter's gun.) "Venison Stew" countered:

In many quarters even among sportsmen, the doe is still the great woodland mother-image—keen-nosed, alert, protective, watchful-animal femininity incarnate.

The fawn is still the woodland sprite, terrified at the hunter's gun, inheritor of herd leadership, Bamby [*sic*] with limpid eyes.

Only the noble buck is worthy quarry, a match for the chase.

There is nothing wrong with this sort of sentiment. It's kind of nice. But it's not conservation.[16]

With no party permits issued in 1961 or 1962, deer kills under the more traditional buck-only seasons resembled numbers from an earlier time: only about 39,000 deer were taken in 1961, and about 46,000 in 1962.

The elimination of the party permit didn't eliminate the need to reduce the deer population in areas of its northern range, where, again, deer were increasingly out of control in parts. The hard winter of 1961–62 brought heavy starvation losses to deer yards. "Without man's help, a winter like this in areas where herds are over carrying capacity, heavy losses could result," wrote Ben Lewis in the *Wausau Daily Record-Herald* in early March of 1962.[17]

As the northern deer herd reached the critical late-winter period, L. P. Voigt, director of the Conservation Department, issued an "emergency order for browse cutting to lessen the impact of widespread deer starvation."[18] His frustration with the lack of increased acceptance of the need for antlerless deer reduction is evident in this statement, quoted in the *Wausau Daily Record-Herald* on March 9, 1962: "This is a repeat performance of a wildlife tragedy that could have been avoided had the department's recommendations for realistic deer seasons been followed."[19]

The roller coaster of Wisconsin deer management was in need of some stability. Changes in store for the 1963 deer season would provide this—as well as set the stage for the future of deer hunting in Wisconsin.

During the winter of 1962, the Conservation Department promoted its "forest-deer policy." "The new policy will mesh management of deer and forests for the benefit of both, aiming at a winter herd of 340,000 animals and an annual harvest of 70,000 to 100,000 deer state-wide," reported the *Rhinelander Daily News*. "The program to place the new policy in operation will start with the deer season of 1963."[20]

The policy represented many advances in the science of game management and established some cornerstones of Wisconsin deer management. Population goals were set for all of the state's deer management units, which first had been established in the mid-1950s. The primary mechanism to maintain these goals was a new and improved party permit.

The party permit of 1963 utilized a new "variable quota" system. A set number of "quota deer" was determined for a management unit in need of reduction to bring the unit closer to the population goal. Party permits were then issued based on the number of quota deer. Under the old party permit system, the number of permits issued was unlimited as long as party tag requirements were met. Those permits also were not specific to a particular management unit.

The Conservation Department, mindful of the past, began using the new variable quota party permit with caution. In 1963 about 4,500 deer were taken in eight deer management units, for a total of 65,000 deer taken statewide. By 1965, quota deer taken rose upward of 30,000, and the statewide harvest neared 100,000 for the second year in a row.

The refinements to deer management during the mid-1960s helped even out the ups and downs of hunter harvests, and provided for optimum hunter opportunity while protecting a sizable deer herd. Advances in deer management, however, were accompanied by great changes in the Wisconsin landscape.

Generations earlier, as old-growth pine forests were logged and replaced by new, brushy growth, the northern Wisconsin deer herd had shown a favorable population blip. As those "second growth" forests aged, the capacity for them to support deer decreased, resulting in a reduction of deer numbers through starvation and disease. In the 1960s, much of the second-growth forest was old enough to be harvested, causing a new forestry boom in Wisconsin, particularly in the north.

New paper, lumber, and veneer mills were built. Public and private forestlands alike were being intensively managed under scientific principles of sustained yields. Increased cutting of forests for lumber and pulpwood provided additional browse available to deer. Policies that promoted the coordination of forest management with deer management recognized for the first time the relationship between deer and the young forest.

Aside from an overall increase in the deer herd, forest cutting provided another benefit to hunters in the 1960s: increased access. Vast areas of second-growth forest were opened up as a result of timber-cutting operations. Werner "Zim" Zimmer, Oneida County forester from 1949 until his retirement in 1981, remembers the long days he spent laying out and building miles of new county forest roads in the 1960s.

"We built the primary roads to allow access for the loggers," Zimmer said. "Big blocks of forest were very inaccessible then, with just a few town roads and fire lanes running through them. The new roads were a big thing for the hunters; they really moved in."[21]

Aiding the development of backwoods roads was a new source of funding established in 1966. A new county conservation fund made $180,000 available to Wisconsin counties to cost-share conservation projects on a fifty-fifty basis. Eligible projects included improving and maintaining logging roads to increase hunter access. The counties' 50 percent share was in the form of labor and equipment.[22]

"Deer hunters in this part of the state will find some new and improved roads as a result of projects carried out under the new county conservation fund program," wrote the *Rhinelander Daily News*.[23]

Robert Wendt, northeast-area game supervisor, commented that woods roads that allow increased access for the logger would benefit those game animals popular with hunters (such as the white-tailed deer and ruffed grouse) by increasing areas of young forest. "Woods roads that allow access to the logger as well as the hunter will assist in improving range conditions for these animals in our northern forests," he told the *Rhinelander Daily News*.[24]

With deer habitat improving statewide, many longtime Wisconsin hunters remember the 1960s as a period of rising deer numbers, not only in the north but in central and southern counties as well. It was reported that central Wisconsin counties were "loaded" with deer, with Clark, Jackson, Monroe, Wood, Juneau, Adams, and Waushara counties having some of the highest deer densities in the state.[25] The presence of high deer populations in central Wisconsin in the mid-1960s resulted in increased hunting pressure there, rather than in the harder-to-hunt woods of northern Wisconsin.[26]

"West central Wisconsin, closest big deer range to state urban centers, is again expecting to attract as many as 30 to 50 hunters per square mile," the Conservation Department stated in 1964.[27]

That year, with ample deer to pursue closer to home, hunters from southern and central Wisconsin didn't need to head north to find hunting opportunities. The large region of northwestern Wisconsin was in danger of once again being under-hunted. Douglas, Bayfield, Washburn, Ashland, Sawyer, Price, Rusk, and Taylor counties were well above goal and in need of reduction. "Hunters looking for the top quality sport should consider the northwestern part of the state," the Conservation Department urged.[28]

The forest and wildlife managers of the Chequamegon National Forest, located in the northwestern region, also were concerned and encouraged hunters to consider hunting the thousands of acres of public land there. "You can't stockpile deer," Chequamegon wildlife biologist Howard Sheldon told the *Rhinelander Daily News*. "If we can harvest two out of five in the forest, there's that much more food for those left."[29]

That year about 387,000 hunters took advantage of the largest deer herd since 1958: more than 90,000 deer were registered, including 19,557 party permit deer. The highest kill came from the northwest, where 24,571 deer were registered com-

Alan Kidd and his hunting party, on Jackson County Forest land, near Bear Bluff, in 1961. Central Wisconsin was a good place to find deer at this time.

COURTESY OF THE KIDD FAMILY

pared to 15,623 in 1963.[30] The nine-day 1964 season kill was the highest since the 1959 season, which had allowed for sixteen days of hunting in the north. J. R. Smith, chief of the Conservation Department's Game Division, stated, "I never saw a season with fewer complaints." But he noted, "We still have too many deer to survive a good old-fashioned winter."[31]

A combination of favorable deer habitat and expanding range, well-balanced management, and increasing hunter access to remote areas was leading to bumper deer harvests in the late 1960s. In 1967, 128,597 deer were registered by hunters, including 47,785 party tag deer. The season's take just slightly edged out the previous record of 128,296 set in the infamous "split season" of 1943.

More than half a million deer hunters took part in the 1969 gun hunting season. Prior to the season, the Wisconsin Department of Natural Resources—which was striving to maintain an overwinter deer herd of 500,000—predicted a harvest of between 90,000 and 100,000 deer.

The Settler Deer Hunting License was available from 1951 through 1966 and was a sort of hybrid between a resident and nonresident license. It allowed a new resident—someone residing in the state less than one year but more than sixty days—to purchase a deer hunting license for five dollars, the same fee as a resident license. Currently, to purchase a resident license a hunter must have lived in Wisconsin at least thirty consecutive days prior to purchasing the license and show proof of residency, such as a driver's license.

COURTESY OF WISCONSIN DEPARTMENT OF NATURAL RESOURCES, BUREAU OF WILDLIFE MANAGEMENT

An opening-day report from the *Rhinelander Daily News* attested to the fact that, despite the social stresses and strains of the 1960s, deer hunting in Wisconsin was as important as ever:

> There were a great many red-coated nimrods in the woods today as the 1969 gun season got underway at 6:30 a.m. While many of those hunters came from cities and towns to the south, a good portion of them were area residents who were given the day off by the boss. In some cases they were the bosses themselves, as about every citizen of the North is caught up in the hunt once opening day is here.[32]

About 98,000 deer were registered during the 1969 season, a testament to scientific deer management that had taken hold in the 1960s.

Worker at a deer registration station examining a deer's teeth to determine its age in the 1960s. Mandatory deer registration began in 1953.
COURTESY OF WISCONSIN DEPARTMENT OF NATURAL RESOURCES, BUREAU OF WILDLIFE MANAGEMENT

Keith McCaffery, longtime northern forest deer researcher for the DNR who retired in 2000, remembers the differing perspectives on the herd population during that decade. "The transition into the variable quota system of harvest management became a bit rocky during the late 1960s because of an unprecedented sequence of severe winters," he recalls. "Just when the variable quota system was really getting under way, a severe winter struck in 1964–65. This was followed by severe winters in 1966–67 and 1968–69. Reduced recruitment of fawns was being blamed by many hunters on the variable quota system, coyotes, even paper mills, and almost anything other than winters."[33]

The severe winters experienced in the 1960s had shown game managers and the public alike the extreme importance of maintaining deer numbers in balance with the winter range. Scenes of weak, emaciated deer succumbing in the deer yards were powerful images, and unfortunately they were not to be left behind as the new decade dawned.

A big storm began quietly in the Sunday evening darkness of January 4, 1971, with a soft, filtering snow. When the snow began to accumulate, county and town employees across the state were called to their plows. By the time they finished their first run, the snow was even deeper than when they had started.

The snow, in combination with the wind, created drifts and blowing conditions that closed roads, schools, and airports from northern Wisconsin to Chicago. And then the cold came, with temperatures dropping well below zero.

"Old timers had to dig deep into their memories today to recall a blizzard like the one that rocked this section on Sunday and Monday," reported the *Rhinelander Daily News*.[34]

The pattern for the winter of 1970–71 was established back in November when a heavy snow fell in the north on the opening day of gun deer season. "Anyone dreaming of a white deer season in the Rhinelander area most certainly got his wish this year," reported the *Rhinelander Daily News*. "A heavy snow which began to fall about 6:45 o'clock this morning completely blanketed the area by 8 a.m., making tracking difficult and hunting uncomfortable."[35]

The opening-day storm brought colder air, along with winds gusting up to forty miles per hour. Northern and central Wisconsin were hit the hardest, but the storm created slippery and hazardous roads across much of the state.[36]

The deer herd of 1970 was estimated at about 600,000. Even before the opening-day blizzard, deer managers were predicting a much lower kill than in 1969. Party permits issued under the variable quota system had been reduced by up to 66 percent in the north by design of the DNR, resulting in a predicted season take of between 65,000 and 75,000 deer.[37]

While heavy snow hampered hunting in the north, other deer areas were little affected. The statewide kill total of 72,844 for 1970 was about 24,000 deer less than the previous season, but right in line with the DNR's estimate. Statewide, the buck kill had changed only slightly from 1969, with most of the harvest reduction attributed to the reduction in quota deer allowed.[38]

The January 1971 storm continued the severe weather pattern. Other storms followed during the long, painful Wisconsin winter of 1970–71. In early February, another blizzard lashed across the state, dropping nearly three feet of snow at Park Falls, and more than two feet at Wausau. High winds produced massive drifts. The space between storms that winter was often filled with raw, uncompromising cold. On February 8, Eagle River claimed the low temperature reading for both the state and the nation with a mind-numbing forty degrees below zero.[39]

In the quiet of Wisconsin's northern deer yards, many deer suffered and died.

"Winter cold and snow are preying on the deer—bringing death as surely, if more slowly, than the hunter's well aimed bullet," reported the Associated Press in March 1971.[40]

"Real bad conditions developed over a short time," recalled Frank Haberland, supervisor of the DNR's big-game department during this period. "We were hit pretty hard in January with heavy snow and extremely cold temperatures. It's one of the worst winters we've had in many a year."[41]

While Associated Press photos of starving deer taken in the northern deer yards appeared in newspapers across the state, game managers tried in vain to keep food available for the animals. Trails were plowed by the state to allow deer to travel between active logging operations, but few deer moved in their weakened condition. "In spite of a major effort to feed deer," reported the *Wisconsin Conservation Bulletin* in the fall of 1971, "an estimated 50,000–60,000 succumbed by spring."[42]

Use of the variable quota system by game managers had been well on its way to accomplishing effective herd management statewide in 1969, but the winter of 1970–71 abruptly halted that progress. The northern deer herd, which had benefited during the early 1960s from a combination of improved habitat and mild winters, was devastated by a series of unusually severe winters, beginning with the winter of 1964–65 and continuing into the early 1970s with harsh winters in 1970–71 and 1971–72—the first back-to-back severe winters since 1950–51 and 1951–52.

"It was this series of severe winters that caused the deer herd to decline to about half the 1964 level," wrote DNR research biologist Bruce Kohn in the *Wisconsin Conservation Bulletin*.[43] In the aftermath of the 1970–71 winter, hunter dissatisfaction ran high. Prospects for the 1971 gun season were bleak.

"Wisconsin's 1971 gun deer season gets underway at daybreak on Saturday with the possibilities of success in the northern part of the state rated as 'very low' by DNR officials for several reasons," reported the *Rhinelander Daily News* prior to opening day. In that article, Don Bragg, administrative assistant with the DNR, is quoted as saying, "Of the past six winters four have been very hard on the deer population. Losses last year were estimated at 60,000 deer dying of starvation alone because of the extreme cold."[44]

OLD CAMP TWO

There stands an old log cabin
Beside a winding trail,
Where gray wolves howl
  and bobcats prowl
And lonely coyotes wail,
It's built of tam'rack timber,
It's rustic through and through,
A two day hike from Settler's
  pike
We call it Old Camp Two.

There's miles of spruce
  and hemlock
That's stood since ancient
  time,
A clean old reach of birch
  and beech
And slopes of virgin pine,
A stretch of wildwood river
Reflecting skies of blue
A swampy dale of black ash
  swale
Way back by Old Camp Two.

When summer days are ended
And autumn's here again,
When snow flakes fall those
  wild haunts call
From ridge and swamp and
  glen!
My thoughts of work are
  blended
With dreams of venison stew,
I pack my sack upon my back
And start for Old Camp Two.
    William McCaffery
    Superior, Wisc.

The poem of "Old Camp Two," which appeared in the *Rhinelander Daily News* in 1971, brings to mind the former logging camps that served as deer camps in an earlier time.

Rhinelander Daily News, November 20, 1971

Compounding the lowered opportunity for hunting in northern Wisconsin because of the herd decrease was the lack of party permit tags. In 1970, the number of party permits issued for the north had been slashed, in part due to new highs in sentiment against the party permit following the large deer kills of the late 1960s.

As deer populations declined due to severe winters, hunters again perceived the party permit as the cause rather than the cure. Despite DNR educational campaigns in the 1960s that focused on the idea that hunters needed to shoot deer—including antlerless deer—in order to save the animals from dying in the winter deer yards, a strong public belief still existed, particularly in the north, that the complete protection of does was necessary to build up a deer population.

A northern Wisconsin assemblyman, Ellsworth Gaulke, wrote in 1971: "There are those who feel, myself included, that the party permit places too much of a strain on the deer herd by allowing doe to be taken.

"For instance, the killing of a buck represents the killing of one deer while the killing of a doe represents the killing of three deer."

Gaulke recommended the elimination of the party permit. In its place, longer seasons should be utilized when necessary, he proposed, "while leaving the productive doe to repopulate."[45]

Due to the backlash, party permits for northern deer management units were eliminated altogether in 1971. About 71,000 deer were taken during the season, the majority in central and southern Wisconsin counties. Another severe "deer-killing" winter in 1972 ensured that few party permits would be issued in the north in the future—at least until the herd could recover to at or above management goals.

With low deer numbers and no party permits, hunting in the big woods of the north was truly tough in the early 1970s, and hunter pressure reflected this. The hunter who sought challenge and solitude could find it on the thousands of acres of northern Wisconsin public lands.

As deer hunting opportunities declined in the north, they expanded in central and southern Wisconsin—areas that were, for the most part, immune to the habitat limitations and extreme winter severity that plagued the north. Fall population size increased sixfold in the farmland region (which included the lower two-thirds of the state, excluding the central forest region) from 1962 to 1984, and population goals there were also revised upward.[46]

"Heaviest hunting pressure is expected in the central part of the state where the DNR says the herd is in good shape and the best hunting last year was found there," reported the *Rhinelander Daily News* in 1971. "There are an estimated 700,000 deer in the woods according to the DNR."[47]

Growing populations were reported for several counties. "Hunters venturing out in Marathon County may have better than average luck because there seems to be an increase in the number of deer in that area," the paper continued. "Records also show that the deer herd is normal or higher in the Wood and Adams county areas."[48]

Hunters concentrated where the deer were, many forsaking a hunting trip to the north. "The population mass in central and southern Wisconsin is expected to lead to heavy hunting pressure in the same 10 central counties which yielded the highest kills last season," it was reported.[49]

By the mid-1970s, more than half a million hunters were participating in the Wisconsin

If you have any questions,
contact any Department fieldman or station.

Courtesy of Wisconsin Department of Natural Resources, Bureau of Wildlife Management

gun deer season, and nearly all of them hunted opening weekend. Intense hunting pressure in the agricultural central and southern counties, where much of the huntable land was in private ownership, was beginning to present some new problems. Concerns were raised about trespass and damage caused by "slob" hunters. Hunters were perceived as becoming increasingly competitive, and many felt the image of the sportsman was deteriorating as a result.

A report by UW–Madison rural sociologist Thomas Heberlein stated: "As hunters concentrate in areas with many deer, competition between hunters for available deer has fostered misunderstandings with property owners and unethical and often

Lakewood Sporting Goods of Wausau offered many items for the deer hunter in 1968, as well as a big buck contest.
Wausau Daily Record-Herald, November 14, 1968

dangerous behavior in the field, and has raised cries of alarm from anti-hunters who seem to view deer hunting not as a sport requiring skill but as a slaughter of helpless animals."[50]

The sport of deer hunting was being scrutinized as never before. When Earth Day was founded by Wisconsin Senator Gaylord Nelson and others in 1970, partly in response to an oil spill in 1969 along the California coast, the nation added environmental protection to the list of political and social issues being hotly debated.[51] As the 1970s progressed, the growing public focus on the environment was a boon to groups that promoted their animal rights agendas as environmental protection issues, and the influence of organizations expressly opposed to sport hunting grew. Seemingly overnight, the more well known of those groups were supported by operating budgets as large as or larger than well-established hunter advocate groups.

As hunters and hunting came under attack, the nonhunting public's perception of deer hunting became increasingly important to game managers. To combat criticisms of deer hunting, as well as address significant safety and quality of the hunt issues, the DNR developed some radical proposals for the 1977 season. The proposed season framework changes were designed to more evenly distribute hunting pressure and also reduce the emphasis on opening weekend.

The "new deer season" proposals consisted of two separate but similar plans. Both included the creation of three deer hunting zones: northern (Zone A), central (Zone B), and southern (Zone C). Within each zone, seasons would vary depending on deer numbers and hunter concentration, but a hunter would be restricted to only one zone.

A long, sixteen-day season for Zone A was proposed in Plan I as a means to increase hunter pressure in more remote, less hunted regions. The northern season would open a week before the regular season. Plan II altered the sixteen-consecutive-day season proposal by creating a split season of three and thirteen days in Zone A.

Both plans allowed for a split season for Zone B to alleviate heavy opening-day pressure. In this zone, a hunter would have to choose between a short season that included opening day or a longer season that began after opening day.

An either-sex season for Zone C was a component of both plans, with Plan I allowing a three-consecutive-day season and the Plan II season consisting of five half-days. Both seasons opened at midweek.

Basically, the proposals allowed for choices and flexibility: a hunter would choose a zone and then a season within that zone, weighing the benefits of hunting a shorter amount of time at the opening of the season versus being able to hunt longer.[52]

The proposals represented some "thinking outside the box" and, if enacted, would definitely set a precedent. They were presented at numerous public meetings held across the state in 1976, with a follow-up survey sent to a representative sample of deer hunters who had attended a meeting. Meeting and survey results showed vehement opposition to most of the proposed changes. It was clear that Wisconsin deer hunters felt strongly about the traditional season framework and wanted no further restrictions on when and where to hunt. The proposals were dropped by the DNR.

Nevertheless, the DNR wondered if there was another segment of hunters out there: those who might support the proposals but did not attend the public meetings.

A survey targeting what was intended to be a more representative cross section of the deer hunting public was conducted by Professor Heberlein. The results of his 1976 survey did show that the participants at the public meeting were more opposed to the proposed season changes than the general deer hunting public, but the differences were insignificant. The bottom line was that Wisconsin hunters did not want these changes, period.[53]

Now knowing what the hunter would absolutely not accept, the DNR's Subcommittee for Improving Wisconsin's Deer Hunt drafted a new set of proposed changes, which were sent as a questionnaire following the 1977 gun deer season. The new proposals were more incentive-based rather than restrictive. The sixteen-day northern season was kept as a proposal, as well as a weekday opener, but there were no restrictions on where or when a hunter could fill his tag within the framework. To make this work, however, there would be a restriction on the number of licenses sold: a hunter would have to apply for a deer license, something Wisconsin hunters had never had to do. The DNR also proposed using the party permit as well as a new spin on the party tag: a "one man, either sex" permit.[54]

Overall reaction to the 1977 proposals was strongly negative, but not quite as harsh as the response to the 1976 proposals. The earlier Plans I and II had met with disapproval of 76 percent and 86 percent, respectively. The proposed limit on license sales was opposed by 83 percent of hunters surveyed. The midweek opener, perceived as a threat to hunting tradition, was bashed by 70 percent of respondents. However, there was one idea the public seemed to like: the "one man, either sex" permit, supported by 71 percent of respondents.[55]

Although few concrete changes came out of the 1976 and 1977 proposals, the UW report on the surveys was able to quantify what deer hunters had always felt in their hearts. The report concluded that there was a commitment to deer hunting not seen in other recreational activities. The majority of deer hunters said that they would miss deer hunting more than most or all of the other interests they had. In other words, there was just no substitute for the deer hunting experience—and Wisconsin hunters wanted the tradition of the experience preserved.

One last severe winter was dished out before the decade came to a close. "Deer will die this winter, as they do every winter," noted the *Wausau Daily Herald*. "But the potential exists for a deer kill larger than Wisconsin sportsmen have seen for years."[56]

The winter of 1978–79 was another tough one for northern deer. The predictions for the autumn hunt of 1979 were not promising. "I can't be super optimistic about this season," admitted Chet Botwinski, DNR wildlife manager at Woodruff in northern Wisconsin. Even central Wisconsin game managers were concerned about low numbers in the area, including Portage, Wood, Adams, and Juneau counties.[57] Dead deer had been found as far south as Governor Dodge State Park in Dodgeville.[58]

Despite the dismal projections, the initial take of bucks in 1979 was higher in the north than expected, a pleasant surprise for game managers. Overall, the statewide take was down from the previous year in which a record-breaking 150,845 deer had been killed. However, the 1979 kill of 125,570 (including 40,848 quota deer) still was one of the highest harvests since mandatory registration began in 1953.

Autumn 1980 was a time of uncertainty. The fifty-three Americans held hostage by young Iranian revolutionaries in Tehran were approaching a year in captivity. The nation was plagued by recession and increasing inflation. The term *acid rain* had recently become a part of the American vocabulary. An intense campaign for the presidency was being waged between President Jimmy Carter and former California governor Ronald Reagan.

Amid the confusion, there was one thing a Wisconsinite could bank on come fall: the arrival of deer season. More than 600,000 hunters were planning to escape the frustration and turmoil of politics and the poor economy by heading to the woods. Another good bet was that these hunters would take a lot of deer.

In the late 1970s statewide deer harvests of more than 100,000 had become common as deer numbers continued to increase in central and southern Wisconsin, and the northern herd began a steady recovery from a devastating series of severe winters in the 1960s and early '70s. A new harvest record had been set in 1978, when more than 150,000 deer were taken statewide.

Prior to the 1980 season, the DNR predicted a seventh straight year of high kills. Frank Haberland, the DNR's big-game biologist, predicted that between 625,000 and 630,000 hunters would be afield in 1980 and would successfully take about 100,000 deer.[59]

"Wisconsin's deer herd totals around 700,000, down perhaps 50,000 from last year. Most deer are within a triangle with lines from Madison to Eau Claire to Green Bay and back to Madison, and nearly all of this land is private land," said Haberland.[60]

Haberland encouraged hunters to secure permission to hunt private lands well in advance. "If they don't, they're going to be disappointed, because virtually all of that land is posted against hunting and trespassing." He also repeated the now familiar refrain that to get away from the crowds and have a crack at a trophy buck, hunters should consider heading north.[61]

Aside from the increase in deer numbers, wildlife managers were also enthusiastic about another aspect of the 1980 hunt: the first use of the "Hunter's Choice" permit. This permit, which replaced the twenty-three-year-old party permit system, allowed an individual hunter the option of taking either a buck or an antlerless deer in a designated management unit. This idea of a "one man, any deer" permit was one of the few new deer season proposals from the DNR that had been positively received by hunters in 1977.

The choice permit was seen as an improvement to the party deer tag, which had been used since 1957 to manage the antlerless deer harvest within the context of a regular buck-only season. The party permit system was cumbersome. It required the four hunters to coordinate on an application and hunt together, with the designated shooter wearing an armband while hunting. There also was a five-dollar application fee.

Advantages of the choice permit included an easier, free application process. DNR officials hoped the new permit system would help disperse hunters by allowing a lone hunter the opportunity to take an antlerless deer. Also, party permit success had averaged about 70 percent, whereas Hunter's Choice antlerless success was expected to be less than half that amount, since only one hunter versus four was attempting to fill a tag. This resulted in an increase in the number of permits issued, thereby enabling more hunters to participate in an any-deer hunt.[62]

The DNR had an idea that the Hunter's Choice permits would be well received by hunters, but the demand was greater than expected. About 350,000 hunters applied for 93,930 available permits. "The demand was somewhat of a surprise," said Haberland. "We didn't think in the first year of a new system we would get so many applications."[63]

Of course, the application process couldn't have been made any easier: the permits were free and applications were included with hunting license materials. The high rate of applications did suggest that more than half of the deer hunters in the state thought it a good idea to have what amounted to an any-deer permit on hand.

Hunters experienced another new development in the 1980 deer season: the requirement that at least 50 percent of a hunter's clothing above the waist—including a hat, if worn—needed to be blaze orange. The "army of redcoats," as the newspapers had referred to the thousands of red-wool-clad hunters who invaded the woods each November, was replaced by an "army of blaze orange." Many hunters had already been wearing blaze orange clothing, or had sewn strips of blaze orange material onto their traditional hunting clothes, and generally supported the new law.

"Many hunters wear a blaze orange vest," Haberland told the press prior to the season. "That would meet the requirements of the law. It's a very unique color that will be very effective in preventing mistakes. It's highly visible in poor light where traditional red was not."[64]

But not every hunter was enthusiastic about the new color requirement: "Some bureaucrat has relegated thousand of dollars worth of excellent red wool coats to the ash bin on a whim. Wear an over-vest? Of cotton, nylon, or plastic? Have you ever compared the noise of yourself or any other hunter going thru the brush in wool material compared to the racket he makes if he wears cotton, nylon or plastic? And you can't wear out these red wool coats in civilian life either—not only because of the color, but because they were all bought large enough to wear over many layers of warm clothing," wrote one disgruntled hunter in a letter to the editor of a northern Wisconsin newspaper.[65]

Wearing their new blaze-orange garb and packing Hunter's Choice permits, hunters experienced a tremendously good season. The actual kill far exceeded expectations, with more than 139,000 deer taken. "Hunters enjoyed one of the safest and most successful seasons in history during the 1980 nine-day Wisconsin gun deer hunt," reported the *Rhinelander Daily News*.[66]

Speaking to the Natural Resources Board, big-game biologist Haberland noted that the DNR was "extremely pleased" with the first season of the Hunter's Choice permit despite the fact that 10,000 more antlerless deer than expected were taken.[67] He noted that the harvest was second only to the 1978 record of 150,845—an indication the state's deer herd was on an upswing. Haberland added that "prospects for next year appear equally as good if another favorable winter occurs."[68]

Haberland's predictions for another large harvest were realized in 1981. As if the hard winter of 1978–79 were the last hurdle to be cleared by the state's deer herd, the population continued to climb. A new record take was made in 1981 when more than 630,000 hunters killed 166,673 deer.

The new record would not stand for long.

The DNR estimated that 640,000 hunters would turn out for the 1982 deer season. Reasons for the predicted jump in hunter numbers from 1981 included the faltering economy. "It seems more hunters will be out as a result of that," Haberland told the press. "Being laid off, unemployed, they've got more time to spend hunting."[69]

The Old Wool Mackinaw

I LOOK FORWARD TO THE WINTER SEASON FOR SEVERAL reasons. I enjoy the brisk, dry air that winter brings and the opportunity to strap on snowshoes once in a while for a hike through the woods.

It also is the time of year when I can wear the old wool mackinaw again.

The red mackinaw had belonged to a hardscrabble northern Wisconsin River dairy farmer. After age and years of backbreaking labor led

The red-and-black "army"
COURTESY OF WISCONSIN DEPARTMENT OF NATURAL RESOURCES, BUREAU OF WILDLIFE MANAGEMENT

The Old Wool Mackinaw (continued)

to the necessity of a nursing home, most of a lifetime's worth of possessions were divided up and carted off, the cattle and little farm sold. Not much left to show for a half century of hard work, just old fence lines enclosing small, rocky pastures.

The coat was rescued from a box of clothes destined for the resale shop by someone who understood that there can be meaning in a piece of clothing. It was given to me as a gift.

Wisconsin outdoors writer Gordon MacQuarrie also understood the power of a seasoned coat and wrote affectionately about an old wool mackinaw that had belonged to his late father-in-law, Al Peck, the first president of the Old Duck Hunters Association, Inc.:

When you open this shed door one of the first things to catch your eye is a brown, checked-pattern mackinaw, about 50 years old, I guess. It belonged to the President of the Old Duck Hunters. I like to keep it there. It belongs there.

Flying squirrels had filled one pocket of the mackinaw with acorns. They always do that, but these avian rodents, so quick to unravel soft, new wool for their nests, have never chewed at the

All the necessary gear
Courtesy of Martin Runge

The Old Wool Mackinaw (continued)

threadbare carcass of Mister President's heroic jacket. Perhaps it is because the wool, felted and tough, has lost its softness and flavor.[1]

The wool mackinaw was the garment of choice for deer hunters in the early days of sport hunting in Wisconsin. Wool was warm and held up well under rugged conditions. As more and more deer hunters took to the field in the early 1900s and firearms accidents increased, many hunters learned the benefits of being readily seen by other hunters and began wearing red or red-and-black plaid. When the wearing of red was mandated by regulation in 1945, deer hunters truly became the "army of redcoats" as they were often described by the press. The red wool mackinaw became this army's uniform.

Red, however, wasn't the most visible color in the spectrum and later legislation allowed first orange (1951) and then yellow (1967) as choices to meet the safety color requirement. Blaze orange, a great advancement in hunter safety, and its adoption as the only allowable safety color in 1980, along with the increasing availability of modern high-tech fabrics, such as Gortex, and insulating materials such as Thinsulate, helped relegate the wool mackinaw to the annals of hunting history.

✦ ✦ ✦ ✦ ✦

I wore my old wool mackinaw during a walk on a cold and damp winter night not too long ago when light rain was turning to snow and the wind was just strong enough to numb my cheeks a little. As I walked, the wet snow gathered on the shoulders of the coat and I noticed the aroma of damp wool. It is difficult to describe the smell to someone who doesn't regularly wear wool in situations—for example, trudging through swamps and deep snow—that might result in it getting wet. It's even harder to explain that the smell can be a pleasant one. I'm not sure myself why I like the smell of wool, but I think it's because it is honest and natural and, like wood smoke and pipe tobacco, it reminds me of deer camp and old times.

On those sorts of nights I think about the old dairy farmer, gone many years now, and how he might have kept the coat on a hook by the back door, throwing it on along with a wool cap as he headed outside in early morning blackness, through cold and snow toward the barn to tend to the cows. I imagine he might have worn the coat while deer hunting along the Wisconsin, wool pants tucked into high leather boots, a .30-30 in his hands.

And I wonder what he may have thought if he could have known that the old wool mackinaw would still be helping someone ward off the northern Wisconsin winter well into a new century.

NOTE

1. Gordon MacQuarrie, *Stories of the Old Duckhunters* (Harrisburg, PA: The Stackpole Company, 1967), 195–96.

Haberland also predicted hunters would take even more deer than the previous season. Although a harsh winter in some parts of northern Wisconsin in 1981–82 had affected populations in that part of the state, the statewide population of about 850,000 was estimated to be the largest in modern history.[70]

Haberland's prediction was accurate. Despite a rainy season in many areas of the state, hunters set a new record with a take of 182,715 deer, which included a Hunter's Choice kill of 71,774.

A few of the deer taken in 1982 were shot with handguns. "Deer hunters, for the first time ever, can pack big caliber handguns instead of shouldering rifles as usual during the nine-day season starting next weekend," reported the *Rhinelander Daily News*. "Under the new rule, hunters can use a .357, .41 or .44 caliber handgun with barrels measuring at least five and a half inches in counties open only to hunting with rifles."[71]

The new rule allowing for the use of handguns was initially "sought by some law enforcement officers, who said they preferred their handguns to rifles."[72] At first, the proposal to legalize the use of large-caliber handguns for deer hunting had met with some opposition from those in the Legislature who imagined the deer hunt turning into a Wild West event. But the measure did pass, although with some restrictions: in addition to bore-size and barrel-length restrictions, a hunter opting for a handgun could not also carry a rifle.[73]

The record kill of 1982 did little to stem the growth of the deer herd. In November 1983, DNR wildlife managers anticipated another banner season for hunters. "Rarely have conditions looked so good for the gun deer season. From north to south, east to west, the reports are favorable. Officials of the Department of Natural Resources are unblushingly forecasting another record year," reported the *Wausau Daily Herald*. "The deer kill is expected to top 200,000 animals by the time the nine-day season ends Nov. 27."[74]

The optimistic forecast was the result of a mild 1982–83 winter combined with an increase in Hunter's Choice permits, particularly in southern management units. The easy winter—a boon to northern deer—translated into good winter survival as well as good fawn production in the spring.

Another factor in the mix may have been that the rainy weather hunters experienced in 1982 reduced hunting pressure and the potential harvest, leaving more deer for 1983. "I don't feel we harvested the number of bucks in Lincoln and Langlade counties that we could have last year," stated a northern wildlife manager.[75]

While hundreds of thousands of Wisconsin deer hunters were primed for the 1983 gun hunt, a new sort of deer hunting conflict had been brewing. Earlier in the year in Chicago, the U.S. Court of Appeals for the Seventh Circuit had made a decision on an appeal brought by the Lac Courte Oreilles Band of Lake Superior Ojibwe Indians. The federal appeals court reversed a 1978 ruling by a federal district court in Madison that had decided Ojibwe bands in Wisconsin did not retain any off-reservation hunting, fishing, and gathering rights.[76]

Known as the Voigt Decision, the ruling stated that an 1854 treaty with Wisconsin Ojibwe, which had followed treaties in 1837 and 1842 and resulted in a final ceding of Indian lands in Wisconsin to the United States, did not terminate Ojibwe hunting and fishing rights in the ceded area. The Voigt Decision touched off a firestorm of controversy as it was unclear what authority the state had in regulating off-reservation hunting and fishing. It would take several more years to sort through the details of the nature and extent of the ceded territory rights, the level of authority held by the state and tribes to regulate tribal members exercising these rights, and the allowable take of fish and game under these rights.[77]

All of this was unclear in the autumn of 1983. As late as November, the state was still negotiating with the Ojibwe to formulate a ceded territory deer hunting structure that was acceptable to the state and the Indian tribes. "The agreement reportedly would issue Chippewas [the Ojibwe] 6,250 free permits for deer of any sex hunted on public lands off reservations through December 31," reported the *Wausau Daily Herald* and Associated Press in early November.[78]

This was uncharted water for the Indian tribes and the state, but it seemed that at least an interim agreement for 1983 could be reached before the state-scheduled gun season. There was, however, one sticking point that infuriated non-Indian hunters: a request to begin the tribal off-reservation treaty deer hunt a week before the regular state season. "Kathryn Tierney of Hayward, representing the Lac Courte Oreilles, said the special Chippewa hunting season should start Saturday because there is no reason involving conservation of the deer herd to delay it," reported the *Wausau Daily Herald*.[79]

While later clarification of ceded territory rights (such as that which Federal Judge Barbara Crabb provided in August 1987) would affirm the authority of the Indian tribes to set their own seasons, the issue went unsettled in 1983. "Chippewa Indians in northern Wisconsin apparently have delayed opening their deer season," reported the *Wausau Daily Herald*. "The tribes had wanted to begin hunting last weekend, a week before the season starts for non-Indian hunters. The Department of Natural Resources and Chippewas tried to settle the issue, but it went unresolved last week."[80]

An editorial from the *Wausau Daily Herald* asked for reason from the hunting public regarding the issue:

> The Indians' newly confirmed rights nearly caused a confrontation that could have had tragic results. They wanted to begin their gun deer season last Saturday, a week before the general season begins for non-Indians.

Anyone who attended a spring Conservation Congress hearing knows it's true: Hunters can get livid when it comes time to set deer quotas. Probably no other issue causes such controversy among Wisconsin sportsmen.

Non-Indians must recognize that treaties give the Chippewas some rights that were ignored for decades and are now being asserted. And the Chippewas should understand that interfering with the state's traditional deer hunt could provoke unwarranted conflict.[81]

With no agreement in place between the tribes and the state allowing for an off-reservation tribal deer hunt prior to the start of the state's regular nine-day gun season in 1983, tribal members who did attempt an early off-reservation hunt were arrested by DNR law enforcement. "Several Indians were arrested for hunting outside reservation boundaries this weekend but wardens said tribal members generally showed restraint following the breakdown of an agreement over deer hunting last week," the *Rhinelander Daily News* reported.[82]

Five days before the start of the 1983 season—and following six and a half hours of negotiations between the principal negotiator for the DNR, George Meyer (then director of law enforcement), and Jim Schlender, lead negotiator for the tribes—an agreement was finally reached for a treaty deer season.[83] While the tribes agreed to begin the off-reservation season on the same day as the state's season, the end date of the treaty season was not at issue and would run until January 31, 1984. A total of 644 deer were taken by Native Americans in this first off-reservation treaty deer hunt.[84]

As the 1983 season opened, rainy weather once again plagued hunters across the state, making back-roads travel difficult and hunting unproductive. "For the second year in a row, the gods of the hunt threw a wet blanket on the opening of the deer season," wrote Jim Lee, outdoor editor for the *Wausau Daily Herald*. "At dusk Saturday, unpaved roads were quagmires and conditions worsened Sunday. Only four-wheel drive vehicles were venturing off the paved roadways."[85] Later in the season a winter storm brought cold and more rain to central Wisconsin and heavy snows to the northwest.

The opening weekend kill was reported to be way down in many areas. However, even though the harvest didn't top 200,000 as predicted, it came close, with a kill of more than 197,000—yet another record-breaking harvest. The following years, however, would meet and exceed the predictions, with new record kills in 1984 and 1985 of about 255,000 and 274,000, respectively.

Keith McCaffery, retired DNR northern forest deer researcher, explained the steady growth of the deer herd during the 1980s. "After the series of bad winters in the 1960s continuing up through 1972, the northern herd really began to recover, getting back to near-management goals by 1983–84," he said. "During a bad winter in 1985–86 we expected to have some losses, but a quick thaw in the spring— just about the time the deer would have been in trouble—may have helped. We still backed off on the quota deer just to be safe. After a record-breaking mild winter in 1986–87, the deer population really took off."[86]

By 1987, the statewide deer population was estimated to be a million deer for the first time. Predictions were for another harvest of much more than 200,000.

1989 Wisconsin Hunting Regulations

This pamphlet does not contain a complete set of Wisconsin hunting regulations, but gives you a summary of the most important ones you should be aware of so you comply with state law.

LYME DISEASE — **Be Wary, Not Worried, When Enjoying The Outdoors!**

Actual Size of Deer Ticks

Adults

LARVAE NYMPH FEMALE MALE

ONE INCH

Write for the facts:
Wisconsin Department of Health and Social Services
1 West Wilson Street, P.O. Box 309
Madison, WI 53701-0309

WANT TO REPORT A VIOLATION?
CALL 1-800-TIP-WDNR
(1-800-847-9367)
Toll Free   Statewide   24-Hour   Confidential
(Please, violation calls only)

All conservation wardens performing their duties may enter private land at any time.

PUBL-WM-004   89REV

COURTESY OF WISCONSIN DEPARTMENT OF NATURAL RESOURCES, BUREAU OF WILDLIFE MANAGEMENT

"Hunters who began hunting in the 1980s have never known times of low deer populations or sustained periods of population decline," said McCaffery.[87]

Ironically, with deer seemingly behind every tree in some locales, increasingly, the deer hunter of the 1980s was also making use of commercial products designed for hunter success. The commercialization of deer hunting exploded in the 1980s, providing hunters with varieties of bottled lures and scents, easier-to-use tree stands, voice-activated headsets for communication between hunters, and hidden, infrared game counters. By the mid-1980s, the majority of hunters used scoped rifles.

"The rifle scope is rapidly earning a place in the front line of Wisconsin deer hunting," wrote Jim Lee of the *Wausau Daily Herald*, in 1985. "Not too many years ago, the scope was viewed as a frill, an adornment to be used by those uncertain of their shooting abilities."[88]

Hunters from the bygone eras of Wisconsin deer hunting—those from the days when a harvest of 30,000 deer was something to marvel at and bucks were pursued by men who used black-powder rifle cartridges and sent their trophies home by express car at the train depots—would no doubt have scoffed at the development of modern hunting aids. But they certainly would have been in awe of the size of the deer population and numbers of deer killed by hunters in the 1980s.

During the 1989 season, near-perfect hunting weather and a deer population estimated at 1.2 million deer allowed hunters to break one more record for the decade: an estimated 700,000 hunters bagged more than 300,000 deer.

The Decade of Opportunity

For tens of thousands of years, we have lived as food gatherers and hunters. In those times, we learned things as the deer learns them; slowly, over long stretches of time and through long immersion in repeated experience. Such instincts do not vanish without a trace simply because a man lives in the age of factories and plastic, and has signed on to work by the hour or the year in a plant or in an office.
—Curtis K. Stadtfeld, *Whitetail Deer*[1]

It had been a long time since I had hunted in Wisconsin. After graduating from college at the University of Wisconsin–Stevens Point in 1983, with a degree in wildlife management, I had set out to find gainful employment in a tough job market, taking seasonal and part-time jobs wherever I could find them. These jobs took me to Nebraska, Arkansas, and Alaska and eventually to permanent employment in New Mexico and then Texas.

In 1990 a job change brought me back to Wisconsin. One of the first things I did was go to the nearest sporting goods store to purchase a lever-action Marlin Model 336CS—chambered, of course, for a .30-30 Winchester, the first smokeless powder hunting cartridge—a box of shells, and a variety of blaze orange clothing. One of the next things I did was meet with my hunting partner to pore over maps, making plans for a northern Wisconsin deer hunt that had been a long time coming.

Although I didn't realize it, I could not have picked a better time to return to the world of Wisconsin deer hunting. The Wisconsin gun deer season of 1990 had everything going for it. Deer populations were at all-time highs, the season was scheduled to open on November 17—the earliest date possible under the traditional nine-day season framework that had become the norm since 1960—and the forecast called for clear, mild weather. Another record-breaking season was predicted.

"This is as good as it gets," wrote Jim Lee in the *Wausau Daily Herald*. The DNR predicted that an estimated 700,000 hunters would take more than 350,000 deer during the gun season, which included the regular nine-day season along with an extended seven-day "antlerless-only" season held in sixty-seven deer management units, primarily in the north.[2]

"We've got more deer on the landscape than we probably ever had," remarked Carl McIlquham, a northern area wildlife manager, prior to the season.[3]

But there was a déjà vu aspect to the enthusiasm regarding the first deer season of the 1990s. "For deer hunters, the advance view of the Wisconsin gun deer season looks like it just can't get much better than this," reported the *Rhinelander Daily News* the year before.[4] Predictions of a record-setting season in 1989 had been fulfilled when more than 310,000 deer were taken from a herd estimated at 1.2 million animals. Near-perfect hunting weather had contributed to the large kill. Bowhunters took an additional 46,394 deer that year.

"We've got a very healthy, very productive deer herd that has benefited literally since 1980 without a severe winter," said DNR Lake Michigan District wildlife supervisor Jim Raber in November 1989.[5] Another mild winter was added to the books following the 1989 deer season. The state's deer population continued to climb into uncharted territory.

In an attempt to keep the herd in check, more than 500,000 quota deer permits were issued for the 1990 season, with the hope of hunters taking at least

Bucks hang heavy on the meat pole of a Price County deer camp in the 1990s.
Courtesy of Ed Zydzik

230,000 antlerless deer. Few hunters who applied for Hunter's Choice permits in northern deer management units were disappointed. In many units, available choice permits exceeded demand, and for the first time in Wisconsin deer hunting history "bonus permits" were distributed to hunters who had applied for Hunter's Choice permits in these "surplus permit" units. The opportunity to take two antlerless deer during the regular gun season was something from Wisconsin's distant past.

As in 1989, the 1990 deer season arrived without rain, or wind, or bone-numbing cold. Opening weekend tallies were on a record pace.

"Hunters registered a record 170,821 deer on opening weekend of the Wisconsin hunt, raising expectations for a record kill during the fall's extended gun season for white-tailed deer, game managers say," the Associated Press reported. Opening weekend of 1989 had seen 143,011 deer taken. A DNR spokesperson said that one factor in the rise in deer registration figures was the weekend's weather, which featured sunshine and temperatures in the fifties.[6]

Accompanied by the sounds of the newly released novelty song by Bananas at Large, "Da Turdy Point Buck," which was to become Wisconsin's version of Da Yoopers' "Second Week at Deer Camp," hunters hurried to get deer registered and processed.

An editorial in the *Wausau Daily Herald* commented that "the phenomenon that propelled Da Yoopers into local stardom and threatens to do the same to Bananas at Large is firmly rooted in one inescapable fact. If you come home empty handed and red-faced after deer camp, you've gotta come home with a sense of humor. It's the only way."[7]

At season's end, a startling new state record of 350,040 deer harvested had been established, a 13 percent increase from the previous record set the year before.

While mild weather and abundant deer numbers had made for an enjoyable 1990 season for most hunters, a few were frustrated by ever-increasing ranks of antihunting protesters. The antihunting movement had grown considerably during the 1980s, and hunting opponents had developed aggressive new strategies.

"Strapping fake hunters on cars and interfering with deer hunters in the field are among the tactics due for discussion at the annual meeting of Alliance for Animals," the *Wausau Daily Herald* reported. "About 30 demonstrators are expected to gather early on opening day at Blue Mounds State Park, near Madison. The demonstration is to protest hunting in state parks and to challenge a recently passed anti-harassment law."[8]

Women and Deer Hunting

CONNIE ROLLMAN OF RHINELANDER REMEMBERS ONE particular day of the 1997 deer season very fondly. "It was a beautiful day, with a crystal blue sky and just enough snow on the ground," she recalled. Rollman, hunting with her son, Jim, was able to tag a buck shot in her favorite hunting grounds along the Noisy Creek in southern Oneida County.[1] It was a special day for another reason as well: it marked her fiftieth consecutive year of Wisconsin deer hunting.

The daughter of a Dutch immigrant, Rollman (née Voermans) grew up on the small farm her father carved from 120 acres of Lincoln County cutover. Learning the value of self-reliance and how to get by on the little they had was an important part of her upbringing, yet deer hunting had not been much of a part of her childhood.

"Dad hunted deer, like everyone did," she said. "But it was more for meat than anything. We really didn't see much of deer on the farm, and he was usually too busy to sport hunt."

Connie Rollman stands beside her eight-point buck taken in 1950, with her two-year-old son, Rick, her father-in-law, Alfred "Rollie" Rollman, and her father, Cornelius "Con" Voermans.
COURTESY OF CONNIE ROLLMAN

Her exposure to hunting came when she married Carl Rollman in August 1947. A dyed-in-the-wool hunter, her new husband spent nearly every free hour during autumn hunting seasons in the woods in pursuit of partridge, ducks, geese, and deer. Carl had previously hunted out of a traditional deer camp in the Sugar Camp area. The "womenfolk" were expected to stay at home, holding luncheons and playing bridge. "We weren't supposed to want to hunt," Rollman said. "I wouldn't have that. I wanted to hunt."

Carl, who wanted to hunt closer to home anyway, changed his deer season plans in 1947: that year, the newlyweds began a new tradition of hunting together in the Wisconsin River country near their home. Rollman took a spike buck her first season.

As the seasons passed, she learned how to read deer sign and locate prime runways; how to track, shoot, and trail deer; and how to field dress those shot. She learned every nook and cranny of their hunting grounds.

Women and Deer Hunting (continued)

In 1950, with a two-year-old at Grandma's and a baby on the way, Rollman took her second deer: an eight-point buck. "I was a little unsure of what to do with it," she said. "I field dressed it and would have tried to drag it out if I hadn't been pregnant."

Rollman continued: "We preferred to hunt alone. I'd pack a lunch for myself and for Carl, and in the morning we would head our separate ways, sometimes not meeting up until the end of the day. I loved to walk and could never sit for very long."

Through the years more notches were added to the stock of a .30-30 Marlin (purchased for fifty dollars in the early 1950s), but the kill was never the most important part of the hunt for Rollman. "I always wanted to see a deer. And I wanted to shoot a deer if I saw one," she said. "But I also liked the excitement of being out alone in the woods."

The very nature of hunting has changed greatly in the more than half a century of hunting experienced by Rollman. "Things began to change in the 1960s," she said. "I used to be able to hunt all day without running into another hunter. That started to change as logging roads provided more access and more hunters arrived from other areas."

Change, however, was one thing Rollman adapted to with ease. "The increase in hunters took a little of the fun out of it," she said. "But I hung in there and found new runways and trails, new places to hunt."

Rollman, who finally had to put away the deer rifle for good when in her early eighties, is a classic example of the type of woman involved in the male-dominated deer hunt of decades past. Typically those women were simply not willing to stay at home to sip tea with other deer hunting "widows." Another key ingredient was a supportive husband or father, for a major roadblock to the participation of women in hunting was the lack of a teacher or mentor willing to pass on hunting skills.

The late Frances Hamerstrom, noted Wisconsin ornithologist and wildlife researcher who collaborated with her husband, Frederick, to conduct groundbreaking research on northern harriers and kestrels at the University of Wisconsin–Stevens Point, also typified the early female sport hunter.[2]

Born in 1907, Hamerstrom was the only girl in a family with three boys. Her father was an avid hunter but as was typical of the times, he did not recognize his young daughter's growing passion for hunting. Not to be discouraged, the strong-willed Hamerstrom attempted to learn on her own, sneaking out of the house at age fifteen for an unsuccessful try at waterfowl hunting with shotgun shells pilfered from her father.[3]

After marrying Frederick in 1931, she became his equal in both academic as well as hunting pursuits, although others weren't so quick to accept this idea. "Hunters tend to be subtle and try various ingenious ways of keeping a female out of the party," she wrote in her 1989

Women and Deer Hunting (continued)

book, *Is She Coming Too?* "'My wife,' says one (having just made the phone call), 'is giving a little party this afternoon and is counting on having you there.'"[4]

Although female deer hunters may not have been common in the early to mid-1900s, despite the obstacles, they weren't exactly rare either. Reporting on the number of deer licenses sold in 1903, the Rhinelander-based newspaper *The Vindicator* noted: "To resident hunters 75,000 licenses have been issued to date, and to non-residents, 351, the odd one going to Mrs. A. D. Dorman of LaGrange Ill., who will hunt at Mellen."[5]

A newspaper story from Oconto in 1912 described how Mrs. Peter Brazeau, hunting with her husband out of an old lumber camp on the Popple River, shot a deer on the first day of the season:

> A young man who heard her shoot came up soon afterward, and she asked him to go into the swamp and drag the deer out for her. He consented and disappeared into the swamp. He had been gone some time before Mr. Brazeau arrived. Mrs. Brazeau told her husband what had happened and he immediately took the trail into the swamp. It was easy to follow, as the deer was bleeding profusely. He had not gone into the woods very far when he came to where the young man had dressed the deer and dragged it out of the swamp on the other side.[6]

The story didn't end there. The Brazeaus' hunting party, after learning of the incident, went out in search of the deer and found it hanging from a tree at the tent camp of the young man and his father. They repossessed Mrs. Brazeau's deer only to have it stolen back during the night.

But such incidents didn't deter women from heading into the woods in pursuit of deer. In 1917 *The New North* reported: "Mrs. E. E. Melton of Superior was the guest of relatives near McNaughton last week and while there she went deer hunting with the result that she brought down a large buck. Mrs. Melton felt justly proud of her prowess with the rifle and her trophy was admired by a large number of friends."[7]

A *New North* story from 1922 reported on the success of another female deer hunter: "This morning the carcass of a 225 buck was strapped to an automobile near the Oneida hotel. The animal was shot in the northern part of the county by a woman whose name could not be learned. It is said that the modern Diana exhibited no little elation over her kill."[8]

"Two Rhinelander women proved their prowess with the rifle when deer hunting near this city," reported *The New North* in 1928. "Mrs. Rose Shedore shot a buck that weighed 165 pounds and Mrs. Elsie Gollwitzer brought down one that weighed 160 pounds."[9]

Clearly women enjoyed hunting deer from the early days of sport hunting, but deer hunting remained a male-dominated activity throughout most of the twentieth century. Those

Women and Deer Hunting (continued)

women who did participate almost always did so accompanied by their husbands, or, less typically, were girls hunting with their fathers. Hunting culture, as well as the mores of the times in the first half of the century, simply did not allow for women to strike out on their own, if they so desired.

The barriers that hampered or prevented more women from hunting were many, but it wasn't until the late 1900s that these barriers began to come down as a result of an educational process that became known as the Becoming an Outdoors-Woman (BOW) program. "The program got started in 1990 when Ray Anderson, a wildlife professor at UWSP, and Bob Jackson, a psychology professor, asked me if I would organize a conference about woman hunters," said BOW program founder Dr. Christine Thomas, dean of the College of Natural Resources at UWSP. "We developed specific questions that the conference could address: why weren't there many women participating in hunting and fishing and what could be done about it?"[10]

The conference, Breaking Down Barriers to Participation of Women in Angling and Hunting, held at UWSP in August 1990 and geared toward an audience of natural resource management agency professionals, was a great success.

"We found that people were very interested in this," said Thomas. "We had sixty-five people from all across the United States attend the conference." One of the primary goals was to determine what hindered women from being more involved in hunting and fishing. "We identified twenty-one barriers," said Thomas. "Fourteen of the barriers were related to women simply not knowing how to do it, not having the skills." With outdoor pursuits, particularly hunting, traditionally dominated by males, it was obvious that women did not have the role models or mentors to teach them outdoor skills and to encourage participation.

Thomas and her UWSP colleagues decided there was no reason why they couldn't begin to teach the outdoor skills that women weren't able to learn in the course of their daily lives. The first BOW workshop was launched in 1991 at UWSP. "We had space for one hundred participants," said Thomas. "But we didn't have much interest early on. Finally, Jay Reed, the outdoor editor for the *Milwaukee Journal Sentinel*, wrote an article on the workshop. Within twenty-four hours we were full."

The participants weren't necessarily greenhorns who had never hunted or fished. Many who attended already had some outdoors experience but really wanted to be a part of the workshop. "They recognized this as something new and important," said Thomas.

Because of the success of the Stevens Point workshop, the National Shooting Sports Foundation offered Thomas a $5,000 grant to organize a workshop in another state, with the caveat that the grant be matched. Safari Club International stepped up to match the grant and with the support of the Nebraska Fish and Game Commission the next workshop was planned for Omaha.

Women and Deer Hunting (continued)

Once again few women initially signed up. "Our break in Omaha came when the *Omaha World-Herald* ran a front-page story on the workshop," said Thomas. "Again, we filled up quickly after the story came out."

The program eventually became a media favorite, which helped keep the momentum going; subsequent workshops were held in Oklahoma, Arkansas, Texas, and Oregon. Thomas, who had a hand in organizing these workshops, soon realized that the BOW program was becoming too big for her to keep up with.

She shifted emphasis to a "train the trainer" workshop in Stevens Point for those who wanted to start the program in their state. This allowed the program to grow rapidly: as of 2007, more than forty states were offering BOW workshops. "Some states hold the basic hunting and fishing workshop," said Thomas. "Other states, such as Wisconsin, have very advanced programs with more specialized workshops."

Has the success of Wisconsin's BOW program translated into an increase in the number of women buying hunting licenses in the state, as well as an increase in numbers in the field? The latest U.S. Fish & Wildlife Service National Survey of Fishing, Hunting, and Wildlife-Associated Recreation revealed that of the U.S. population age sixteen and older, 1 percent of females participated in hunting in 2006.[11] While this percentage may seem low, 1 percent nationally accounts for 1.2 million female hunters. Perhaps more significantly, the survey showed a 50 percent increase in the number of girls ages fifteen and under

hunting from 2001 to 2006, accounting for more than 300,000 young female hunters.[12]

As might be expected, the trend is clearly exhibited in Wisconsin, a state that consistently ranks near the top in terms of percentage of residents who hunt. In his 2006 Deer Season Report, Wisconsin Department of Natural Resources Chief Warden Randy Stark wrote: "In the 12–16 cohort age range, females comprised nearly 21% of the licensed gun hunters. This is a reflection of the hunting community becoming more inclusive as hunting parents are introducing their daughters to deer hunting, and the success of programs like Becoming an Outdoors-Woman."[13]

Although there is no hard data that directly links the increase in women hunters and the sale

More than 20,000 students attend Becoming an Outdoors-Woman programs nationwide annually. The organization is based in Stevens Point.
COURTESY OF PEGGY FARRELL, BOW

Women and Deer Hunting (continued)

of hunting licenses to women with the BOW program, Peggy Farrell, International and Wisconsin BOW director, based at UWSP, believes there is a connection. "There must be something that explains the increase in women hunters while the traditional male hunter base has declined," she said. "I believe the BOW workshops are at least one component to the increase."[14]

The greater significance of the program's success is not simply in the teaching of outdoor skills to thousands of women but in actually changing the hunting culture altogether. BOW does more than teach outdoors skills: it empowers women and gives them the moral support needed to pursue a pastime that has long excluded females. The extensive media coverage of BOW workshops also helped to put a female face on a historically male activity.

With the help of BOW workshops and society's changing attitudes toward women and hunting, it is likely that the question that once raised the ire of Fran Hamerstrom—"Is she coming too?"—won't be heard as much when deer hunting season rolls around.

———

NOTES

1. Connie Rollman, interview by the author, August 2000.
2. Keith L. Bildstein, "In Memoriam: Frances Hamerstrom, 1907–1998," *The Auk*, October 1999.
3. Frances Hamerstrom, *Is She Coming Too?* (Ames: Iowa State University Press, 1989), 5–8.
4. Ibid, 83.
5. "An Army of Hunters," *The Vindicator*, November 25, 1903.
6. "Woman Kills Deer," *Wausau Daily Record-Herald*, November 16, 1912.
7. "Woman Kills Deer," *The New North*, December 6, 1917.
8. "Hunters Invade Woods for Deer," *The New North*, November 16, 1922.
9. "Women Kill Deer," *The New North*, November 29, 1928.
10. Dr. Christine Thomas, interview by the author, February 13, 2008.
11. U.S. Department of Interior, Fish & Wildlife Service, and U.S. Department of Commerce, U.S. Census Bureau, 2006 National Survey of Fishing, Hunting, and Wildlife-Associated Recreation.
12. Marty Roney, "Girls, Women, Aim for Hunting," USAToday.com, March 31, 2008.
13. Randy Stark, "2006 Deer Season Report," Memo to DNR Secretary Matt Frank, December 5, 2007.
14. Peggy Farrell, interview by the author, February 28, 2008.

The Monday following opening day, two of the antihunting demonstrators who attempted to disrupt the hunt at Blue Mounds claimed they were harassed. "Two opponents of deer hunting say they were threatened and harassed after following hunters in a state park," it was reported. The harassment allegedly included a threatening message on an answering machine and some deer parts left on a driveway.[9]

Another mild winter in 1990–91 guaranteed that the burgeoning deer herd would not be checked anytime soon: the 1991 pre–deer season population was estimated at 1.3 million animals. More than half of the state's 122 deer management units were above their over-winter goals. A record 586,000 Hunter's Choice permits were issued prior to the 1991 season, and more than 120,000 bonus permits were sold through the mail at twelve dollars (twenty dollars for nonresidents) each. Hunters were allowed to buy up to two bonus tags. Surplus bonus permits (those not sold through the mail) could be purchased at DNR stations. Wisconsin deer hunters had not had such ample opportunity to take deer since the late 1800s.

"Game managers will make more than 98,000 bonus antlerless deer permits available on a first-come, first-served basis Saturday in hope of killing off more of Wisconsin's record deer herd this fall," reported the *Wausau Daily Herald*.[10] The DNR was unsure if all could be sold. "Being this is the first time for this kind of thing, it is sort of a toss-up on how many will be sold," a DNR spokesperson told the press. "I don't think we are going to sell out of them Saturday or Sunday."[11]

In contrast to the early season of 1990, with its springlike weather, the 1991 season opener fell on the latest date possible under the existing framework: November 23. Confounding things further was a Halloween blizzard that dumped as much as thirty inches of snow north and west of a line from Grantsburg to Ashland, prematurely forcing deer into yards. Going into opening day, heavy snow fell centered on a line from Prairie du Chien in the southwest to Niagara in the northeast. In the north, hunters faced a wet, heavy snow that steadily accumulated throughout opening day. In the southeast, a cold rain soaked hunters and made back roads impassable. With a less-than-expected opening weekend harvest, an "emergency" seven day extension was implemented in seventy-two central and northern Wisconsin deer management units. Nevertheless, despite the late season date and bad weather, hunters took a total of 352,000 deer, just slightly edging out the record set the previous year.

The option of obtaining both Hunter's Choice and multiple bonus permits in northern deer management units was allowing for greatly increased hunter success in the North Woods, a real difference from the lean 1980s. "Our deer populations up here are at a thirty-year high," said Cliff Wiita, a DNR wildlife manager at Park Falls. "There's no question the deer are out there. We've had four mild winters in a row. We've had super production. Our yearling class is excellent and we have a better than normal crop of bucks."[12] There would be an unprecedented six consecutive mild winters from 1989–90 through 1994–95, although early blizzards dampened recruitment in 1991–92.[13]

The trend toward increased hunting pressure in central and southern Wisconsin, which had begun in the 1970s, was now being reversed. Central Wisconsin wildlife managers began to notice reductions in the number of hunters. "We've noticed a significant decline in hunters in the past few years," said Joe Haug, DNR wildlife manager for an area that included Wood, Portage, Juneau, and Adams counties. "Hunting pressure is down as many as five to 10 hunters per square mile on public hunting lands on opening weekend. We don't know why, but we think they are being drawn up north by all the hunter's choice and bonus permits."[14]

However, a reduction in Hunter's Choice and bonus deer permits for the north was in store for 1992, particularly in the northwest. The previous winter had taken a toll on fawn production in many areas. Deer driven into yards by the snow were

Deer population estimates - statewide

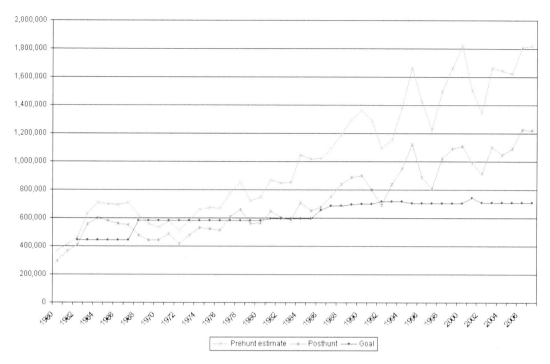

— Prehunt estimate — Posthunt — Goal

While the hunting season generally brought population estimates closer to goal, it became
increasingly more difficult to do so by the mid-1990s.

COURTESY OF WISCONSIN DEPARTMENT OF NATURAL RESOURCES, BUREAU OF WILDLIFE MANAGEMENT

easy targets for hunters, and many of the thousands of Hunter's Choice permits
and bonus tags were filled due to the early snowfall. The ensuing northern winter
of 1991–92 also took a toll on young deer.[15]

Antlerless deer permits were slashed by 40 percent in a six-county area that
included Douglas, Bayfield, Burnett, Washburn, Polk, and Barron counties.[16] "We
may be close to having the herd under control," commented DNR wildlife manager Arlyn Loomans in Rhinelander.[17]

"That means the days of every northern hunter finding a hunter choice permit
in the mail and bags of bonus tags to choose from may be over," said Dave Daniels,
DNR public information officer.[18]

Despite there being fewer antlerless permits in the north for 1992, many DNR
northern region wildlife managers were predicting that the harvest of older bucks—
those two and a half years and older—might actually be greater than the previous
year. Although the antlerless kill was high during the 1991 season, the buck take
was decidedly below expectations—setting the promise of a larger percentage of
older bucks in the herd for 1992.

"The buck kill should definitely show an increase," predicted wildlife manager Cliff Wiita at Park Falls. "Just how much is hard to tell. Our '91 buck kill was down 33 percent in some areas. It wasn't because the bucks weren't there. We definitely have a bulge in our buck population this year."[19]

The combination of snowfalls during the 1991 season had a variable effect on buck harvest according to Keith McCaffery. "First there was the Halloween blizzard that prematurely put deer into winter yards in far northwest Wisconsin, mainly west of U.S. Highway 63," said McCaffery. "This increased buck exploitation there above normal, as everyone seemed to know where the deer were. Secondly, there was a blizzard on opening weekend that traveled from Prairie du Chien to Niagara, laying down up to eighteen inches of snow. This blizzard reduced buck exploitation." This made using the 1991 harvest data questionable for validating the 1991 herd size and thus confounded the base for predicting the herd status in 1992.

"The SAK [Sex-Age-Kill] assumes equal buck exploitation from year to year," said McCaffery. "As this assumption was badly violated in 1991, we had to use 1990 data to set the season for 1992—in effect a double prediction." This was the first time since the inception of the SAK in 1961 that it was not applied annually.[20]

At 1.25 million deer, the 1992 prehunt population prediction showed a slight reduction for the first time in several years, but it was still much larger than was comfortable for deer managers. One emerging dilemma was getting hunters to take a sufficient number of deer in the mostly private land areas of central and southern Wisconsin—a new twist on the age-old access problem of getting hunters to where herd reduction was needed.

A state audit report earlier in the year took the DNR to task for its difficulties in managing the state's deer herd. The report focused on the DNR's failed attempt to extend the deer season to sixteen days as a means of keeping the herd in check, even though the proposal had been withdrawn after intense opposition from the public. The report also questioned the DNR's methods of estimating deer numbers but stated, "We found no evidence that the basic principles of the process used to estimate the deer population are incorrect, but we identified several measures that would assist the department in further improving the accuracy of its estimates."[21] The main recommendation was to include road-kills in the SAK formula. This recommendation was disregarded for the simple reason that this adjustment, along with other nonharvest losses, had already been incorporated into the SAK.[22]

With antlerless permits reduced in northern units and an opening day that brought heavy rains right before sunrise, the 1992 harvest dipped below 300,000 to 288,000 thousand. Farm regions also had their share of problems. Testament to a wet autumn, seven times more standing corn than usual provided convenient escape cover for whitetails. Flooded lowland areas also provided refuges for deer throughout the season.[23] Despite the problems encountered by hunters, the season take ranked as the fourth highest deer kill in the recorded history of Wisconsin deer hunting.

Deer Season Dollars and Cents

It is a Saturday afternoon exactly three weeks before opening day of the nine-day Wisconsin gun deer season. I have just driven about sixty miles from my home in Rhinelander to Wausau, to the enormous sporting goods store located there. Instinctively I push a cart, although I came with plans to purchase only a few essentials for the coming season.

Early November in the middle of a sporting goods store is when and where economic common sense—the good fiscal responsibility that I may have adhered to most of the year—goes out the window. The fact is, aside from the essentials I know I will need—rifle cartridges, batteries, maybe a bottle or two of Indian Buck Lure (it worked so well in 1990)—I always come across something else I must have for the hunt.

Earlier in the year I may have agonized over some mundane purchase, such as a new toaster. But on the Saturday three weeks before opening day, the decisions are cut and dried. The thought process is basically this: "It's almost deer season; this would be nice to have." Done. Or "I could really use another one of these." Done again. And that is why I push the cart.

Of course, a visit to the superstore is not my only pre–deer season sporting goods store trip. I have already made several visits to my local Rhinelander store, a family-owned business that has existed since the 1940s. Shopping there is like a step back in time, the old wooden floor creaking as you survey aisles packed with a little bit of everything. But the lure of the big store, with its gleaming racks of new rifles and

Deer hunting has a long history of bringing additional revenue into local communities each fall. This window at Badger Sporting goods on Madison's State Street lured many hunters preparing for a northern Wisconsin deer hunt in 1944.
WHi Image ID 13190

aisles of hunting clothes, draws me at least once each year. After checking out, not worried in the least about how much I just put on the credit card (there is plenty of time for that after deer season), I head to another part of town where I find an even bigger superstore full of groceries. The cart is definitely needed here, as I plan to fill it with more than a weeks' worth of groceries—

Deer Season Dollars and Cents (continued)

and not just the normal stuff but *deer camp* groceries.

Shopping for deer camp grub is the time when nutritional common sense frequently flies out the window to join the economic common sense previously jettisoned. Again the reasoning is simple: this is for deer camp, *the* most important nine days out of the entire year, and I need to be prepared. So into the cart go the bacon and kielbasa, a block of cheese, big cans of baked beans, a bag of potatoes, maybe muffins and pastries for breakfast, and many other items that are neither organic nor low in cholesterol.

A couple of days before the heralded opening day I'll pack all of my old gear and all of my brand-new gear and my bountiful supply of camp groceries for the hundred-mile drive to the Bayfield County hunting cabin. In Ashland I'll stop at the grocery store to pick up the items I remembered I needed while on the drive, and I'll also eat lunch there before proceeding to camp. The camp's living quarters, though primitive, still require some purchases: propane for the tanks that fuel the cook stove, a supply of firewood previously bought from a local logger and stacked in between trees in front of the cabin, some cleaning supplies.

As fellow camp members arrive, I can tell by the bags and boxes and coolers they unload from their pickup trucks that they have done pretty much the same as I did. Variations of these economic scenarios are played out by the thousands each year. But while all of us hunters are planning and buying and traveling, we really aren't thinking about the enormous positive impact we are having on the state's economy.

I don't think I've ever heard a deer hunting buddy remark, "I am really excited about the great contribution I am making to the state's economy this deer season."

While deer hunters may have other things on their minds, most certainly the owners of motels, restaurants and taverns, gas stations, feed mills, sporting goods and grocery stores, and meat processors—particularly those located in smaller, rural communities—are focused on cash flow.

There's no doubt about it: deer season is big business in Wisconsin, with estimates of the total direct and indirect spending associated with the hunt at $250 million to more than $1 billion annually.[1] "Deer hunting in Minnesota and Wisconsin isn't just about getting out in the woods and getting together with friends and relatives, it's about getting out the wallet," wrote John Myers of the *Duluth News-Tribune* in 2004.[2]

A survey conducted by the Wisconsin Department of Tourism found that deer hunters spent $233 million during the 2000–2001 deer season on travel-related expenses alone.[3] The survey also found that 31 percent of deer hunters stayed in paid accommodations, such as a motel or rented cabin or condo, and that those hunters who traveled to their hunting locations spent twice as much each day as those hunting from home.[4]

Deer Season Dollars and Cents (continued)

Retail sales from deer hunting–related purchases—rifles, scopes, cartridges, blaze-orange clothing, boots, knives, tree stands, binoculars, porta-potties, hand warmers, and more—are huge. A report from the International Association of Fish and Wildlife Agencies (IAFWA) on the economic importance of hunting in the United States found that, on average, each hunter spends about $2,000 annually on hunting-related purchases, or about 5.5 percent of the average wage earner's annual income.[5]

"These expenditures then 'ripple' through the economy generating three times more impact for the U.S. economy," the report stated. "For many communities, hunting dollars keep them afloat."[6] The report ranked Wisconsin third (behind Texas and Pennsylvania) in annual hunting-related retail sales with more than $960 million.[7]

"Deer hunting pumps big bucks into the Wisconsin economy. Not only do retailers who sell hunting supplies benefit, but so do meat processors, businesses that handle registrations and other places where hunters go to fuel up both themselves and their vehicles," reported the *Appleton Post-Crescent*.[8]

Some estimates put the economic impact from deer hunting above that generated by the Green Bay Packers. "Deer hunting in Wisconsin generates about $890 million per year. Compare that with the $60 million that Green Bay officials say the Packers bring into that community," reported the *Milwaukee Journal Sentinel* in 1999.[9]

The economic might of deer season translates into jobs, too. In 1995 Jay Reed of the *Milwaukee Journal* wrote: "Deer hunting in Wisconsin supported 7,860 full- and part-time jobs in 1991. These are not only jobs that are directly associated with hunters, but also are jobs in industries that indirectly support hunting-related activities."[10] On the flip side, however, deer season may lead to fewer workers. A deer season economic factor not too well known is the impact on unemployment rates in the state. "Initial claims for unemployment insurance shot up 95% last week in Wisconsin, an annual spurt that labor officials attributed to deer hunting," reported Joel Dresang in the *Milwaukee Journal Sentinel* in December 2004.[11] "Each year at Thanksgiving, which coincides with Wisconsin's nine-day gun deer-hunting season, herds of business owners suspend operations to accommodate the call of the wild," wrote Dresang. "Often, the layoffs allow employees to file for unemployment benefits.

"Employers tend to schedule deer-related downtime for a combination of reasons: business is slack, most of their work force hunts, and outdoor employees such as loggers and construction workers might be exposed to hunters."[12]

"The shooting sports are so much more than simply pulling a trigger or releasing a bow-string," says the IAFWA. "They represent financial opportunity for every American community, especially rural economies. Each purchase made by hunters sets off a chain reaction of economic benefits."[13] The fact that deer hunting is a highly

Deer Season Dollars and Cents (continued)

profitable industry in Wisconsin, however, should not be construed as the reason why hundred of thousands of Wisconsinites take to the woods each fall; it is simply a nice result.

Tom Heberlein, professor emeritus at the University of Wisconsin–Madison Rural Sociology Department, told the *Milwaukee Journal Sentinel* in 1999:

> When people—particularly wildlife managers—strive to show that hunting is important, they talk about matters of the pocketbook. Deer hunting is not about economic impact. We deer hunters don't do this to be useful.
>
> Certainly, money will be spent in rural areas by people from cities. But you'll never find a hunter who will say they're hunting to cause an economic transfer.[14]

NOTES

1. Pete Bach, "Wisconsin Sportsmen Spend Millions Gearing Up," *Appleton Post-Crescent*, November 21, 2004.
2. John Myers, "Deer Hunt Bolsters Northern Minnesota, Wisconsin Economy," *Duluth News-Tribune*, November 13, 2004.
3. "Deer Hunting Season Generated $233 Million in Wisconsin Last Year," Wisconsin Department of Tourism, http://agency.travelwisconsin.com/Research/EconomicImpact_Active/hunters.shtm.
4. Ibid.
5. "Economic Importance of Hunting in America," International Association of Fish and Wildlife Agencies, http://georgiawildlife.dnr.state.ga.us/assets/documents/Hunting%20Economic%20Impact%202001.pdf.
6. Ibid.
7. Ibid.
8. Pete Bach, "Wisconsin Sportsmen Spend Millions Gearing Up."
9. Tom Vandenbrook, "Big Buck$: Deer Hunters Make Huge Impact on Wisconsin Economy," *Milwaukee Journal Sentinel*, November 20, 1999.
10. Jay Reed, "National Survey Puts Price Tag on Deer Hunt," *Milwaukee Journal*, March 5, 1995.
11. Joel Dresang, "Hunt for Benefits: Jobless Claims Rise Again in Deer Season," *Milwaukee Journal Sentinel*, December 2, 2004.
12. Ibid.
13. "Economic Importance of Hunting in America," International Association of Fish and Wildlife Agencies.
14. Tom Vandenbrook, "Big Buck$," *Milwaukee Journal Sentinel*, November 20, 1999.

Still, herd predictions in eighteen northern units were found to have been overly optimistic.[24] This caused a huge outcry from the Conservation Congress and resulted in very conservative antlerless quotas in 1993.[25]

By 1993 hunters planning to head north had little expectation of receiving a Hunter's Choice permit, as many deer management units offered few, if any, quota deer permits. "After years of bonus permit bonanzas, North Central Wisconsin hunters are returning to their roots," suggested Jim Lee in the *Wausau Daily Herald*. "Older hunters may relish restoration of the challenge to tag antlered deer only."[26]

With a herd now estimated at closer to one million animals, hunters took 217,584 deer during the season. Statewide deer population reductions would not continue, however, as a series of mild winters helped to push deer numbers to the 1.5 million mark by 1995.

"Some 650,000 hunters were expected to take to the fields and woods this weekend, stalking a whitetail herd estimated at 1.5 million animals—more than any time since settlers arrived and some 500,000 more than two years ago," reported the Associated Press.[27]

In 1995, to address the burgeoning deer herd the DNR issued an unprecedented 607,335 bonus permits in an effort to reduce antlerless deer numbers. So many bonus tags were available that supply exceeded demand: the DNR licensing division reported that 39,000 bonus permits were still available the Friday before opening day.[28] Incredibly, hunters could not shoot enough deer to keep the herd in check—the effect of a record six mild winters and increasing amounts of supplemental energy provided to deer by baiting and feeding piles.[29]

Great increases in quota deer permits in the north had hunters once again heading to the North Woods for the opportunity to fill a bonus tag (or two or three) as well as the chance to find a big buck. Northern wildlife managers were becoming concerned about too much hunting pressure. "Last year there were as many hunters up here as I've ever seen and it looks like there certainly will be more this year," stated one northern manager.[30] Jim Lee of the *Wausau Daily Herald* wrote: "On some northern units, particularly in the state's 'cottage country,' hunters may outnumber deer on opening day."[31] The DNR cautioned that although the herd was at near-record numbers in the north "there's not a deer behind every bush."[32]

In other areas in the state, however, it seemed as if there *were* a deer behind every bush. Deer numbers in central and southern Wisconsin continued to be well above management goals in most deer management units. Deer damage to agriculture, as well as deer-vehicle collisions, continued to drive the need to reduce numbers.

Despite incredible deer hunting opportunities due to the sheer numbers of antlerless permits available, and the call from the state and many in the press for hunters to step up and play a greater role in the management of a potentially out-of-control deer herd, the generations-old ideas of protecting does still persisted in the minds of many hunters in 1995. Outdoor writer Jim Lee addressed the issue. "Without an antlerless harvest, the state's deer herd would balloon to well over 2 million deer by next summer, a circumstance that would quickly lead motorists and farmers to label the animal as a pest and demand an eradication program be initiated," Lee wrote. "Currently, hunting is the preferred form of managing deer numbers in Wisconsin. It is likely to remain so as long as hunters understand their roles."[33]

Hunters did step up. "A statewide deer kill record-shattering pace was set early by Wisconsin hunters, who enjoyed nearly perfect weather conditions on opening weekend," wrote Jim Lee. "The final deer kill is expected to approach 400,000 animals as the nine-day season winds down today."[34]

In the end, about 690,000 hunters managed to break yet another state harvest record with 398,002 whitetails taken.[35] An additional 69,269 deer were taken by archers that fall—a harvest greater than the total gun deer kill in some years in the 1950s and '60s.

Despite the record harvest in 1995 and a severe winter prior to the 1996 season, the herd—estimated at more than 1.5 million—remained unchecked in many areas. In an attempt to counter this growth in the worst of those locations, a new type of deer season was established.

"Nearly 90,000 hunters have free tags allowing them to do something unprecedented in Wisconsin this century—use their guns to shoot whitetail deer in October," reported the press. "It's the latest evidence of the radical steps being taken to corral the growth of the state's deer herd—now the largest in history at 1.6 million deer."[36]

The special herd control deer season, known as the "Zone-T" season (an antlerless hunt allowed only in deer management units designated as Zone-T due to being well above population goals), began October 24, and ran for four days in nineteen of the state's most overpopulated deer management units. The units covered all or parts of thirty counties, predominantly agricultural areas in southern and central Wisconsin. It would be the first time since the 1800s that Wisconsin hunters could legally hunt deer with a gun in October.[37]

"Hunters have taken to the woods to help the Department of Natural Resources snuff out a goal of 100,000 whitetail deer. The new, four-day deer hunting season has begun here in an attempt to thin an out-of-hand herd," reported the Associated Press.[38]

These first Zone-T management units in 1996 had an "Earn-a-Buck" provision, which required any hunter who wanted to hunt for bucks in Zone-T units during the regular gun season to first harvest an antlerless deer prior to the regular November hunt. This provision was controversial but effective, and was dropped from subsequent Zone-T seasons.

During the first October Zone-T hunt, nearly 25,000 antlerless deer were taken—far fewer than what the DNR would have liked.[39]

"The first October gun deer season held in Wisconsin this century was almost accident-free but may not have trimmed the state's oversized deer herd as much as anticipated, game managers say," reported the Associated Press.[40] After the season, DNR officials stated that nearly 100,000 deer would have to be taken during the regular season in those nineteen units to bring deer numbers closer to management goals.[41]

Earn-a-Buck

DURING THE SUMMER AND EARLY AUTUMN OF 2004, I heard bits and pieces about "Earn-a-Buck" (EAB), a deer hunting regulation that requires a hunter to harvest an antlerless deer before being authorized to take a buck in designated deer management units (DMUs) during the gun and archery deer seasons. But, truthfully, I wasn't paying much attention. I did know that twenty-six DMUs as well as all of the chronic wasting disease (CWD) zones had been designated EAB units for the 2004 season.[1] I also knew that the EAB regulation was an extraordinary measure enacted to reduce the herd in units where deer numbers were chronically well above the Wisconsin Department of Natural Resources' goals.

I wasn't paying much attention for two reasons. The first was I assumed these EAB units were nowhere near where I hunted in DMU 3, the northernmost DMU (with the exception of DMU 79, which covered the Apostle Islands). The second was that DMU 3, like other northern units,

had a low over-winter goal: just twelve deer per square mile as compared to central Wisconsin DMUs, which had goals of twenty to thirty deer or more per square mile. After more than a decade of hunting Unit 3, I'd concluded that deer were few and far between—at least on the county forest land where I hunted. I felt lucky to even see deer during the season.

When I finally began studying the 2004 regulations pamphlet a few weeks before the season opener, I was surprised to discover that Unit 3 had in fact been designated an EAB unit. Many conversations ensued between me and my hunting partner, Steve Lane, about what EAB meant and how the procedure to get authorized to take a buck would actually work. We sorted through the various tagging options. Unit 3 had been a Zone-T unit (now referred to as a herd control unit) since 2000. The Zone-T designation essentially made a DMU an "any deer" unit, as there were an "unlimited" number of antlerless permits available.[2] Units gained EAB status if the herd

2007-2008 Earn-a-Buck Unit
Buck Authorization

114065

WISCONSIN
DEPT. OF NATURAL RESOURCES

DNR Customer #

Must be attached to back of regular gun or archery carcass tag before tagging the deer. Not valid if numbers are changed. This sticker is **not** replaceable.

The required buck authorization sticker for EAB units.
COURTESY OF WISCONSIN DEPARTMENT OF NATURAL RESOURCES,
BUREAU OF WILDLIFE MANAGEMENT

Earn-a-Buck (continued)

control designation alone did not bring down deer numbers closer to goal two years in a row.

When we purchased our licenses, we automatically received a free antlerless tag to use during the season. The EAB status in 2004 required a hunter to use the antlerless tag *before* legally taking a buck. We would have to tag and register our antlerless deer to receive a buck authorization sticker. However, a provision in the regulation allowed a hunter to take an antlerless deer, tag it, and keep hunting in the same location for a buck—bringing both to the registration station if successful.[3] A new level of complexity was definitely added to the hunt that year.

While it was new to us, EAB had first surfaced as a herd control measure in 1996, when sixteen DMUs were designated, largely in agricultural areas.[4] That also was the first year the early, four-day October herd control antlerless season was established, taking place only in the Zone-T units with EAB status.[5] Gun hunters had the opportunity to harvest an antlerless deer during the October season in order to receive authorization to take a buck during the regular season in these units. The early season resulted in a kill of 24,954 antlerless deer.[6] Those not taking part in the October season had to take an antlerless deer during the regular nine-day season if they wanted to kill a buck in EAB units; however, antlerless deer taken during the early archery season was another way to qualify.

Overall, the first EAB season was a success in terms of increasing the antlerless harvest in those sixteen DMUs. But EAB was hugely

unpopular with hunters who did not like the idea of having to pass up a shot at an adult buck— something not experienced in Wisconsin during a November gun season since the "antlerless-only" five-day season of 1949. The result was the eight-year disappearance of EAB from the hunting scene, except for in CWD zones.

The resurrection of EAB in 2004 was a result of recommendations from the "Deer Management for 2000 and Beyond" ("Deer 2000," for short) process. Deer 2000 was an exhaustive public process initiated by the Wisconsin Natural Resources Board and carried out by the Conservation Congress that sought input from a wide variety of user groups regarding the future of deer management in the state.[7]

While I was initially surprised that EAB included DMU 3, I realized that with a population goal of only twelve deer per square mile, it didn't take many extra deer to push the numbers above goal. The over-winter goal is developed by the DNR based on the biological carrying capacity of the habitat as well as the social carrying capacity—the number of deer acceptable to the public with considerations for agricultural damage, deer-vehicle collisions, damage to ornamental plantings, and public health concerns.[8] In northern forest DMUs, the social carrying capacity wasn't as much of an issue as biological carrying capacity: a productive deer herd could outgrow its habitat quickly, becom-

Earn-a-Buck (continued)

ing prone to die-offs—precisely the issue that spawned the deer wars of the 1940s and what the DNR was attempting to prevent in 2004 through the EAB system.

Eight northern forest region DMUs, eleven eastern farmland region DMUs, and five DMUs in the southern farmland region were designated EAB units in 2004 (two EAB units were in the west-central region).[9] Farmland DMUs had over-winter goals that were based more on a combination of biological and social carrying capacity. These units—patchworks of farm fields and woodlots, as well as towns and roads—are home to more deer due to better habitat and milder climate but also more people, farms, towns, and roads.

On opening day for Deadfall Camp in 2004, luck was with both camp members as Steve and I were able to take antlerless deer on that first day. Happily, we headed into town to register the deer and receive our coveted buck authorization stickers. Our herd reduction job accomplished, we settled into buck hunting for the remainder of the season. Unfortunately, but par for the course, we were not successful. But we had taken deer—although not the mature North Country bucks we always hope for—and were satisfied with the venison and the season overall.

That season, as had occurred in 1996, EAB was a definite factor in increasing antlerless kill in designated zones. "In units with Earn-a-Buck rules in place, antlerless deer registrations were running ahead of previous years," reported the

Rhinelander Daily News.[10] However, not every hunter was satisfied with the EAB provisions, and they made their feelings known to their local Conservation Congress delegates as well as their legislators. In doing so, another Wisconsin deer management strategy became primarily political. Voiced opposition to EAB once again affected the program. There would be no EAB for 2005.

"Faced with widespread hunter dissatisfaction and strong opposition from the Conservation Congress and other groups, the Natural Resources Board voted unanimously last week to reject a Department of Natural Resources recommendation that eight deer management units have the Earn-a-Buck requirement this fall," reported *Milwaukee Journal Sentinel* outdoor columnist Bob Riepenhoff in 2005.[11]

The Conservation Congress held the position that they would support the designation of Zone-T units but no EAB units for the 2005 season. The DNR had proposed eight EAB units and forty-one Zone-T units. In a quick compromise with the Conservation Congress, the DNR agreed to convert the proposed EAB units to Zone-T units and to remove four other units (9, 13, 18, and 73B) from Zone-T designation.[12] The final recommendation, approved by the NRB, was for forty-five Zone-T units and no EAB units, leaving fifty-six units as standard buck-plus-quota hunting.

In 2005 gun hunters harvested a total of 387,310 deer, with about 325,000 coming from the regular nine-day season and the remainder

Earn-a-Buck (continued)

from October and December herd control seasons in herd control units, the youth hunt, and the muzzleloader season.[13]

"Wisconsin hunters did a great job holding projected herd growth to 12 percent over last season given the 2005 season's reduced emphasis on herd control measures, no Earn-a-Buck Units, and an extremely mild northern winter," Keith Warnke, DNR big-game ecologist, told *Outdoors Weekly*.[14] However, with the deer herd estimated by the DNR at 1.5 million to 1.7 million prior to the 2006 hunting seasons (a statewide herd at or near population goals would be slightly more than a million deer), it was clear that more aggressive herd control strategies were needed in some DMUs.[15]

EAB would be back in twenty-one DMUs for 2006—with a well-received change: despite the fact that there were no EAB units in 2005, a new system had been put into effect that allowed hunters to prequalify for EAB by taking an antlerless deer in any DMU that was to be designated EAB the next year. For example, an antlerless deer taken in a herd control unit in 2005 could qualify a hunter for buck authorization in any EAB unit in 2006 if the unit where the antlerless deer was taken was designated EAB for 2006. In subsequent years hunters could plan to meet EAB requirements by reviewing an EAB "watch list" of DMUs likely to receive EAB designation the following year. This provision allowed greater flexibility and opportunity to conform to EAB requirements.

"Many . . . deer management units had EAB restrictions last year. However, the ability to use a doe tag from the previous year to meet the requirement helped offset opposition," wrote Lee Fahrney of the *Monroe Times* in January 2007.[16]

The effectiveness of EAB in those units in need of more aggressive harvest was readily apparent after the 2006 season. A total of 393,306 deer were killed during the 2006 gun hunting seasons, including more than 250,000 antlerless deer.[17] According to Keith Warnke, in the twenty-one Earn-a-Buck units the number of antlerless deer killed increased 30 percent from 2005, when the areas were designated Zone-T.[18] Hoping to keep the herd reduction momentum going, the DNR recommended EAB designation for thirty-five DMUs for the 2007 hunting seasons.

The Conservation Congress grudgingly agreed to the expanded EAB units but hoped the program would not become a permanent fixture on the Wisconsin deer hunting scene. Conservation Congress chairman Ed Harvey was quoted in an Associated Press story in March 2007: "This year we're taking what we're getting. We've got to get past these earn-a-bucks. The complaints are just constant about earn-a-buck seasons and getting into them and never getting out of them."[19]

Others saw that EAB had become a valuable tool in the deer manager's toolbox. Jim Lee, writing for Gannett Wisconsin Newspapers, urged hunters to be proactive when it came to EAB:

Central Wisconsin hunters should keep two aspects in mind when they take to the

Earn-a-Buck (continued)

woods Nov. 17, the opening of the 2007 gun deer season. No.1—Earn-a-buck has become an essential tool in the state's deer management plan. No. 2—Earn-a-buck is likely coming to your deer management unit in 2008—if it isn't in effect already—and the ability to prequalify for the 2008 season under earn-a-buck has begun.[20]

Whatever the perspective of the individual deer hunter, it was becoming clear that EAB would be around for as long as it was necessary for herd control.

NOTES

1. "2004 Wisconsin Big Game Summary," Wisconsin Department of Natural Resources, 2.
2. Ibid.
3. "Wisconsin Earn-a-Buck Fact Sheet," Wisconsin Department of Natural Resources, 2004, www.dnr.state.wi.us/org/land/wildlife/HUNT/DEER/EABfactsheet.pdf.
4. Keith McCaffery, retired Wisconsin Department of Natural Resources northern forest deer researcher, personal communication, January 2, 2008.
5. "A Chronology of Wisconsin Deer Hunting from Closed Seasons to Antlerless Permits," Wisconsin Department of Natural Resources, news release, November 12, 2006.
6. Ibid.
7. Kevin Wallenfang, "Deer on the Agenda," *Wisconsin Natural Resources*, October 1998, 17–18.
8. "Wisconsin's Deer Management Program: The Issues Involved in Decision Making," Wisconsin Department of Natural Resources, Madison, 1998, http://dnr.wi.gov/org/land/wildlife/hunt/deer/Deerbook.pdf.
9. Gary F. Martin, "Wisconsin's 2004 Deer Outlook, Part 2," *Wisconsin Sportsman*, www.wisconsinsportsmanmag.com/hunting/whitetail-deer-hunting/wi_aa115904a/.
10. "Preliminary Count Shows Increase in Deer Harvest," *Rhinelander Daily News*, November 28, 2004.
11. Bob Riepenhoff, "Unpopular Earn-a-Buck Plan Rejected: Eight Hunting Units Instead Designated as Zone-T," *Milwaukee Journal Sentinel*, March 3, 2005.
12. Ibid.
13. "2005 Wisconsin Big Game Summary," Wisconsin Department of Natural Resources, 21–25.
14. "Wisconsin Outdoors: 2006 Regional Deer Season Forecast: Wisconsin Deer Season: What You Need to Know," *Outdoors Weekly*, August 25, 2006, www.outdoorsweekly.com/news_wisconsin/06_0825_wisc.html.
15. Keith McCaffery, personal communication, January 2, 2008.
16. Lee Fahrney, "Concealed Carry, CWD Management Among the Hot Topics for 2007," *The Times Plus, Monroe Times*, January 18, 2007.
17. "2006 Wisconsin Big Game Summary," Wisconsin Department of Natural Resources, 16.
18. Associated Press, "Wisconsin DNR Wants More Earn-a-Buck Areas," *La Crosse Tribune*, March 22, 2007.
19. Ibid.
20. Jim Lee, "Outdoors: Earn-a-Buck Permeates Hunt," *Stevens Point Journal*, November 11, 2007.

The weekend before opening day 1996, my hunting partner, Steve Lane, and I were doing some hard scouting in the Chequamegon National Forest north of Clam Lake. This last scouting trip the weekend before the season had become a tradition since we started hunting out of an outfitters-type deer camp in the Clam Lake area in 1990. I was excited about some prime-looking hunting locations I had discovered on Saturday. Sunday afternoon we scoped out some new territory. That was when the rain started—a cold, bone-numbing November rain.

When we noticed it was turning to sleet and covering the forest roads with ice, we decided to head back home, which for me was Rhinelander and for Steve was Sugar Camp. About six hours later I arrived at my front door—a trip that normally took just two hours. We crept along major highways coated with freezing rain at a top speed of twenty miles an hour. When we approached Minocqua well after sunset, we could see that trees along the road were bent, heavy with ice. Closer to town, Minocqua was eerily dark. Branches too weak to withstand the tremendous weight of their ice coating were crashing to the ground. Tree tops brought down power lines.

"More than 70 two-person crews from throughout the state worked at restoring power to the more than 12,000 Wisconsin Public Service customers without service in Lincoln, Oneida and Vilas counties," the press reported the next day.[42]

Farther north, in the Lake Superior "snowbelt," the storm had dumped snow. The *Wausau Daily Herald* reported: "The first day of the gun deer season is a week away but it may already be over in brief parts of the far north. . . .

"Storms off Lake Superior brought snow down by the bucketful last weekend in counties near the Michigan border."[43]

The ice storm may have been a hint of what was in store for the gun season, at least in the north. Because Thanksgiving Thursday fell on a later than usual date, opening day also fell on the latest date possible: November 23. For northern Wisconsin that meant no hope of catching the tail end of the rut. Also, game managers were predicting fewer deer in the north due to the harsh winter of 1995–96—a winter not unlike the severe ones of the 1970s. In January, the Lake Superior snowbelt town of Hurley broke a state record for snow depth with sixty inches on the ground. A record temperature for the state was set that February when thermometers bottomed out at an incredible minus 55 degrees Fahrenheit near Couderay in Sawyer County.[44]

As had become second nature twenty years earlier, sportsmen's groups and concerned citizens did what they thought necessary to help the deer survive. "Many individuals, groups and organizations pitched in last year to feed during our severe winter. In those areas, the deer herd moved into the spring season in better shape than we might have expected," stated DNR wildlife manager Arlyn Loomans in Rhinelander.[45]

While the supplemental feeding helped some local deer populations, overall, the northern herd suffered significant losses due to the effects of winter and the high proportion of young deer in the overabundant herd.[46] "Around Spooner, in northern forest areas, there probably was a 10 percent loss, while the area along Lake Superior and Michigan's Upper Peninsula may have lost a quarter of the herd," reported the DNR.[47]

As in the previous year, there were none of these dismal reports for central and southern Wisconsin. "The deer population in Marathon County is at record levels," stated a DNR wildlife manager in 1996.[48]

Although the late season opener probably meant missing the rut for central Wisconsin hunters as well as northern hunters, antlerless quotas were still high for most central and southern deer management units. Overall expectations were high as well. "For the second consecutive year, wildlife experts predict a record number of whitetail deer could be killed during Wisconsin's nine-day gun season," reported the press. "If DNR projections prove true, gun and bow and arrow hunters this fall could shoot a record 500,000 deer from a statewide herd estimated at 1.5 million animals. That number is astounding when considering the state whitetail population in 1962 didn't even total 500,000 deer."[49]

A look back to seasons of the past shows the incredible rise of the whitetail and the whitetail hunt in Wisconsin that had occurred during the 1980s and continued into the 1990s. In 1906 the estimated legal deer kill was fewer than 5,000 animals. Jumping ahead to 1926, the estimated statewide take was just 12,000 deer, with fewer than 50,000 deer tags sold. In 1943, the harvest surpassed 100,000 for the first time in history as a result of the infamous split season; it surpassed 100,000 only seven times between 1943 and 1973. It wasn't until 1974 that gun season kills began surpassing 100,000 on a regular basis, breaking the 200,000 mark in 1984. From then on, it seems, there was no looking back as deer numbers and season takes continued a steady climb upward. The vast majority of this herd increase occurred in the southern two-thirds of Wisconsin where farmland deer populations increased sixfold from 1962 to 1984.[50]

Opening weekend results in 1996 seemed to confirm the preseason predictions. In central and southern Wisconsin counties the opening take was on par with the 1995 hunt.[51] Also as predicted, registration stations in northern counties reported significantly fewer registrations as compared to the year before.[52]

Despite fewer deer in the north and fewer antlerless permits in the hands of northern hunters, along with the Earn-a-Buck provision in nineteen deer management units, the statewide deer kill for the 1996 season was only about 10,000 deer shy of the 1995 record. License sales had increased by about the same amount that the kill declined, resulting in 684,780 licensed hunters harvesting 388,791 deer.[53] Archers took an additional 72,941 deer. Hunters of the 1990s were experiencing deer hunting opportunities as never seen before. As DNR deer biologist Bill Mytton said at the time, "The good old days are right now."[54]

My own hunt during that season caused me to believe Mytton. A week after the ice storm, the weather in the Chequamegon National Forest was crisp and for the most part clear. Just the right amount of fresh snow covered the ground. It was the seventh year my partner and I had made camp at Deadfall in the Chequamegon woods. During the season, I had discovered the largest bobcat tracks I had ever seen, watched a full moon rise behind a grove of hundred-year-old hemlocks, heard a chorus of wolf howls early one morning while walking to a blind, and, on a very cold morning the day before Thanksgiving, when the woods seemed as quiet as an empty church, I shot a young buck deer. It truly was the best hunting season of my life.

The winter that had started with the northern ice storm progressed into another hard one for the north. The temperature extremes of 1995–96 were replaced by unusually high snow accumulations. Always subject to huge amounts of snow, Hurley again broke records during the winter of 1996–97: the greatest monthly snowfall total was given to Hurley for 103.5 inches in January 1997, which was just a portion of the 301 inches (more than twenty-five feet) to hit Hurley that winter—enough for it to take the honors for the greatest seasonal accumulation of snow.[55]

The impacts of two back-to-back severe winters, the first since 1971 and 1972, once again had deer managers predicting a reduced deer kill in northern Wisconsin. "We're feeling the effects of those two bad winters and hunters shouldn't be too optimistic heading into this season," said a DNR biologist in Rhinelander.[56] However, a central Wisconsin wildlife manager stated that Marathon County should be "as good as ever."[57]

With deer numbers uncertain, the Zone-T units were cut back from nineteen the year before to just seven deer management units and three state parks. The very unpopular Earn-a-Buck provision was eliminated, at least for the time being. Early-season October four-day hunts in the Zone-T units resulted in a take of only about 7,000 antlerless deer.

Snow and sleet welcomed deer hunters in northern Wisconsin on opening weekend. The weather, along with another year of fewer antlerless permits, and forecasts for a bleak season, probably had many deer hunters back to the cabin or home in time to watch the Green Bay Packers take on the Dallas Cowboys on Sunday. "Last year's Super Bowl winners play the arch rival Dallas Cowboys in Green Bay on Sunday, the second day of the deer season for gun hunters. The game's lure—Dallas has beaten the Packers eight straight times—will have hunters hanging up their guns for a few hours, observers say," reported the press.[58]

Whatever the reasons, the 1997 deer harvest was dramatically less than the previous two years. Overall, at 292,513, the gun season harvest was about 96,000 deer fewer than the 388,791 of 1996 and 105,000 fewer than the record-breaking season of 1995. Nevertheless, the 1997 kill still ranked as one of the highest in the history of regulated deer hunting in Wisconsin.

A meteorological phenomenon known as El Niño became well known during the winter of 1997–98 as it abruptly put a stop to the pattern of severe winters. At the time, the winter of 1997–98 was the warmest in the state since the inception of modern record keeping in 1895.[59] Daytime temperatures were only somewhat higher than average, but nighttime temperatures ranged from 10 to 14 degrees

Fahrenheit warmer than average.[60] In many locations, ice out came earlier than anyone could remember.

Statewide the Wisconsin deer herd sailed through winter in excellent condition with does and young deer surviving in good shape. Consequently fawn production in the spring also was high. Mild winter conditions translated into a deer herd once again expanding beyond the capacity of the habitat to support it.

The El Niño effect continued through to the season of 1998. "Nearly ideal weather and a healthy white-tailed deer herd in most parts of the state provided excellent hunting conditions for the opening weekend of the 1998 Wisconsin nine-day gun deer hunting season," reported the DNR.[61] The mild weather during the season allowed hunters in blinds or on stands to stay sitting much longer than in colder weather.

Opening weekend registrations ran much higher than the previous year, a combined result of the need to get harvested deer processed quickly due to the warmer weather as well as increased hunter success. Buck deer made up about 90,000 of the 170,000 deer registered opening weekend. Harvested bucks showed above-average antler development, something attributed to the mild winter.

"Buoyed by excellent weather conditions and benefiting from a deer herd in superb shape, hunters in the northern counties registered bucks exhibiting some of the best antler development seen in recent years," reported the *Wausau Daily Herald*.[62] Yearling bucks—those fawns from the year before that are one-and-a-half years old during the hunting season—generally are spike bucks or four-point forked bucks during their second autumn. Deer registration stations were reporting numerous yearling bucks with forked antlers, some with six- and eight-point racks.[63]

With the need to check deer herd growth again imperative, the number of antlerless deer permits was increased for 1998, although the October Zone-T season was held in only one management unit. With an increased antlerless take coupled with a significantly greater take of bucks during the nine-day season, the total gun kill for 1998 was 332,254—the fifth highest harvest in Wisconsin history. Archers took another 75,301 deer.

The mild winter of 1998–99 kept herd growth on the upswing. With deer numbers consistently well over one million animals, it was becoming clear to deer managers that hunting, the number one deer management tool, was increasingly losing its ability to control numbers. Underappreciated at this time was the impact of increased baiting and recreational feeding of deer. Clearly, this and mild winters were causing unprecedented herd increases, requiring the state to set aggressive harvest recommendations.[64]

"Biologists who predict hunters will shoot 400,000 deer this month say this will not sufficiently reduce a Wisconsin herd that has gotten too large," reported the press.[65]

The Great Bait Debate

PRIOR TO THE LATE 1980S, THE PLACEMENT OF PILES of food—corn, apples, potatoes, rutabagas, and similar foodstuffs—to attract deer and keep them in an area before the hunting season was not a widespread practice. The use of bait as an aid to hunting whitetails was not illegal, and existing bait regulations were mainly for bear hunting.

According to retired Wisconsin Department of Natural Resources northern forest deer researcher Keith McCaffery, some level of baiting and feeding of deer has likely always occurred. State-sponsored programs to feed deer during harsh northern winters were well accepted and supported by the public from the mid-1930s until 1960.[1] For decades, hunters relied on the time-honored practice of seeking out hunting locations where deer would be drawn to natural food sources: acorns on an oak ridge, grassy forest openings, apples in abandoned orchards, edges of farm fields. The actual placement of bait wasn't a common practice, although a bowhunter might toss some apples around a stand to get a deer to pause for a better shot.

Deer baiting has it proponents—and staunch opponents.
PHOTO BY ROBERT C. WILLGING

In the 1980s baiting became a major component to the strategy of a growing number of hunters. Rather than seeking out areas where deer might be found and hunting there—even if it might be a cornfield or apple orchard—the hunter using bait relies on the food he or she placed to lure deer. Baiting generally involves finding a stand or blind location that allows for ease of access as well as clear shooting, and then establishing a feeding site. Since the goal in most situations is to attract deer to the area and keep them there until hunting season, the bait site needs to be maintained. This often requires the hunter to purchase large quantities of bait—typically in the form of fifty-pound sacks of corn or apples—to regularly replenish the bait site. According to McCaffery, it is the repeated replacement of feed at a site that distinguishes baiting and feeding from all natural foraging by deer.[2]

The Great Bait Debate (continued)

The use of baiting to hunt deer exploded in popularity seemingly overnight. In Michigan, where deer-baiting surveys were instituted in the mid-1980s, the amount of bait being used by hunters increased fourfold between 1984 and 1991.[3] A similar situation began somewhat later in Wisconsin.

"It is my recollection that deer baiting was not an issue in Wisconsin or Minnesota in 1991, but that Michigan reported at the Great Lakes Deer Group meeting that their hunters reported placing 13.1 million bushels of bait in 1991—up from 3.3 million bushels in 1985. For decades, biologists from Minnesota and Wisconsin looked to Michigan for trends that would likely affect them later," said McCaffery. "Minnesota went home and banned deer baiting statewide by Commissioners Order in 1991 and before baiting became an issue. But Wisconsin ran into some objections from the leader of the Conservation Congress who insisted on a long-term study. The first [time] that I saw bait sold at a gas station in Rhinelander was 1995, and it included sugar beets from Michigan. By the time of the 'Deer 2000' studies, baiting was controversial in Wisconsin. So, I've been arguing that baiting was not much of an issue in Wisconsin until the 1990s."[4]

There has been a lot of discussion and speculation as to why this way of deer hunting became so favored in such a short amount of time. The method may have mirrored changes in the hunting population; with less and less time available to devote to scouting hunting locations prior to the season and less time to spend on the stand or still-hunting the woods during the season, the idea of baiting to draw deer to a site became increasingly acceptable. The time and effort that must be expended to maintain bait sites may be outweighed by the reduced amount of time needed to take a deer.

Another change in the 1980s and 1990s was simply the likelihood of more money in the hunter's pocket due to a good economy. Hunters relying on baiting incurred the expense of not only hundreds of pounds of bait but also the transportation to get it to the site on a regular basis. For hunters living considerable distances from their bait sites, this cost could be significant.

Land ownership changes also contributed to the increase in baiting. The 1990s saw sharp growth in the demand for recreational hunting lands in the state. Many of the hunters who bought their own chunk of hunting land resorted to bait or food plots to attract, concentrate, and hold deer on or near their private properties.[5]

Some other reasons for the rise of baiting might include the simple idea that as more hunters began to bait, many more hunters realized that baiting was not illegal. "Some growth in baiting can probably be attributed to growing awareness that it was legal," said McCaffery. "It had been popularly believed that baiting was illegal since it had been illegal to use any form of bait to hunt waterfowl or to use salt to bait deer."[6]

Whatever the reasons, the sudden increase of hunting over bait generated plenty of con-

The Great Bait Debate (continued)

troversy. Early in the debate the issues largely centered on ideas of ethics and fair play. As with any good Wisconsin deer hunting or management debate, there was polarization. At one pole were those hunters who did not bait—never did and never would—and who considered baiting highly unethical and unsportsmanlike. The other pole was occupied by those who had no ethical qualms whatsoever and had made baiting their hunting method of choice. Of course, most deer hunters fell into the complex world between the poles: there were those who felt baiting would be acceptable if it was just regulated more, and there were others who felt baiting was all right in certain situations, such as for the younger and older hunters, or when bowhunting.

There was growing support within the DNR for a baiting ban as Wisconsin deer managers learned from Michigan, where biologists had been the first in the region to document the baiting phenomenon.[7] Some in the DNR took a middle-of-the-road approach at first. In 1987 outdoor writer Jim Lee noted, "Even some wildlife managers believe that as long as the deer herd remains at high levels and that baiting isn't proven to have an adverse effect on the buck population . . . DNR will be hard put to justify banning it altogether."[8]

Early in the new century, however, the nature of the bait debate was changed forever when tissue samples from three deer taken near Mt. Horeb during the 2001 season tested positive for chronic wasting disease (CWD). The test results caused immediate alarm. Concerned that CWD

could be elsewhere in the state or could spread to other areas and threaten herd health as well as the Wisconsin deer hunting tradition itself, the DNR acted quickly to develop a CWD action plan. The resulting management plan incorporated a range of strategies to attempt to combat the disease, including the removal of thousands of deer through landowner out-of-season permits and the use of government sharpshooters in the core management area (parts of Iowa and Dane counties) as well as a massive statewide testing program during the 2002 hunting seasons.[9]

Another important component of the plan was an emergency statewide ban on deer baiting (defined as the practice of putting out food for the purpose of hunting) and feeding (defined as placing food for purposes other than hunting, such as wildlife viewing) that went into effect in July 2002.[10] Suddenly the deer baiting issue transcended hunter ethics and became a matter of deer herd health.

A DNR information leaflet stated: "On July 3, 2002, it became illegal to feed or bait deer in Wisconsin. Prohibiting feeding and baiting is a part of the state's efforts to control Chronic Wasting Disease (CWD) and reduce the chance that CWD will become established in new areas of Wisconsin."[11] A violation of the new baiting ban could earn a hunter a $2,091 fine along with revocation of hunting, fishing, and trapping privileges for up to three years. The penalties for a feeding violation also included possible revocation of privileges, but the fine was only up to $300.[12]

The Great Bait Debate (continued)

At the time of the ban, DNR surveys indicated that about 40 percent of bowhunters used bait, while only about 17 percent of gun hunters did. Also, the DNR estimated, conservatively, that nearly four million gallons of bait had been used by deer hunters in northern Wisconsin during the 2001 season.[13]

While there were many unknowns about CWD and exactly how it spread, the possibility of transmission through deer to deer contact was very real. Saliva was suspected as a mode of transmission as early as 1999.[14] It was clear to deer managers and scientists that a ban on feeding and baiting could help control the spread of the disease.

In September 2002, when the Legislative Joint Committee for Review of Administrative Rules (JCRAR) extended the emergency ban, set to expire November 23, to April 30, 2003, it became certain that the archery and gun deer hunting seasons of 2002 would be conducted completely without the use of bait.[15]

Public opposition to the ban came from both those who hunted with bait and those who profited by selling bait—particularly in northern Wisconsin, where stacks of fifty-pound bags of corn and apples outside sporting goods and convenience stores had become an autumn fixture. Baiting was very popular among those hunting the north's large acreages of public land where lower deer densities made hunting more difficult.

"Hunters using bow and arrow—who often lure deer to their tree stands with piles of corn—

are griping about the ban. So far this year, 35,000 fewer archery licenses have been sold, a 22% drop compared with the same time last year," reported the Milwaukee Journal Sentinel in November 2002. "Sales have plummeted at feed mills, particularly in the north, where many mills sell bags of corn and mineral blocks to hunters and to people who like to see deer in their backyards."[16]

While the bait ban was one component in the decline of both archery and gun license sales in 2002, the hunting public's fear of possible CWD transmission to humans eating venison from sick animals probably contributed significantly.

Organizations with the goal of fighting a permanent baiting and feeding ban quickly formed and preempted DNR-sponsored public meetings by holding meetings of their own. A northern Wisconsin group calling itself Voices of Wisconsin organized a series of public meetings to rally against the ban, the first of which was held in Ashland in January 2003. "Frustration and anger about what is perceived as the Wisconsin DNR's intrusion into people's lives without representation filled the auditorium of the Northwoods Visitor Center last night as hundreds of hunters and other deer enthusiasts gathered to discuss the agency's emergency ban on baiting and feeding," wrote Kevin O'Brien of the Daily Press in Ashland.[17]

Patti Rantala, co-owner with her husband, Ron, of the Country Feed and Pet Store in Iron River, in northwestern Wisconsin, became active in fighting the ban, forming her own pro-baiting

The Great Bait Debate (continued)

organization, Wisconsin Baiting and Feeding. She had seen profits rise from the sale of deer feed in the years preceding the 2002 ban. "We were in the black for the last four years," Rantala told the *Ashland Daily Press*. "Last year, we lost well over $26,000 on our bottom line."[18] Other northern feed mills and stores also reported high revenue losses due to the ban.[19]

On April 23, just days before the emergency ban was set to expire, the Natural Resources Board (NRB) voted—after a lengthy meeting at which more than fifty citizens on both sides of the issue testified—to send a proposal to the Legislature for a permanent ban.[20] In May, with vocal public opposition to the baiting and feeding ban mounting, the Legislature was searching for a compromise. The Assembly Natural Resources Committee and Senate Environment Committee held a joint hearing on the proposed permanent rule. The result was a compromise proposal allowing two gallons of bait in units other than CWD management zones and feeding in units north of Highway 29.

In June, at its next meeting, the NRB rejected the compromise proposal, again voting to submit a proposal for a permanent statewide baiting and feeding ban.[21] During the ensuing months, continued wrangling between the NRB and the Legislature produced no acceptable compromise. With the approach of the 2003 deer hunting seasons, the DNR again requested an emergency rule to regulate baiting and feeding. However, the rule that went into effect September 11 was vastly different from the emergency rule of 2002:

it banned baiting and feeding within CWD eradication, herd reduction, management, or intensive harvest zones but allowed the practices throughout the rest of the state.

About this same time, an Assembly bill with similarities to the emergency rule and previous Legislature compromise proposals was passed by a vote of 84-15. The bill, AB 519, moved quickly through the State Senate (Act 240) and was signed into law by Governor Jim Doyle in Eau Claire on April 13, 2004; a ceremonial signing was held later that day in Ashland.

"This compromise legislation provides some balance to the regulation of baiting and feeding," Doyle said. "It will allow many small businesses that depend on the sale of feed to stay in business. And most importantly, it will help curb the spread of this disease."[22]

Basically, AB 519 allowed for the use of bait for deer hunting anywhere outside of those counties closed to baiting and feeding due to being designated as a CWD management, eradication, or intensive harvest zone. As of the 2007 deer season, there were twenty-six counties closed to baiting and feeding, all in southern or central Wisconsin.[23]

The law also placed some tougher restrictions on the use of bait, including a daily bait placement limit of two gallons; no more than two gallons of bait on each contiguous area of forty acres or less; and a hundred yards was required between bait sites.[24]

While AB 519 may have tightened restrictions on baiting and feeding somewhat and

The Great Bait Debate (continued)

definitely helped silence some of the rancor over the issue, the debate did not go away. As the initial panic over CWD receded in the years following the discovery of the disease in the state, the push by the DNR and many conservation and sportsmen's groups for a statewide ban on hunting with bait did not. Disease concerns may have thrust the baiting and feeding issue to the forefront, but many other issues—the ethics of baiting; negative effects baiting has on deer distribution, survival, and behavior; and the alteration of the landscape (due to the impact on vegetation resulting from artificially high deer numbers)—are also concerns.

McCaffery argues that baiting and feeding practices result in thousands of tons of food artificially entering the natural system each year. "This energy changes productivity, survival, distribution, and behavior of deer," he wrote in *Wisconsin Outdoor Journal* in 2004. According to McCaffery, artificially high deer populations lead to a host of problems, including negative impacts on habitat and the need for more complex harvest strategies, such as Earn-a-Buck.[25]

A growing number of hunters seem to agree, as evidenced by public input at 2006 Conservation Congress spring hearings. (These annual hearings, held in every county in April, are a process unique to Wisconsin, one that allows the public to voice opinions on a variety of conservation issues.) Five separate advisory questions regarding the regulation of baiting were on the ballot.

Sportsmen and conservation organizations, such as the Wisconsin Wildlife Federation, con-

cerned about the negative impact of baiting were pleased to see that a question asking individuals if they would support a statewide ban on baiting ten days before the gun deer season had the support of 62 percent of those who voted.[26] It was clear that the hunting public had become better informed about the pros and cons of baiting since 2002.

However, a question asking whether there should be a complete statewide ban resulted in a stalemate: a near fifty-fifty split, evidence that, like so many deer hunting and management issues of the past, baiting was sure to generate heated debate for years to come.

———

NOTES

 1. Keith R. McCaffery, "Even Limited Baiting and Feeding Poses Threat," *Wisconsin Outdoor Journal* 18, no. 7 (Fall 2004), 22–24.
 2. Ibid.
 3. Ibid.
 4. Keith McCaffery, "Deer Baiting and Feeding Issue," paper presented to joint meeting of the Midwest and Northeast Deer Study Groups, Hillman, MI, 2000.
 5. Ibid.
 6. McCaffery, "Even Limited Baiting and Feeding Poses Threat," 22–24.
 7. McCaffery, "Deer Baiting and Feeding Issue."
 8. Jim Lee, "Deer Hunters Find Success in 50-lb Sack," *Wausau Daily Herald*, November 15, 1987.
 9. Robert E. Rolley, "Controlling Chronic Wasting Disease in Wisconsin: A Progress Report and Look Toward the Future," Wisconsin Department of Natural Resources, PUB-CE 461 2005.
10. "NRB Affirms Its Proposed Ban on Deer Baiting and Feeding," Wisconsin Department of Natural Resources press release, August 15, 2003.
11. "The Ban on Baiting and Feeding in Wisconsin," Wisconsin Department of Natural Resources informational brochure, 2003.
12. Ibid.

The Great Bait Debate (continued)

13. Ibid.
14. C. J. Sigurdson, et al., "Oral Transmission and Early Lymphoid Tropism of Chronic Wasting Disease PrPres in Mule Deer Fawns (*Odocoileus hemionus*)," *Journal of General Virology* 80 (1999), 2,757–2,764.
15. "NRB Affirms Its Proposed Ban on Deer Baiting and Feeding," Wisconsin Department of Natural Resources press release, August 15, 2003.
16. Meg Jones, "Opposition Grows for Ban on Deer Baiting," *Milwaukee Journal Sentinel*, November 1, 2002.
17. Kevin O'Brien, "Deer Enthusiasts Unite in Opposition to Baiting and Feeding Ban," *Ashland Daily Press*, January 9, 2003.
18. Kevin O'Brien, "Iron River Businesswoman Takes on the DNR," *Ashland Daily Press*, August 7, 2003.
19. Kevin O'Brien, "Deer Feeding Ban Sparks Strong Reaction," *Ashland Daily Press*, January 3, 2003.
20. Minutes, Natural Resources Board, April 22–23, 2003.
21. "NRB Affirms Its Proposed Ban on Deer Baiting and Feeding," Wisconsin Department of Natural Resources press release, August 15, 2003.
22. "Gov. Doyle: Governor Signs Bill to Limit Baiting and Feeding Only in Areas Where CWD Is Present in Deer Herd," Governor's Office Press Release, April 13, 2004.
23. "Wisconsin Deer Baiting and Wildlife Feeding Regulations," Wisconsin Department of Natural Resources, WM-456-2007.
24. Ibid.
25. McCaffery, "Even Limited Baiting and Feeding Poses Threat," 22–24.
26. Robert Imrie (Associated Press), "Deer Bait Limits Backed, Await DNR Board OK," *Capital Times*, April 12, 2006.

"The numbers of animals are above goal statewide mostly due to mild winters and winter feeding and baiting during the season," deer biologist Keith McCaffery told the *Rhinelander Daily News* in 1999. "Most of the herd consists of younger individuals because the population growth has occurred relatively recently."[66]

Before the 1999 season, the deer herd was estimated at a staggering 1.7 million animals.[67] For hunters this meant incredible opportunities once again to take more than one deer home from the hunt.

"The 1999 gun deer season might be as good as it gets in north central Wisconsin," wrote outdoor writer Jim Lee, ironically echoing a similar statement he had made back in 1990.[68]

While high deer numbers would potentially translate into success for hunters, for deer managers the 1999 deer season represented another battle with an out-of-control herd. When at management goals, the fall herd should number about 1.1 million deer.[69] DNR officials wanted hunters to take at least 420,000 deer—more deer than had ever been taken before in a single season—in an attempt to turn the corner on herd growth.

"Wildlife experts are hoping hunters, using luck and skill, walk away from the nine-day gun season with an all-time record of 420,000 deer," reported the Associated Press.[70] The DNR established a statewide harvest quota of 335,000 antlerless deer. Accounting for hunter success rates, more than one million antlerless permits in the form of Hunter's Choice and bonus permits were made available. Once again, however, supply exceeded demand; nevertheless, a whopping 764,256 antlerless permits were issued.[71]

Dry, mild weather and the abundance of antlerless deer permits enabled hunters to set a new state gun season harvest record during the 1999 season, with more than 402,000 deer killed. Archers added a record 92,203 to the tally.

As the 1990s came to a close, so, too, did the twentieth century. Nine of the century's ten highest deer harvests had taken place during this decade. At the beginning of the century, many concerned Wisconsin citizens warned of the pending demise of those "swift-footed animals of our American forests," as rising hunter numbers whittled away at a deer population numbering perhaps fewer than 30,000 animals.[72] Never in their wildest dreams could they have imagined the abundance of deer—and the strength of the Wisconsin hunting tradition—that existed on the eve of the new millennium.

The Prion That Changed the Hunt

*There is no describing the frustrations of deer management
to persons who have not been exposed to it.*
—Ernest Swift, *A Conservation Saga*[1]

During autumn 2001, in a patch of fields and woodlots in the dairy-farm country of Dane County, southwest of Madison, a two-and-a-half-year-old buck whitetail was dying. Its mind confused, unable to function as it should, its body becoming increasingly uncoordinated, no longer able to run and leap, the deer was a weak shadow of what it once had been. Always thirsty in the September heat the buck had difficulty drinking, could not easily swallow the water it craved. Eating was even more difficult, and the buck had stopped feeding altogether weeks before, its body now gaunt, bones poking against skin. The deer was literally wasting away.

There was no reason for anyone in the Mt. Horeb area to think that there were sick and dying deer in the woods as the 2001 nine-day gun hunting season began, but when the eighteen-year-old son of a local dairy farmer shot and killed that emaciated whitetail buck, it became apparent that something wasn't right.[2] What exactly that "something" was no one would know until well after the season's end.

The Wisconsin Department of Natural Resources had begun disease sampling of a small percentage of whitetails killed during the hunting season of 1996, initially looking for tuberculosis (TB) in response to the discovery of TB-infected captive elk in Manitowoc County.[3] Michigan had already battled an outbreak of TB in its wild deer herd in the northeastern part of the state. In 1999 testing for chronic wasting disease (CWD)—a disease known to infect only cervids (including mule and white-tailed deer and elk)—was added to the annual disease sampling program when it was discovered that captive elk from CWD-infected herds in western states may have ended up at game farms in Fond du Lac, Dodge, Jefferson, Sheboygan, and Washington counties.[4] In the fall of 2000, a total of 400 deer were sampled in Wisconsin. The results were negative for both TB and CWD.[5]

Those 400 deer were but a drop in the bucket out of a herd estimated at 1.7 million prior to the 2000 hunting season. That year, the state once again was aiming for a record harvest to check herd growth.

"Department of Natural Resources wildlife officials are hoping that many hunters will use permits that allow them to shoot antlerless deer to help control a statewide deer herd that is estimated to be 1.7 million, the highest on record. Two free Zone-T antlerless permits were issued with the purchase of every license, and hunters can purchase additional bonus permits for most of the state's non-Zone T deer management units," reported the press.[6]

It appeared that there would be an ample number of hunters to take all those permits to the field. A total of 694,957 gun season licenses were sold—a number that ranked just below the record of 699,275 set in 1990.[7] "As of noon Friday, the last day to buy a license, statewide sales transactions were averaging 80 per minute," reported the *Rhinelander Daily News*.[8]

Even in the first year of a new century, deer hunting was still one of Wisconsin's biggest events of the year and still rated as a school holiday for many kids across the state. "Wisconsin's deer hunting season is so steeped in tradition that many school districts call off classes so that students won't miss it," reported a northern Wisconsin newspaper. "Twenty-three school districts cancelled classes this week for what they listed as fall vacations, according to the state Department of Public Instruction."[9] The Webster School District in northwestern Wisconsin, typical of many other school districts, had taken Thanksgiving week off for the past nineteen years.

Kids on "fall vacation" and adults alike enjoyed almost perfect opening weekend weather as they helped set an opening weekend record harvest of 200,206 deer—an 8 percent increase from the previous year's season start. "All the elements really came together to produce what I'd call the best opener in years," said Bill Mytton, the big-game ecologist with the DNR.[10]

A heavy harvest of deer in the north contributed to a record nine-day gun season take of 437,737 deer. "Almost 20,000 more deer were killed during the 2000 hunt in the Northern region, a 15.5% increase on last year's total. The Northern Region reported the highest percentage increase in deer killed," reported the press.[11] The total 2000 take—including the October and December antlerless hunts and the muzzleloader hunt—exceeded 528,000 deer. This was an all-time record kill for any state.

✦ ✦ ✦ ✦ ✦

The great success of the 2000 season had indeed helped to achieve a needed reduction in deer numbers. With a herd estimated at more than 1.5 million deer approaching the next season, most deer management units were still over goal, and deer managers wanted to keep the momentum going. The 2001 hunt would be another season of plentiful antlerless permits. With a statewide quota harvest goal set at about 540,000 antlerless deer, the DNR issued 1.2 million antlerless permits in an attempt to reach that goal.[12] Again the antlerless permits came in a mix of free Zone-T permits (one for each type of deer license purchased), Hunter's Choice permits in non-Zone-T units, and bonus permits. Leftover bonus permits could be purchased over the counter.

Sixty-seven DMUs and nine state parks were designated as Zone-T for 2001. For the sixth year in a row, a four-day October gun hunt was held in Zone-T units, resulting in an early season harvest of 44,503 antlerless deer.[13]

The regular gun season was set to open on November 17— nearly a week earlier than the latest date the Wisconsin deer season can begin under the traditional Saturday before Thanksgiving opener. An early opening date can be good and bad. While it increases the likelihood that hunters will catch the end of the rut, it also means it can be touch and go with weather conditions, since temperatures above 40 degrees Fahrenheit at this time of year tend to reduce deer activity.[14]

Opening weekend in 2001 brought news that the benefit of the rut was being enjoyed by hunters across the state. "Reports from around the state this week indicate the deer are still in the midst of their mating season," reported the *Rhinelander Daily News*.[15]

However, weather conditions were decidedly not on the side of the hunter. "Instead of snow and cold that sometimes greets hunters on opening day, the forecast called for high temperatures in the 60's statewide under sunny skies," reported a northern Wisconsin newspaper. "That meant hunters donned blaze orange baseball caps, T-shirts and sweatshirts rather than the parkas and snowsuits they used to bundle up in colder years. It also meant no snow for tracking deer and tougher visibility in the woods, where everything was brown."[16]

The situation didn't improve after opening weekend. "Hunting conditions during most or all of the 9-day season were considered poor to very poor throughout the state," reported the DNR. "The majority of the state experienced no snow cover with temperatures well above normal throughout the week. Fog and above average temperatures on opening weekend may have reduced vision and hunter movements in most of the state."[17]

Each deer season seems to present something to remember aside from the usual ups and downs of the weather and hunting conditions. Despite less-than-optimum deer hunting weather, hunters who looked upward in the prehunt darkness of November 18 were treated to a rare sight: the Leonid meteor shower, the special perk for the 2001 season. I remember stepping outside the Deadfall Camp cabin, about two hours before sunrise, and immediately noticing stars streaking across the sky, one right after another. The press reported later: "Thousands of shooting stars provided a dazzling light show Sunday that amazed veteran and novice stargazers alike as the Leonid meteor show made the moonless sky appear to rain light."[18]

Without having heard anything about the Leonid beforehand, I found it a strange, mystical event. As I settled into my tree stand about half an hour before sunrise, the stars were still catching my eye above the trees.

My deer season typified the early start date season scenario that many hunters across the state experienced. Although I glimpsed a buck full of rut and still checking his scrape line opening day—with no opportunity for a shot—the remainder of the season was spent with the wool clothes and heavy-duty thermals left at the cabin as I worked up a sweat traversing ridges covered with wet leaves instead of snow. While there was absolutely no need to make excuses for an opening weekend harvest of 151,929 deer, comparisons to the record harvest of the year before, when more than 200,000 deer were taken opening weekend, were to be expected.

"The deer kill number is down approximately 24 percent from 2000's record opening weekend harvest . . . but is still near the 10-year opening weekend average of about 155,000," reported the *Rhinelander Daily News*.[19] Though a reduction of Zone-T units and fewer antlerless permits available in 2001 (each gun hunter received one free Zone-T permit, instead of the two they received in 2000) may have caused a lower antlerless deer take, most blamed the numbers on the weather. The article noted another influence on the hunt: "DNR wildlife managers cited a variety of factors for the reduced deer harvest, but the overriding one was the weather: Last year's opening weekend was near perfect hunting weather, while this year hunters were greeted with near balmy weather. With temperatures reaching in to the high 60's and low 70's, some hunters actually reported hearing tree frogs and seeing dragon flies."[20]

While the warm weather may have impacted overall numbers, hunting the rut allowed for "a large percentage of older bucks with very nice racks registered across the state."[21] In the end, with the sheer abundance of deer on the landscape, ample permits for antlerless deer in hand, and weather that, while not perfect for hunting, still allowed hunters to spend more hours in the woods than a cold season normally allows, hunters managed to take 361,264 deer—the fifth highest gun kill on record.[22]

One of those deer was the bag-of-bones buck killed on the Mt. Horeb dairy farm. Tissue samples from the sickly buck along with samples from about eighty other deer in that area were tested as part of the DNR's disease monitoring program. Deer from other areas of the state, including Crivitz, Black River Falls, and

Lab technicians removing samples for CWD testing.
COURTESY OF WISCONSIN DEPARTMENT OF NATURAL RESOURCES, BUREAU OF WILDLIFE MANAGEMENT

Spooner, were slated for sampling in 2001; the Mt. Horeb area was added at the last minute, when a DNR employee living in the area became available to take samples.[23]

The DNR explained the testing program: "Bovine tuberculosis (TB) and chronic wasting disease (CWD) are important emerging diseases in the United States, but have not yet been found in Wisconsin's free ranging white-tailed deer herd. Continued monitoring for these two diseases is important."[24]

Everything changed in February 2002, when the results of the 2001 disease sampling were released. Chronic wasting disease had found Wisconsin.

Since it was initiated in 1999, sampling for CWD in Wisconsin had been focused on counties near game farms that had received elk from western herds where CWD was present. Tests of these tissues, until now, had come back negative. The testing at Mt. Horeb unexpectedly, and perhaps fortuitously, hit a CWD hotspot: three of the deer tested from the area—all bucks—were positive for CWD.

The always-fatal disease that some hunters knew about from trips to the west suddenly landed on the front pages in the spring of 2002—rocking the world of the deer hunter. This was true not only for Wisconsin hunters but for hunters and wildlife biologists nationwide. Initially it sounded like something straight from the script of a bad horror movie: the culprit, they were told, was a not a virus or a bacteria, something more easily understood, but an abnormal protein called a prion. Infectious versions of prions, sometimes referred to as mutant proteins, could be insidious killers, something that could attack and destroy healthy protein.[25] There was no known treatment, no cure. Death was preceded by a cruel, slow destruction of the brain until it was pockmarked like a sponge and could no longer function. Slowly the animal is robbed of the ability to run, to feed, to survive.

To make everything even more frightening, the disease was transmittable, perhaps easily, by deer-to-deer contact, possibly passed on at contaminated communal watering or feeding areas. To top it all off, the deadly prions were virtually indestructible in nature and could persist in the soil, such as that underneath the decayed carcass of an infected deer, for decades.

The discovery of CWD shook the very foundation of deer management in Wisconsin. The implications were profound: as opposed to the western states, which had been coping with CWD in free-ranging herds since the 1980s, the discovery of the disease in Wisconsin's super-high-density whitetail herd could possibly spell disaster for Wisconsin's time-honored deer hunting tradition.

The press was quick with gloom-and-doom prophecies, which included catastrophic economic losses as well as potential health concerns. "Wisconsin's hunting industry could lose as much as $96 million if deer hunters afraid of chronic wasting disease stay home this fall, a University of Wisconsin–Madison researcher said," reported the Associated Press. "Fears over the deadly brain disease could keep 10 to 20 percent of hunters out of the woods, according to a projection by UW Agriculture and Applied Economics Department chairman Richard Bishop."[26]

While Bishop did conclude that lost hunter revenue might be as high as $96 million, he also believed that since most of this spending decline would be from state residents (who represent the vast majority of Wisconsin hunters) the money would not "evaporate," it would simply be spent elsewhere.[27] If out-of-state hunters decided to stay away because of CWD fears, Bishop concluded, a net loss to Wisconsin's economy of $5 million to $10 million might be realized.[28] However, while this loss in hunter revenue might not be significant to the overall Wisconsin economy, it would certainly impact the sporting goods stores and local cafés, taverns, motels, and resorts that look forward to the deer-season boost.

Speculation about the health implications of CWD also ran rampant in the spring and summer of 2002. CWD is one of several diseases in a group of transmissible spongiform encephalopathies, or TSEs, which meant very little to the general public at the time. What did mean something was that other TSE diseases, first cousins to CWD, were BSE (bovine spongiform encephalopathy), better known as mad cow disease, and something called Creutzfeldt-Jakob disease (CJD). BSE infection causes symptoms in cattle that are similar to what CWD causes in deer. CJD does the same for humans.

Most people were familiar with mad cow disease from the graphic news reports covering the outbreaks in England and the subsequent slaughtering of millions of cattle in the mid-1980s. CJD was less well known, but, after the discovery of CWD in Wisconsin, it was widely reported that an increase in the usually very rare illness possibly was linked to human consumption of BSE-infected cattle. The dots were there and many decided to connect them.

While the thought of a disease that might kill large numbers of whitetails was bad enough, the very idea that eating venison could cause the same type of disease in humans was unthinkable. Soon news reports regarding hunters that had contracted CJD possibly by eating venison from infected deer flashed across the state. The most widely reported story was of three men from Wisconsin who had died of CJD-like diseases. They had participated in wild game dinners at the North Woods cabin of one of the men, who had fed more than fifty people at wild game dinners there since the 1970s.[29] Many of them had hunted in western states and had brought game back to Wisconsin.

It was presumed that the three men had all eaten CWD-infected game, probably from western killed animals, and had contracted CJD as a result. Since the occurrence of CJD in humans is extremely rare (normally about one in a million), it seemed logical that the common denominator between the men was CWD. However, the facts didn't support the premature news articles or the rumors that followed. Eventually the Centers for Disease Control and Prevention (CDC) investigated the deaths of the men and determined that only one of the men had actually died from CJD, and there was no evidence to suggest a link between CWD and the deaths of any of the three men.[30]

The CDC, however, did not rule out CWD as a potential threat to human safety and recommended that animals with evidence of CWD be "excluded from the human food or animal feed chains."[31] CDC also advised that hunters follow some precautionary guidelines to prevent possible exposure to the CWD agent. The bottom line was that CWD was a new and potentially dangerous addition to the landscape, but there just wasn't enough known about the disease in 2002 to make any solid connections.

Saddled with the unwanted responsibility of being the first eastern state wildlife department forced to react to the CWD threat, and without any precedent to guide the way, the Wisconsin DNR felt enormous pressure to act quickly.

The first step was to assess how widespread the disease was. The scary reality was that once a deer became infected with CWD it might be months or even years before the disease caused noticeable signs. Flash back to the sickly Mt. Horeb buck. When and where had that animal—clearly in the final stages of infection—contracted the disease? That question and its implications were enough to send chills down the spines of wildlife managers and hunters alike.

To answer the basic question of how widespread CWD was in the Mt. Horeb area, within a week of learning the test results, the DNR initiated a plan to sample more deer in late March and early April 2002 inside a 415-square-mile area around the initial CWD-positive locations. Rather than rely solely on government sharpshooters to sample deer, the DNR wanted landowners to take part. "Landowners are breaking out their rifles and taking to their fields and woods as part of an unprecedented whitetail deer hunt that will allow the state to see how far a fatal brain disease has spread," reported the Associated Press. "Deer infected with the disease, which has no known cure, threaten the rite of autumn in Wisconsin, where deer hunting is as much a part of the state's tradition as cheese and Green Bay Packers football."[32]

Between March 6 and April 9, a total of 516 deer were collected. By the end of April the test results were in: eleven more deer in the Mt. Horeb area were positive, bringing the total to fourteen.[33] In mid-May, a more accurate testing method using lymph node tissue rather than brain stem tissue resulted in an additional four positives from the initial 516-deer sample. The CWD infection tally grew to eighteen.[34]

With the discovery of more CWD-positive deer, the spring hunt confirmed what many expected—the disease was established in the area—and what most had hoped for—the infection rate was low and CWD seemed to be confined to a relatively small area. The knowledge that the disease was probably not yet widespread led to the tantalizing idea that it could be contained or even eradicated, thus avoiding a statewide catastrophe.

With so little known about CWD, the impetus was to act quickly and aggressively—to "cut deep and wide," as one veterinarian put it.[35] The April hunt was followed up with more extensive plans to remove—as well as test—a greater number of deer in a larger area. The initial plan called for two zones. A 287-square-mile eradication zone (EZ), later known as the intensive harvest zone, was established by the DNR based on the sampling results. Plans were developed to kill the estimated 15,000 deer within the zone.[36] Outside of the EZ was a larger CWD management zone that covered all or part of fourteen counties. The goal in this management zone would be to reduce deer numbers by as much as 50 percent.[37]

The original EZ was expanded to 361 square miles on May 22, when the additional lymph node test positives came in and one was located just outside the initial zone. "Our goal there is to eliminate the disease by bringing the white-tailed population just as low as we possibly can, as close to zero as we can get it," stated a DNR spokesperson in the spring of 2002.[38]

The reduction of the deer population in the hot zone began in June with the first of four weeklong summer hunts. About 900 special permits were issued to landowners in the eradication zone.

The eradication effort was garnering national attention. "Landowners and hunters in Wisconsin this week will begin the unprecedented killing of all the white-tailed deer—up to 15,000—in a part of the state where deer are affected by a disease similar to Britain's mad cow disease," reported *USA Today*.[39]

The first weekend of the special June hunt yielded about one hundred deer taken mostly by landowners but also by agency sharpshooters. It was clear that although hunters understood the need to control the disease, it was difficult for them to reconcile their deeply held personal beliefs about the meaning of deer hunting with the necessity to address the disease issue. A local hunter quoted in an Associated Press news report stated: "I love deer hunting, but I don't particularly feel great about doing this."[40]

By the end of the week a total of 262 deer were killed—170 by landowners and 92 by agency personnel—in the first hopeful step to eradicate most, if not all, the deer in the EZ. When test results from the deer taken in the hunt came back, another six CWD positives were tallied, bringing the state total to twenty-four. Since two of the new positives occurred near the edge of the EZ, the zone was expanded to 374 square miles.[41]

The June hunt kicked off a frenzy of activity that continued through the summer and fall of 2002 as the DNR and other government agencies (including the U.S. Department of Agriculture), landowners in the CWD management zones, sportsmen's groups, and individual hunters from across the state grappled with the CWD monster. Other weeklong summer hunts were held, one each in July, August, and September. By the end of October the CWD positive tally was at forty, and the EZ had expanded to 389 square miles.[42]

While the four summer hunts did little to reduce numbers in the EZ, they were important in helping further define the size of the infected area. "Every deer that we can get for sampling is a bonus to us," stated a DNR administrator.[43]

While steps toward CWD control were occurring on the ground, action to support those steps occurred at a rapid pace in the capital. In May 2002, Governor Scott McCallum signed into law Wisconsin Act 108—Management of Chronic Wasting Disease. The act did many things to assist the DNR in fighting CWD, including authorization for spending from existing sources (such as the wildlife damage surcharge on hunting licenses) for CWD testing and expanding the deer season in the management zone. It also gave the DNR authority to establish rules on recreational feeding of deer (the agency already had authority to regulate the use of bait for hunting).

The use of bait for hunting deer—something that had increased in popularity throughout the 1990s but reigned as one of the great deer hunting controversies of the day—was banned by emergency order in July as a CWD control measure. Recreational feeding was also included in the ban. "Any practice that concentrates deer—including baiting and feeding—is likely to increase the spread of CWD," stated the DNR.[44]

Although some hunters were unhappy with the ban, most seemed to understand the need. It was supported by major sportsmen's organizations, including Whitetails Unlimited, a national organization that promotes the preservation of deer hunting tradition.

"CWD is a very serious problem, and all of the health and wildlife experts are in agreement that this will help contain the spread of the disease," said Peter J. Gerl, the group's executive director, in May 2002. "Whatever your ethical stance is concerning baiting and feeding, the health of the entire deer herd is threatened. It's just common sense that you should do whatever is possible to control the spread of the disease from one deer to another."[45]

It was certain that deer season 2002 would be one for the history books. Southern Wisconsin hunters would see an unprecedented liberal hunt in and around CWD zones. Statewide hunters would enter the woods with a baiting ban in place and thoughts, and possibly fears, of CWD in their heads.

Questions were many: Would CWD transform or somehow diminish Wisconsin's great deer hunting tradition? Would fear of the unproven link between CWD and Creutzfeldt-Jakob disease keep hunters home? Perhaps the biggest question was, would CWD rear its ugly head somewhere else in the state, far from Dane and Iowa counties?

"On the eve of the most important deer hunt in Wisconsin history, 88% of state residents surveyed who held deer hunting licenses last year are planning to head back to the woods this year, according to a *Journal Sentinel* poll," wrote *Milwaukee Journal Sentinel* outdoor writers Lee Bergquist and Bob Riepenhoff. "The poll suggests that, despite the presence of chronic wasting disease, the number of hunters this year might not be as low as the sluggish sales of hunting licenses have indicated."[46]

The *Journal Sentinel* poll put into black and white what most already felt: it would take more than CWD to break the back of the Wisconsin deer hunt. The poll found that most would hunt, most would still take the deer home and butcher it or have it processed, and most hunters would still enjoy their venison as they had in past years—even if the nonhunting neighbor might refuse the posthunt gift of venison sausage.

While hunters would be in the woods en masse during the nine-day gun season (although perhaps minus a few thousand comrades), there was certain to be some trepidation. In part to allay those fears but primarily to shed light on the status of CWD infections statewide, the DNR launched an ambitious statewide sampling and testing program. Prior to opening day, the DNR told hunters:

> Statewide Wisconsin will be testing over 40,000 deer for CWD from the fall 2002 hunt. Hunters will be asked to provide tissue samples from their deer for testing. About 500 deer will be tested from every county in the state. Additional deer will

Deer being processed by DNR staff at a CWD registration and sampling station.
COURTESY OF WISCONSIN DEPARTMENT OF NATURAL RESOURCES

Deer brought in for CWD sampling are assigned a tracking number so that test results can be matched with a hunter's venison.
COURTESY OF WISCONSIN DEPARTMENT OF NATURAL RESOURCES

be tested in the area of known infection. Achieving the sampling goal of about 500 deer/county will allow scientists to say with confidence whether the disease is present or not in any county.[47]

At registration stations across the state DNR officials were on hand to ask successful hunters whether they would be willing to let the DNR take the head of their deer for CWD testing. Each deer head and carcass were given corresponding numbers so that, if they wished, hunters could wait for test results before eating any of the venison, a peace-of-mind bonus (even though CWD testing was not a food-safety test). Although it would take several months for all the results to be known, as results came in they were posted on a DNR website for easy access by hunters.

Those not willing to wait for the results from the DNR tests, or those unable to have their deer sampled by the state (the DNR stopped taking heads once the county goal for sampling was met), could purchase their own CWD test kit for about fifty dollars. The promoters of the commercial kits promised a five-week turnaround time. The kits included everything needed to submit a lymph node sample to the testing facility along with detailed instructions for hunters on how to remove the needed tissue sample from their deer. Kits were available at some sporting goods stores, including the Gander Mountain chain.[48]

It was important for hunters to be in the woods. Heavy harvests of the past few years were having an impact, slowly nudging deer numbers closer to management goals. However, the winter of 2001–02 had been another mild one. With the deer herd estimated at 1.3 million animals, many management units were still well over goal. The possibility that reduced hunter effort would allow deer numbers to shoot upward was a concern of the Wisconsin Farm Bureau Federation.

"Wisconsin farmers are worried hunters won't kill enough deer to stem a growing herd capable of destroying their crops," reported the Associated Press.[49]

Farm Bureau President Dan Poulson pushed for stronger action on CWD, saying that the state needed to be vigilant in controlling the disease. "The concern is widespread," he said.[50]

The hunters who did intend to pursue their favorite pastime—CWD be damned—would be taking advantage of great opportunity. "Prospects for the nine-day hunt, which opens November 23, have rarely been more optimistic," reported the *Wausau Daily Herald*.[51]

With the exception of the CWD zones in the south, the rest of the state would experience what had become a modern deer season pattern: a combination of Zone-T units (forty-five of them), the seventh year for the early October gun hunt, and an ample supply (1.1 million) of antlerless permits (including the one free permit for each gun and bow deer license and bonus tags to be purchased at will).[52] Following up the regular nine-day gun season would be another December antlerless-only season south of Highway 8.

According to an Associated Press story in the *Capital Times*, "The DNR had submitted its plan for a statewide deer hunt in December to the Assembly Natural Resource Committee, but members opposed the idea because they thought it would conflict with other winter recreational activities."[53] State Representative DuWayne Johnsrud, then chairman of the Assembly Natural Resources Committee, said, "We had skiers opposed. We had snowmobilers opposed."[54]

When registration data began to roll in after opening weekend it quickly became apparent that the kill was much lower than in previous years. In Langlade County, the opening weekend buck kill was down 35 percent while the antlerless harvest was down 20 percent.[55] Similar results were repeated across the state.

As is tradition after any lackluster Wisconsin deer season, explanations were numerous and varied: the late opening date, which guaranteed little if any buck rutting activity; poor hunting weather with a lack of snow; the baiting ban; fewer antlerless permits issued. The role CWD played in the reduced harvest was unclear. Certainly fears of the perceived health implications of CWD, or simple discomfort with the idea of the disease being "out there," had a negative impact on the deer take. In the end, license sales were down by about 10 percent, so there were definitely fewer hunters in the woods. In addition, hunters may have been more conservative in their use of antlerless permits, perhaps not wanting more than one deer to take home. The specter of CWD in southern Wisconsin may also have led some hunters north into unfamiliar, and less productive, hunting territory.

The most pronounced difference between the nine-day gun seasons of 2002 and 2001 was in the buck harvest: 121,959 to 140,632, respectively. The

2002 antlerless harvest showed a decline of less than 2,000 deer from the year before. Another 8,000 deer were harvested during the December Zone-T season (south of Highway 8 only), for a total 2002 gun deer take of 317,888 deer—the tenth highest harvest on record.[56]

All of the time and effort and a cost of about $1 million to take deer heads from the 2002 season for CWD testing began to pay dividends as early as mid-December as test results started coming in. By December 22, no positives had been found in the 5,045 deer tested from outside the CWD zones.[57] Through the winter and into the spring of 2003, results poured in. By February 8, 16,119 tests results were in; by early May, all of the test results were known. Hunters across the state could breathe a collective sigh of relief: with more than 41,000 deer tested, 207 cases were positive and all were within the CWD management zone.[58] It seemed that CWD had not found its way out of the original infection area.

The DNR's testing of hundreds of deer from every county in the state—the largest single CWD monitoring effort of all time—was an enormously important action. As test results began to be reported and it became clear to hunters that CWD really was contained in a relatively small geographic area, almost overnight the CWD issue transformed from being *the most important* deer management concern in the minds of Wisconsin hunters to almost an afterthought in the minds of those outside of the counties where the disease had been found.

However, in the minds of deer managers, CWD hadn't gone away; it was still an enormously complex problem that warranted continued research, monitoring, and intensive management. Of concern to biologists was the knowledge that radio-collared deer occasionally dispersed more than a hundred miles in a single year. A further concern was the nearly 1,000 deer and elk farms scattered across Wisconsin; the health condition of the animals was an unknown.[59]

The difference of perception between hunters and state deer managers quickly manifested itself in a hot controversy over deer baiting. The emergency baiting and feeding ban that had been enacted in 2002 had been extended to April 30, 2003, by the Legislative Joint Committee for Review of Administrative Rules (JCRAR). The DNR, supported by the Natural Resources Board (NRB) and scientists from across North America, felt that a permanent ban on baiting and feeding was a very necessary component of CWD management and should follow the emergency ban. "The available science, field research and the professional opinions of dozens of nationally recognized animal health experts all support banning baiting and feeding as a means to limit spread of CWD," said Tom Hauge, director of the DNR's Bureau of Wildlife.[60]

Deer hunters on the other side of the baiting issue, as well as those who benefited from the sale of deer bait, closed ranks and began to work through their legislators. One player in the battle was a feed store owner from Iron River in northern Douglas County. Patti Rantala and her husband, Ron, had come to depend on the dollars brought into their operation through the sale of feed to bait and feed deer (the farming community formerly served by the feed mill had largely disappeared). In an interview with the *Ashland Daily Press*, Rantala claimed they had lost "well over $26,000 on our bottom line" due to the 2002 baiting ban.[61] Not content to simply voice her opinion, Rantala mobilized others and formed a group, Wisconsin Baiting and Feeding, to fight the permanent ban. A second group, VOW (Voices of Wisconsin), was led by Casey Edwards, a Mason deer farmer. VOW hired a lobbyist, Barbara Linton (a former Assembly representative) to work the Legislature.[62]

Other North Woods feed mill owners echoed Rantala's viewpoint on the baiting and feeding issue. "It's killed the North Woods," an owner of a Rib Lake feed mill told the *Milwaukee Journal Sentinel*.[63]

Through early 2003, the controversy really began to heat up. Organized anti–baiting ban groups held several public meetings in the north. As legislators began to hear from more and more constituents opposed to the ban, the NRB and JCRAR squared off.

In March JCRAR voted unanimously to direct the DNR to halt its restrictions against baiting and feeding, but extended the emergency ban to April 10; on April 9, they extended it again, to April 30. On April 23, the NRB again proposed that the emergency ban become permanent. In May, after the emergency ban finally expired, the Assembly and Senate held a joint committee hearing to address the issue and ended up proposing a compromise solution to the NRB that would allow regulated baiting and feeding outside the CWD zones. Again the NRB stood firm with its proposal to keep a statewide ban.[64] Through several more months of wrangling, the final outcome was another emergency rule, this one allowing regulated baiting and feeding, but prohibiting any sort of baiting and feeding within the CWD zones.[65]

In short, for most of the state, baiting was back in for the 2003 deer hunt, after an absence of only one year. The baiting ban controversy highlighted the incredible complexities of managing an overpopulated deer herd in the age of CWD. While the results of the intensive CWD testing had been welcome news by the state's deer hunters, it also opened the door for disagreement on how CWD should be managed. Approaching the gun season of 2003, fears and anxiety about CWD had been replaced with the older debate on baiting—but with a CWD tint.

Regardless of a hunter's stance on the baiting debate, it was clear that there would be none of the CWD hysteria seen the year before. Scott Helberger of the *Wausau Daily Herald* wrote: "A year ago at this time we were up to our back tags in chronic wasting disease anxiety. What a difference a year makes. The anxiety is dialed way down."[66]

With baiting back in place and CWD anxiety reduced, the compelling issue for the 2003 deer season was once again high deer numbers. "With the kill from last year's gun season down 10% and little snow so far across much of the state, there is growing concern that Wisconsin's already large deer population could grow out of control," wrote Lee Berquist of the *Milwaukee Journal Sentinel*.[67]

There was no doubt that the multitudes of Wisconsin deer hunters were willing to step up once again and were looking forward to the 2003 season with renewed vitality. The now "traditional" season structure—with an early Zone-T antlerless hunt from October 30 through November 2 in the forty-seven deer management units designated as Zone-T, the regular nine-day season with a million antlerless permits available, and the late Zone-T season in December south of Highway 8—would allow hunters ample opportunity to trim the herd.

Something that the state hoped might add a little urgency to the need to harvest antlerless deer was the prospect of numerous Earn-a-Buck (EAB) units for the 2004 season if chronically over-goal units couldn't be brought to within 20 percent of goal: at least thirty deer management units could potentially be designated EAB units the next year if the 2003 harvest didn't measure up. EAB was in place in CWD zones but had not been used widely in other areas of the state.

Big harvests for the regular nine-day season can be promoted by the issuance of huge numbers of antlerless permits. But the single most important factor is usually one that is the most uncontrollable: the weather. As hunters across the state poked their heads outside in the predawn hours of November 22, opening day, most found high winds and sleet, rain, or a mixture of both.

"Wisconsin deer hunters had to cope with a lack of snow and intermittent rain in north central Wisconsin as the state's gun deer season opened at daylight Saturday," wrote Jim Lee of the *Wausau Daily Herald*.[68] To the south, Dane County experienced nearly two inches of rain Saturday night and into Sunday. Weather conditions improved during the week.

Hunter numbers had begun to bounce back substantially from the twenty-year low experienced the year before. "Lessening concerns about the implications of Chronic Wasting Disease and the ability to once again bait deer in 2003 is being credited with returning the area deer harvest to near normal levels," reported the *Ashland Daily Press*.[69]

Statewide, the harvest from the nine-day season did return to "near normal" and beyond in some areas. Overall, about 46,000 more deer were taken during the regular 2003 season than in the CWD-depressed 2002 season. About 16,000 more bucks were registered and a healthy 30,000 more antlerless deer. The combined total of all 2003 gun seasons was 388,791, making it the fifth highest gun deer harvest on record. Archers added another 73,000 deer to the take.

The return to a "near normal" harvest in 2003, however, wasn't enough to prevent a big jump in herd growth in 2004. An extremely mild 2003–04 winter led to excellent deer health coming into spring and a high population of new fawns. The prehunt deer population was estimated at 1.7 million deer, which mean that, once again, many deer management units would be well over goal going into the fall. A continued concern of deer managers was that, in addition to the trend of mild winters, the continued provision of high-quality feed to deer through baiting and feeding would make it difficult to reach management goals.[70]

In the early 1960s, when deer managers first began setting goals, the DNR had an over-winter (post–hunting season) statewide goal of 441,900 deer.[71] This was in the days when severe winters regularly devastated northern and central deer herds, and hunter numbers nearly equaled deer numbers. Between 1962 and 1984, the over-winter deer population estimate averaged only about 1 percent over the statewide goal.[72] As deer range expanded and whitetail populations grew through the years, hunter numbers kept pace. The state gradually increased the over-winter goal to more than 700,000 deer,[73] with the vast majority of the goal increases occurring in the farmland deer range. For many years, hunter effort—helped along by Mother Nature—kept an expanding herd in check. In the 1980s, the scene began to change.

In the ten years from 1985 through 1994, the over-winter estimate average had crept up to 16 percent above goal.[74] In the next ten years the over-winter average grew to 43 percent above goal. The Wisconsin deer herd—promoted by mild winters, an ever-increasing food supply, and a leveling off of hunter numbers— became an unwieldy, difficult-to-manage multitude.

"A whitetail deer herd that state wildlife experts say has grown 21 percent from a year ago sets the stage for hunters to kill a record number of deer in the tradition-steeped season opening Saturday," wrote Associated Press reporter Robert Imrie in 2004. "But the burgeoning herd—estimated at 1.7 million deer—also prompted a new hunting rule in some parts of the state that requires [a hunter] to shoot an antlerless deer—a doe or yearling buck [*sic*, fawn]—to earn the chance to shoot the more coveted big, adult buck with large antlers."[75]

Sounding like some sort of grocery store shopping incentive program Earn-a-Buck was here. Although used successfully in CWD zones and a limited number of east-central units in 1996, the reality of EAB was something new to most Wisconsin hunters. Twenty-six over-goal deer management units that had not been brought closer to goal as Zone-T units in 2003 were designated as EAB units in 2004. Forty-eight units remained Zone-T.

Since my hunting camp is located at the north end of the most northerly deer management unit in the state (with the exception of DMU 79 covering the Apostle Islands) and also has one of the lowest over-winter goals (twelve deer per square mile), I had become accustomed to Zone-T and the free antlerless-deer tag. (With such a low over-winter goal, it didn't take much for DMU 3 to be over goal.) I also was accustomed to seeing few deer during the season. It seemed that, due to a relatively low deer density coupled with traditionally low hunter pressure, deer could spread out pretty well along the oak ridges and steep ravines of the county forest where we hunted.

Our deer management unit was one of the twenty-six designated EAB units for the 2004 deer season. It took some careful scrutinizing of the deer hunting regulations and a DMU map showing a mosaic of gray-shaded and cross-hatched units (Zone-T, EAB, CWD, and regular units) for my hunting partner, Steve, and I to decipher exactly which procedures we needed to follow in our first EAB season. Only twenty-nine of the state's 135 DMUs would have what might be called the "traditional" season framework.[76]

Emotions regarding EAB generally replaced any latent CWD worries as hunters affected by EAB voiced their opinions. "There certainly are a lot of hunters who are expressing concern and disappointment with Earn-a-Buck," the DNR's big-game specialist told *Milwaukee Journal Sentinel* outdoor writer Bob Riepenhoff. "But there is also a very strong participation in the Earn-a-Buck program. Hunters are earning their bucks."[77]

The big question discussed at every deer camp in an EAB unit was, what would a hunter do if presented with the opportunity to bag the buck of a lifetime before obtaining the authorization to take the buck through the registration of an antlerless deer? The vast majority of hunters knew the right answer to that one, but the speculation was intriguing.

Kevin O'Brien of the *Ashland Daily Press* wrote: "For many Wisconsin hunters, the opening weekend of the 2004 deer season will be remembered as the time they let that big buck get away . . . on purpose."[78]

Opening weekend, stories at the registration stations in EAB units included a good share of missed-buck tales. "Josh Michels of Madison and his friend said they watched three bucks go by Saturday, including one that stopped and lingered within shooting range," reported the *Ashland Daily Press*.[79]

As fate would have it, I had my own EAB story to tell as well when a small fork horn trotted past my blind a few minutes into the opener. Not more than a half hour after that a small doe entered a clearing across the ravine I was hunting and paused long enough for me to make a solid shot. I had earned my buck and actually felt pretty good about getting my blue EAB sticker at the registration station in Washburn. I headed back to the woods that afternoon with high expectations. Now that I had "earned" my buck, I expected to get him.

I didn't see another deer the rest of the season.

In 2004, hunter numbers, still rebounding from the low of 2002, were similar to 2003 figures: about 640,000 licensed hunters. The total 2004 gun kill (early Zone-T, nine-day, muzzleloader, and late Zone-T) came in at 413,794, about 40,000 deer higher than in 2003 and the third highest on record—a direct result of the increase in antlerless deer killed in EAB units.

Despite the complexities or the dislike of EAB, it served its stated purpose of increasing the antlerless deer kill. Only one previous hunting season had seen a higher antlerless take: the record gun season of 2000, with 356,741 antlerless deer killed. The flip side to the story was a reduction in the take of bucks: down about 14,000 from the year before, but still pretty close to the previous ten years' average. EAB had the effect of doubling the antlerless kill (compared to buck-plus-quota) while reducing the antlered kill by about 40 percent.[80]

"Deer registrations were up in many areas of the state after opening weekend fueling anticipation that a banner year might be in progress," wrote Jim Lee for the *Wausau Daily Herald*. "However, preliminary tallies following the conclusion of the nine-day hunt indicates buck registrations are down from a year ago in many counties, leaving nods of understanding in some circles and shakes of perplexion in others."[81]

At the conclusion of the 2004 hunt there would be plenty of controversy to keep deer management issues in the forefront until the next season. Earn-a-Buck, however well intentioned or needed, collided head-on with some deeply held beliefs regarding Wisconsin deer hunting. Even though numerous Wisconsin hunters travel to western states to hunt, where the ability to hunt a buck or a bull is often based on successfully drawing a permit, the Wisconsin tradition of the hunt had always been first and foremost a buck hunt. The taking of antlerless deer—while accepted as necessary and routine by the vast majority of hunters—still had some stigma attached to it for a significant number of hunters.

One EAB unit hunter quoted by the *Ashland Daily Press* said: "I got my fawn, and I'm ashamed of myself."[82]

To varying degrees, many Wisconsin hunters shared a low opinion of EAB after the 2004 season. A rising tide of sentiment against the antlerless-only October Zone-T hunt was occurring as well. Many of these hunters communicated their dissatisfaction and frustration to their local Conservation Congress delegates.

At a January 2005 meeting, the Conservation Congress Executive Council passed two resolutions calling for major deer season framework changes, including the elimination of both EAB and the October Zone-T hunt.[83]

"We will take other routes to change the seasons if we have to," Congress Chairman Steve Oestreicher told the *Milwaukee Journal Sentinel*. "We do the best job we can to represent outdoorsmen on these issues, and we heard loud and clear the past two years that . . . deer hunters are not happy."[84]

The Executive Council also decided to add a question to the Conservation Congress's Spring Hearing (held annually in April in every county in the state) questionnaire to determine whether hunters would support the proposed changes (a regular nine-day hunt without an October Zone-T hunt but with a statewide December Zone-T season).[85]

Voters supported the proposed changes by a margin of about two to one.[86] It was clear that a segment of Wisconsin deer hunters wanted change.

"In March, faced with widespread hunter dissatisfaction and opposition from the Conservation Congress, the Natural Resources Board voted unanimously to reject a DNR recommendation that eight deer management units have the Earn-a-Buck requirement this fall," reported Bob Riepenhoff of the *Milwaukee Journal Sentinel*.[87] There would be no EAB (outside of CWD control zones, that is) for the 2005 deer season.

When the NRB met in Spooner on August 17, members listened to a multi-faceted rules package proposal presented by DNR—a compromise hammered out between DNR, the Congress, and several hunting interest groups back in June, which included a two-year "trial" moratorium on an October Zone-T hunt (effective in 2006 and 2007). Other components of the package were a two-day youth hunt in September, unrestricted antlerless tags in herd control units, and the replacement of Hunter's Choice with the sale of bonus tags (available in regular DMUs based on antlerless quotas).[88]

While the compromise package put the October Zone-T hunt on hold, the DNR's caveat was that the take of antlerless deer for the nine-day season must increase during the two-year trial period to prevent a return to the October season. The NRB unanimously passed the rules package at their December meeting in Madison.

The 2005 gun seasons, which were in place before any new proposals could affect them, were similar to 2004. The framework included an October Zone-T antlerless hunt in forty-five DMUs south of Highway 8 and a December Zone-T season in Herd Reduction Zones statewide, as well as the traditional nine-day hunt. The total harvest from these three seasons plus the muzzleloader season totaled 387,310 deer.[89] Unlike 2004, however, there were no EAB units outside of CWD zones.

The new year brought CWD to the forefront again when results of a study published in the *Journal of Science* indicated that the prions associated with CWD infection could be found in the muscle tissue of deer.[90] (Previously it had been thought that CWD prions were only found in brain and central nervous system tissue.[91]) This finding resulted in cautions from DNR and health officials for hunters to not eat venison from deer taken in CWD zones until a negative test result had been returned.

The new year also brought some wrangling between the NRB and the Legislature over the new deer hunting season framework approved by the NRB in December. "In response to a first legislative request, the board modified the rule package

Mike Edwards and his twelve-year-old son pose with Austin's first buck, a very nice eight-pointer taken in November 2005 in Douglas County.

<small>COURTESY OF MIKE AND MICHELLE EDWARDS</small>

at a special January 31 meeting, moving a two-day youth hunt and limiting the December antlerless hunt to . . . north of Highway 8," reported a news wire in February.[92]

The NRB refused to meet a second legislative request to move the December hunt to the week following the regular nine-day season, overlapping muzzleloader season.[93] At the crux of the issue was opposition from snowmobile interest groups, who felt a December season would delay the opening of trails and negatively impact winter tourism.[94] This impasse threatened to stall the implementation of the rules package until 2007.

"Despite opposition from state deer hunting organizations, this fall's deer hunting rules will be the same as last year and will include a four-day antlerless-only Zone-T hunt in October," reported Bob Riepenhoff.[95]

The standoff between the NRB and the Legislature wasn't resolved until May, when the Legislature's Joint Committee for Review of Administrative Rules rejected the call for an earlier December hunt and instead asked the NRB to limit the proposed hunt changes to a one-year trial.[96] The NRB agreed, paving the way for implementation of components of the original rules package, including a statewide December antlerless hunt the second Thursday after Thanksgiving for the 2006 season.[97]

While the October Zone-T hunt was suspended for 2006, EAB was back in twenty-one DMUs after the 2005 hiatus. However, there was some added flexibility this time: the DNR began designating some DMUs as EAB "watch units." A hunter shooting an antlerless deer in a watch unit could prequalify for buck authorization if that unit became EAB the next year.[98] More than 80,000 hunters were able to prequalify in 2005, which allowed them to take a buck in 2006 without having to take an antlerless deer first.[99]

With above-average temperatures across most of the state for the opener, hunters harvested 342,411 deer during the regular nine-day season, which included an antlerless take of 213,894 deer.[100] The total harvest for all gun seasons (youth hunt, regular nine-day, and December herd reduction) totaled 393,306 deer.[101]

About every five to eight years, the traditional nine-day deer season framework gives deer hunters a little bonus: opening day falls on November 17, allowing some increased chance that hunters, particularly those in the north, will be able to take advantage of the rut, or at least the end of it.

A November 17 opener was just one of the reasons hunters could be very optimistic about the 2007 gun season. A mild 2006–07 winter, with a Winter Severity Index of 32 (anything below 50 is considered mild), meant little winter mortality and does coming out of winter in good shape, ready to produce fawns.[102] An estimated 1.6 million to 1.8 million deer awaited hunters.[103] Again, there would be no October antlerless herd control hunt, but there would be a second year of a statewide December antlerless hunt, December 6–9.

All hunters were issued one free antlerless permit with the purchase of a license (archery and gun), valid in any herd reduction, EAB, or CWD zone. In regular units, hunters could purchase antlerless permits over the counter on a first-come, first-served basis, rather than having to apply under the more cumbersome Hunter's Choice system that existed prior to the new rules.

One move not welcomed by many deer hunters was the expansion of DMUs designated as EAB. "The state Natural Resources Board voted Wednesday to expand the contentious earn-a-buck program for this fall's deer hunt," reported the *Wisconsin State Journal* in March.[104] The number of EAB units was raised from twenty-one to thirty-five outside CWD zones, and all CWD zones were designated EAB.[105]

Weather for the nineday opener varied across the state, from damp and dreary conditions in the south to seasonally cold in the north

COURTESY OF WISCONSIN DEPARTMENT OF NATURAL RESOURCES, BUREAU OF WILDLIFE MANAGEMENT

2007 Unit Recommendations

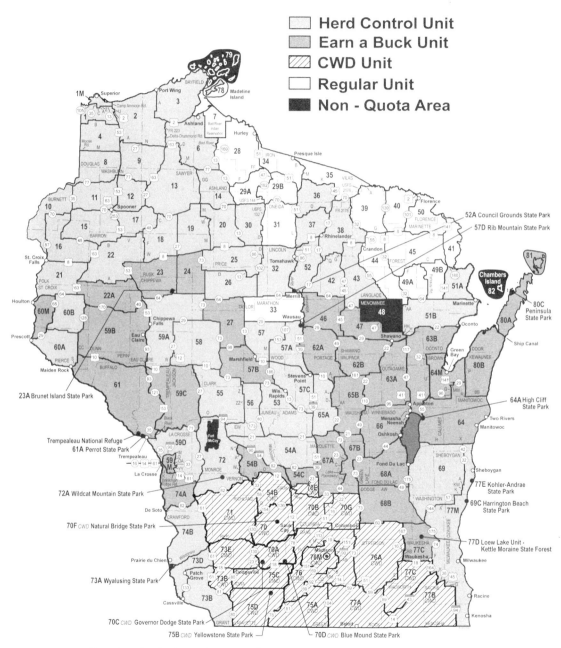

Deer hunting in the early twenty-first century means deciphering the deer management unit mosaic.

Courtesy of Wisconsin Department of Natural Resources, Bureau of Wildlife Management

with some snow cover. "In what were mixed but generally good hunting conditions across the state, hunters registered a preliminary tally of 171,584 deer over the first two days of the 2007 gun deer hunting season. This compares to an opening weekend preliminary count of 167,573 in 2006," reported the press.[106]

While opening weekend has traditionally been the busiest two days for deer harvest during the nine-day season, it seemed even more so in 2007—a trend that Chief Warden Randy Stark noted in the DNR law enforcement bureau's annual deer hunting report to the DNR secretary: "The methods used by hunters continue to change in Wisconsin. Many wardens attribute these changing methods to the changing age and structure of the hunting community. While there was good participation in the hunt on opening day, it is becoming more and more evident that the amount of sustained effort put forth throughout the season by hunters appears to be decreasing annually."[107]

Stark also noted that, as of 2007, more hunters seem to be opting for comfort, using "comfortable tower blinds, with an increasing number with four walls, roof, windows, radio, TV, and heater."[108] Wardens have also begun seeing fewer organized deer drives, according to Stark, as the size of hunting groups decreases and rural residential development increases.[109]

However, by the end of the nine-day season, hunters had taken an impressive 354,384 deer. The total for all 2007 gun seasons was 402,563 deer, which included 4,609 deer taken by youths, ages twelve to fifteen, during the increasingly popular youth hunt held October 6–7.[110] The 2007 gun season harvest was the third highest on record.

Wisconsin deer management and hunting issues never seem to take a break during the winter: in January 2008, CWD management was in the news again. "The DNR, smarting from criticism of its CWD policies, formed a citizen advisory group that is expected to make recommendations in January on new ways to control the spread of the disease," reported Ron Seely in the *Wisconsin State Journal*.[111]

Known as the CWD Stakeholder Advisory Group, the group met on seven Saturdays from July through January with the task of developing recommendations to improve CWD management in the state.[112] "State wildlife officials should sim-

The diversity of the deer camp tradition, 2007. This crew makes its annual camp near Richland Center.
COURTESY OF THE DANIELS FAMILY

plify their chronic wasting disease policies, consolidate disease zones into a new zone and dump earn-a-buck in the new zone for one season, a citizens group tasked with rethinking Wisconsin's struggles against CWD recommended in a report released Wednesday," wrote Associated Press reporter Todd Richmond in February.[113]

However, with several minority opinions and one panel member even calling the work of the group a "failure," the recommendations were far from a mandate from the public.[114]

To further assess public opinion regarding CWD management the NRB held public hearings in March. In April, it approved a new CWD management plan for the state. The *Capital Times* reported: "The plan for the 2008 hunt reflected input from citizens during eight public hearings around the state that were called to try to generate cooperation in CWD management efforts. Previous attempts to stop the spread of the contagious disease by killing as many deer as possible in the core disease area in south-central Wisconsin have been unpopular with hunters and many residents."[115]

The primary components of the new plan included (1) combining the core Disease Eradication Zone and the surrounding Herd Reduction Zone into one CWD management zone with the same season and consistent regulations, and (2) raising population goals from five deer per square mile in the core area and ten per square mile in the reduction zone to goals of 20 percent below the population goals that were in place in deer management units in 2001—the year before CWD was discovered.[116]

Time will tell if the new plan will adequately balance the desires of the public with the need to keep CWD in check.

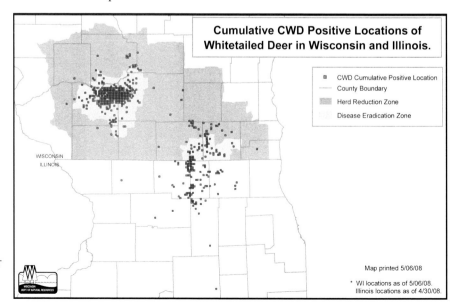

More than six years after the discovery of CWD in the Wisconsin deer herd, positive tests are still concentrated in a relatively small area.

COURTESY OF THE WISCONSIN DEPARTMENT OF NATURAL RESOURCES AND THE ILLINOIS DEPARTMENT OF NATURAL RESOURCES

Wisconsin whitetail deer hunting is a phenomenon that defies explanation or analysis. It has survived through days of wanton butchery and disregard for the law. It has survived through closed counties and seasons and the "deer wars." It has served as a rock of tradition while the country experienced world wars, social upheaval, natural disasters, and the horrors of terrorism. It has provided countless hours of enjoyment, excitement, and satisfaction for large numbers of hunters through the years.

The first decade of the new century has already presented an array of trials and tribulations for both deer manager and hunter alike. However, it is safe to say that Wisconsin deer hunting and all of its glorious tradition will survive—without doubt amid heated discussion and controversy—well into the future for new generations to enjoy.

The Upshot

Then came the gadgeteer, otherwise known as the sporting goods dealer. He has draped the American outdoorsman with an infinity of contraptions, all offered as aids to self-reliance, hardihood, woodcraft, or marksmanship, but too often functioning as substitutes for them. Gadgets fill the pockets, they dangle from the neck and belt. The overflow fills the auto trunk, and also the trailer.
—Aldo Leopold, "Wildlife in American Culture"[1]

Spring had been late in coming to the North Woods. After some pleasantly warm early April days that sent the snow banks trickling down the roads and seeping into the ground, the weather pattern had settled into a repetition of cold and gray, sometimes with rain, sometimes with snow flurries depending on which side of freezing the temperature ended up.

It was a surprise then to see the doe and her newborn fawn about the third week of May. It seemed much too early for fawns, as I was still stuck in a late winter–early spring frame of mind. Fawns signified the end of spring and the beginning of summer to me, the season of exploding vegetation growth, the chorus of frogs at night, raccoon tracks in the sand. Spring had become grossly behind schedule, the trees that had thought about leafing out a month earlier were now at a standstill. The fawn had just crossed the blacktopped road on which I was traveling toward home. Startled by the approach of the vehicle, the doe had headed down a grassy logging road, with the fawn obediently bounding with amazing speed behind her. The little deer was no bigger than a medium-sized dog, with impossibly thin legs and a coat spattered with white.

It was an early fawn that by hunting season in November would be a good six months old and would have transformed from the delicate baby into a youngster weighing perhaps sixty pounds, possessing all the innate abilities of the species, the keen ears, sharp eyesight, and uncanny ability to catch a scent. What the fawn would lack, however, would be its mother's experience. As each year passes and the fawn survives to yearling and then to adulthood, that experience would be added to the mix.

The old logging road and the woods around it were now part of a subdivision, just a few miles from town and consisting of large lots, all more than five acres. The chunk of land that became the subdivision had not too many years before been a favorite of local hunters with its oak ridges, aspen stands, and wetlands. As new houses are constructed, the deer in the area will not suffer. They will flourish as hunting pressure declines and the natural browse they seek is supplemented by the seed from backyard bird feeders, exotic plants from the flower garden or shrubbery, and the corn set out for the specific purpose of attracting them so they may be seen from the living room window.

One effect of human encroachment on deer habitat
COURTESY OF LINDA GRANT

About two weeks later I saw another doe and her fawn while I was driving. The fawn was about the same size as the one I had seen earlier and was nursing from the doe, a sight I had seen only once before. The doe was standing, patiently allowing the fawn to suckle beneath her. I had little time to enjoy the sight, as I was driving along at sixty-five miles per hour on I-39 near the Central Wisconsin Airport just south of Mosinee. Doe and fawn were exhibiting one of nature's most intimate moments for all to see on the grassy median of the Interstate—cars, trucks, SUVs roaring past north and south. The deer had probably been caught between the fences that ran along both sides of the highway, and when the time came for the fawn to feed, necessity became more important than location.

The amazing thing to me was that the doe seemed, as far as I could tell, perfectly fine with the situation despite the obvious dangers.

Odocoileus virginianus, the animal that fed and clothed the Paleo-Indian and occupied the wintertime dreams of Ojibwe and Potawatomi hunters, the animal that played a vital role in the colonial battles for dominance of the northeastern United States, fed the early Wisconsin pioneers, fueled a tremendous market-hunting trade that nearly caused deer in the Badger State to become merely a memory, and, in more recent years, had become the respected quarry of the sportsman and the scourge of the farmer and the backyard gardener, has had an extraordinarily intimate relationship with people.

The deer-human relationship has changed as humankind has changed. Today the diverse Wisconsin landscape supports well in excess of a million deer. That's an incredible number when you consider that by 1900 there may have been as few as 350,000 deer left in the entire United States.[2] The boy Aldo Leopold would not like to own if his "hair does not lift his hat when he sees his first deer" is the norm today as deer are seen practically everywhere on a regular basis, from the inner suburbs of Milwaukee to the soccer fields and parks of nearly every small town in the state, and, yes, even nursing fawns on the median strip of an Interstate.

Deer are so common today that they are simply ignored by many people, until one whacks into the front end of a vehicle, as happens thousands of times annually on Wisconsin roads, with the mangled and blood-smeared carcasses of whitetails left on the gravel shoulders or grassy ditches bearing testimony to the carnage. (In 2007 the Wisconsin Department of Natural Resources reported that more than 35,000 road-killed deer were either picked up by contractors or salvaged for use by the public.[3]) In fall, a road-killed buck will soon have its antlers sawed off by some passing motorist who leaves behind the desecrated carcass of the once magnificent animal to decay.

I remember my first experience with a car-killed deer. While in college at Stevens Point in the early 1980s an excited dorm mate came running into my room to announce that someone had killed a deer with a car near the campus nature preserve and "they didn't even want to keep it!" We rushed to where the deer had been hit only to find out that the city police had taken it away. If we had been able to get the deer somehow I'm not sure what we would have done with it, but the feeling was the deer would have been a prize—a deer killed out of season and available for the taking.

Today deer-car collisions are so common and deer so plentiful that few people even bother to salvage the deer freshly killed by their automobile.

Deer-vehicle accidents have increased along with the growth of Wisconsin's deer population.
WHi Image ID 41284

Insurance agents can expect several calls every week regarding deer damage to a vehicle. In 1979 deer-related accidents accounted for 4.7 percent of all reported vehicle accidents in Wisconsin. From 1996 to 2006 deer-vehicle accidents averaged 15.4 percent of all reported accidents.[4]

Thoughts of this wholesale waste of deer killed by collisions with vehicles bring to mind something I read in the newspaper regarding another, but more sinister, waste of our deer resource. The story described the arrests of several juveniles and a young adult on charges of "thrill killing" whitetails. This group would travel the back roads of a rural county shooting at and injuring or killing whatever wildlife they could find, primarily deer, for the fun of it.

As I did a little research on thrill killing I discovered that it wasn't an isolated event, but is a behavior that is actually on the rise. According to a *Milwaukee Journal Sentinel* article, a DNR warden surveyed fellow wardens across the state and found that there had been more than twenty thrill killing incidents investigated.[5] The vast majority of the cases involved participants in their teens or early twenties. In most instances, the perpetrators were eventually arrested.

In one of the worst cases two teens and a twenty-year-old had shot more than one hundred times at deer seen while spotlighting on a remote country road. One of the three had told a DNR warden that "it became kind of fun and we were surprised we [ever] got caught."[6]

Many people have speculated on the motivation behind thrill killing: boredom, too many violent video games, or even too many unrealistic hunting shows that focus exclusively on the kill, not the hunt. I have absolutely no answers for the many questions a detestable act such as thrill killing deer poses in regard to our relationship to deer.

Aldo Leopold had strong words for those hunters back in his day, the 1930s and 1940s, who shot at any deer until they killed a legal buck, leaving does and fawns to rot in the woods. "Such deer-hunting is not only without social value," he wrote, "but constitutes actual training for ethical depravity elsewhere."[7]

With Wisconsin history firmly implanted in my brain, I think of the thrill killers and then of the Ojibwe hunter of three hundred years ago, so careful not to offend the spirit of the deer, aware of how important deer were to the very survival of his wife, his children. And I think of the early Wisconsin settler, whose children wore pants and shirts made from the buckskin of deer killed by their father and whose supper was by necessity frequently venison. I think about how misguided these kids today must be, not to believe or understand that a living white-tailed deer is anything more than a target. The survival toolbox filled through thousands of years of pursuit and escape could not help a deer shot to death at night by a bored teenager in a car with a spotlight and a gun.

The thrill killing incidents contrast sharply with the ethics and parameters of the modern deer hunt and engender disgust in the minds of sportsmen. Unfortunately, a sizeable portion of the nonhunting public doesn't understand how incredibly wide that contrast is. Hunters in general often get accused of hunting for the sheer enjoyment of killing an animal by those who use hunters as the symbol for everything that is wrong with the world. They throw hunters into a world view that includes wild animals that are benign, friendly, and cute—a world view shaped by constant doses of movies and television shows depicting wild animals as people in animal bodies. A world view that is sanitized, digitized, and nearly devoid of meaningful contact with the realities of nature. A view that does not leave room for the idea of people killing wild animals as part of a regulated, ethical activity. A view that cannot understand that your typical, law-abiding Wisconsin sportsman would be the first to condemn thrill killing.

My thoughts turn to my own hunting experiences. The countless hours I have spent perched on a tree stand, bow or rifle across my knees, through every kind of weather, with a hope that I would at least see a deer, never daring to jinx myself with the thought of actually killing a deer, or the double-whammy curse of hoping to kill a great big buck deer. I remember passing an entire afternoon until sunset during one bow season planted motionless on the stand while a howling late-autumn storm swirled around me, the tree bending back and forth with the wind gusts, hard ice pellets hitting my face.

What got me there, up in that tree on that dark afternoon, was a report from a friend in the area that he had seen a nice buck saunter down the trail the day before. What kept me there, in the wind and cold, was not simply the desire to kill the deer; there was much more to it than that. There was something in my brain that told the other something in my brain (the something that longed to get out of the tree, into the warm truck, and as quickly as possible back home and into a warm bed) that we all needed to stay just a little bit longer, that the buck could be near. That something that made me stay, despite the weather, despite the ache in my legs and numbed fingers, is the reason we hunt. It's been that something that has me sitting in a tree stand or ground blind two hours before daybreak on opening morning and staying put until sunset. It is that something that all of us who hunt the Wisconsin whitetail have somewhere deep inside that will never let the sight of a whitetail become commonplace or boring.

The North Woods subdivision where I live, where I saw the doe and small fawn early in the spring, supports many deer. Nearly every day I pass several on my drive home, on the grassy slopes between the woods and the blacktop. As the car approaches, the adults raise their heads and watch, unconcerned until the vehicle gets to within thirty yards or so, and by this time the smaller deer are watching, too. As a certain distance is closed, the adults leap into the woods, tails up, followed by the younger deer. They don't go far, just what they perceive as a safe distance into cover. There they stop, turning their heads to watch the car pass by.

Toward the end of one summer, an adult doe with two fawns and a yearling doe spent a lot of time in our front yard, usually feeding on the lawn during the day and, under the cover of darkness, tasting the perennials, shrubs, and hosta plants that my wife tends close to the house. One late afternoon while watching television, I saw movement out of the corner of my eye, deer ears moving along the edge of our elevated front deck. The red-coated doe soon moved into plain view, intent on reaching a little garden patch of shrubs and flowers. She was moving cautiously, occasionally stopping to raise her nostrils to test the air, ears twitching. Suddenly the television show I was watching cut to a loud commercial. The doe heard it and froze in her tracks, head up, senses all in high gear, assessing. With no movement to catch her eye and no new scent on the breeze she resumed her stalk toward the garden.

The same animal that quickly adapted to feeding on the early Wisconsin pioneer's crops has adapted very well to living in the very heart of human society. Its ancient survival mechanisms are working as well as ever, used today to assess the dangers of a loud commercial rather than the sound of an approaching saber-toothed cat. As man has plowed, cut, dozed, paved, and otherwise altered the natural landscape to meet his needs, the whitetail has met the challenge.

In Wisconsin, I don't believe there is a better example of how quickly and completely we're altering the landscape than in Dane County. Many times a year work duties bring me to Sun Prairie, once a small farming community distinctly separated from urban Madison, but now merging with rapidly expanding Capital City growth.

As late as a decade ago, there was a clear demarcation where Sun Prairie, the small village, stopped and the cornfields began. But then the boom began. The early 1990s saw interest rates drop and development skyrocket. As each year passed, I witnessed immense new housing developments and office parks rise from the cornfields. Farm fields and oak woodlots soon were nothing but rooftop and blacktop. Streetlights brighten the night. A few of the vestiges of old remained, a single dairy farm or farm house, some wetlands, and here and there an old sentinel tree that had once provided shade for a farmer working his fields. These landmarks won't last long. The chopping and changing continues.

According to the American Farmland Trust, southern Wisconsin is the third most threatened area in the entire United States for the loss of prime farmland.[8] Statewide, Wisconsin has lost a third of its farmland to sprawl—more than eight million acres—since 1950. Southeastern Wisconsin loses ten square miles of farmland each year.[9]

For better or for worse, however, sprawl development is a boon to the ever-adaptable whitetail. Haphazard and hopscotch development, where a subdivision plops down next to a working farm and suddenly acres of lawn, palatable shrubs, and people more than willing to provide handouts are added to the old habitat mix of fields and woodlots, allowing deer numbers to flourish. Hopscotch sprawl is perfect for deer because of the great amount of edge habitat it creates, mixing cover with increased foraging opportunities.[10]

Perhaps to address the phenomenon of deer populations at the interface of urban sprawl, it seems that, of late, every major hunting magazine runs an article prior to deer hunting season espousing the great bowhunting opportunities found in urban or suburban environments. The stories usually go something like this: A guy, maybe the author, was able to bag the trophy buck that had been living in a patch of thicket in a city park and using a railroad right-of-way to travel the neighborhoods at night. Set up in an old oak tree in someone's backyard, within sight of some brushy cover as well as a kid's plastic play gym, he arrows the buck as it crosses between areas of cover. The kill is always clean; the buck always drops within a few yards.

I'm all for increased hunting opportunity, but urban deer hunting presented as sport hunting is another modern twist to the eons-old relationship between people and whitetails that makes me a little uneasy. Aside from the complexities of city regulations, tracking wounded animals across backyards (or worse yet, highways), and a huge concentration of antihunter sentiment, suburban or urban hunting can be disturbing to me.

Gordon MacQuarrie, I believe, would have agreed. In his partridge hunting story, "A Brace Apiece," he wrote about how Mr. President (a character based on his father-in-law) was incensed that someone was "shooting up coveys that have hung around the place all summer" after he discovered someone had been hunting birds living close to MacQuarrie's cabin on Middle Eau Claire Lake.

MacQuarrie wrote: "Next to a pot-shooter who busts 'em on the ground, he despises the kind who hunt the lake-cabin precincts, picking up birds that have learned a fatal friendliness for man. When you hunt partridge with Mister President, you get back there in the bush where the wild, wise brethren scuff in the leaves and success is measured by the soundness of your legs."[11]

MacQuarrie was communicating in a not-so-subtle way that it is the hunter's responsibility to determine the parameters of the hunt, that hunters need to be involved in maintaining the integrity of the hunting experience. There would be little to gain from shooting down the grouse that feels at home in the front yard. Aldo Leopold was more direct: "Voluntary adherence to an ethical code elevates the self-respect of the sportsman, but it should not be forgotten that voluntary disregard of the code degenerates and depraves him."[12]

Maybe there is nothing ethically wrong with killing a buck in someone's backyard at the edge of suburbia. But, in my mind, the promoters of "hunt the suburbs" are in a way giving in to the idea that urban sprawl combined with an adaptable species like the whitetail is somehow good—a boon for outdoorsmen.

We have more deer today than at any other time in recent history. Mild winters, urban-suburban sprawl, and more people than ever willing to provide additional food through recreational feeding or the baiting of deer for hunting, along with other factors, have all contributed to herd growth that allows harvest records to be broken year after year but that also may be diminishing our respect and admiration for the whitetail—perhaps even generating contempt and loathing for the animal by some.

Cities and towns across the state are grappling with dangerously high urban deer numbers. Often a solution is a well-planned and regulated control hunt conducted by trained marksmen—something clinical, in a way, and very different from the traditional hunting experience, but necessary.

Whitetails in the backyard clipping off tulips at night, grazing on the edge of the soccer field, becoming the target of control hunts; whitetails getting whacked by the thousands across our highways and left as food for crows, turkey vultures, bears, and coyotes; whitetails nibbling away well over a million dollars' worth of crops each year[13] as well as forest resources such as northern white cedar (deer browsing of saplings has hugely affected cedar regeneration[14])—all of these are signs of an extremely high deer population in our state. And, as has been the case throughout the history of scientific deer management, these new developments, new conflicts and problems call for new ways of thinking and creative strategies. In the past, we've seen this take the form of antlerless seasons, party permits, and Hunter's Choice. More recently, we've experienced herd reduction hunts, bonus antlerless permits, and Earn-a-Buck.

Despite how these changes in deer management might affect the hunt, in my mind there will always be two archetypal Wisconsin deer hunting scenarios. There is the farmland hunt: the family affair, with a lunch break back at the house or shack to warm up and discuss the morning's adventures and plan the afternoon drive. The deer are the corn-fed, fast-growing deer of the farm country of central and southern Wisconsin—deer bounding across open fields surrounded by hardwoods, the patchwork habitat with plenty of edge that deer do so well in.

One indicator of an overpopulation of hungry deer is evident in these trees in southwestern Wisconsin. The browse line ends where the deer are unable to reach.

Photo by William Ishmael, Wisconsin Department of Natural Resources

And there is the North Woods hunt: the deer camp in the pines, the crack of the .30-30, the frigid cold and occasional deep snow. Acres of public land with few hunters—and fewer deer—but the chance to maybe bag a buck of a lifetime, a deer that has survived for five, six, or seven years. The legendary swamp buck.

I believe there is a great purpose to deer hunting.

While we must, we are told, adapt and accept the constant barrage of changes thrown at us by an ever-changing world of technological hype, the very core of deer hunting's value to us as individuals and to society lies in the conscious effort to not change.

Although deer hunting is exciting and full of surprises, every hunt a different tale to tell, it is the sameness, the lack of change and hype, that is most important. The woodlots, farm fields, oak ridges, or big timber hunted by your grandfather in his youth may or may not be the same ones you hunt today, but they look and feel the same, for the alder swamp hunted last year looks and smells just like an alder swamp from a hundred years ago, the same as 1,000 years ago. The deer Grandpa pursued are the same incredible species we pursue today. The venison tenderloin cut from a freshly killed deer, cooked to perfection in a cast-iron skillet and shared with hunting camp members of old smells and tastes just as good as the meal of venison prepared in a modern-day kitchen and enjoyed with family and friends around the dinner table.

Time-honored deer hunt and deer camp traditions seek to carry on this sameness as well. If only for a few days out of each year, the hunt is a respite from the modern world. We know what to expect when we deer hunt: life becomes simpler, decisions easier to make, sense of self and purpose in the world become clear.

Deer Camp Traditions

WHEN EMIL FALK AND SEVEN OTHER COLUMBIA COUNTY farmers—all of whom knew one another from working together on the "threshing ring" that rolled to each of their farms every year to do the hot, back-breaking work of threshing oats— decided almost on a whim to do something a little different in November of 1938, they had no idea that their plan would set in motion a tradition that would endure more than sixty-five years.

The simple decision those farmers made was to get together some warm clothes, boxes of provisions, a canvas tent, and an assortment of rifles and drive by automobile and truck on the mud or gravel or oil-topped roads to find the famous Wisconsin North Woods. Somewhere along the way they bought licenses to hunt deer, and when they finally reached the big woods and settled on a location from which to hunt, another Wisconsin deer hunting camp was born.

Hard work and deprivation was all a part of life back on the farm, and no one thought twice about the rustic conditions of their first

Deer Camp Traditions (continued)

The first camp, 1938. Emil Falk is third from left.

1940

1964

1958

1987

1963

1990

1992

Deer Camp Traditions (continued)

1992

2002

Brittney Falk, Emil's great-granddaughter, with her first deer, 2007
ALL PHOTOS OF CROOKED HORN CAMP COURTESY OF LEWIE FALK

camp. A community bed, on which all eight men slept, was constructed by placing tree limbs and evergreen boughs on the cold ground. The small canvas tent was hung above the bed and secured. In this fashion, the men had a soft place to unroll their assorted blankets and quilts.

The farmers had come to this unfamiliar country, so different from the prairie and savannas of Columbia County, with hopes of shooting deer. Deer were scarce back home—nonexistent in much of the county—and even if one of the farmers actually glimpsed a fat buck loping across a field, there was no legal opportunity to shoot it. Columbia County had no open season on deer in 1938.[1]

The necessity to head north, and away from home and family, in the early years of Wisconsin

Deer Camp Traditions (continued)

sport deer hunting directly led to the evolution of the traditional Wisconsin deer camp. The term *North Woods* eventually became inseparable from the term *deer camp*.

Emil Falk and the other farmers loved what they had discovered: the freedom of the northern woods, the thrill of the hunt, and the unique camaraderie of the camp. It was like nothing else they had known. They returned annually to the area they had claimed for their deer camp, all the time sleeping on their evergreen bough beds on the ground, for ten-plus years. In 1949, their deer camp became somewhat more established— and more comfortable—when the men, a few more years of threshing behind them, decided to forsake the tent and hunt from a cabin at a nearby resort.

Lewie Falk, a retired Wisconsin DNR employee from Poynette, remembers the first year at the resort well. It was his first hunt, his first trip to deer camp with his father, Emil. "I thought it was just great," recalled Falk. "I was thirteen years old and had heard Dad and his friends talk about deer camp. It was a thrill to be able to go."[2]

The love of deer hunting and the northern Wisconsin deer camp was passed from father to son. "We liked the freedom of the big country in the north," Falk remembered. "Sometimes we would hunt the last weekend of the season back home, but it wasn't the same. You always had to worry about boundaries and private property."

When his father passed away in 1957, Falk felt a sort of responsibility to keep the deer camp tradition alive. In the 1950s he began keeping records of each hunt, each deer taken by members of the camp.

When the Vilas County resort that had been the camp's home base for nearly thirty years was sold to new owners in 1978, the hunting group decided the deer camp should have a permanent location. One member bought some nearby land, and all the members contributed their many talents to build a hunting cabin. The new camp was quickly christened Crooked Horn thanks to the unusual rack taken by a bow that season by one member.

That same year, the Falk deer camp tradition was passed to another generation when Falk's son Jim began to hunt. His youngest son, Jeff, started hunting in 1980.

"The deer camp experience helps the younger generation grow up," Falk said. "They learn from the older hunters. They find out how important it is to follow the rules and help with the work."

First-time hunters at Crooked Horn receive both a new compass and a serious lecture on safety. "We always stress safety," said Falk. "After a year or two the younger fellas start to watch out for each other and point things out that aren't right."

The deer season of 2007 marked nearly seventy years of Falk's deer camp. A fourth generation, under the watchful eyes of older hunters, now participates in the annual tradition. "We have two grandchildren, Brittany and Cody, who will hunt at camp this year," said

Deer Camp Traditions (continued)

Falk. "Cody was eleven years old last season and walked with his dad. I asked Cody this summer if he was ready to go back to deer camp. He said he's been ready since the day he left camp last year."

In today's age of instant communication and high-tech entertainment it is a constant battle to keep the old ways. But the members, young and old, of Crooked Horn are doing their share to keep the Wisconsin deer camp tradition alive.

NOTES

1. Otis S. Bersing, *A Century of Wisconsin Deer* (Madison: Game Management Division, Wisconsin Conservation Department, 1956), 74.
2. Lewie Falk, interview by the author, October 2000.

Is having a lot of deer—more deer, it seems, than we know what to do with—something that should be welcomed by deer hunters? Is the heavy use of baiting to take deer—a phenomenon that may be exacerbating the population issue but also might be keeping more people in the woods, thereby allowing more deer to be killed—something that needs to be regulated or not worried about? Will chronic wasting disease ever go away, ever spread through other regions of the state? While we strive for tradition and sameness in our deer hunt, the "outside" world—the world of politics and lobbyists and, yes, of change—cannot be ignored. The deer hunt of the twenty-first century, for all of its similarities to deer hunting in the previous century, has indeed changed from the days of Grandpa's youth.

When pondering just how much the hunt has changed through the years, here's something to consider: with all the press about record deer numbers and record deer harvests, the one record that hasn't been broken for sixty years is the peak number of deer in northern Wisconsin. According to Keith McCaffery, retired Wisconsin DNR northern forest whitetail researcher, the record was set in 1943—the year of the infamous split season, right in the middle of the good old "original" deer wars—and hasn't been broken yet. This means we're probably doing something very right here in Wisconsin in the way we manage our deer herd. It also means the hackneyed old adage "the more things change, the more they stay the same" may apply more aptly to Wisconsin deer hunting than anything else.

I realized this truth one late winter evening when I attended a public meeting in the gymnasium of a local junior high. The bleachers were half filled with people, mostly men, mostly men in flannel shirts and jeans. They had come to listen to a diverse panel of speakers: some legislators, some members of conservation groups, and a preponderance of DNR employees. The purpose of this panel was to allow the people in the bleachers to ask questions and vent their anger and frustration at the panel members (primarily the panel members from the DNR) regarding wildlife issues dear to their hearts. The role of the legislators, as far as I could tell, was to agree with the crowd and rally their support for the next election.

As I sat quietly at the back in the highest row of bleachers, I gazed across the gym. On one wall hung an American flag, just above a large map of the world. The basketball hoops were raised to the ceiling. Down on the court were seven long tables placed end to end. Legislators clustered at one end; DNR people, including the DNR secretary, clustered at the other. A moderator, a local radio personality, sat in the middle.

Twenty minutes were allowed for questions and answers for each of three major issues: the deer season framework, a proposed license fee increase, and wolf management. The time was put on the scoreboard clocks and began ticking down.

Comments regarding the deer season framework and deer hunting license increases came fast and furious:

"Earn-a-Buck creates frustration. There was more criticism of deer hunting last year than I have heard in all my years of hunting."

"I don't see deer anymore. I got an e-mail from the DNR that said wolves don't have a negative impact on deer."

"Next thing I'm expecting is a buck stamp and a doe stamp."

"Someone with three sons will give up hunting if fees fee increases go through—can't afford the licenses, and will have to take up some other activity."

"Deer is like religion in this state, and we need to make sure we keep them the majestic animal that God intended them to be."

For well over an hour, the questions, complaints, and comments were aimed at those on the floor. The managers tried their best to explain, to sympathize, to stand their ground.

This occurred in 2004. It could have been 1978 or 1943 or 1930 or any other year Wisconsin has had a formal deer season. No other issue in Wisconsin has been so hotly discussed, argued, debated, and complained about for as many years as has been deer management and the deer hunting season. Wars, poverty, highway spending, terrible storms—they've all had their place on the front pages. But nothing captivates the interest, and the wrath, of Wisconsin citizen sportsmen as much as deer hunting.

In a 1956 Wisconsin Conservation Department publication, *The White-Tailed Deer in Wisconsin*, Burton Dahlberg and Ralph Guettinger wrote:

We can be fairly certain that as each necessary change [in deer management] evolves there will be a lament from sportsmen, "Hunting aint what it used to be," followed by a tale of the "Good Old Days." The "Good Old Days" may indeed be old or they may be days of more recent vintage, depending upon the individual, the vicissitudes of memory, and the character of the experiences encountered.[15]

The Wisconsin deer hunt is like no other thing on earth: a curious mix of ancient and modern technologies, of old and new ideas, young and old people, wet wool socks and space-age thermal underwear, tradition and television, heated "cabin stands" and hand-built balsam fir blinds, pain and suffering, frustration and great satisfaction, deer that eat rose bushes and deer that eat aspen and birch twigs and deer that eat corn, the believers and the nonbelievers, venison brats and cheese and beer and dem Packers, long hours and lucky shots, disappointment and elation, buck fever and frozen toes.

Maybe the adage could use an update for the twenty-first century: The more the world changes, the more the Wisconsin deer hunt stays the same.

William Damm marks nearly forty-five years of hunting—and another successful outing in Columbia County—in 2006.
PHOTO BY MARK MARTIN

The tradition continues: The first
buck for Jenny Engstrom (2004)
and first hunt for Wes Braker (2006).
Both young hunters were mentored
by their moms.
Courtesy of Jenny Engstrom (top),
Courtesy of Nancy Braker (right)

Appendix Gun Season Data, 1900–2007

Year	Start Date	Season Length	Legal Take for Regular Season	License/ Tag Sales	Total Estimated Kill	Comments/ Regulations
1900	Nov. 1	20 days	Any two deer	32,086	3,500[1,2]	
1901	Nov. 11	20 days	Any two deer	41,000	4,000[1,2]	
1902	Nov. 11	20 days	Any two deer	72,635	4,000[1,2]	
1903	Nov. 11	20 days	Any two deer	78,164	4,250[1,2]	
1904	Nov. 11	20 days	Any two deer	81,000	4,500[1,2]	
1905	Nov. 11	20 days	Any two deer	73,474	4,250[1,2]	
1906	Nov. 11	20 days	Any two deer	82,000	4,500[1,2]	
1907	Nov. 11	20 days	Any two deer	90,000	4,750[1,2]	
1908	Nov. 11	20 days	Any two deer	100,000	5,000[1,2]	
1909	Nov. 11	20 days	Any one deer	103,000	5,550[1,2]	First one-deer season
1910	Nov. 11	20 days	Any one deer	113,000	5,750[1,2]	
1911	Nov. 11	20 days	Any one deer	125,000	9,750[1,2]	
1912	Nov. 11	20 days	Any one deer	123,000	8,500[1,2]	
1913	Nov. 11	20 days	Any one deer	147,000	9,700[1,2]	
1914	Nov. 11	20 days	Any one deer	155,000	9,850[1,2]	
1915	Nov. 11	20 days	One buck	149,000	5,000[1,2]	First one-buck law
1916	Nov. 11	20 days	One buck	139,000	7,000[1,2]	
1917	Nov. 21	10 days	Any one deer	53,593	18,000[1]	Tags required for first time. Cost: 10 cents
1918	Nov. 21	10 days	Any one deer, no fawns	50,260	17,000[1]	
1919	Nov. 21	10 days	Any one deer	70,504	25,152[1]	
1920	Nov. 21	10 days	One buck, horns not less than 3"	69,479	20,025[1]	First use of metal tags
1921	Nov. 13	10 days	One buck, not less than one year old	63,848	14,845[1]	
1922	Nov. 13	10 days	One buck, not less than one year old	59,436	9,255[1]	
1923	Nov. 13	10 days	One buck, not less than one year old	51,140	9,000[1]	
1924	Nov. 13	10 days	One buck, not less than one year old	50,212	7,000[1]	
1925	No open season[1]					First closed season
1926	Dec. 1	10 days	One buck, not less than one year old	47,330	12,000[1]	
1927	No open season[1]					
1928	Dec. 1	10 days	One buck, not less than one year old	69,049	17,000[1]	
1929	No open season[1]					
1930	Dec. 1	10 days	One buck, not less than one year old	77,284	23,001[1]	
1931	No open season[1]					
1932	Nov. 21	10 days	One buck, not less than one year old	70,245	36,009[1]	Greatest number of closed counties (50)

Year	Start Date	Season Length	Legal Take for Regular Season	License/ Tag Sales	Total Estimated Kill	Comments/ Regulations
1933	No open season[1]					
1934	Nov. 24	7 days	One buck, not less than one year old	83,938	21,251[1]	
1935	No open season[1]					
1936	Nov. 21	7 days	One buck, fork or larger	97,735	29,676[1]	At least 1" fork required
1937	Nov. 26	3 days	One buck, fork or larger	90,906	14,835[1]	Shortest Wisconsin deer season
1938	Nov. 19	7 days	One buck, fork or larger	103,721	32,855[1]	
1939	Nov. 25	7 days	One buck, fork or larger	109,630	25,730[1]	
1940	Nov. 23	8 days	One buck, fork or larger	105,198	33,138[1]	
1941	Nov. 22	9 days	One buck, fork or larger	124,305	40,403[1]	
1942	Nov. 21	9 days	One buck, fork or larger	120,605	45,188[1]	
1943	Nov. 18 Nov. 25	4 days 4 days	One buck, fork or larger Doe or fawn	157,824	66,252[1] 62,044[1]	Infamous split season
1944	Nov. 25	6 days	One buck, fork or larger	127,643	28,537[1]	
1945	Nov. 24	5 days	One buck, fork or larger	133,548	37,527[1]	Red clothing required for first time
1946	Nov. 23	9 days	One buck, fork or larger	201,061	55,276[1]	
1947	Nov. 22	9 days	One buck, fork or larger	222,935	53,520[1]	
1948	Nov. 20	9 days	One buck, fork or larger	248,609	41,954[1]	
1949	Nov. 19	5 days	Antlerless or buck with fork less than 2"	286,299	159,112[1]	First antlerless-only hunt
1950	Nov. 18	7 days	Any one deer	312,570	167,911[1]	First any-deer season since 1919
1951	Nov. 17	7 days	Any one deer	296,795	129,475[1]	Orange added as safety color option
1952	Nov. 22	7 days	One buck, fork or larger	238,287	27,504[1]	
1953	Nov. 28	7 days	One buck, fork or larger	234,032	19,823[1]	Mandatory registration begins
1954	Nov. 20	7 days	One buck, fork or larger	247,310	24,698[1]	
1955	Nov. 19	9 days	One buck, fork or larger	267,612	30,000[1]	
1956	Nov. 17	9 days	One legal buck	284,645	35,561[1]	Spike bucks first allowed as legal bucks
1957	Nov. 16	9 days	One legal buck, party deer	288,903	67,870[1]	First party permit year
1958	Nov. 15	16 days	One legal buck, party deer	335,866	95,234[1]	Longest season since 1916; extended one week in north
1959	Nov. 14	16 days	One legal buck, party deer	349,443	105,596[1]	Season opened one week earlier in north
1960	Nov. 19	9 days	One legal buck, party deer	338,208	61,005[1]	
1961	Nov. 18	9 days	One legal buck	307,863	38,722[1]	
1962	Nov. 17	9 days	One legal buck	331,035	45,835[1]	
1963	Nov. 23	9 days	One legal buck, party deer	360,552	65,020[1]	
1964	Nov. 21	9 days	One legal buck, party deer	386,519	93,445[1]	
1965	Nov. 20	9 days	One legal buck, party deer	405,023	98,745[1]	
1966	Nov. 19	9 days	One legal buck, party deer	432,111	110,062[3]	

Year	Start Date	Season Length	Legal Take for Regular Season	License/ Tag Sales	Total Estimated Kill	Comments/ Regulations
1967	Nov. 18	9 days	One legal buck, party deer	470,782	128,527[3]	
1968	Nov. 23	9 days	One legal buck, party deer	503,190	119,986[3]	
1969	Nov. 23	9 days	One legal buck, party deer	506,526	98,008[3]	
1970	Nov. 21	9 days	One legal buck, party deer	501,799	72,844[3]	
1971	Nov. 20	9 days	One legal buck, party deer	509,447	70,835[3]	
1972	Nov. 18	9 days	One legal buck, party deer	517,724	74,827[3]	
1973	Nov. 17	9 days	One legal buck, party deer	514,626	82,105[3]	
1974	Nov. 23	9 days	One legal buck, party deer	556,815	100,405[3]	
1975	Nov. 22	9 days	One legal buck, party deer	582,113	117,378[3]	
1976	Nov. 20	9 days	One legal buck, party deer	589,590	122,509[3]	
1977	Nov. 19	9 days	One legal buck, party deer	617,823	131,910[3]	
1978	Nov. 17	9 days	One legal buck, party deer	644,594	150,845[3]	
1979	Nov. 17	9 days	One legal buck, party deer	617,109	125,570[3]	
1980	Nov. 22	9 days	One legal buck, plus Hunter's Choice	618,333	139,624	First year of Hunter's Choice
1981	Nov. 21	9 days	One legal buck, plus Hunter's Choice	629,034	166,673[3]	
1982	Nov. 20	9 days	One legal buck, plus Hunter's Choice	637,320	182,715[3]	
1983	Nov. 19	9 days	One legal buck, plus Hunter's Choice	649,972	197,600[3]	
1984	Nov. 17	9 days	One legal buck, plus Hunter's Choice	657,969	255,726[3]	
1985	Nov. 23	9 days	One legal buck, plus Hunter's Choice	670,329	274,302[3]	
1986	Nov. 22	9 days	One legal buck, plus Hunter's Choice	662,771	259,240[3]	
1987	Nov. 21	9 days	One legal buck, plus Hunter's Choice	660,400	250,530[3]	
1988	Nov. 19	9 days	One legal buck, plus Hunter's Choice	653,790	263,424[3]	
1989	Nov. 18	9 days	One legal buck, plus Hunter's Choice	661,713	310,192[3]	
1990	Nov. 17	16 days	One legal buck, plus Hunter's Choice/bonus	699,275	350,040[3]	Regular 9-day season, plus 9-day antlerless-only extension
1991	Nov. 23	16 days	One legal buck, plus Hunter's Choice/bonus	674,422	352,520[3]	Regular 9-day season, plus 9-day antlerless-only extension
1992	Nov. 21	9 days	One legal buck, plus Hunter's Choice/bonus	666,570	288,820[3]	
1993	Nov. 20	9 days	One legal buck, plus Hunter's Choice/bonus	652,491	217,584[3]	
1994	Nov. 19	9 days	One legal buck, plus Hunter's Choice/bonus	670,778	307,629[3]	

Year	Start Date	Season Length	Legal Take for Regular Season	License/ Tag Sales	Total Estimated Kill	Comments/ Regulations
1995	Nov. 18	9 days	One legal buck, plus Hunter's Choice/bonus	684,944	398,002[3]	
1996	Nov. 23	9 days	One legal buck, plus Hunter's Choice/bonus	677,072	388,791[3]	First October herd control hunt
1997	Nov. 22	9 days	One legal buck, plus Hunter's Choice/bonus	671,706	292,513[3]	October herd control hunt
1998	Nov. 21	9 days	One legal buck, plus Hunter's Choice/bonus	668,958	332,254[3]	October herd control hunt
1999	Nov. 20	9 days	One legal buck, plus Hunter's Choice/bonus	690,194	402,204[3]	October herd control hunt
2000	Nov. 18	9 days	One legal buck, plus Hunter's Choice/bonus	694,712	528,494[3]	October and first December herd control hunts
2001	Nov. 17	9 days	One legal buck, plus Hunter's Choice/bonus	688,540	361,264[3]	October and December herd control hunts
2002	Nov. 23	9 days	One legal buck, plus Hunter's Choice/bonus	618,945	317,888[3]	October and December herd control hunts
2003	Nov. 22	9 days	One legal buck, plus Hunter's Choice/bonus	645,369	388,344[3]	October and December herd control hunts
2004	Nov. 20	9 days	One legal buck, plus Hunter's Choice/bonus	654,812	413,794[3]	October and December herd control hunts
2005	Nov. 19	9 days	One legal buck, plus Hunter's Choice/bonus	643,673	387,310[3]	October and December herd control hunts
2006	Nov. 19	9 days	One legal buck, plus Hunter's Choice/bonus	645,609	393,306[3]	October youth hunt and December herd control hunt
2007	Nov. 17	9 days	One legal buck, plus Hunter's Choice/bonus	643,172	402,563[3]	October youth hunt and December herd control hunt

[1] Otis S. Bersing, *A Century of Wisconsin Deer* (Madison: Wisconsin Conservation Department, Game Management Division, 1956).

[2] Burton L. Dahlberg and Ralph C. Guettinger, *The White-Tailed Deer in Wisconsin*. Technical Bulletin No. 14 (Madison: Wisconsin Conservation Department, Game Management Division, 1956), 208–209.

[3] "2007 Wisconsin Big Game Hunting Summary," Wisconsin Department of Natural Resources, April 2008, 62.

Notes

Preface

1. Aldo Leopold, *A Sand County Almanac: With Other Essays on Conservation from Round River* (New York: Oxford University Press, 1966), 210.

Chapter 1

1. Ernest Thompson Seton, *The Nature Library: Animals* (Garden City, NY: Doubleday and Company, 1926), 18.
2. Ian M. Lange, *Ice Age Mammals of North America: A Guide to the Big, the Hairy, and the Bizarre* (Missoula, MT: Mountain Press Publishing Company, 2002), 44.
3. Ibid., 21.
4. Donald R. Prothero and Robert M. Schoch, *Horns, Tusks, and Flippers* (Baltimore, MD: Johns Hopkins University Press, 2002), 80.
5. Rollin H. Baker, "Origin, Classification and Distribution" in *White-Tailed Deer: Ecology and Management*, ed. Lowell K. Halls (Harrisburg, PA: Stackpole Books, 1984), 5.
6. Ibid.
7. Ibid.
8. Ibid.
9. C. W. Severinghaus and E. L. Cheatum, "Life and Times of the White-Tailed Deer," in *The Deer of North America*, ed. Walter P. Taylor (Mechanicsburg, PA: Stackpole Books, 1956), 58.
10. Lange, *Ice Age Mammals of North America*, 109.
11. Prothero and Schoch, *Horns, Tusks, and Flippers*, 176.
12. Valerius Geist, *Deer of the World: Their Evolution, Behavior, and Ecology* (Mechanicsburg, PA: Stackpole Books, 1998), 255.
13. Ibid., 281.
14. Geist, *Deer of the World*, 282.
15. Peggy R. Sauer, "Physical Characteristics," in *White-Tailed Deer: Ecology and Management*, ed. Lowell K. Halls (Harrisburg, PA: Stackpole Books, 1984), 78.
16. Geist, *Deer of the World*, 283.
17. Ibid., 284.
18. Ibid., 285.
19. Sauer, "Physical Characteristics," 78.
20. Leonard Lee Rue III, *The Deer of North America: An Illustrated Guide to Their Lives, Their World, Their Relationships with Man* (New York: Crown Publisher, 1978), 162.
21. Ibid.
22. L. David Mech, "Predators and Predation," in *White-Tailed Deer: Ecology and Management*, ed. Lowell K. Halls (Harrisburg, PA: Stackpole Books, 1984), 198.
23. Larry Marchington and David H. Hirth, "Behavior," in *White-Tailed Deer: Ecology and Management*, ed. Lowell K. Halls (Harrisburg, PA: Stackpole Books, 1984), 142.
24. Richard Nelson, *Heart and Blood; Living with Deer in America* (New York: Vintage Books, 1997), 14.

Chapter 2

1. Jon Manchip White, *Everyday Life of the North American Indian* (New York: Holmes and Meir Publishers, 1979), 54.
2. Most sources agree that the Paleo-Indian people who found Wisconsin about 11,000 to 12,000 years ago were descendants of the people who immigrated from Asia (Siberia) across the Bering Sea land bridge during the last Ice Age at least 14,000 years ago. However, it is currently debated whether these people were truly the first humans to enter North America. There may have been an earlier wave of immigration,

perhaps 20,000 to 30,000 years earlier than previously believed, based on recent archaeological discoveries and linguistics analysis (Thomas C. Pleger, PhD, "The First People in Wisconsin," UW–Fox Valley, Anthropology, 2000, www .uwfox.uwc.edu/academics/depts/tpleger/ paleoindian.html; "The Midwestern U.S. 16,000 Years Ago," www.museum.state.il.us/ exhibits/; Museum Link Illinois, "Native Americans, Paleo-Indian," www .museum.state.il.us/muslink; Adam Boyle, "Retrace the Trek of First Americans," MSNBC Technology and Science, February 16, 1998, www.msnbc.com/news).

3. Clovis points, which characterize the Paleo-Indian, have been found in nearly every state south of Canada, suggesting rapid colonization of the Clovis people in North America (Robert Boszhardt, "Common Projectile Points of the Upper Mississippi River Valley," Mississippi Valley Archaeology Center at the University of Wisconsin–La Crosse, www.uwlax.edu/ mvac/PointGuide/PointGuide.htm).

4. Thomas C. Pleger, PhD, "The First People in Wisconsin," UW–Fox Valley Anthropology, 2000, www.uwfox.uwc.edu/ academics/depts/tpleger/paleoindian.html.

5. Ibid.

6. "Early Cultures: Pre-European Peoples of Wisconsin, Paleo Tradition, Nomadic Lifestyle," Mississippi Valley Archaeology Center at the University of Wisconsin–La Crosse, www.uwlax.edu/mvac/ PreEuropeanPeople/EarlyCultures/paleo_ nomadic.html.

7. Robert Claiborne and the Editors of Time-Life Books, *The First Americans* (New York: Time-Life Books, 1973), 41.

8. George Irving Quimby, *Indian Life in the Upper Great Lakes: 11,000 BC to AD 1800* (Chicago: University of Chicago Press, 1960), 27.

9. "The Midwestern U.S. 16,000 Years Ago," State of Illinois, Museum Link Illinois, www.museum.state.il.us/exhibits.

10. National Park Service, Effigy Mounds National Monument Online Teachers Guide, "Prehistory," www.nps.gov/efmo/ parks/prehist.htm.

11. Ian M. Lange, *Ice Age Mammals of North America: A Guide to the Big, the Hairy, and the Bizarre* (Missoula, MT: Mountain Press Publishing Company, 2002), 168.

12. Ibid., 139–141.

13. Grant Keddie, "The Atlatl Weapon," The Royal BC Museum, Human History, www.bcarchives.bc.ca/Content_Files/The AtlatlWeaponNewest.pdf.

14. Although some sources date the first use of the atlatl in North America as occurring in the early Archaic period, or about 8,000 years ago, others say the tool was developed and used in Europe and Asia perhaps as many as 30,000 years ago. Numerous sources believe the atlatl was used in North America at least 10,000 to 12,000 years ago, which means it would have been used by the early Paleo-Indians. There is a difference of opinion as to whether the atlatl came with the Paleo-Indian across the Bering Sea land bridge, or was developed independently by them in North America. It is probable that the Paleo-Indians did use atlatls with large Clovis-point tipped darts to hunt. Atlatls may have been used in North America for many thousands of years, even after the development of bows and arrows (Claiborne, *The First Americans*, 41; Keddie, "The Atlatl Weapon," www.bcarchives.bc.ca/Content_ Files/The AtlatlWeaponNewest.pdf.

15. Dr. Kiisa Nishikawa, Department of Biological Sciences, Northern Arizona University, "The Mathematics of the Atlatl," http://oak.ucc.nau.edu/ratliff/ ccligrant/Atlatl.html.

16. Thomas J. Elpel, "The Atlatl and Dart: An Ancient Hunting Method," www .hollowtop.com/atlatlbob.htm.

17. "Clovis," Mississippi Valley Archaeology Center at the UW–La Crosse, www.uwlax .edu/mvac/PointGuide/clovis.htm.

18. Ibid.

19. Indian Country Wisconsin, "Archeological History," www.mpm.edu/wirp/ICW-22 .html.

20. Quimby, *Indian Life in the Upper Great Lakes*, 33.
21. "Native Americans, Archaic," State of Illinois, Museum Link Illinois, www.museum.state.il.us/muslink/nat_amer/pre/htmls/archaic.html.
22. Ibid.
23. Thomas C. Pleger, PhD, "The Old Copper Complex of the Western Great Lakes," UW–Fox Valley Anthropology, www.uwfox.uwc.edu/academics/depts/tpleger/oldcopper.html.
24. "Native Americans, Archaic," State of Illinois, Museum Link Illinois, www.museum.state.il.us/muslink/nat_amer/pre/htmls/archaic.html.
25. "Hunting," in *Encyclopedia of North American Indians*, ed. Frederick E. Hoxie (New York: Houghton Mifflin, 1996), 261.
26. White, *Everyday Life of the North American Indian*, 55.
27. "Early Cultures: Pre-European Peoples of Wisconsin: Archaic Tradition" Mississippi Valley Archaeology Center at the UW–La Crosse, www.uwlax.edu/mvac/PreEuropeanPeople/EarlyCultures/archaic_hunting.html.
28. Ibid.
29. Elpel, "The Atlatl and Dart: An Ancient Hunting Method."
30. Keddie, "The Atlatl Weapon."
31. "Native Americans, Woodland, Technology," State of Illinois, Museum Link Illinois, www.museum.state.il.us/muslink/nat_amer/pre/htmls/w_tech.html.
32. White, *Everyday Life of the North American Indian*, 65.
33. Gad Rausing, "The Bow: Some Notes on Its Origin and Development," *Acta Archaeologica Lundenesia* Series in 8. No. 6, 1967, 13.
34. "Native Americans, Woodland, Technology, Weapons," State of Illinois, Museum Link Illinois, www.museum.state.il.us/muslink/nat_amer/pre/htmls/w_weapons.html.

Chapter 3

1. Charles Claude Le Roy de La Portherie, *Adventures of Nicolas Perrot 1665–1670*, Wisconsin Historical Society Digital Library and Archives, American Journeys Collection, http://content.wisconsinhistory.org, Document No. AJ-046, 87.
2. Robert E. Bieder, *Native American Communities in Wisconsin, 1600–1996* (Madison: University of Wisconsin Press, 1995), 48–49.
3. Carol I. Mason, *Introduction to Wisconsin Indians: Prehistory to Statehood* (Salem, WI: Sheffield Publishing Company, 1988), 63.
4. Barthelemy Vimont, *The Journey of Jean Nicolet, 1634*, Wisconsin Historical Society Digital Library and Archives, American Journeys Collection, http://content.wisconsinhistory.org, Document No. AJ-043, 16.
5. Ibid.
6. Mason, *Introduction to Wisconsin Indians*, 69–70.
7. Ibid., 74.
8. Bieder, *Native American Communities in Wisconsin*, 31.
9. Ibid., 34.
10. Jacqueline Denbar Greene, *The Chippewa* (New York: Franklin Watts, 1993), 31.
11. Mason, *Introduction to Wisconsin Indians*, 106.
12. Bieder, *Native American Communities in Wisconsin*, 34.
13. Ibid.
14. Greene, *The Chippewa*, 34.
15. A. W. Schorger, *Wildlife in Early Wisconsin* (Stevens Point: University of Wisconsin, Student Chapter of The Wildlife Society, 1982), 52.
16. Greene, *The Chippewa*, 35.
17. Edmund Jefferson Danziger Jr., *The Chippewas of Lake Superior* (Norman: University of Oklahoma Press, 1978), 14.
18. Sister M. Carolissa Levi, *Chippewa Indians of Yesterday and Today* (New York: Pageant Press, 1956), 243.
19. Ibid.

20. Ibid.
21. Sister M. Inez Hilger, *Chippewa Child Life and Its Cultural Background* (Washington, DC: U.S. Government Printing Office, 1951), 170.
22. Ibid., 121–122.
23. Ibid., 120.
24. Mason, *Introduction to Wisconsin Indians*, 106.
25. Ibid., 95.
26. Bieder, *Native American Communities in Wisconsin*, 43.
27. Mason, *Introduction to Wisconsin Indians*, 126.
28. Bieder, *Native American Communities in Wisconsin*, 38.
29. Ibid., 42.
30. Ibid., 43.
31. Schorger, *Wildlife in Early Wisconsin*, 57.
32. J. G. Kohl, *Kitchi-Gami: Wanderings Round Lake Superior* (Minneapolis, MN: Ross and Haines, 1956), 311.
33. Schorger, *Wildlife in Early Wisconsin*, 58.
34. *The Story of American Hunting and Firearms from Outdoor Life* (New York: Books Division, Times Mirror Magazines, 1976), 18.
35. Richard E. McCabe and Thomas R. McCabe, "Of Slings and Arrows: An Historical Retrospection" in *White-Tailed Deer Ecology and Management*, ed. Lowell K. Halls (Harrisburg, PA: Stackpole Books, 1984), 49.
36. Victor Barnow, *Wisconsin Chippewa Myths and Tales* (Madison: University of Wisconsin Press, 1977), 263–264.
37. Charles F. Waterman, *Hunting in America* (New York: Holt, Rinehart and Winston, 1973), 32.
38. Schorger, *Wildlife in Early Wisconsin*, 57–58.
39. McCabe and McCabe, "Of Slings and Arrows," 48.
40. Ibid., 39.
41. Ibid., 43.
42. Kohl, *Kitchi-Gami*, 122–123.
43. McCabe and McCabe, "Of Slings and Arrows," 48.
44. Mason, *Introduction to Wisconsin Indians*, 107.
45. McCabe, and McCabe, "Of Slings and Arrows," 54.
46. Ibid., 37.
47. Kohl, *Kitchi-Gami*, 212.
48. McCabe and McCabe, "Of Slings and Arrows," 40.
49. Mason, *Introduction to Wisconsin Indians*, 117.
50. Ibid., 107.

Chapter 4
1. Junius Henderson and Elberta L. Craig, *Economic Mammalogy* (Baltimore, MD and Springfield, IL: Charles C. Thomas, 1932), 140.
2. McCabe and McCabe, "Of Slings and Arrows," 59.
3. Ibid., 61.
4. Ibid.
5. Ibid., 60.
6. Calvin Martin, *Keepers of the Game: Indian-Animal Relationships and the Fur Trade* (Berkeley: University of California Press, 1978), 145.
7. McCabe and McCabe, "Of Slings and Arrows," 59.
8. James Lewis, "The Blackhawk War of 1832," Abraham Lincoln Historical Digitization Project, http://lincoln.lib.niu.edu/blackhawk/index.html.
9. Otis S. Bersing, *A Century of Wisconsin Deer* (Madison: Wisconsin Conservation Department, Game Management Division, 1956), 6–7.
10. McCabe and McCabe, "Of Slings and Arrows," 62.
11. Schorger, *Wildlife in Early Wisconsin*, 56–57.
12. McCabe and McCabe, "Of Slings and Arrows," 68.
13. Ibid.
14. Ibid., 63.
15. Ibid.
16. Ibid.
17. Ibid.
18. Ibid.
19. Schorger, *Wildlife in Early Wisconsin*, 62.
20. Bersing, *A Century of Wisconsin Deer*, 10.
21. Burton L. Dahlberg and Ralph C. Guettinger, *The White-Tailed Deer in Wisconsin*. Technical Bulletin No. 14 (Madison: Wisconsin Conservation Department, Game Management Division, 1956), 25.
22. McCabe and McCabe, "Of Slings and Arrows," 66–67.
23. Ibid., 67.

24. Ibid.
25. Bersing, *A Century of Wisconsin Deer*, 12.
26. Schorger, *Wildlife in Early Wisconsin*, 62.
27. McCabe and McCabe, "Of Slings and Arrows," 65.
28. Ibid., 69.
29. Ibid.
30. Schorger, *Wildlife in Early Wisconsin*, 64–65.
31. Ibid., 65.
32. Ibid., 65–66.
33. Ibid., 66.
34. Ibid., 93.
35. Ibid., 75–76.
36. Ibid., 76.
37. Ibid., 88.
38. Ibid., 98.
39. Ibid., 83.
40. Ibid., 92.
41. Ibid., 79.
42. Ibid., 94.
43. Ibid., 78.
44. Ibid., 91.
45. Ibid., 67.
46. Bersing, *A Century of Wisconsin Deer*, 15.
47. Ibid., 9.
48. Walker D. Wyman, *The Lumberjack Frontier* (Lincoln: University of Nebraska Press, 1969), vii.
49. Wisconsin Woodland Owners Association, *One Hundred Years of Wisconsin Forestry, 1904–2004* (Black Earth, WI: Trails Custom Publishing, 2004), 6.
50. Ibid.
51. Wyman, *The Lumberjack Frontier*, viii–ix.
52. Wisconsin Woodland Owners Association, *One Hundred Years of Wisconsin Forestry, 1904–2004*, 8.
53. Ibid.
54. Ibid., 9.
55. Ibid., 12.
56. Schorger, *Wildlife in Early Wisconsin*, 69.
57. Ibid., 70.
58. Ibid., 77.
59. Ibid., 81.
60. Ibid., 94.
61. Ibid.
62. Bersing, *A Century of Wisconsin Deer*, 11.
63. Schorger, *Wildlife in Early Wisconsin*, 62.
64. Frederick Hale, *Swedes in Wisconsin* (Madison: The State Historical Society of Wisconsin, 1983), 20.
65. Robert Gough, *Farming the Cutover: A Social History of Northern Wisconsin* (Lawrence: University Press of Kansas, 1997), 21.
66. Ibid., 66.
67. Ibid.
68. Dahlberg and Guettinger, *The White-Tailed Deer in Wisconsin*, 26.

Chapter 5

1. Gene Hill, *A Listening Walk . . . and Other Stories* (Piscataway, NJ: Winchester Press, New Century Publishers, 1985), 95.
2. "Wisconsin: Population of Counties by Decennial Census: 1900 to 1990," www.census.gov/population/cencounts/wi190090.txt
3. "Deer Slaughter Is On," *The New North*, November 11, 1901.
4. Ibid.
5. "Open Season for Deer," *The New North*, November 9, 1905.
6. "Official Railroad Map of Wisconsin" (Milwaukee, WI: Knell Publishing Co., 1904).
7. "Many Hunters Are in the Northern Woods," *The New North*, November 17, 1910.
8. "Unusually Good Deer Season Ended Sunday," *The New North*, December 5, 1901.
9. "Deer Season to Open Nov. 21," *The New North*, November 18, 1920.
10. "Game Warden Capture," *The New North*, November 27, 1902.
11. "Woodruff," *The New North*, November 22, 1906.
12. "Estimates Dead Deer at 10,000," *The New North*, December 19, 1907.
13. "Many Deer Are Killed," *The New North*, November 19, 1908.
14. "Organize Hunting and Fishing Club," *The New North*, January 14, 1909.
15. Ibid.
16. "Many Deer Are Killed," *The New North*, November 19, 1908.

17. "Organize Hunting and Fishing Club," *The New North*, January 14, 1909.

18. Ibid.

19. Sears, Roebuck & Co., Chicago, Illinois. Catalogue No. 117. 1908.

20. Ibid.

21. "All Aboard for Hunting Grounds," *Wausau Daily Record-Herald*, November 10, 1910.

22. "Wausau Hunter Gets First Deer," *Wausau Daily Record-Herald*, November 14, 1910.

23. Ibid.

24. "Opening of Deer Season Is Close," *Wausau Daily Record-Herald*, November 8, 1910.

25. "Deer May Be Shot Monday," *Rhinelander News*, November 8, 1912.

26. "Set Gun Causes Teacher's Death," *The New North*, November 7, 1912.

27. "Game Is Very Plentiful," *Rhinelander News*, August 23, 1912.

28. "Kill Many Deer in This County?" *The New North*, November 28, 1912.

29. "Deer Hunters Are Already in Woods," *The New North*, November 3, 1910.

30. "Governor McGovern Here: Chief Executive on Way to Glidden for Deer Hunt," *The New North*, November 21, 1912.

31. "Kill Many Deer in This County?" *The New North*, November 28, 1912.

32. "Hunters Are Ready," *Rhinelander News*, November 7, 1913.

33. "Kill Less Deer than Last Year," *The New North*, December 4, 1913.

34. Ibid.

35. "Deer Hunting in Full Swing," *The New North*, November 19, 1911.

36. Dahlberg and Guettinger, *The White-Tailed Deer in Wisconsin*, 26.

37. Bersing, *A Century of Wisconsin Deer*, 15.

38. "May Attempt to Repeal Buck Law," *The New North*, December 7, 1916.

39. "Many Does Lie Dead in Woods," *Wausau Daily Record-Herald*, November 17, 1915.

40. "Garner Condemns 'One Buck' Law," *The New North*, November 23, 1916.

41. "Claims Buck Law Checks Accidents," *The New North*, November 30, 1916.

42. "Pleads for Care in the Northwoods," *Wausau Daily Record-Herald*, November 19, 1917.

43. Ibid.

44. Ibid.

45. "Predicts Closed Season on Deer," *The New North*, November 20, 1919.

46. "Big Deer Leaps on Automobile," *The New North*, November 13, 1924.

47. "Sold Over 2,100 Hunting Licenses," *The New North*, November 25, 1920.

48. "Buck Shipment Is Not Heavy," *The New North*, December 7, 1922.

49. "Deer Season to Open Nov. 21," *The New North*, November 18, 1920.

50. "Sportsmen Meet," *The New North*, December 23, 1920.

51. "Buck Shipment Is Not Heavy," *The New North*, December 7, 1922.

52. "Favors Closed Season on Deer," *The New North*, December 11, 1924.

53. Bersing, *A Century of Wisconsin Deer*, 87–90.

54. "Favors Closed Season on Deer," *The New North*, December 11, 1924.

55. Ibid.

56. Ibid.

57. "Ikes for Better Game Protection," *The New North*, January 15, 1925.

58. "Hunting Season Soon to Open," *The New North*, September 9, 1926.

59. "Protest on Late Hunting License," *The New North*, November 18, 1926.

60. "Set Aside Land for Game Refuge," *The New North*, September 16, 1926.

61. John Madson, *The White-Tailed Deer* (New Haven, CT: Winchester-Western Press, 1961), 51.

Chapter 6

1. Gordon MacQuarrie, "Just Look at This Country," in *Stories of the Old Duck Hunters* (Minocqua, WI: Willow Creek Press, 1990), 44.

2. "Last Pine Plank Cut at Drummond," *The New North*, November 13, 1930.

3. "Larger Loggers Are Quitting," *The New North*, July 10, 1930.

4. "Big Demand for Hunting Licenses," *The New North*, October 16, 1930.

5. Dahlberg and Guettinger, *The White-Tailed Deer in Wisconsin*, 208.

6. "Hunters Consider 1930 Deer Season Successful," *The New North*, December 31, 1930.

7. Ibid.

8. "Deer Season Facts Listed," *The New North*, November 17, 1932.

9. Dahlberg and Guettinger, *The White-Tailed Deer in Wisconsin*, 208.

10. Ibid., 151.

11. Ibid.

12. "Hunters Consider 1930 Deer Season Successful," *The New North*, December 31, 1930.

13. "Deer Hunters Are Satisfied," *The New North*, December 4, 1930.

14. "Conservation Notes, Refuges," *The New North*, January 7, 1937.

15. "New Game Refuge," *The New North*, November 19, 1936.

16. Aldo Leopold's 1933 book, *Game Management*, is widely thought to be the first textbook on scientific game management, and Leopold himself is considered the father of modern wildlife management. However, it took until the late 1940s before wildlife management moved from protection to biology (Keith McCaffery, retired Wisconsin Department of Natural Resources northern forest deer researcher, personal communication, October 11, 2005).

17. "Conservation Notes, Forest Crop Lands," *The New North*, December 19, 1938.

18. History of the Chequamegon-Nicolet National Forests, www.fs.fed.us/r9/cnnf/general/history/detailed_history.pdf.

19. "Conservation Notes, Tree Planting," *The New North*, December 29, 1938.

20. Wisconsin Bowhunters Association, www.wbhassoc.com.

21. M. R. James, *Unforgettable Bowhunters* (Amherst Junction, WI: IHUNT Communications, 2007).

22. "Deer Season to Open Here November 24," *Rhinelander Daily News*, November 21, 1934.

23. "New Hunting Rules in Effect," *The Wisconsin Sportsman*, September 1936, 1–2.

24. "Whirring Arrows Whiz as Archers Prepare for Their Special Season," *The Wisconsin Sportsman*, October 1936, 1.

25. "Just One Buck Falls Victim to Bow & Arrow," *The Wisconsin Sportsman*, November 1936, 1.

26. "Archers Expect Twenty Day Bow Season in 1937," *The Wisconsin Sportsman*, February 1937, 1.

27. "Conservation Notes," *The New North*, November 4, 1937.

28. "Conservation Notes," *The New North*, October 19, 1939.

29. Ibid.

30. L. H. Kingston, "Claims Illegal Deer Kill Heavy," *The New North*, December 15, 1938.

31. "Conservation Notes: Deer Heads," *The New North*, December 16, 1937.

32. "Hunters Flock to Northwoods," *The New North*, November 23, 1939. Ordway's buck may have been beaten by a buck shot in Cook County, Minnesota, in 1922 by Carl J. Lenander Jr. of Minneapolis, which had a dressed weight of 402 pounds ("The White-Tailed Deer of Minnesota," Minnesota Division of Game and Fish, Technical Bulletin No. 5, 1961).

33. Ibid.

34. "Wisconsin Hunter Bags Record Breaking Buck," *The Wisconsin Sportsman*, December–January 1937, 1.

35. "The 1937 Deer Hunting Season: Digest of the Arguments," *The Wisconsin Sportsman*, August 1937, 3.

36. Ibid.

37. Ibid.

38. Ibid.

39. Ibid.

40. Ibid.

41. Dahlberg and Guettinger, *The White-Tailed Deer in Wisconsin*, 208.

42. Ernest Swift, "The Problem of Managing Wisconsin Deer" (Madison: Wisconsin Conservation Department, 1939), 11–12.

43. Ibid., 2.

44. Ibid., 3.

45. Ibid., 4.

46. Ibid., 6.

47. Ibid., 4.

48. Ibid., 17.

49. Ibid., 18.

50. Ibid., 18–19.

51. Ibid., 13. Retired DNR northern forest deer researcher Keith McCaffery noted that Swift's concerns regarding imbalanced

sex ratios were likely misplaced unless the herd was not recruiting young deer into the population. According to McCaffery, we know today that normal recruitment will swamp sex ratios back to two does per buck or better each fall under buck-only hunting (Keith McCaffery, personal communication, October 11, 2005).

52. Aldo Leopold, "Deer Irruptions," in *Wisconsin's Deer Problem* (Madison: Wisconsin Conservation Department, 1943), publication 321, 9–10.

53. Ibid., 10.

54. Ibid.

55. Ibid., 9.

56. W. S. Feeney, "Wisconsin Deer Today and Tomorrow," in *Wisconsin's Deer Problem* (Madison: Wisconsin Conservation Department, 1943), publication 321, 12.

57. Ibid., 12–13.

58. Citizens' Deer Committee, "Majority Report of the Citizens' Deer Committee to Wisconsin Conservation Commission," in *Wisconsin's Deer Problem* (Madison: Wisconsin Conservation Department, 1943), publication 321, 20–21.

59. Ibid., 21.

60. Ibid., 20.

61. Ibid., 22.

62. "Deer Hunters Go Out Tomorrow," *Rhinelander Daily News*, November 17, 1943.

63. "'County Strewn with Blood,' Says Game Warden," *Rhinelander Daily News*, November 26, 1943.

64. "Record Sale of Deer Hunting Licenses Expected," *Rhinelander Daily News*, November 23, 1943.

65. "State Press: Deer Slaughter (*Oshkosh Northwestern*)," *Rhinelander Daily News*, December 3, 1943.

66. "State Press: Slaughter of Deer (*Capital Times*)," *Rhinelander Daily News*, December 8, 1943.

67. "State Press: 1943 Conservation (*Forest Republican*)," *Rhinelander Daily News*, December 14, 1943.

68. "State Press: Faulty Deer Season (*Vilas County News-Review*)," *Rhinelander Daily News*, December 7, 1943.

69. "State Press: Success or Failure? (*Marshfield News-Herald*)," *Rhinelander Daily News*, December 10, 1943.

70. Keith McCaffery, personal communication, October 11, 2005.

71. "Record Sale of Deer Hunting Licenses Expected," *Rhinelander Daily News*, November 23, 1943.

72. "Deer Hunters Go Out Tomorrow," *Rhinelander Daily News*, November 17, 1943.

73. "Deer Hunters Get OPA Warning," *Rhinelander Daily News*, November 2, 1943.

74. "Servicemen Get Their Deer, Too," *Rhinelander Daily News*, December 2, 1943.

75. "Kid Brother Beats Ace to Buck," *Rhinelander Daily News*, November 18, 1943.

76. Bersing, *A Century of Wisconsin Deer*, 104.

77. Ibid., 105.

78. "Antlerless Season Open Tomorrow," *Rhinelander Daily News*, November 18, 1949.

79. "Meat Hunt," *Rhinelander Daily News*, November 23, 1949.

80. "Fine Tracking Aids Hunters in Area," *Rhinelander Daily News*, November 19, 1949.

81. "North's Plea for Change in Deer Season Rejected," *Rhinelander Daily News*, November 9, 1949.

82. Bersing, *A Century of Wisconsin Deer*, 105.

83. "No Luck in Woods," *Rhinelander Daily News*, November 20, 1951.

84. Bersing, *A Century of Wisconsin Deer*, 84.

85. Dion Henderson (Associated Press), "Deer Hunt Dawns, and Yelps of Old Not Being Heard," *Rhinelander Daily News*, November 17, 1950.

86. "Deer Tales," *Rhinelander Daily News*, November 21, 1950.

87. "State Press: Deer Question (*Vilas County News-Review*)," *Rhinelander Daily News*, October 20, 1951.

88. Ibid.

89. "*Marinette Eagle-Star*: Deer Hunting," *Rhinelander Daily News*, November 20, 1951.

90. "State Press: Deer Management (*Green Bay Press-Gazette*)," *Rhinelander Daily News*, November 29, 1951.

91. Keith McCaffery, personal communication, October 11, 2005.

92. "Deer Season Time to Eye Future of Herd, Says Swift," *Rhinelander Daily News*, November 17, 1951.

93. "Deer Tales," *Rhinelander Daily News*, November 21, 1955.

94. "Deer Tales," *Rhinelander Daily News*, November 19, 1951.

95. "Heavy Snow Closes Some Schools, Strands Hunters," *Rhinelander Daily News*, November 21, 1956.

96. Lewie Falk, interview with the author, October 2000.

97. Ibid.

98. "Deer Kill May Double 1956 Take," *Rhinelander Daily News*, November 18, 1957.

99. "Men in Red Poised for Big Deer Kill," *Rhinelander Daily News*, November 14, 1958.

100. "Extra Week of Season in North May Curb Herd," *Rhinelander Daily News*, November 28, 1958.

101. Most current Wisconsin wildlife managers would probably say that the "deer wars" never really ended, as deer management continues to be the most controversial and hotly debated wildlife management issue in the state. However, according to Keith McCaffery, the traditional idea of the "deer wars" refers to the period of 1935–51 (Keith McCaffery, personal communication, October 18, 2005).

Chapter 7

1. Stephen J. Bodio, *On the Edge of the Wild* (New York: The Lyons Press, 1998), 199.

2. "Jack Slays Deer, Friend Gets Bruised," *Rhinelander Daily News*, November 18, 1960.

3. "Crandon Editor Decries Nicolet Hunt Promotion," *Northern Lakes Advertiser*, November 3, 1960.

4. Ibid.

5. Dick Hemp, "Deer Herd Keeps Flourishing Despite 'Wiped Out' Charges," *Wausau Daily Record-Herald*, November 17, 1960.

6. "Party Permit Still Basic Tool of Deer Management," *Northern Lakes Advertiser*, November 10, 1960.

7. Ibid.

8. Ibid.

9. Ibid.

10. "Opinions on Size of Deer Herd Spice Start of Hunt," *Rhinelander Daily News*, November 18, 1960.

11. Ibid.

12. Ibid.

13. "Area Kill Surpasses Forecast," *Rhinelander Daily News*, November 21, 1960.

14. "Many Reasons Offered for Light Deer Kill," *Rhinelander Daily News*, November 22, 1960.

15. "Venison Stew . . . With Ingredients for Good Deer Management" (Madison: Wisconsin Conservation Department, 1961), 1.

16. Ibid.

17. Ben Lewis, "Touch of Ugliness in Snow's Beauty," *Wausau Daily Record-Herald*, March 2, 1962.

18. "Browse Cutting Ordered: Says Many Deer Will Starve," *Wausau Daily Record-Herald*, March 9, 1962.

19. Ibid.

20. "Forest-Deer Plan to Be Discussed at Congress Meet," *Rhinelander Daily News*, December 4, 1962.

21. Werner Zimmer, interview with the author, September 2000.

22. "Area Counties Improve Roads to Hunting Hotspots," *Rhinelander Daily News*, November 17, 1966.

23. Ibid.

24. Ibid.

25. " 'Biggest Herd Since '58' Awaits Deer Hunters," *Rhinelander Daily News*, November 14, 1964.

26. According to Keith McCaffery, the rapid growth of the deer herd during the early 1960s was, in part, caused by the two-year moratorium on party permits and the conservative approach used to introduce the variable quota system (Keith McCaffery, personal communication, October 21, 2005).

27. " 'Biggest Herd Since '58' Awaits Deer Hunters," *Rhinelander Daily News*, November 14, 1964.

28. Ibid.

29. "Chequamegon to Offer Heaviest Concentration," *Rhinelander Daily News*, November 19, 1964.

30. "Northeast Deer Kill 18,811, Well Above 1963," *Rhinelander Daily News*, December 3, 1964.

31. Ibid.

32. "Hunting Season Opens Under Ideal Conditions," *Rhinelander Daily News*, November 22, 1969.

33. Keith McCaffery, personal communication, October 21, 2005.

34. "Storm Closes Schools, Brings Traffic to a Halt," *Rhinelander Daily News*, January 4, 1971.

35. "Heavy Snow Hampers Deer Hunters Today," *Rhinelander Daily News*, November 21, 1970.

36. Ibid.

37. "Buck Kill Down Only Slightly After All," *Rhinelander Daily News*, December 7, 1970.

38. Ibid.

39. "Eagle River's 40 Lowest in Nation," *Rhinelander Daily News*, February 8, 1971.

40. William E. Schultz (Associated Press), "Winter's Cold and Snow Bring Slow Death to North Area's Deer Herd," *Rhinelander Daily News*, March 3, 1971.

41. Ibid.

42. Edward J. Frank, "Hunting Prospects–1971," *Wisconsin Conservation Bulletin*, September–October 1971.

43. Bruce E. Kohn, "What's Happened to the Northern Forest Deer Herd?" *Wisconsin Conservation Bulletin*, September–October 1972.

44. "Predict Deer Hunting in North to Have 'Poor' Season," *Rhinelander Daily News*, November 19, 1971.

45. Ellsworth K. Gaulke, "Would Extend Season, Ban Party Permits," *Rhinelander Daily News*, November 17, 1971.

46. According to Keith McCaffery, deer population goals in the farmland region were initially set by the DNR in 1962 near the existing deer population—the thought being that the herd was at a level well tolerated by farmers. As the herd increased, farmers' tolerance was tested. It was determined that goals could be increased until the population hit about twenty-five deer per square mile, which was when acceptance declined (Keith McCaffery, personal communication, April 30, 2008).

47. "Predict Deer Hunters in North to Have 'Poor' Season," *Rhinelander Daily News*, November 19, 1971.

48. Ibid.

49. "Area Hunters Find Success in Deer Opener," *Rhinelander Daily News*, November 20, 1971.

50. Thomas A. Heberlein and Laybourne, "The Wisconsin Deer Hunter: Social Characteristics, Attitudes, and Preferences for Proposed Hunting Season Changes," iv.

51. James A. Swan, "What to Do About Earth Day?" ESPN.com, http://sports.espn.go.com/espn/print?id=2031384&type=story.

52. Heberlein and Laybourne, "The Wisconsin Deer Hunter: Social Characteristics, Attitudes, and Preferences for Proposed Hunting Season Changes," iv.

53. Ibid.

54. Ibid., v.

55. Ibid.

56. Tom Berger and Harvey Rockwood, "Snow Depths Threaten State's Large Herd," *Wausau Daily Herald*, January 26, 1979.

57. Jim Lee, "Status of Deer Herd Somewhat of a Mystery," *The Wausau Daily Herald*, November 9, 1979.

58. Keith McCaffery, personal communication, October 21, 2005.

59. "DNR Forecasts Another Large Deer Kill," *Rhinelander Daily News*, November 16, 1980.

60. Ibid.

61. Ibid.

62. Keith McCaffery, personal communication, October 21, 2005.

63. "DNR Forecasts Another Large Deer Kill," *Rhinelander Daily News*, November 16, 1980.

64. Ibid.

65. "Blaze Orange Law Insult to Hunter Intelligence," E. N. Foltz letter to the editor, *Rhinelander Daily News*, December 7, 1980.

66. "Wisconsin Deer Kill Second Highest in History," *Rhinelander Daily News*, December 21, 1980.

67. Ibid.

68. Ibid.

69. "Record Deer Kill Is Anticipated," *Rhinelander Daily News*, November 14, 1982.

70. Ibid.

71. Ibid.

72. Ibid.

73. Ibid.

74. Jim Lee, "Record Year? DNR Predicts Deer Kill Will Top 200,000," *Wausau Daily Herald*, November 17, 1983.

75. Ibid.

76. Indian Country Wisconsin: Ojibwe Treaty Rights, Peace Treaties, Milwaukee Public Museum, www.mpm.edu.wirp/ICW-110.html.

77. Ibid.

78. Associated Press, "No Early Hunting for Indians," *Wausau Daily Herald*, November 11, 1983.

79. Ibid.

80. "Chippewas Delay Start of Their Deer Season," *Wausau Daily Herald*, November 14, 1983.

81. "Let's Be Reasonable About Deer Hunting," Opinion, *Wausau Daily Herald*, November 15, 1983, 1.

82. Roland Barker, "Tribes Show Restraint: Wardens Arrest Indian Hunters," *Rhinelander Daily News*, November 14, 1983.

83. "Task Force State Reach Pact," *Masinaigan*, December 1983.

84. Jonathon H. Gilbert, GLIFWC Administrative Report Summary of the 1983–84 Off-Reservation Treaty Deer Season, March 1984.

85. Jim Lee, "Rainy Days Dampen Deer Hunting Success," *Wausau Daily Herald*, November 21, 1983, 1.

86. Keith McCaffery, personal communication, October 21, 2005.

87. Ibid.

88. Jim Lee, "The Scope Earns Status as Valuable Hunt Accessory," *Wausau Daily Herald*, November 17, 1985.

Chapter 8

1. Curtis K. Stadtfeld, *Whitetail Deer: A Year's Cycle* (New York: The Dial Press, 1975), 91.

2. Jim Lee, "Deer Hunt Aims at Record," *Wausau Daily Herald*, November 11, 1990.

3. Ibid.

4. "Record Year for Deer Possible," *Rhinelander Daily News*, November 12, 1989.

5. "Hunters Bag More than 313,000 Deer Statewide," *Rhinelander Daily News*, November 29, 1989. Actually, there were tough winters in 1981–82 and 1985–86, but the mildest on record was in 1986–87 (Keith McCaffery, personal communication, March 7, 2006).

6. "Hunters on Record Pace," *Wausau Daily Herald*, November 20, 1990.

7. "Season Drives Them Bananas," editorial, *Wausau Daily Herald*, November 20, 1990.

8. Associated Press, "Battle Plan: Hunting Foes Ready for Action," *Wausau Daily Herald*, November 13, 1990.

9. "Hunting Foes Claim Harassment," *Wausau Daily Herald*, November 20, 1990.

10. "Bonus Deer Permits Available Saturday," *Wausau Daily Herald*, November 14, 1991.

11. Ibid.

12. Ibid.

13. Keith McCaffery, personal communication, March 7, 2006.

14. Jim Lee, "Record Deer Herd Awaits Hunters," *Wausau Daily Herald*, November 17, 1991.

15. Jim Lee, "Buck Kill Is Up 104% in Marathon County," *Wausau Daily Herald*, November 24, 1992. According to Keith McCaffery, the average Winter Severity Index for the north was only fifty (the dividing line between mild and moderate). However, fawn/doe ratios in 1992 were at record low levels.

16. Jim Lee, "Cards Stacked in Hunters' Favor," *Wausau Daily Herald*, November 15, 1992.

17. Jim Lee, "Buck Kill Is Up 104% in Marathon County," *Wausau Daily Herald*, November 24, 1992.

18. Ibid.

19. Jim Lee, "Cards Stacked in Hunters' Favor," *Wausau Daily Herald*, November 15, 1992.

20. Keith McCaffery, personal communication, March 7, 2006.

21. Associated Press, "Deer Management Questioned: Report Doubts DNR's Deer Population Estimate," *Wausau Daily Herald*, November 17, 1992.

22. Keith McCaffery, personal communication, March 7, 2006.

23. Ibid.

24. According to Keith McCaffery, the DNR's expectation prior to the 1992 hunt was the reduced exploitation of bucks in most of northern Wisconsin, excluding the far northwest, thus saving some older bucks for the 1992 season. But since SAK data from 1991 could not reliably be used to predict the 1992 population (and 1990 data was used to "double predict" for 1992), herd status in eighteen northern deer management units was overestimated (Keith McCaffery, personal communication, June 11, 2008).

25. Keith McCaffery, personal communication, March 7, 2006.

26. Jim Lee, "Reality Returns to Deer Hunt," *Wausau Daily Herald*, November 14, 1993.

27. Associated Press, "DNR: Thousands of Bonus Tags Unsold," *Wausau Daily Herald*, November 18, 1995.

28. Ibid.

29. Keith McCaffery, personal communication, March 7, 2006.

30. Jim Lee, "Deer Hunt Aims at Record," *Wausau Daily Herald*, November 12, 1995.

31. Ibid.

32. Ibid.

33. Jim Lee, "Deer Hunter Is a Game Manager, Like It or Not," *Wausau Daily Herald*, November 19, 1995.

34. Jim Lee, "Season Noteworthy for Big Bucks," *Wausau Daily Herald*, November 26, 1995.

35. "Wisconsin Deer Harvest and License Sales," Wisconsin Department of Natural Resources, www.dnr.state.wi.us/org/land/wildlife/hunt/deer/histharv.htm.

36. Associated Press, "October Hunt Unprecedented in Wisconsin," *Rhinelander Daily News*, October 7, 1996.

37. "A Chronology of Wisconsin Deer Hunting," Wisconsin Department of Natural Resources, http://dnr.wi.gov/news/DNRNews_Lookup.asp?id=40#art8.

38. Associated Press, " 'Earn a Buck' Hunt Underway," *Rhinelander Daily News*, October 25, 1996.

39. "A Chronology of Wisconsin Deer Hunting," Wisconsin Department of Natural Resources http://dnr.wi.gov/news/DNRNews_Lookup.asp?id=40#art8.

40. Associated Press, "Deer Hunters Play It Safe," *Rhinelander Daily News*, October 29, 1996.

41. Ibid.

42. Jay Faherty, "8,000 Still Without Power," *Wausau Daily Herald*, November 17, 1996.

43. Jim Lee, "Northern Deer Herd Taken by Storm," *Wausau Daily Herald*, November 17, 1996.

44. "Wisconsin's Winter Awareness Week, November 7–11, 2005," Wisconsin Department of Military Affairs, Wisconsin Emergency Management, press release, October 28, 2005, http://emergencymanagement.wi.gov/docview.asp?docid=5199.

45. "Deer in Local Counties Down from Last Year," *Rhinelander Daily News*, November 17, 1996.

46. Keith McCaffery, personal communication, March 7, 2006.

47. Associated Press, "Hunters Might See Fewer Deer in North," *Wausau Daily Herald*, November 17, 1996.

48. Jim Lee, "Northern Deer Herd Taken by Storm," *Wausau Daily Herald*, November 17, 1996.

49. Robert Imrie (Associated Press), "Watch for Blaze Orange as Hunters Hit the Woods," *Wausau Daily Herald*, November 23, 1996.

50. Keith McCaffery, personal communication, March 7, 2006.

51. Associated Press, "Opening Weekend Hunt Results Mixed," *Rhinelander Daily News*, November 25, 1996.

52. Ibid.

53. "Wisconsin Deer Harvest and License Sales," Wisconsin Department of Natural Resources, www.dnr.state.wi.us/org/land/wildlife/hunt/deer/histharv.htm.

54. Imrie, "Watch for Blaze Orange," *Wausau Daily Herald*, November 23, 1996.

55. "Wisconsin's Winter Awareness Week, November 7–11, 2005," Wisconsin Department of Military Affairs, Wisconsin Emergency Management, press release, October 28, 2005, http://emergencymanagement.wi.gov/docview.asp?docid=5199.

56. Jim Lee, "Plenty of Questions as Gun Deer Hunt Nears," *Wausau Daily Herald*, November 16, 1997.

57. Ibid.

58. Robert Imrie (Associated Press), "Cowboys Might Affect Deer Hunt," *Wausau Daily Herald*, November 17, 1997.

59. Winter 1997–98 in Wisconsin, Wisconsin State Climatology Office, www.uwex.edu/sco/win9798.html.

60. Ibid.

61. "Wisconsin Outdoor Report," Wisconsin Department of Natural Resources, November 17, 1998.

62. "Hunters Bag Big Bucks on Opener," *Wausau Daily Herald*, November 22, 1998.

63. "Wisconsin Outdoor Report," Wisconsin Department of Natural Resources, November 17, 1998.

64. Keith McCaffery, personal communication, March 7, 2006.

65. Associated Press, "Hunting Falls Short of Helping Natural Balance," *Rhinelander Daily News*, November 19, 1999.

66. Daryl Youngstrum, "1999 Deer Population Setting Records," *Rhinelander Daily News*, November 3, 1999.

67. "1999 Wisconsin Big Game Hunting Summary," Wisconsin Department of Natural Resources, April 2000, 2.

68. Jim Lee, "Deer Prospects Couldn't Be Better," *Wausau Daily Herald*, November 14, 1999.

69. Keith McCaffery, personal communication, March 7, 2006.

70. "Hunters Find Success on Opening Day," *Rhinelander Daily News*, November 21, 1999.

71. "1999 Wisconsin Big Game Hunting Summary," Wisconsin Department of Natural Resources, April 2000, 2.

72. "Woodruff," *The New North*, November 22, 1906.

Chapter 9

1. Ernest F. Swift, *A Conservation Saga* (Washington, DC: National Wildlife Federation, 1967), 254.

2. Robert Imrie (Associated Press), "Wisconsin Hunters to Shoot Diseased Deer," Forest Conservation Portal, March 26, 2002, http://forests.org/articles/reader.asp?linkid=9327.

3. "State's White-Tailed Deer Test Negative for TB, Chronic Wasting Disease," Wisconsin Department of Natural Resources, News and Outdoor Report, July 3, 2001.

4. Mary Van de Kamp Nohl, "The Killer among Us," *Milwaukee Magazine*, December 2002, 56.

5. "State's White-Tailed Deer Test Negative for TB, Chronic Wasting Disease," Wisconsin Department of Natural Resources, News and Outdoor Report, July 3, 2001.

6. "2000 Nine-Day Firearm Season Underway," *Rhinelander Daily News*, November 19, 2000.

7. "2000 Wisconsin Big Game Hunting Summary," Wisconsin Department of Natural Resources, April 2001, 56.

8. "Deer Kill Up from 1999," *Rhinelander Daily News*, November 22, 2000.

9. "Deer Hunting Tradition Leads to Cancellation of Classes," *Rhinelander Daily News*, November 26, 2000.

10. "Deer Kill Up from 1999," *Rhinelander Daily News*, November 22, 2000.

11. "One-Third of All Deer Taken in Northern Area," *Rhinelander Daily News*, November 30, 2000.

12. "2001 Wisconsin Big Game Hunting Summary," Wisconsin Department of Natural Resources, April 2002, 2.

13. Ibid.

14. Keith McCaffery, personal communication, April 25, 2006.

15. Associated Press, "Deer Hunt Underway," *Rhinelander Daily News*, November 18, 2001.

16. "Deer Hunt Opens Under Sunny Skies," *Rhinelander Daily News*, November 18, 2001.

17. "2001 Wisconsin Big Game Hunting Summary," Wisconsin Department of Natural Resources, April 2002, 3.

18. Associated Press, "Leonid Meteor Shower Dazzles Stargazers Across the United States," *Rhinelander Daily News*, November 19, 2001.

19. "Weather Responsible for Reduced Gun Season Harvest," *Rhinelander Daily News*, November 25, 2001.

20. Ibid.

21. Ibid.

22. "2001 Wisconsin Big Game Hunting Summary," Wisconsin Department of Natural Resources, April 2002, 3. The gun season kill totals include deer taken in the early and late Zone-T hunts. In 2001, 58,107 antlerless deer were taken in the antlerless-only October and December hunts.

23. Nohl, "The Killer among Us," *Milwaukee Magazine*, December 2002, 56.

24. "2001 Deer Hunting Season Wildlife Report," Wisconsin Department of Natural Resources, November 29, 2001, www.dnr.state.wi.us/org/caer/cs/reports/2001/wildlife.htm.

25. "Wisconsin Hunters Asked to Help Fight Chronic Wasting Disease," Medical College of Wisconsin Healthlink, http://healthlink.mcw.edu/article/1029352007.html.

26. Associated Press, "Hunting Industry in State Could Lose Up to 96M," *Capital Times*, July 15, 2002.

27. Richard C. Bishop, "The Economic Effects in 2002 of Chronic Wasting Disease in Wisconsin," Department of Agricultural and Applied Economics, University of Wisconsin–Madison, Staff Paper No. 450, July 2002.

28. Ibid.

29. "Fatal Degenerative Neurologic Illnesses in Men Who Participated in Wild Game Feasts–Wisconsin, 2002," *Morbidity and Mortality Weekly Report MMWR* 52(07) (February 21, 2003), 125–127.

30. Ibid.

31. Ibid.

32. Robert Imrie (Associated Press), "Wisconsin Hunters to Shoot Diseased Deer," APOnline, March 26, 2002.

33. Robert Manwell, "CWD Update," *Wisconsin Natural Resources*, August 2002, 26.

34. Ibid.

35. Robert Imrie (Associated Press), "Wisconsin Hunters to Shoot Diseased Deer."

36. "Wisconsin Mobilizes to Battle Chronic Wasting Disease," *Journal of the American Veterinary Medical Association*, June 15, 2002, www.avma.org/onlnews/javma/jun02/020615b.asp.

37. Ibid.

38. Ibid.

39. Anita Manning, "Outbreak Spurs a Record Deer Kill in Wisconsin," *USA Today*, May 6, 2002.

40. Associated Press, "Hunters Shoot Fewer than 100 deer," *Wisconsin State Journal*, June 9, 2002.

41. "Chronic Wasting Disease in Deer: Detailed CWD Timeline," Georgia Department of Natural Resources, Wildlife Resources Division, http://georgiawildlife.dnr.state.ga.us/content/displaycontent.asp?.

42. Ibid.

43. Associated Press, "Hunters Shoot Fewer than 100 Deer," *Wisconsin State Journal*, June 9, 2002.

44. "Deer Feeding and Baiting Banned," Wisconsin Department of Natural Resources fact sheet, 2002.

45. "Whitetails Unlimited Supports Ban on Baiting and Feeding in Response to Chronic Wasting Disease," Whitetails Unlimited, press release, May 16, 2002,

http://wideerhunters.org/articles/
WTUposition.html.

46. Lee Bergquist and Bob Riepenhoff, "88%
Plan to Hunt this Fall, Survey Says,"
Milwaukee Journal Sentinel, November 17,
2002.

47. "The Facts About White-Tailed Deer
and Chronic Wasting Disease," WDNR
Pub-WM-450-2002. The 500 deer per
county testing goal would allow for a
statistical confidence of 95 percent.

48. Jim Lee, "Two CWD Test Options
Available to Hunters," *Wausau Daily Herald*,
November 17, 2002.

49. Associated Press, "Farmers Fear Larger
Deer Herd Will Destroy Crops," *Wausau
Daily Herald*, December 1, 2002.

50. Ibid.

51. Jim Lee, "Deer Hunting Prospects
Excellent," *Wausau Daily Herald*, November
10, 2002.

52. "2002 Season Wisconsin Big Game
Hunting Summary," Wisconsin
Department of Natural Resources, April
2003, 2.

53. Associated Press, "December Hunt Nixed,"
Capital Times, January 11, 2002.

54. Ibid.

55. Jim Lee, "2002 Season Difficult to Read,"
Wausau Daily Herald, December 1, 2002.

56. "2002 Season Wisconsin Big Game
Hunting Summary," Wisconsin
Department of Natural Resources, April
2003, 1.

57. "Chronic Wasting Disease in Deer:
Detailed CWD Timeline," Georgia
Department of Natural Resources, Wildlife
Resources Division, http://georgiawildlife.
dnr.state.ga.us/content/displaycontent.asp?.

58. Ibid.

59. Keith McCaffery, personal communication,
April 26, 2006.

60. "NRB Affirms Its Proposed Ban on
Deer Baiting and Feeding," Wisconsin
Department of Natural Resources, news
release, August 15, 2003.

61. Kevin O'Brien, "Iron River
Businesswoman Takes on the DNR,"
Ashland Daily Press, August 7, 2003.

62. Keith McCaffery, personal communication,
April 25, 2006.

63. Meg Jones, "Opposition Grows for Ban on
Deer Baiting," *Milwaukee Journal Sentinel*,
October 31, 2002.

64. "NRB Affirms Its Proposed Ban on
Deer Baiting and Feeding," Wisconsin
Department of Natural Resources, press
release, August 15, 2003.

65. Senator Joe Leibham, "To Bait or Not to
Bait," News Columns, September 24, 2003,
www.legis.state.wi.us/senate/sen09/news/
Press/2003/col2003-012.htm.

66. Scott Helberger, "CWD Fears Subside, but
Problem Simmers," *Wausau Daily Herald*,
November 30, 2003.

67. Lee Berquist, "State Considers Longer
Deer Hunt," *Milwaukee Journal Sentinel*,
January 22, 2003.

68. Jim Lee, "Weather Conditions, CWD
Concerns Dominate First Hunting
Day," *Wausau Daily Herald*, November 23,
2003.

69. Rick Olivo, "As CWD Fears Drop, 2003
Hunting Season Returns to More Typical
Pattern," *Ashland Daily Press*, February 11,
2004.

70. Keith McCaffery, personal communication,
April 25, 2006.

71. "Deer Population Goals," Wisconsin
Department of Natural Resources, www
.dnr.state.wi.us/org/land/wildlife/hunt/
deer/popgoal.htm.

72. Ibid.

73. Ibid.

74. Ibid.

75. Robert Imrie (Associated Press), "Huge
Herd Awaits State's Deer Hunters," *Wausau
Daily Herald*, November 15, 2004.

76. Bob Riepenhoff, "New Season Brings
Change," *Milwaukee Journal Sentinel*,
November 13, 2004.

77. Ibid.

78. Kevin O'Brien, "Earn-a-Buck Weighs
Heavy on Hunting Opener," *Ashland Daily
Press*, November 22, 2004.

79. Ibid.

80. Keith McCaffery, personal communication,
April 25, 2006.

81. Jim Lee, "2004 Deer Season Faded at Finish," *Wausau Daily Herald*, December 5, 2004.

82. O'Brien, "Earn-a-Buck Weighs Heavy on Hunting Opener," *Ashland Daily Press*, November 22, 2004.

83. Tim Eisele, "Program Under Fire," *Milwaukee Journal Sentinel*, January 16, 2005.

84. Ibid.

85. Ibid.

86. Bob Riepenhoff, "Compromise on Deer Hunt Prepared," *Milwaukee Journal Sentinel*, July 24, 2005.

87. Ibid.

88. Bob Riepenhoff, "Deer Hunt Package Clears Hurdle," *Milwaukee Journal Sentinel*, December 11, 2005.

89. "2005 Big Game Hunting Summary," Wisconsin Department of Natural Resources, April 2006, 17.

90. Franzen, "Chronic Wasting Disease: Extra Caution With Deer Meat," *Milwaukee Journal Sentinel*, January 30, 2006.

91. Ibid.

92. U.S. Federal News Service, Including U.S. State News, "Deer Hunting Rules Not to Change for 2006 Wisconsin Seasons," February 10, 2006.

93. Ibid.

94. Bob Riepenhoff, "Deer Hunt Proposals Put On Hold," *Milwaukee Journal Sentinel*, February 26, 2006.

95. Ibid.

96. Bob Riepenhoff, "Deer Hunting: Board Approves New Rules," *Milwaukee Journal Sentinel*, May 14, 2006.

97. Ibid.

98. Associated Press, "Earn-A-Buck Returns, to Some Hunters' Dismay," *Dubuque Telegraph-Herald*, March 29, 2006.

99. Ibid.

100. "2006 Wisconsin Big Game Summary," Wisconsin Department of Natural Resources, May 2007, 29.

101. Ibid.

102. U.S. Federal News Service, Including U.S. State News, "2007 Deer Season Forecast," November 2, 2007.

103. Mike Heine, "Season to Feature Plenty of Deer," *Janesville Gazette*, September 15, 2007.

104. Associated Press, "Earn-A-Buck Is Broadened for Fall Deer Season," *Wisconsin State Journal*, March 29, 2007.

105. Ibid.

106. U.S. Federal News Service, Including U.S. State News, "Preliminary Count Shows Hunters Registering More than 171,000 Deer Over Opening Weekend of 2007 Gun Deer Season," November 19, 2007.

107. Randy Stark, "Memo to DNR Secretary Matt Frank," December 5, 2007, http://dnr.wi.gov/org/es/enforcement/2007_Deer_Gun_Season.pdf.

108. Ibid.

109. Ibid.

110. Brian Dhuey and Keith Warnke, "2007 Wisconsin Deer Hunting Summary," Wisconsin Department of Natural Resources, http://dnr.wi.gov/org/land/wildlife/harvest/reports/deerharv07.pdf.

111. Ron Seely, "Cease-Fire Declared in Chronic Wasting Disease Dispute," *Wisconsin State Journal*, November 17, 2007.

112. Ibid.

113. Todd Richmond (Associated Press), "Deeply Divided Panel Suggests CWD Policies," *Wisconsin State Journal*, February 7, 2008.

114. Ibid.

115. Anita Weier, "Deer Hunt Rules Eased on CWD," *Capital Times*, April 24, 2008.

116. Ibid.

Chapter 10

1. Aldo Leopold, "Wildlife in American Culture," in *A Sand County Almanac: With Other Essays on Conservation from Round River*, (New York: Oxford University Press, 1966), 198.

2. McCabe and McCabe, "Of Slings and Arrows," 72.

3. "Deer Vehicle Collisions," Wisconsin Department of Natural Resources, http://

dnr.wi.gov/org/land/wildlife/hunt/deer/cardeer.htm.

4. "Motor Vehicle–Deer Crashes in 2006," Wisconsin Department of Transportation, www.dot.wisconsin.gov/safety/motorist/crashfacts/docs/deerfacts.pdf.

5. Bob Riepenhoff, " 'Thrill Killing' on the Rise," *Milwaukee Journal Sentinel*, October 15, 2005, http://jsonline.com/outdoors/oct05/363167.

6. "Blanchardville Men Fined, Lose Hunting and Fishing Licenses over Deer 'Thrill Killings,' " Wisconsin Department of Natural Resources, news release, February 28, 2005.

7. Leopold, "Wildlife in American Culture," 197.

8. "Farmland Protection Program Wisconsin Summary," Natural Resources Conservation Service, December 2001, 1.

9. "Deer & Development: How Sprawl Impacts the Deer Herd, Hunters, Auto Safety and Your Pocket Book," 1000

Friends of Wisconsin, www.1kfriends.org/Publications/Online_Documents/Deer_Development.htm.

10. Ibid.

11. Gordon MacQuarrie, "A Brace Apiece," in *More Stories of the Old Duck Hunters*, ed. Zack Taylor (Minocqua, WI: Willow Creek Press, 1990), 121.

12. Leopold, "Wildlife in American Culture," 197.

13. Brad Koele and Laurie Fike, "Wildlife Damage Abatement and Claims Program, 2006," Wisconsin Department of Natural Resources, http://dnr.wi.gov/org/land/wildlife/damage/progreport.pdf.

14. Thomas P. Rooney, Stephen L. Solheim, and Donald M. Waller, "Factors Affecting the Regeneration of Northern White Cedar in Lowland Forests of the Upper Great Lakes Region, USA," *Forest Ecology and Management* 163 (2000), 129.

15. Dahlberg and Guettinger, *The White-Tailed Deer in Wisconsin*, 236.

Index